Traditional Anti-Torah Church Doctrines

The Curses of Our Fathers

Cornie Banman

TRADITIONAL ANTI-TORAH CHURCH DOCTRINES
THE CURSES OF OUR FATHERS

iUniverse books may be ordered through booksellers or by contacting:

iUniverse
1663 Liberty Drive
Bloomington, IN 47403
www.iuniverse.com
1-800-Authors (1-800-288-4677)

ISBN: 978-1-4917-4312-6 (sc)
ISBN: 978-1-4917-4313-3 (hc)
ISBN: 978-1-4917-4314-0 (e)

Library of Congress Control Number: 2014914200

Print information available on the last page.

iUniverse rev. date: 09/04/2015

CONTENTS

INTRODUCTION

I was born in a small farming community in La Crete, Alberta, Canada, in the spring of 1959. My wife, Sara (Wolfe), from southern Manitoba, and I got baptized in a local Church in La Crete in the spring of 1981, and we got married in the summer of that year. Sara has a tremendous passion for children, including the handicapped, and all children love her. She is a very serious gardener. She is a blessing to me and to all who know her. God blessed us with a wonderful daughter, Kathryn, in the summer of 1996; she also enjoys gardening and doing yard work.

My wife and I both grew up in a culture of very religious and sincere churchgoing Anabaptist Mennonites. Mennonites are a people who take after the faith of a man called Menno Simons, an Anabaptist who broke away from the Roman Catholic system in the early sixteenth century and started his own denomination.

After I finished the eighth grade at age fifteen, I started working in the sawmill industry. I have built and maintained sawmills for other people for a few decades. I am presently employed at one that I set up in 1991 for eight local businessmen. I still enjoy that line of work.

In 1998, greed motivated me to become a partner with a friend in a business venture, which failed financially. New partners got involved and eventually purchased the business, but they didn't pay for it as promised. I tried to settle through the legal system but was forced to back off by the church of which I was a member, with a promise of settlement. Since I was brought up in the church system, I obeyed them. But settlement never came. We felt extremely betrayed by that church system. This brought me down very low, to a point where it humbled me enough that I eventually surrendered myself to my Creator. I repented, turned away from that system, and turned to God for my first time. Thus, the healing process began.

We do not belong to any *denominational* church now. But we have, as a family, committed ourselves to obey the God of heaven and earth. We belong to God's congregation now—the Israel of God (Gal. 6:16)—and He provides our spiritual food, and His blessings are overwhelming. But this comes with a price tag, because it means committing to the laws and commandments of the creator God, for which much criticism comes from *traditional* Christianity. All the years that we did attend the Mennonite churches, we were fully convinced that the congregations were, as a whole, fully keeping the Ten Commandments. We were indoctrinated with a belief that our congregations were the only ones that were living by the commandments of God. We didn't wake up to realize, until we severed from that system, that they not only did not keep God's commandments but also, in a hideous and deceitful way, advocated that one ought *not* keep them, because they are burdensome. In order to reason around not needing to keep them, they professed that God gave them to the Jews only, thus justifying the enforcing of their own *traditional* doctrines as divine commandments of God. Their doctrines rub shoulders with the Ten Commandments, but they are mixed with traditions and customs of men and, as such, are preached as God's divine Word. The catechism, which is a question-and-answer tool wherewith to teach teenagers about God's divinity, includes the rehearsing of the Ten Commandments. Then, ironically, five questions after the actual Ten Commandments are rehearsed, it is professed that those commandments were only a teacher for the people of ancient times and don't apply to us today.

Going through this experience has developed within us a tremendous passion to share with the world what we have learned from God's truth; especially how the scriptures revealed to us what changes we would have to make in our life to be able to be healed from those troubles. Thus, we feel moved and obliged to share our experience with all who have ears to hear, in hopes that it may deliver some hope and encouragement to others who may find themselves in similar situations, that they also might find healing through and by God's truth.

I don't declare myself to be a prophet or anything of that sort. I'm an average, wage-earning family man with a strong passion to share what we have learned from God's truth. And new revelations and convictions confront us daily. These experiences are what motivated me to start publishing books and tracts, and also a website to share with the world. If any good comes from it, I pray that *all* honor and glory goes to our creator God.

Love,
Cornie Banman

I've done a lengthy study and research on today's traditional church system, which I refer to as traditional Christianity or the traditional church system; by which terms I mean the Protestant reformation religion (protesting Catholics). These terms relate to the church denominations that can trace their genealogy back to the Roman Catholic system.

My wife and I started out by looking into God's Word to confirm that the doctrines that were taught in the churches in our area were backed up by the Holy Scriptures. And we were truly convinced that they were, as we were always assured of by our parents and the preachers. We were shocked to discover that the doctrines of these churches were merely traditions of men, and as such were usually the exact opposite of the Holy Scriptures. They claim that the Ten Commandments are binding upon us, but they refuse to abide by certain ones, which they shrug off as being commanded only for the wicked and evil Jews, whom they've labeled as the murderers of our Lord. This shocked us to the core. So we studied the Holy Scriptures along with other resources to try to find out how a church system that swears to be unanimously scripture based could have gone so tragically wrong.

The results of that study motivated me to publish a book to show that God's moral laws are eternal and still apply to us today, for our benefit—not as a burden, as is taught by traditional Christianity. That book is called *The Commandments of God. Are they burdensome? Are they abolished?* It can be obtained through my website, http://corniebanman.com, through the publisher iUniverse (www.iUniverse.com), and from most online bookstores. On my website I also have a few tracts in English and German. Feel free to print them to share with friends.

What I learned from writing that book motivated me to continue the study to see how the early church fathers could have borne such an apostasy. It will help to more readily understand the concept of this book if you have already read that book. However, this book is only a slight continuation of it, and more of an explanation of how and why traditional Christendom has rejected the Ten Commandments, and how that belief has inevitably created an anti-God messiah.

In *Traditional Church Doctrines* I show how a subtle and extremely powerful philosophy of anti-Jew doctrines has, with sobering success, indoctrinated millions, or perhaps billions, of traditional Christians into believing that the Messiah's First Coming was to abolish the Ten Commandments. I will show how the philosophy of a few demon-inspired and God-hating church fathers has successfully accomplished that mission by elevating man-made traditions to commandment status through traditional church doctrines. We'll see how an extreme anti-Jew philosophy plays a key role in that mission, and thus expose its foundation and maybe—with the help of God—start shattering some of those beliefs.

In section 2 I describe how the God of Abraham has given mankind a very simple formula to test and measure all doctrines against His Word. I occasionally demonstrate that test throughout this book, and by the time we get to the end you will see how anyone who has a willing mind to learn God's truth can use that test to prove all doctrines to see whether they are inspired by the God of the scriptures, or perhaps by the god of this world. Then I will show how a person who's snared by deceived indoctrination can get back into alignment with God's true Word.

I'm not judging or condemning the churches, or people to whom this applies, but I do abhorrently rebuke the traditional law-done-away doctrines that I am unveiling in my books and tracts. Any congregation that is unanimously scripture based need not wear this shoe. Please read this entire book with an open and unbiased mind before judging it.

Important Notice: Most of the New Testament, which was written between about AD 40–100, was originally written in Greek and translated to other languages many centuries later. The King James Version (KJV) was translated into English from 1604 to 1611. The Old Testament was originally written in Hebrew. I have a Hebrew-Greek-English interlinear scriptures set, in which every Hebrew and Greek word is numbered for the purpose of cross-checking in the concordance dictionary. I have studied the contents of the articles in this book and have included a number of definitions in hopes that it will help you to understand the contents of this book and, moreover, the scriptures.

Throughout this book you will see endnote numbers, such as [22], which indicates that you will find the Hebrew or Greek word from which the previous word or words were translated, with the definition, in section 13. I have emphasized texts in scripture verses by setting text in **boldface,** <u>underlining</u> text, and sometimes *italicizing*, throughout this book. Words and phrases among scripture citations in [square brackets] are added by me for emphasis only. All citations are as they appear in the scripture, with the exception of the words or phrases that I have set in boldface or otherwise emphasized (which is done for clarification purposes only, so that you can see what I am emphasizing at the time). No words or phrases have been altered to any extent beyond what I've mentioned. All scripture verses are quoted from the KJV unless otherwise stated. The Ten Commandments from the scriptures (Ex. 20:2–17) and the Ten Planks of the Communist Manifesto are cited on pages 378-382.

1. WHERE DID THE CHURCH TRADITIONS BEGIN?

We need to start way back in time, a few millennia ago or so. In the book of Genesis God told Abraham—a man who had great and absolute faith in Him—that He would give him much property in which He would raise up many people through his seed, by which He would bless the whole world: "For all the land which thou seest, to thee will I give it, and to thy seed for ever. And I will make thy seed as the dust of the earth" (Gen. 13:15–16; read also Gen. 12:3, 7; 15:5–7; 17:7–8; 18:18; 22:17; 24:60; 26:3–5; 28:13–14; 32:12; Ex 32:13; Deut. 9:5–6; Acts 3:25; Rom. 4:17; Gal. 3:8, 17; Heb. 11:12). God made an eternal promise and covenant with Abraham: "And I will establish my covenant between me and thee and thy seed after thee in their generations for an **everlasting <`owlam>**[1] covenant, to be a God unto thee, and to thy seed after thee And I will give unto thee, and to thy seed after thee, the land wherein thou art a stranger, all the land of Canaan, for an **everlasting <`owlam>**[1] possession; and I will be their God" (Gen. 17:7–8; read also Gen. 26:24; 28:13; Rom. 9:8; Gal. 3:17; Heb. 11:16).

God foretold Abraham that his descendants would be oppressed in a land of strangers from among whom He would later redeem them with great substance. Abraham had a son Isaac, who had a son Jacob. And because of Abraham's faith and obedience to God's laws and commandments, which God knew he would also teach to his children (Gen. 18:19), God transferred the covenants and promises to his descendants: "Sojourn in this land, and I will be with thee, and will bless thee; for unto thee, and unto thy seed, I will give all these countries, and I will perform the oath which I sware unto Abraham thy father; And I will make thy seed to multiply as the stars of heaven, and will give unto thy seed all these countries; and **in thy seed shall all the nations of the earth be blessed; Because that Abraham**

obeyed my voice, and kept my charge <mishmereth>[2]**, my commandments <mitsvah>**[3]**, my statutes <chuqqah>**[4]**, and my laws <towrah>**[5]" (Gen. 26:3–5; read also 22:16; 28:15; Ps. 105:9–10; Heb. 11:9). In Genesis 32:28 God changed Jacob's name to Israel, meaning that Jacob's descendants would be powerful and would rule as God: "And he said, Thy name shall be called no more Jacob, but **Israel <Yisra'el>**[6]: for as a prince hast thou power with God and with men, and hast prevailed" (Gen. 32:28). From that moment on, Abraham's descendants—flesh-born and also adopted Gentiles (Ex. 12:38; Rom. 2:28–29; 10:12; Gal. 3:28–29; Col. 3:11)—are *all* together called Israelites; the Israel of God (Gal. 6:16), named after the congregation of Jacob/Israel (Deut. 33:4), through whom the covenantal promises can be obtained.

In Exodus chapters 1 to 11, we read of how the Egyptians forced brutal labor upon the Israelites for a few centuries. Four hundred thirty years, to the day (Ex. 12:40–41), after God made the covenant with Abraham (Gen. 17:21; Gal. 3:17), He demonstrated His sovereignty and mighty powers while He delivered the Israelites, Abraham's children of promise, out of the Egyptian bondage and slavery. God set appointed times for the special events that pertain to the fulfillment of these covenantal promises (Gen. 15:13; Gen. 17:21; Gen. 18:10, 14; Gen. 21:2; Acts 7:6; Rom. 9:9; Gal. 3:17) because the whole of these plans reveals to us how He is restoring His kingdom back into the state in which it was before the archangel Lucifer, called Satan, the devil (Rev. 12:9; 20:2), rebelled against God, thus defiling it.

It's interesting to note that the 430 years go back to the day after Isaac was born, which was also exactly, to the day, one year after Isaac was promised to Abraham and Sarah: "But my covenant will I establish with Isaac, which Sarah shall bear unto thee at this **set time <mow`ed>**[7] in the next year" (Gen. 17:21). So the day on which God promised Abraham a son, the day on which that son was born, and the day of the Lord's Passover, when God redeemed the Israelites from Egypt, happened to be on the same day of the year—God's appointed time. The Messiah also kept the Passover on that same day in the New Testament (Luke 22:13-20), when He became the Passover Lamb of God (1 Cor. 5:7; 1 Peter 1:19).

After about four centuries of being enslaved, the Israelites were glad to be redeemed from that bondage. But they soon forsook the God of their father Abraham and worshipped the Baal gods of the pagan nations around them. The whole book of scriptures is full of testimonies and examples of these accounts: "And the LORD said unto Moses, Behold, thou shalt sleep with thy fathers; and this people will rise up, **and go a whoring after the gods of the strangers of the land**, whither they go to be among them, **and will forsake me, and break my covenant** which I have made with them" (Deut. 31:16). After their forty-year journey through the wilderness and desert, Moses reminded them of exactly that fault: "Ye have been rebellious against the LORD from the day that I knew you" (Deut. 9:24).

The gods with whom they flirted were *always* pagan deities from the heathen world around them. The heathen gods continually enticed them with worldly lusts and desires of the flesh in order to seduce them away from the God of Abraham, who delivered them from bondage. This type of flirting, which started with Adam and Eve in the garden of Eden still continues today, inspired by that same satanic spirit. And we are still descendants of that same Adam (Gen. 5:3; 1 Cor. 15:22, 45).

God made a covenant—a binding agreement, or contract—with the Israelites in Exodus 19–24, which was agreed upon and ratified by blood. This married them to the eternal God. He became their husband (Jer. 3:14; Ezek. 16:8, 32), and likewise they became His wife. He established them and bought them (Deut. 32:6). This God—the God of Israel, which is the God of Abraham, of Isaac, and of Jacob—is a sovereign God with endless power, and He is jealous when other gods get His credit. He calls it adultery or whoring when that happens, and He warned them about that:

> Observe thou that which I command thee this day: behold, I drive out before thee the Amorite, and the Canaanite, and the Hittite, and the Perizzite, and the Hivite, and the Jebusite. Take heed to thyself, lest thou make a covenant with the inhabitants of the land whither thou goest, lest it be for a snare in the midst of thee: But ye shall

> destroy their altars, break their images, and cut down their groves: For thou shalt worship no other god: for the LORD, whose name is Jealous, is a **jealous God**: Lest thou make a covenant with the inhabitants of the land, and they go a whoring after their gods, and do sacrifice unto their gods, and one call thee, and thou eat of his sacrifice; And thou take of their daughters unto thy sons, and their daughters go a whoring after their gods, and make thy sons go a whoring after their gods. (Ex. 34:11–16)

Mankind's fear of man, which has developed a tremendous selfish desire to serve man rather than God, seems to be the overall theme of most of the Old and New Testament scriptures. The prophets and writers of the Holy Scriptures have great and terrible warnings for us and for future generations for following the traditions of men because they come directly from the god of this world—Satan, the devil.

God promised that He would at a certain time send a Redeemer who would destroy Satan and his influences (Gen. 3:15). That Redeemer—the Messiah—was manifested about two thousand years ago to remove the penalty of sin for repentant believers: "Behold the Lamb of God, which taketh away the sin of the world" (John 1:29). Although there are many prophecies in the Old Testament about that Redeemer, there is much more prophesied about His Second Coming than there is about the first. The Second Coming is when He will come to rule this earth while opening the way to unprecedented peace and prosperity. The Jews—Israelites—of old were eagerly looking forward to the events of His coming, but because of their self-righteous and prideful hearts, they ignorantly overlooked the events and purpose of His First Coming. Therefore they overlooked the *need* for what was prophesied to be delivered by His First Coming. After all, they didn't need to be delivered or redeemed from the penalties of sin, because as you can read in John chapters 5 through 10 (you need to read these six chapters to understand this vital point), they claimed that they were already free *because* they were Abraham's descendants, and because of the fact that they were circumcised in the flesh.

As a result of their boastful, control-mongering pride, they preached their traditional doctrines as divine commandments wherewith God's commandments were automatically forsaken: "Thus have ye made the commandment of God of none effect **by your tradition**" (Matt. 15:6; read also Mark 7:6–9). That's what kept their hearts uncircumcised, wherefore God blinded/veiled their hearts: "But their minds were blinded: for until this day remaineth the same vail untaken away in the reading of the old testament; which vail is done away in Christ" (2 Cor. 3:14; read also Deut. 29:4; Isa. 29:10; John 12:40; Rom. 11:7–8). When one realizes that the New Testament does *not* abolish or contradict the Old, but that, rather, through it God reveals events that fulfill His great salvation plan and the hope of mankind *by* the manifestation of its prophecies, God removes the veil.

So the Pharisees argued that this professing Son of Man was not their promised Messiah, because according to *their* understanding of the prophecies of His coming, He would come as their Jewish Lord and King. After all, He was born to be the King of the Jews (Matt. 2:2). Therefore, they thought that, if He were the promised king of the Jews, He would come and bring peace *to* and *for* Israel, as was prophesied that He would do. They believed He would come and *prove* to them that He was the true Messiah of which the prophets had spoken and written. According to their understanding, he had come to literally be their Jewish king, and as such He would judge the Romans and whoever else was in opposition to *their* beliefs, and kick them out of existence forever!

Yes, one of His great promises is that He will rule as King of Kings and Lord of Lords to remove wickedness from this world; but He will do so at His *Second* Coming. He clearly stated that His First Coming was not to make peace but war: "Think **not** that I am come to send peace on earth: I came **not** to send peace, **but a sword**. For I am come to set a man at variance against his father, and the daughter against her mother, and the daughter in law against her mother in law. And a man's foes shall be they of his own household" (Matt. 10:34–36). These are trials with which we will be tested until He returns: "I am come **to send fire on the earth**; and what will I, if it be already kindled?" (Luke 12:49).

He is looking forward to the time when *all* will be fulfilled, after fire will kosher this earth together with the whole universe as we know it—"And ye shall tread down the wicked; for they shall be ashes under the soles of your feet in the day that I shall do this, saith the LORD of hosts" (Mal. 4:3; read also Matt. 24:35; Mark 13:31; Rev. 20:11; 21:1; Isa. 34:4; 47:14; 51:6; 2 Peter 3:10-12)—for to fulfill the establishment of His Father's holy kingdom (Matt. 5:18).

Peter wrote about an end-time fire by which the earth together with its surroundings will be koshered and made holy: "But the day of the Lord will come as a thief in the night; in the which the heavens shall pass away with a great noise, and the elements shall **melt with fervent heat**, the earth also and the works that are therein shall be **burned up"** (2 Peter 3:10). Joel prophesied that there will be war on this earth until the Messiah returns: "Beat your **plowshares into swords**, and your **pruninghooks into spears** ... for the day of the LORD is near in the valley of decision" (Joel 3:10, 14). After His return, the Messiah will deliver peace and salvation, which the Jews of His day expected of His First Coming: "And he shall judge among the nations, and shall rebuke many people: and they shall **beat their swords into plowshares**, and their **spears into pruninghooks**: nation shall not lift up sword against nation, neither shall they learn war any more" (Isa. 2:4; also read Mic. 4:3). After the Messiah returns to put an end to the deadliest war to ever have occurred in this world (the Great Tribulation/Jacobs trouble; Jer. 30:7; Dan. 12:1; Matt. 24:21) and lock Satan away, people's efforts, through love for one another, will be focused on peace and prosperity the likes of which the human mind cannot even imagine.

Even the Messiah's chosen disciples, also yet deceived and blinded, believed that the Messiah had come at that time to rule the earth: "When they therefore were come together, they asked of him, saying, Lord, wilt thou at this time restore again the kingdom to Israel?" (Acts 1:6; read also Matt. 24:3; Luke 19:11; 24:21). Not until the Messiah presented Himself to them after the resurrection did they begin to understand the *true* gospel of the kingdom of God on earth, of which the prophets of old have written. Only then did they begin to understand what the Messiah had meant when He spoke to them—that He was expounding on the order of the fulfilling of the setting up of His Father's kingdom here on earth—which is spelled out in the Law and the Prophets (or, as it is called in Hebrew, the Torah)—instructions with which they were familiar in the carnal and physical manner. Now they began to understand that the crucifixion and resurrection of the Messiah—as vital, holy, and essential as those events were—were merely the beginning of the prophetic events that must be fulfilled in order for the Messiah to restore and set up God's holy kingdom: "And they said one to another, Did not our heart burn within us, while he talked with us by the way, and **while he opened to us the scriptures**? ... And he said unto them, These are the words which I spake unto you, while I was yet with you, that **all things must be fulfilled, which were written in the law of Moses, and in the prophets, and in the psalms, concerning me**. **Then opened he their understanding, that they might understand the scriptures,** And he said unto them, Thus it is written, and thus it behoved Christ to suffer, and to rise from the dead the third day: And that repentance and remission of sins should be preached in his name among all nations, beginning at Jerusalem. And ye are witnesses of these things" (Luke 24:32, 44–48); thus a Torah test. He removed the veil from their hearts so that they could understand that the Old Testament prophecies were in the process of being fulfilled. Torah prophecies were brought to their remembrance, causing them to understand and thus believe.

The Messiah always spoke in parables because the uncalled people weren't supposed to understand him:

> And the disciples came, and said unto him, Why speakest thou unto them in parables? He answered and said unto them, Because **it is given unto you to know the mysteries of the kingdom of heaven**, but **to them it is not given**. For whosoever hath, to him shall be given, and he shall have more abundance: but whosoever hath not, from him shall be taken away even that he hath.

> **Therefore speak I to them in parables**: because they seeing see not; and hearing they hear not, neither do they understand. And in them is fulfilled the prophecy of Esaias, which saith, By hearing ye shall hear, and shall not understand; and seeing ye shall see, and shall not perceive: For this people's heart is waxed gross, and their ears are dull of hearing, and their eyes they have closed; lest at any time they should see with their eyes, and hear with their ears, and should understand with their heart, **and should be converted, and I should heal them**. But blessed are your eyes, for they see: and your ears, for they hear [He unveiled their hearts]. (Matt. 13:10–16; read also Isa. 6:9–10; Mark 4:10–13; John 12:40; Acts 28:27)

After receiving the Holy Spirit during the next Pentecost (Acts 2:1–4), His called-out ones began to understand the spiritual aspects of those events.

God blinded the Pharisees for a purpose—they were not yet called. Thus, still to this very day, they cannot understand. And most of them will remain veiled from the truth until God calls them; and He will, in His time. We will see more of this as we progress along.

This lays the foundation and sets the stage for what I will focus on in this book, because many of these very same prophecies are also being overlooked by today's traditional church system in a similar manner, but with a twist. By the time we get to the end of this book, we will see that the traditional church doctrines are cunningly established upon extreme anti-Jewism, which reveals their anti-Torahism. We will see how a vicious anti-Jewism in their philosophy inevitably forces them to use different rationale and reasoning than the Pharisees did regarding righteousness. Therefore, they have, *just like the Pharisaic Jews*, misappropriated the purpose and the timing of the vital events of the Messiah's First *and* Second Comings.

The extreme anti-Jew doctrines of traditional Christendom come from a very powerful fourth-century Roman Emperor—Constantine the Great. While he was in power, he made a couple of very bold and powerful life-and-death anti-Jew decrees, which stated, "It is our duty not to have anything in common with the murderers of our Lord... " "...We should have nothing in common with the Jews." He called it a divine command "...the divine favour, and this truly divine command." And his decree goes on to say that "...All our brethren in the East who formerly followed the customs of the Jews are henceforth to celebrate the said most sacred feast of Easter at the same time with the Romans... " That decree was penciled between AD 317 and 325, and it was canonized (made Roman Catholic Bible doctrine) around AD 341 by a later successor emperor (Philip Schaff and Henry Wace, eds., *Nicene and Post-Nicene Fathers: Second Series*, vol. 14, [Peabody, MA: Hendrickson Publishers, 1996], 54–56, 108). The Easter decree became canonized at a later point at Antioch in Syria (Canon I, page 108).

Constantine also traded the seventh-day Sabbath for the first-day Sunday, which became Canon XXIX at Laodicea, in Phrygia: "CHRISTIANS must not judaize by resting on the Sabbath, but must work on that day, rather honouring the Lord's Day; and, if they can, resting then as Christians. But if any shall be found to be judaizers, let them be anathema from Christ" (page 148). Thus, because of Constantine's extreme hunger for power and control, he amalgamated all the beliefs of that time into one universal religion; hence the Roman Catholic Church was born. All beliefs were welcome, as long as they had nothing in common with the beliefs of the Jews and paid homage to the Roman Empire and its deities—like Mithras—the sun god which Constantine worshipped.

Since the Pharisaic Jews believe only in the Old Testament scriptures, the believers of the universal Roman Catholic Church system, because of their anti-Jew mind-set, *cannot* use the scriptures from the Old Testament but only from the New Testament—because their beliefs can't have anything in common with those of the Jews. Therefore, both sects are unable to understand the truth of God's Word; they remain veiled/blinded from the truth. On the philosophies of such hateful anti-Jew apostates hinge most, if not all, of the traditional doctrines that the early church fathers invented, thus establishing the foundation of today's traditional church's doctrinal system. I realize that dedicated traditional churchgoers will take issue with this statement, but unless you study and prove these things for yourself and *believe* what you find in God's Word, it's impossible to even begin to understand this great apostasy. It's very important to study this prayerfully with an unbiased mind-set, because if you're determined to defend doctrines of a traditional law-done-away church system, your heart *will* remain veiled! Bear this point in mind throughout this book, and moreover when studying the Holy Scriptures.

The apostle Paul reminds us that we've been deceived through religious systems by false, blinded, and glory-seeking theologically trained teachers: "But I fear, lest by any means, **as the serpent beguiled Eve** through his subtilty, so **your minds should be corrupted** from the simplicity [singleness] that is in Christ. For if he that cometh preacheth **another Jesus**, whom we have not preached, or if ye receive **another spirit**, which ye have not received, or **another gospel**, which ye have not accepted, ye might well bear with him" (2 Cor. 11:3–4). Today's anti-Law advocates teach a gospel consisting of God's truth mixed with lies in a way that portrays a spirit of a messiah who came specifically to abolish God's commandments. Paul reminded us to not mix God's truth with paganism: "But I say, that the things which the Gentiles sacrifice, they sacrifice to devils, and not to God: and I would not that ye should have fellowship with devils. **Ye cannot drink the cup of the Lord, and the cup of devils: ye cannot be partakers of the Lord's table, and of the table of devils**" (1 Cor. 10:20–21). One *cannot* truthfully profess God's Word while serving and advocating paganism.

Lies such as these, and the Pharisees' arguments with the Messiah (John chapters 5–10), must be what inspired John to remind us about how we can know whether we are worshipping the true Messiah—the One who forgives sins when we repent for breaking a commandment: "My little children, these things write I unto you, **that ye sin not. And if any man sin, we have an advocate with the Father, Jesus Christ the righteous**: And he is the propitiation for our sins: and not for ours only, but also for the sins of the whole world. And **hereby** we do know that we know him, **if we keep his commandments. He that saith,**

I know him, and keepeth not his commandments, is a liar, and the truth is not in him" (1 John 2:1–4).

With a law-done-away mind-set (supposedly making sinning impossible), a person cannot feel a need for a redeemer to forgive sins. The pride of the Pharisees caused them to not be able to see their sin, because they professed to be keeping God's commandments. Their trouble was that they kept them according to their perverted version, whereby God's commandments were forsaken. Traditional Christendom advocates that God's commandments don't exist anymore, wherefore they keep the traditions of *their* church, whereby they also forsake God's commandments—just like the Pharisees. God says we are still sinning: "If we say that we have no sin, we deceive ourselves, and the truth is not in us. If we confess our sins, he is faithful and just to forgive us our sins, and to cleanse us from all unrighteousness. **If we say that we have not sinned, we make him a liar**, and his word is not in us" (1 John 1:8–10).

John gave us these strong warnings decades after the commandments were apparently abolished. He knew that to transgress a law, there must first be a law to transgress: "All unrighteousness is sin" (1 John 5:17); "sin is the transgression of the law" (1 John 3:4; read also Matt. 5:17–19; James 2:8–11); "all thy commandments are righteousness" (Ps. 119:172). To not sin is to keep God's commandments. To sin is to not keep them. If God's laws and commandments were abolished, then John's warning to not sin, and his encouragement that we have forgiveness upon confession in case we do sin, would have been totally in vain! He knew, as also Paul did, that we are still carnal and thus able to sin: "For we know that the law is spiritual: but I am carnal, sold under sin" (Rom. 7:14; read also 1 Cor. 3:3–4). And they believed the Messiah when He said that not one jot or tittle would be destroyed from God's laws: "Think **not** that I am come to destroy the law, or the prophets: I am not come to destroy, but to fulfil. For verily I say unto you, Till heaven and earth pass, **one jot or one tittle shall in no wise pass from the law, till all be fulfilled. Whosoever therefore shall break one of these least commandments**, and shall teach men so, he shall be called the least in the kingdom of heaven: but whosoever shall do and teach them, the same shall be called great in the kingdom of heaven" (Matt. 5:17–19).

Satan does not necessarily present himself as a gruesome, fire-spitting devil, as he is typically portrayed; else he could not deceive people: "For such are false apostles, deceitful workers, **transforming themselves** into the apostles of Christ. And no marvel; for **Satan himself is transformed into an angel of light**. Therefore it is no great thing if **his ministers also be transformed as the ministers of righteousness**" (2 Cor. 11:13–15). They come with great authority: "For we wrestle not against flesh and blood, but against principalities, against powers, **against the rulers of the darkness of this world**, against spiritual wickedness in high places" (Eph. 6:12).

Jeremiah lamented about the spiritual tragedy that Satan delivers through false ministers: "My people hath been lost sheep: **their shepherds have caused them to go astray, they have turned them away**" (Jer. 50:6). In chapter 23 Jeremiah explains how Satan's ministers deceive God's flock and lead them astray, thus warning such preachers *and* their followers. It's addressed to specifically convict pastors and to warn and inspire their listeners to, as Paul warns, "Prove all things" (1 Thess. 5:21). As the Bereans did, "they received the word with all readiness of mind, and searched the scriptures daily, whether those things were so" (Acts 17:11). The Bereans compared the teachings of the apostles with the only scriptures they had—the Old Testament scrolls. In Deuteronomy chapter 12:28–13:5, the God of Abraham commands His people to do exactly that, and I will expound a bit upon that before going any further. Throughout this book, I will be focusing on what I will describe in section 2, which I will call the Torah test.

2. THE TORAH TEST

The theme of this book hinges on the aspects of a few very important scriptures regarding prophets and preachers who prophecy and do miracles. God gives us a very strong command to heed their sayings: "I will raise them up a Prophet from among their brethren, like unto thee, and will put my words in his mouth; and he shall speak unto them all that I shall command him. And it shall come to pass, that **whosoever will not hearken unto my words which he shall speak in my name, I will require it of him"** (Deut. 18:18–19).

But, He says, if he claims to be a prophet of God and his prophecies do *not* come to pass, he is a false prophet and as such is to be put to death. "But the prophet, which shall presume to speak a word in my name, which I have not commanded him to speak, or that shall speak in the name of other gods, even that prophet shall die. And if thou say in thine heart, How shall we know the word which the LORD hath not spoken? When a prophet speaketh in the name of the LORD, if the thing follow not, nor come to pass, that is the thing which the LORD hath not spoken, but the prophet hath spoken it presumptuously: thou shalt not be afraid of him" (Deut. 18:20–22). That seems quite simple, straightforward, and fair: if a person prophecies and it doesn't come to pass, it's *not* from the God of Abraham.

If the prophecies of one who professes to be sent by God come to pass, does that inherently warrant that he is speaking for the creator God of heaven and earth? Not necessarily. The God of Abraham commanded us to measure *all* doctrines and commandments that prophets and preachers impose upon us against His Torah truths, to confirm whether they are coming from Him, or perhaps from the god of this world. He says that He will allow prophets to come at us with *real* works and *real* wonders and *real* miracles to see if that will be able to seduce us away from His Torah teaching. This is a specific test to prove whether we truly love Him with all our heart and mind, which is the result of faithfully keeping **His** commandments. And we can always be assured that the Eternal God will change nothing without first revealing it to His people: "Surely the Lord GOD will do **nothing**, but he revealeth his secret unto his servants the prophets" (Amos 3:7).

No matter what the doctrine, prophecy, wonder, or sign may be; no matter from whom it's coming—regardless of authority—we are to use this test prophecy to discern between God's commandments and man's. That's the prophecy with which God warned His people before they crossed over the Jordan River, which took them into the then Gentile-occupied land that He promised to Abraham and his descendants. He gave them—and us—that test so that we would *always* be able to tell if *any* doctrines that might be imposed upon us were actually coming from Him, or from man (or Baal). God designed that test prophecy to be a powerful tool, which mankind would need to be able to tell when the true Messiah showed up on the scene. They would need it to test Him against His teaching to make sure it was not an imposter from Baal. Satan has this world overflowing with his doctrines and commandments, which he foists upon humanity. By mixing truth with lies—adding words and taking away words and doing miracles, thus appeasing the appetite of mankind's lusts and desires—he advocates that philosophy as divine doctrines through traditional ministers. But God forbade the mixing of truth and lies: "Ye shall not add unto the word which I command you, neither shall ye diminish ought from it, that ye may keep the commandments of the LORD your God which I command you" (Deut. 4:2).

Those words of warning were repeated a while later with some more details and reasoning added:

> Observe and hear all these words which I command thee, **that it may go well with thee**, and with thy children after thee **for ever <`owlam>**[1], when thou doest that which is good and right in the sight of the LORD thy God. When the LORD thy God shall cut off the nations from

> before thee, whither thou goest to possess them, and thou succeedest them, and dwellest in their land; **Take heed to thyself that thou be not snared by following them**, after that they be destroyed from before thee; and that thou **enquire not after their gods**, saying, How did these nations serve their gods? even so will I do likewise [celebrating Christmas, Easter, Halloween, Sunday, Lent, birthdays, et cetera, et cetera]. Thou shalt not do so unto the LORD thy God: for every abomination to the LORD, which he hateth, have they done unto their gods; for even their sons and their daughters they have burnt in the fire to their gods. **What thing soever I command you, observe to do it: thou shalt not add thereto, nor diminish from it.** (Deut. 12:28–32)

The Messiah echoed that truth to His disciples while He was on the scene with them, assuring them that God's Laws would not change: "For verily I say unto you, Till heaven and earth pass, **one jot or one tittle shall in no wise pass from the law**, till all be fulfilled" (Matt. 5:18). He came to witness to that truth: "Pilate therefore said unto him, Art thou a king then? Jesus answered, Thou sayest that I am a king. To this end was I born, and for this cause came I into the world, that I should bear witness unto the truth. Every one that is of the truth heareth my voice" (John 18:37). He specifically warned them about false prophets who *would* come and do miracles to deceive many—potentially including them: "For there shall arise false Christs, and false prophets, and shall shew **great signs** and **wonders**; insomuch that, if it were possible, **they shall deceive the very elect**" (Matt. 24:24; 7:22–23; Rev. 13:13–16; 2 Thess. 2:3-4). Those prophecies echo throughout the Scriptures, and they got sealed upon the conclusion of the New Testament: "For I testify unto every man that heareth the words of the prophecy of this book [Genesis to Revelation], If any man shall add unto these things, God shall add unto him the plagues that are written in this book: And if any man shall take away from the words of the book of this prophecy, God shall take away his part out of the book of life, and out of the holy city, and from the things which are written in this book" (Rev. 22:18–19).

The commandments referred to in Deuteronomy chapters 4 and 12 are obviously everything God has commanded up to that point in time, particularly the Ten Commandments, which He engraved into stone tablets about forty years earlier (Ex. 20:2–17; Deut. 5:6–21). *Every* law that God ever created hinges on the love-toward-God (the first table) and love-toward-neighbor (the second table) elements of the Ten Commandments. That's the divine standard against which God commands His children to measure all doctrines:

> If there arise among you a prophet, or a dreamer of dreams, and giveth thee a sign or a wonder, **And the sign or the wonder come to pass**, whereof he spake unto thee, saying, Let us go after other gods, which thou hast not known, and let us serve them; Thou shalt not hearken unto the words of that prophet, or that dreamer of dreams: for **the LORD your God <u>proveth</u> you, to know whether ye love the LORD your God with all your heart and with all your soul. Ye shall walk after the LORD your God, and fear him, and keep <u>his</u> commandments, and obey his voice, and ye shall serve him, and cleave unto him. And that prophet, or that dreamer of dreams, shall be put to death; because he hath spoken to turn you away from the LORD your God, which brought you out of the land of Egypt, and redeemed you out of the house of bondage** [redeemed from sin's bondage], **to thrust thee out of the way which the LORD thy God commanded thee to walk in**. So shalt thou put the evil away from the midst of thee. (Deut. 13:1–5)

God commands that *anyone* who teaches *any* doctrines and commandments other than those He taught us in the Torah is to be stoned to death. That's how strong God's desire is to remove false doctrines from among His people. The time is coming when He Himself will come down to earth and take care of that very business. Bearing this strong test commandment in mind is absolutely vital to be able to measure any preacher, any prophet, or any church doctrines against God's Holy Scriptures. It's also absolutely essential to use this test to prove the Messiah's doctrines, because if we believe that He changed or abolished God's commandments, then, according to His own Word, that would have made Him an imposter, which would have required Him to be stoned to death. Although a preacher or prophet is doing great miracles and wonders, and his prophesies come to pass; if he is not keeping *and* advocating *all* of the Lord's Ten Commandments, you can know with all certainty that it's a test for you and that that preacher or prophet is not speaking for the God of Abraham but is an absolute fraud from Satan, in which case you should flee from him (James 4:7). That message is commanded loud and clear over and over throughout the Old *and* New Testaments. Without being open, honest, willing to learn the truth, and willing to change if and when convicted; *all* information of this type will be totally alien and offensive to you!

According to the Pharisaic Jews' dispute with the Messiah (John chapters 5–10), they were fully convinced that they did not need the freedom He offered them. That's the freedom He has given us from the death penalty incurred by sinning, which He took with Him to the tree, reconciling us to God in doing so. But they rejected that freedom by claiming that they were already justified and free because they were of Abraham's seed. The Messiah told them that even though that they were of Abraham's seed, Abraham really was *not* their father, else they would love Him, and not seek to kill Him for telling the truth; because Abraham believed (had total faith and trust) in Him (Melchisedec, Gen. 14:18) and His Father (God, Gen. 15:6), and believed that the truth (God's Word and instructions, the Torah), would set them free:

> Then said Jesus unto them, When ye have lifted up the Son of man, then shall ye know that I am he [Num. 21:7–9; Gen. 3:15—Torah test proof], and that **I do nothing of myself; but as my Father hath taught me**, I speak these things. And he that sent me is with me: the Father hath not left me alone; for **I do always those things that please him**. As he spake these words, many believed on him. Then said Jesus to those Jews which believed on him, **If ye**

> **continue in my word, then are ye my disciples indeed; And ye shall know the truth, and the truth shall make you free.** They answered him, We be Abraham's seed, and were never in bondage to any man: how sayest thou, Ye shall be made free. (John 8:28–33; read also 3:14–16; 12:32).

Verse 28 predicts a Torah test that would come to pass when they put Him on the stake to prove who He was. As Moses was commanded to put a fiery serpent up on a stake that whoever would look at it after being bitten by a snake would be healed, the Messiah would die on the stake to remove the death penalty of man's sins—thus healing mankind.

The Messiah agreed that they were of Abraham's lineage, but they did not reflect his Godly character: "I know that ye are Abraham's seed; **but ye seek to kill me, because my word hath no place in you**. I speak that which I have seen with my Father: and ye do that which ye have seen with your father. They answered and said unto him, Abraham is our father. Jesus saith unto them, **If ye were Abraham's children, ye would do the works of Abraham. But now ye seek to kill me, a man that hath told you the truth, which I have heard of God: this did not Abraham"** (John 8:37–40). The Messiah made it very clear that if they were Abraham's children, they would then know Him and love Him.

According to the Messiah's own words, if He commanded us to continue in any words other than those from the Old Testament Torah, He would be an imposter—a false prophet. He challenged the Pharisees, and us, to measure Him against God's Word: "Jesus answered them, and said, **My doctrine is not mine, but his that sent me. If any man will do his** [God's] **will, he shall know of the doctrine, whether it be of God, or whether I speak of myself"** (John 7:17). He stated very directly that anyone who knew of God's doctrine — the Torah teaching— would thereby know whether or not He was the true Messiah, by comparing His doctrines and commands with the Torah. He said this about a decade before a word of the New Testament was written, thus He had only the Torah to refer to as God's doctrines.

He advocated that we should live by every word of God: "But he answered and said, It is **written** [not the **oral** Talmud], Man shall not live by bread alone, **but by every word that proceedeth out of the mouth of God** (Matt. 4:4; read also Luke 4:4). He cited this phrase directly from the Old Testament Torah (Deut. 8:3). John 7:17 holds a very powerful command to measure Him against His Father's truth in the Torah, as Deuteronomy 12:28–13:5 commands us to do. And because of this powerful testimony, many did believe Him (verse 30), because those of faith realized that He made no changes to God's laws—not one jot or tittle—thus truly validating Him as the true promised Messiah, **in complete and absolute accordance with the Torah test** and all other Scriptural prophecies concerning Him.

Consider this: those of faith knew of God's commandments and laws from nowhere else but from the Torah. Given that, if the Messiah had advocated any changes to God's commandments and laws, just **one jot or tittle**, they would have been obligated by the creator God / Messiah Himself to stone Him to death.

Nevertheless, the proud, arrogant, control-mongering, greedy, and covetous Pharisees reasoned that if Abraham wasn't good enough, God was their Father. The Messiah told them that if God were their Father, they would know Him and love Him, because He came from God; wherefore they were not even of God; at which point He told them that because of their lusts and desires, they had made Satan their father: "Ye are of your father the devil, and **the lusts of your father ye will do**. He was a murderer from the beginning, and abode not in the truth, because there is no truth in him. When he speaketh a lie, he speaketh of his own: for he is a liar, and the father of it. And **because I tell you the truth, ye believe me not**" (John 8:44–45). Their own demon-inspired traditional doctrines caused them to not be able to understand the truth, and they were thereby able to believe *only* lies. They could believe only the god of this world, because that's whom they served—and thus worshipped—by teaching their traditions and doctrines as divine commandments of God (Matt. 15; Mark 7; 2 Cor. 4:4).

As we can see, the God of heaven and earth has given us a simple and honest way to measure up any church doctrines, or any preachers or prophets, to see whether or not they truly are of Him, or whether they are perhaps wolves in sheep's clothing using His name to deceive us in order to seduce us away from Him—the true Lord God. Typical mainstream traditional Christians will measure up prophets and preachers by declaring that if they can do wonders, they must be of God. But according to this test prophecy, that is not the only rule by which to measure a prophet to see whether or not he is of God. God commands that if any of the least commandments (one jot or tittle) is denied—not kept *and* advocated—the person or thing denying the commandment *cannot* be of Him! John commands us to test the spirits to see if they are of God: "Beloved, believe not every spirit, but **try the spirits whether they are of God**: because many false prophets [theologians—traditional ministers] are gone out into the world" (1 John 4:1). Remember, the God of Creation *allows* false prophets to do miracles and wonders to test us to see whether we love Him by keeping His commandments, against which the prophet can be measured. Just as the Messiah said in John 7:17, if you know the doctrines of God, His Father, then you can know whether He is speaking of Himself or for *and* of God. Accordingly, He was absolutely sure that He made no changes to the Torah teachings.

A very powerful Torah test: The Messiah said to the argumentative Pharisees that He spoke only what His Father commanded Him to speak: "For **I have not spoken of myself; but the Father which sent me**, he gave me a commandment, what I should say, and what I should speak" (John 12:49). That phrase is another powerful Torah test proof, because God the Father promised a Messiah who would speak and do His will: "I will raise them up a Prophet from among their brethren, like unto thee, **and will put my words in his mouth; and he shall speak unto them all that I shall command him**" (Deut. 18:18). The Messiah told the Pharisees that if they were following the laws of Moses, who advocated the laws and commandments of the God of Abraham (which would inherently include the keeping of the Ten Commandments), they would then be able to know for certain whether He was of the God of Abraham or not: "Jesus answered them, and said, **My doctrine is not mine, but his that sent me. If any man will do his** [God's] **will, he shall know of**

the doctrine [the Torah], **whether it be of God, or whether I speak of myself**. He that speaketh of himself seeketh his own glory: but he that seeketh his glory that sent him, the same is true, and no unrighteousness is in him. Did not Moses give you the law, and **yet none of you keepeth the law?** Why go ye about to kill me?" (John 7:16–19).

Had they believed Moses (whom they *falsely* professed to be following), they would thereby—because the Messiah made no changes to those Words—have been able to measure Him up against God's Word from the Torah, whereby they would've been able to believe Him: "For had ye believed Moses, ye would have believed me: for he wrote of me. But **if ye believe not his writings, how shall ye believe my words?**" (John 5:46–47; read also 2 Cor. 3:14 to 4:4). Since they had not believed (trusted) Moses, they *could* not believe (trust) Him. The Old Testament prophesied of Him—the Redeeming Messiah, which He came to manifest. After all, the Messiah was the one who gave the laws and commandments to them through Moses; thus they had forsaken both of them—Moses and the Messiah.

The Messiah made it very plain that in order to understand His words, one must *first* understand and believe what He taught in the Torah, through Moses. They had only the Old Testament to measure the Messiah's doctrines against. The trouble with the Pharisees and Rabbis—the very thing that caused their spiritual blindness, thus keeping them veiled from the truth—was that they measured the Messiah's doctrines against the *oral* commandments of *their own* devised code of laws and commandments (the Talmud) while judging Him in accordance with the *written* commandments of the Old Testament Torah, specifically Deuteronomy 12:28–13:5. So they falsely preached the Talmud as being the divine commandments of God. And since, according to Deuteronomy 12:28–32 and 4:2, no one had any authority to change any part of God's laws, they used the authority from Deuteronomy chapter 13 to pass judgment on the Messiah, thus declaring—as that judgment does command—death to the Messiah for changing God's laws. Thus the Messiah was *not* keeping the commandments in accordance with the Talmud. That's the very reason they remained veiled from the truth.

The apostle Paul addressed *exactly* that issue (as recorded in 2 Cor. 3:14–4:4) while he explained the blindness with which the traditionally indoctrinated people were, and still are, struck, and why this is so: "But their minds were blinded: for **until this day remaineth the same vail untaken away in the reading of the old testament; which vail is done away in Christ**. But even unto this day, when Moses is read, the vail is upon their heart. Nevertheless when it [the heart] shall turn to the Lord [the God/ Messiah of the Old and New Testaments], the vail shall be taken away" (2 Cor. 3:14–16). They did read the Old Testament (the *written* Torah), but they elevated their Talmud (their *oral* Torah) to a higher status than the written Torah through their church system, by their tradition—the Talmud: "Thus have ye made the commandment of God [the written Torah] of none effect **by your tradition** [the oral Torah—the Talmud]" (Matt. 15:6; read also Mark 7:6–9). Thus, if they would go back to the written Torah and believe it, they would then be able to believe and understand the Messiah and His purpose.

When we believe and have faith in the true Messiah of the Old Testament prophecies and believe His promised purpose, thus turning to Him, God takes away the veil so that we can understand His Torah prophecies. Paul continued to explain that the people who are blinded with that veil are proud Baal worshippers: "But if our gospel be hid, it is hid to them that are lost: In whom **the god of this world hath blinded the minds of them which believe not**, lest the light of the glorious gospel of Christ, who is the image of God, should shine unto them" (2 Cor. 4:3–4). As we read earlier in John 8:44–45, the Messiah explained very bluntly that it's because of who the father of *traditionalized* doctrine is, that people can't understand—or believe—*any* truth.

Let's put ourselves into the time in which the Messiah spoke the words recorded in John 7:16–19. Not a word of the New Testament had been written yet, and none would be for at least another decade. He commanded us to measure Him up according to God's will, which is written in the Torah—including the Ten Commandments. As true believers who have put total trust in the God of Abraham, we would be committed to the written Torah teaching, meaning then that we would use the Torah test prophecy to measure up all doctrines and prophecies of our teachers (prophets and preachers) to see whether they were coming from the teaching of the God of Abraham, or perhaps from the god of this world—and it would be one or the other. Now, as in accordance with mainstream traditional Christian teaching, we'll assume that the Messiah said that He was sent by His Father to abolish the Ten Commandments, or even just a jot or tittle of them. Now, according to God's will (John 7:17), *we are commanded* to measure the Messiah's doctrines against the Torah teaching. That's exactly what the Messiah plainly challenges the Pharisees to do in John 7:16–19. And He's commanding us to do the very same thing—to measure His doctrines against God's instructions (the Torah teaching). What else can we measure *any* doctrines against?

So, according to His own words, if He was in any minutest way out of tune with the Old Testament Torah teaching, *He was then admittedly a false prophet*. Read John 7:16–19 again. To me it's extremely sobering to think of accusing the Messiah of having made any changes to God's commandments, especially after He gives us such strong and absolute definitive testimonies that He spoke according only to God's will. According to His own words, if He had made any change to God's commandments while professing to be the Son of God—or a prophet or minister of the God of Abraham, for that matter—He would literally have been committing religious suicide.

If we choose to believe (trust) in the God of Abraham and commit to follow His instructions, He reveals His truths to us in simple terms. His plans are not complicated or confusing: "For God is **not** the author of confusion" (1 Cor. 14:33). To people who commit themselves to follow Him, His instructions are simple, so that a child (a humble, willing, and submissive person) can understand: "I thank thee, O Father, Lord of heaven and earth, **because thou hast hid these things from the wise and prudent** [anti-Law theologians—Satan's ministers], **and hast revealed them unto babes** [submissive, truth-seeking people] (Matt. 11:25; read also Luke 10:21). It's just that plain. So the sobering moral is that if the Messiah did away with, or even just changed, one jot or tittle of God's laws and commandments—other than what the Torah prophesied would change—He *cannot* be the true Messiah, because to be the promised Redeemer of Israel required of Him to be *totally* and *absolutely* sinless and blameless, (Isa. 53:9; Luke 23:41; 2 Cor. 5:21; Heb. 4:15; 1 Peter 2:22; 1 John 3:5), as in accordance with God's laws and commandments—the Torah teaching. That means that He *must* measure up against the Old Testament prophesies in accordance with the Torah test. And John 7:16–19 is one of His strongest testimonies wherewith He challenges us to test His doctrines against the Torah in order to prove Him and see whether He's the Messiah as He claimed to be, or perhaps a false prophet; He must be one or the other! And if we believe what the Messiah states in Matthew 5:17–19, He did not change an iota of God's laws and commandments.

The Bereans used the Torah test *daily*. They measured the teachings of the gospel of God's kingdom as taught to them by the apostles against the Torah teachings—the only scriptures by which they had been trained. Although the apostles' teachings were in total opposition to the laws and decrees of Caesar (Acts 17:7); after confirming that the apostles' doctrines harmonized with the Scriptures, they believed them, thus causing even Gentiles to believe, *because* the apostles taught *nothing* contrary to the Torah prophecies: "These were more noble than those in Thessalonica, in that they received the word [the apostles' teachings] with all readiness of mind [they were teachable - humble truth seekers], and **searched the scriptures** [the Torah] **daily, whether those things were so**. **<u>Therefore</u>** [since the apostles' teaching coincided with the Torah] **many of them believed**; also of **honourable women which were <u>Greeks</u>** [Gentiles]**, and of men**, not a few" (Acts 17:11–12).

The Messiah kept God's commandments perfect (John 15:10). But according to traditional teaching He violated them by abolishing them in order to liberate us from the supposed burdens of keeping them. But according to His own Words, He would have sinned by doing so (1 John 3:4; Matt. 5:17–19; James 2:8–11), which would have disqualified Him for that position of being a blameless redeeming Messiah. And such a lawless messiah is what the traditional anti-Law ministry is advocating through the pulpits!

Fortunately—*very fortunately*—that's not the case, praise the Lord, because He proved in every way that he was the promised Redeemer and Savior who kept and advocated every jot and tittle of God's commandments, which in itself qualified Him as the only unblemished Lamb of God sacrifice, of which much was prophesied in the Torah: "But with the precious blood of Christ, as of **a lamb without blemish and without spot"** (1 Peter 1:19; read also Ex. 12:5; Lev. 22:18–21; 23:12; Isa. 53:7; John 1:29; Acts 20:28; 1 Cor. 5:7; Eph. 1:7; Heb. 9:12–14; Rev. 5:9). He went to the tree *absolutely* sinless and blameless ("For he hath made him to be sin for us, **who knew no sin**" [2 Cor. 5:21; read also Heb. 4:15; 1 Peter 2:22; 1 John 3:5]) because of His **<agape>**[8] love for us, which, according to scriptures, He attained through keeping God's commandments. If you will read the Scriptures referenced above, you'll see that the New Testament scriptures are all—each and every one of them—Torah test confirmations of the Old Testament prophecies about what they were to expect of the Messiah when He showed up on the scene. And that's what gave the disciples and apostles—and all who were looking for the promised Redeemer—the assurance that the Messiah was exactly what God had promised. If He had made a slight change, they would have had a legitimate reason to rebuke Him, in accordance with His own commandments.

When we study the Ten Commandments and imagine that a man would obey them willingly and joyfully from the depth of the heart, greater love could no man have: "**If ye keep my commandments <entole>**[9]**, ye shall abide in my love <agape>**[8]; even as I have kept my Father's commandments, and abide in his **love <agape>**[8]. These things have I spoken unto you, that my joy might remain in you, and that your joy might be **full <pleroo>**[10]. This is my **commandment <entole>**[9], That ye love one another, as I have loved you. **Greater love <agape>**[8] **hath no man than this, that a man lay down his life for his friends**" (John 15:10–13). And that's what the Messiah did for us when He willingly—because of His **<agape>**[8] love—laid down His innocent life for our sins: "Hereby perceive we the **love <agape>**[8] of God, **because he laid down his life for us:**

and we ought to lay down our lives for the brethren?" (1 John 3:16). Because the Messiah kept every jot and tittle of His Father's commandments is the reason He had God's sacrificial-type charitable **<agape>**[8] love in His heart, which *caused* Him to willingly sacrifice His life for mankind: "No man taketh it from me, but **I lay it down of myself"** (John 10:18; read also 1 John 1:9). And Paul also testified to the fact that the Messiah willingly humbled Himself and gave His life for us—exactly as prophesied—in order to deliver us from this world's wickedness: "**Who gave himself for our sins**, that he might deliver us from this present evil world, **according to the will of God** and our Father" (Gal. 1:4). And we're commanded to follow in His steps if we love Him (John 14:15) and desire His gift of eternal life (Matt. 19:17).

The Greek word**<agape>**[8] specifically describes God's sacrificial-type charitable love. That's a love that can come only from the depth of one's heart when God's love **<agape>**[8] dwells in it. John described its scriptural meaning as keeping God's commandments, which explains why they are not burdensome: "For this is the **love <agape>**[8] of God, that we keep his **commandments <entole>**[9]: and his commandments are **not** grievous" (1 John 5:3). The love that mankind is familiar with is denoted by the Greek word **<agapao>**[8a], which describes a moral-social love. God's **<agape>**[8] love is a sacrificial-type charitable love that makes no difference between people, accepts no bribes, and plays no favors; it is a love established upon a character of never-ending mercy and grace for one another. And that's the type of character God needs His followers to have in order to belong to His Family. An **<agape>**[8] love can come only from God, which is why we need His Holy Spirit in our heart—His dwelling in us: "And hope maketh not ashamed; because the **love <agape>**[8] of God is shed abroad in our hearts by the Holy **Ghost <pneuma>**[11] [Spirit] which is given unto us" (Rom. 5:5). And God gives His Holy Spirit and salvation only to those who obey Him: "And we are his witnesses of these things; and so is also **the Holy Ghost** [Spirit]**, whom God hath given to them that obey him ...** And being made perfect, he became the author of eternal salvation **unto all them that obey him**" (Acts 5:32; Heb. 5:9).

Side Note: Those are words and teachings of an *unchanging* God and Messiah and not an evolutionary god (Mal. 3:6; Heb. 13:8; James 1:17); they are the words and teachings of the God who cannot lie (Titus 1:2; Heb. 6:18). That's to our benefit, because if God were evolutionary (ever-changing)—as is the outcome of the teachings of the mainstream traditional anti-Law ministry—we could *never* be sure if any doctrine was from God. How would we be able to know whether or not He changed it the previous night, or the day before? This raises a question that all religious people should answer at least for themselves: How can a Christian prove that the god he serves is the God of heaven and earth? How can a Jew prove likewise? and a Muslim? How can any of these sects prove which god is the *true* God and which one is a false god? It's impossible to prove either, unless you go back to the Torah and closely follow the prophecies of the *true* God of Creation, who promised to deliver such a Redeemer. Therefore it requires that we prove whatever theory wherewith we profess our Redeemer, with the Holy Scriptures—starting from Genesis 1:1 and on to the end of the scriptures—and measure *all* doctrines against it. There is *no other way* to prove that vital point.

Let's consider for a moment the religious argument between traditional Christians, Muslims, and Jews regarding each one's savior. What evidence do Christians have to prove that the Jesus whom they preach and advocate is the true Messiah of the scriptures? How can the Muslims prove that Mohammed is the true Messiah or Prophet and that traditional Christendom's Jesus is not the One? We already know that the Pharisees proved the Messiah as being an imposter by measuring Him against *their* Talmud. What evidence does either sect have to prove the other's savior as a fraud, and thereby prove their savior as legit and holy? And they all profess that they have the one and only true Savior and that the others have a false one. There are extremely vicious ongoing arguments between these religious sects—serious enough to start wars because of it—and it's prophesied to get much worse in the future. So they all profess to be following the only true God and Savior of mankind—according to what, I ask. As Paul admonished us to do, we must "prove all things" (1 Thess. 5:21).

Everyone who makes it into God's kingdom will have the Torah—which includes God's laws and commandments—inscribed into his or her heart eternally, making it possible to live by every word of God: "It is written, Man shall not live by bread alone, but **by every word that proceedeth out of the mouth of God"** (Matt. 4:4; read also Luke 4:4). The Messiah cited this directly from the Old Testament—another powerful Torah test proof: "... that he might make thee know **that man doth not live by bread only, but by every word that proceedeth out of the mouth of the LORD doth man live"** (Deut. 8:3). Thus, God's commandments perpetually inscribed into our heart will enable us to live by every Word of God, hence truly loving Him and the neighbor from the heart! That's what the Ten Commandments and all of God's laws teach—God's sacrificial-type, mercy-packed charitable **<agape>**[8] love.

The Messiah confirmed that God's commandments *are* eternal life: "And I know that his **commandment <entole>**[9] **is life everlasting"** (John 12:50). This is another Torah test proof, because God stated in the Old Testament that keeping His commandments and statutes is life; not keeping them is death:

> See, I have set before thee this day **life and good, and death and evil**; In that I command thee this day to love the LORD thy God, to walk in his ways, and to **keep his commandments and his statutes and his judgments, that thou mayest live** and multiply: and the LORD thy God shall bless thee in the land whither thou goest to possess it. But if thine heart turn away, so that thou wilt not hear, but shalt be drawn away, and worship other gods, and serve them; I denounce unto you this day, that ye shall surely perish, and that ye shall not prolong your days upon the land, whither thou passest over Jordan to go to possess it. I call heaven and earth to record this day against you, that I have set before you **life and death, blessing and cursing: therefore choose life**, that both thou and thy seed may **live**: That thou mayest love the LORD thy God, and that thou mayest obey his voice, and that thou mayest cleave unto him: for **he is thy life**, and

> the length of thy days: that thou mayest dwell in the land which the LORD sware unto thy fathers, to Abraham, to Isaac, and to Jacob, to give them. (Deut. 30:15–20)

The Messiah frequently expounded to the people upon the prophecies of the Torah, with which the Pharisees were boastful because they had a lot of knowledge of it. But because of their own invented traditions, which inevitably perverted the Torah, they couldn't understand the truth of it (John 5:46–47; 2 Cor. 3:14–4:4). He made it very plain: if we don't believe—trust—in the old writings, we will be blinded so that we will not be able to understand Him, because the Torah (the old writings) is the only book in which the prophecies that He was beginning to reveal are contained, and it is against these writings that we are commanded to measure Him, as well as all doctrines!

Peter testified that the Messiah had performed signs, wonders, and miracles as part of a proof that He was the promised Messiah: "Ye men of Israel, hear these words; Jesus of Nazareth, **a man approved of God among you by miracles and wonders and signs, which God did by him in the midst of you, as ye yourselves also know"** (Acts 2:22). Peter knew that the Messiah kept every jot and tittle of God's commandments, which—coupled with all the miracles that He did—proved in every way that the Messiah was of the true God of heaven and earth. How did Peter know whether those miracles were coming from God or Baal? He saw proof that this was the promised Son of God Messiah because, as the Messiah Himself states in Matthew 5:17–18, He made no changes to God's laws, thus harmonizing perfectly with the Torah test prophecies.

The Pharisees also knew of the test prophecy, and they also witnessed the miracles. But the miracles were not proof to them that He was the promised Messiah, because He did not keep God's commandments in accordance with their traditional talmudic version of them, as we can read in Matthew chapters 15 and 23, and Mark chapter 7:

> Then came to Jesus scribes and Pharisees, which were of Jerusalem, saying, Why do thy disciples transgress

> the **tradition of the elders** [talmudic traditions]? for they wash not their hands when they eat bread. But he answered and said unto them, **Why do ye also transgress the commandment of God** [the *written* Torah] **by your tradition** [the *oral* Torah—the Talmud]**?** For **God commanded** [in the *written* Torah]**, saying, Honour thy father and mother** [the sixth commandment (Ex. 20:12)]**: and, He that curseth father or mother, let him die the death** [a *written* commandment of God (Ex. 21:17; Lev. 20:9)]. But **ye say** [the *oral* Torah—the Talmud]**, Whosoever shall say to his father or his mother, It is a gift, by whatsoever thou mightest be profited by me** [for their convenient profit]**; And honour not his father or his mother, he shall be free. Thus have ye made the commandment <entole>**[9] **of God** [from the *written* Torah] **of none effect by your tradition** [by the *oral* Torah—talmudic tradition]**.** Ye hypocrites, well did Esaias prophesy of you, saying, This people draweth nigh unto me with their mouth, and honoureth me with their lips; but their heart is far from me. But **in vain they do worship me, teaching for doctrines the commandments <entalma>**[9a] **of men** [religious traditions] (Matt. 15:1–9; read also Mark 7:1–13; Isa. 29:13).

This leaves absolutely no wiggle room to justify traditions as doctrines, whether they're coming from the Pharisees, the Muslims, traditional Christendom, or from any religion! Tradition is tradition is tradition, no matter under which man's stripes it comes!

> **Note:** While being interrogated during trial, Paul made a very powerful testimony to prove that he was measuring his doctrines against the Torah test prophecy. He preached of no changes other than those which were prophesied to occur: "Having therefore obtained help of God, I continue unto this day, witnessing both to small and great, **saying none other things than those which the prophets and**

> **Moses did say should come**" (Acts 26:22). He goes so far as to even specify the changes that are in question, and none other: "That Christ should **suffer**, and that he should be the first that should **rise from the dead**, and should **shew light unto the people**, and **to the Gentiles**." (Acts 26:23). Paul referred to the prophecies of Isaiah chapter 53, which the Messiah came to fulfill. These events are scattered throughout the Old Testament scriptures (Gen. 3:15; 22:7–14; Deut. 18:15–18; 32:21; Ps. 16:10; Isa. 9:2; 42:6; 49:6; 55:5; 60:1–3; Joel 2:28–29), and Paul stated only the specific events that had already been fulfilled. If *any* of God's commandments had been changed or abolished, there would likely never have been a better time and place for Paul to bring it to the table than right then and there, for his court case at the time, and for you and me today, and most of all for God's honor and glory. Paul preached absolutely no other doctrines than what he could confirm in the Old Testament Torah prophecies!

Nevertheless, since traditional Christianity has been indoctrinated to believe that the Messiah abolished God's commandments, they tragically have absolutely nothing to measure *any* doctrines against in order to prove them. Everything will then qualify as doctrine, to which mainstream traditional Christendom actually is a strong testimony. Mainstream traditional Christians have been indoctrinated to believe that as long as it comes from the pulpit, that doctrine is divine. No wonder there is so much religious confusion in this Babylonian world today; it's all about doctrines of men. Church doctrines are compared between the different religions instead of being measured against the Torah.

Traditional Christendom will typically interpret 2 Corinthians chapter 3 in a way to make it say that the Old Testament is done away in the Messiah, which is the exact opposite of its true intent. Please read those paragraphs again. Paul is in perfect harmony with what the Messiah told the Pharisees, in that a man will understand the Messiah and His purpose (as our Passover Lamb—for Jew and Gentile) only after coming into agreement and alignment with God's word in the Old Testament—the Torah—which prophesied of Him and of His sole purpose. That *veil* (verse 14) is done away with upon one's belief in the Old Testament prophecies that told of the coming Messiah as the Redeemer of Israel, and how He would come to glorify God by *magnifying* His law, not by abolishing it: "The LORD is well pleased for his righteousness' sake; **he will magnify the law, and make it honourable**" (Isa. 42:21). Paul did not say that the Old Testament was done away by accepting the Messiah as Savior. Read again John 5:46–47, which harmonizes with what Paul stated in 2 Corinthians chapter 3. The New Testament scriptures reveal and confirm the Messianic prophecies of the Old Testament, because they manifest the Messiah together with His sole purpose, **exactly** as was prophesied in the Old Testament. And there are many more wonderful prophecies that the Messiah will yet fulfill in the future, of which we can read in the Old *and* New Testaments. When the Messiah begins to fulfill more of the Old Testament prophecies, we will need Torah knowledge to measure them against in order to confirm whether they come from the God of Creation or from the god of this world. How else can we know whether it is coming from God / the Messiah or from Baal?

So, in essence, the New Testament scriptures help to understand the prophecies of the Old Testament, but they do so only if you believe and accept the true manifested Messiah as the prophesied Old Testament Redeemer of Israel. That's why it's so important to understand the Old Testament. Without that understanding, one cannot prove the Messiah's doctrines, or a preacher's, because as the test prophecy states, God will allow false prophets to test us with signs and wonders that He will allow to come to pass. Only by holding fast to the Torah will one be able to prove if such a one is of the true God of Abraham, or of the god of this world. If *one* of the Ten Commandments is not kept and advocated by that person or prophet, *it **cannot** be from the God of Abraham*. It's just that simple! What else can we measure it against to be sure? That test prophecy is a tremendous benefit for all who want to make sure that the doctrines that are being advocated to us are coming from the right God—the God who brought us out of Egypt (sin), as stated in the first commandment: "I am the LORD thy God, which have brought thee out of the land of Egypt, out of the house of bondage. Thou shalt have no other gods before me" (Ex. 20:2–3; Deut. 5:6-7).

As we've seen, the Pharisees could not accept the Lord and Savior as their promised Messiah, because the Messiah's word—although it was in perfect harmony with the Torah—did not align with their perverted version of it. That's why the Pharisees could not believe Him. That's the whole argument in John chapters 5–10. It's absolutely vital that we understand this principle, because there's more prophesied in the Old Testament about the Messiah's Second Coming than in the New Testament. And there's more prophesied about His Second Coming than about His First Coming in both the Old *and* New Testaments. Thus, by rejecting the Old Testament scriptures, the truth and sole purpose of the Messiah's role in God's salvation plan in the Old *and* New Testaments cannot be understood.

If we don't measure doctrines against the Old Testament, we are apt to believe anything. If we believe that the Messiah came to compromise any part of God's Word from the Old Testament other than what was prophesied to occur, then the harsh penalties that are promised in both the Old *and* New Testaments for adding or taking away words from His Holy Scriptures are totally in vain, and the Messiah would then have been an imposter!

The Torah contains everything that the Messiah referred to, of which He was a testimony. According to the Messiah's words, the people of His day should have known all about Him with gladness. But the glory-seeking Pharisees had perverted, or Judaized, most of the Torah's writings—particularly the ones that would by doing so become a gain to their proud, control-mongering religion. And as we saw, they made judgments according to their perverted version of God's commandments (while using God's judicial instructions from Deut. 12:28–13:5, which they had, to their benefit, *not* perverted) to lay charges against the Messiah to frame Him as an imposter. Remember, God commanded that if anyone comes along and teaches *anything* different from the Torah, he or she is to be killed by stoning. And because of the Pharisees' perversion of God's commandments and laws against which they measured the Messiah's works, they often conspired to stone Him: "Then took they up stones to cast at him" (John 8:59; read also 10:31, 39; 11:8). The Messiah's teaching of the true laws of God did not line up with *their* perverted version of God's laws. Our God and Messiah laid the foundation in the beginning, which stands fast forever (Ps. 111:7–8; Matt. 5:17–19; 1 Cor. 3:11). And no one has any authority to change a jot or tittle of it; not even the Messiah, because that would make Him a liar—which is impossible (Rom. 3:4; Heb. 6:18).

The Messiah, likely bearing the Torah test prophecy in mind, reminded and warned us that the religious people *will* do miracles in His name to deceive us. If we believe and practice God's truth, we can compare their fruit against it and know with certainty whether that prophet or preacher is true or false: "Wherefore **by their fruits ye shall know them. Not every one that saith unto me, Lord, Lord**, shall enter into the kingdom of heaven; but **he that doeth the will of my Father** which is in heaven. Many will say to me in that day, Lord, Lord, have we not **prophesied in thy name**? and **in thy name have cast out devils**? and **in thy name done many wonderful works** [the test miracles of Deuteronomy chapter 13]? And then will I profess unto them, I never knew you: depart from me, **ye that work iniquity** [lawlessness] **<anomia>**[12]" (Matt. 7:20–23). In plain words, He's referring to lawless preachers whom He will *allow* to do miracles in order to test the people who profess to be following Him. Remember, doing miracles while professing His Name does not alone prove that it is from the God of heaven and earth, as He might be allowing it as a test for us! This is a very true and hard test for mankind. Just as God allowed Satan to turn sticks into snakes through Pharaoh's gods (Ex. 7:11–12), He still allows Satan to do miracles before our eyes to test us by.

Inset: In the end-time, as the ultimate test of all time, God will allow Satan to do extraordinary wonders and miracles in order to try to steer believers away from the God of Abraham, just as the Torah test warned us about. God will continue to allow Satan's miracles to come to pass:

> And he [Satan] doeth great wonders, so that **he maketh fire come down from heaven** on the earth in the sight of men, **And deceiveth them that dwell on the earth by the means of those miracles which he had power to do** in the sight of the beast [to test us]; saying to them that dwell on the earth, that they should make an image to the beast, which had the wound by a sword, and did live. **And he had power to give life unto the image of the beast**, that the image of the beast should both speak, and cause that as many as would not worship the image of the beast should be killed. **And he causeth all, both small and great, rich and poor, free and bond, to receive a mark in their right hand, or in their foreheads** (Rev. 13:13–16). What an awesome test that will be!

According to the Messiah, all people, including the elect, will eventually succumb to Satan, unless He intervenes: "For then shall be great tribulation, such as was not since the beginning of the world to this time, no, nor ever shall be. And **except those days should be shortened** [the Messiah steps in], there should no flesh be saved: but **for the elect's sake those days shall be shortened**. Then if any man shall say unto you, Lo, here is Christ, or there; believe it not. **For there shall arise false Christs, and false prophets, and shall shew great signs and wonders; insomuch that, if it were possible, they shall deceive the very elect**" (Matt. 24:21–24). Only His people—the elect, who keep God's commandments, from which they receive His identifying sign (Ex. 31:13–18; Deut. 6:1–9; Ezek. 9:4; 20:12, 20)—will be able to discern whether those miracles come from the God of Abraham or from the god of this world.

For the people who believe that God's commandments and laws have been changed or abolished, what will they measure the signs and miracles against which the man of sin, Satan, the devil, will perform to impress the world, including even the elect—God's chosen? According to law-done-away philosophy, whatever laws or commandments they will use to measure Satan's works against might be changing every century, decade, year, month, week, day, hour, minute, or maybe even every second. Do you get the picture? Actually, the inventor of the law-done-away doctrines is the same one who continually changes the doctrines as required by its followers—and that's the man of sin himself: "Let no man deceive you by any means: for that day shall not come, except there come a falling away first, and that man of sin be revealed, the son of perdition; Who opposeth and exalteth himself above all that is called God, or that is worshipped; so that he as God sitteth in the temple of God, shewing himself that he is God" (2 Thess. 2:3-4). So whatever commandments he will advocate from the authoritative throne upon which he will be sitting will always be in absolute harmony with the traditional church doctrines, because he designed them to match so as to deceive his followers.

So if any laws have changed other than what was prophesied in the Old Testament, then there's absolutely nothing to measure Satan's doctrines against. The whole world is deceived (Rev. 12:9); of which the anti-commandment religions throughout the world are a living testimony. That's why the Messiah warned us that all would succumb to the falsehood of Satan's doctrines unless He intervened to save His elect remnant (Matt. 24:22). The Messiah will return to cut it short; we'll learn more of this in section 5a.

So the Pharisees, by using the authority of the Torah test (as it does command us to do) and measuring the Messiah's works against their perverted Judaized talmudic version of God's commandments, felt compelled by God to put Him to death, which they eventually accomplished. And the Messiah warned us that the religious leaders of the day will do the same to us if we follow His commandments instead of theirs: "They shall put you out of the synagogues: yea, the time cometh, that whosoever killeth you will **think that he doeth God service"** (John 16:2; read also John 9:22, 34; Rev. 13:15).

In John chapter 8 the Pharisees boldly state that they are not in any bondage to sin. Because of that belief, which was established by using their traditional Judaized doctrines (the Talmud) as commandments, they ignorantly overlooked the vital events of the Messiah's First Coming. Paul referred to that philosophy as self-righteousness, or pride: "For I bear them record that they have a zeal of God, but not according to knowledge. For they **being ignorant of God's righteousness**, and going about to **establish their own righteousness, have not submitted themselves unto the righteousness of God**" (Rom. 10:2–3). Why not? "Because they sought it not by faith" (Rom. 9:32; read also Hebrews 4:2). What is righteousness? "All thy commandments are righteousness" (Ps. 119:172). Instead of obeying God's commandments, they established their own—hence the Talmud—which the Messiah condemned (Matt. 15, 23; Mark 7).

Similarly, today's traditional church system also has established its own traditional doctrines whereby followers become righteous. There it's preached that it's impossible to keep God's commandments, wherefore it's a sin to try. Based on that philosophy, they have invented theological doctrines to explain away the need to obey God's commandments to be saved. Saved from what, sin? What is sin? Sin is breaking God's commandments (1 John 3:4)! No sin will enter God's kingdom. And they take it yet a step further, to a point where they preach that one will end up in the fires of hell for keeping the Ten Commandments. But if the commandments were really done away with, then no one has sinned since the crucifixion, and thus everyone—commandment keepers and commandments breakers—will be in God's kingdom.

According to scriptures, God's commandments are righteousness: "And **it shall be our righteousness, if we observe to do all these commandments** before the LORD our God, as he hath commanded us" (Deut. 6:25). The New Testament states that Zacharias and Elizabeth were righteous before God for keeping His commandments: "And **they were both righteous <dikaios>**[13] **before God, walking in all the commandments <entole>**[9] **and ordinances <dikaioma>**[13a] **of the Lord blameless**" (Luke 1:6). This is another Torah test proof. What should we believe, the scriptures or the anti-Law preachers who proclaim that God designed the Ten Commandments in such a way that they couldn't be, and hence shouldn't be, kept?

Paul openly admitted in his testimonies that he had been an extremely aggressive and zealous Pharisee. Before he was converted, he was one of their top mob-ring leaders: "For ye have heard of my conversation in time past in the **Jews' religion** [the Talmud—Judaized commandments], how that **beyond measure I persecuted the church of God**, and wasted it: And profited in the Jews' religion above many my equals in mine own nation, being more **exceedingly zealous of the traditions of my fathers** [commandments of men—the Talmud]" (Gal. 1:13–14). "The Jews' religion" refers to the traditions of his fathers, who were Pharisees: "Why do thy disciples transgress the **tradition of the elders**?" (Matt. 15:2). The Messiah condemned the use of those traditions:

> He answered and said unto them, Well hath Esaias prophesied of you hypocrites, as it is **written**, This people honoureth me with their lips, but their heart is far from me. Howbeit in vain do they worship me, teaching for doctrines the **commandments <entalma>**[9a] **of men** [talmudic doctrines]. **For laying aside the commandment** <entole>[9] **of God, ye hold the tradition of men**, as the washing of pots and cups: and many other such like things ye do. And he said unto them, **Full well ye reject the commandment** <entole>[9] **of God, that ye may keep your own tradition. Making the word of God of none effect through your tradition** ... (Mark 7:6–9, 13; read also Matt. 15:6–9 and chapter 23)

This is a very important testimony to remember whenever studying the laws that Paul refers to throughout his ministry, because in some instances where he speaks about laws or circumcision, he's referring to these *traditional* laws, mixed with the works of the animal sacrificial rituals, and then all together syncretized with God's commandments. That's how Judaism is borne, hence the Talmud.

Please note: the translators used the English word "commandments" as the translation of two different Greek words in the above scripture. In verse 7 they translated the Greek word "*entalma*" into the English word "commandment," which means "a **religious** precept or commandment." In verse 9 they used the word "commandment" as the translation of the Greek word "*entole*," which means "an **authoritative** commandment and precept." "Entole" designates precepts of God, while "entalma" designates religious precepts that come from doctrines of men. The word "entalma" describes the traditional doctrines of the Jews and the traditional doctrines of Christians. Tradition is tradition is tradition, no matter which religious label we hang on it.

Paul's testimony continues:

> Circumcised the eighth day, of the stock of Israel, of the tribe of Benjamin, an **Hebrew** of the Hebrews; as touching the law, **a Pharisee**; Concerning zeal, persecuting the church; touching the righteousness which is in the law, blameless. (Phil. 3:5–6)
>
> I am a **Pharisee**, the son of a Pharisee. (Acts 23:6)
>
> After the most **straitest sect** of our religion **I lived a Pharisee"** (Acts 26:5).

In Judaism, they justified themselves according to their own traditional Judaized commandments **<entalma>**[9a], which they preached as God's divine commandments **<entole>**[9]. Before conversion, Paul was a highly respected minister of that talmudic system.

Common theologians, taking after the early anti-Jew church fathers, such as Emperor Constantine I and reformer Martin Luther, have taken these perverted Judaized traditions, syncretized with God's commandments and laws as they were, and labeled them all together as burdensome and grievous rudiments of this world. So they label the Ten Commandments with that philosophy, thus claiming that to be the reason why they were nailed to the tree together with the Messiah. And according to that philosophy is how the anti-commandment doctrines are preached in the whole of today's traditional church system. Thus they have invented an anti-Jew, anti-Law, and anti-Torah philosophy, from which is borne an extreme hatred for the Jews—thus through this inherently causing a hatred for God's commandments and laws, because the Jews whom they condemn profess to be keeping them. A proverbial saying comes to mind: "Hence they've thrown out the baby [God's commandments—**<entole>**[9]] with the bathwater [man's commandments—**<entalma>**[9a]].

We need to study this with an unbiased, open, reverential, and God-fearing mind to understand how such an apostasy could take place. Let's examine it further.

3. HEBREWS—ABRAHAM'S DESCENDANTS

To better understand that apostasy as a whole, it will help to gain some insight into the history of the Pharisaic Jews. We will find out who they are and aren't, where they come from, and some of the things that they did and didn't do, and why. Then we can better give credit where it's due. This will help to understand some of the terms used, in order to be able to put many of the misrepresented and perverted doctrinal issues into a better perspective. After we get a better grip on that, and see some of their motive as to *why* they did what they did, and hence see the results of those decisions, we will be able to better understand what actually took place. First of all, we'll take a brief look at our faithful father, Abraham. It is through his faith in God that we have received the great promises. We will begin with him and his descendants, to see who his children really are.

God started His creation of humankind in the garden of Eden about six thousand years ago when he created the *first* Adam, and shortly thereafter, Eve. They rejected God and worshipped Satan instead, which mankind—as descendants of Adam—still prefers to this day. Those who repent of this world's Satan worship and worship the creator God through the Messiah—the *last* Adam—and accept Him as their personal Lord and Savior, are promised eternal life (the tree of life, Gen. 3:22), thus taking us back to the paradise in the garden of Eden: "Blessed are they that **do his commandments <entole>**[9], that they may have right to the **tree of life**, and may enter in through the gates into the city" (Rev. 22:14). This time Satan and his influences (Rev. 20) are not present in the garden; I will explain more about this in section 5a.

Around 1400 BC, God chose to Himself a peculiar people, the Israelites, Hebrew descendants of faithful Abraham, through whom He would reveal His sovereignty and almighty power to the world. They were to be His nation of people here on earth. God also accepted many Gentiles into that family (Ex. 12:38). All who had faith in Him were redeemed—a theme that is unbroken throughout the Scriptures (Ex. 12:38; Matt. 3:9; Acts 13:26; Rom. 2:28–29; 4:11; 9:6–8; 10:12; chapter 11; 1 Cor. 7:19; 12:13; Gal. 3:28–29; 4:28–29; 5:6; Eph. 2:14–16; Col. 3:11). He would demonstrate to the world how, through faith in Him, He would redeem His children from the Egyptian bondage and slavery by His grace and mercy. Through great miracles, wonders, and judgments He did demonstrate His power to the world, and He proved with all certainty that He was the great eternal God of heaven and earth and everything in it! And that theme of how He redeems people by His grace, through faith in Him, remains unbroken. That's how He proved to the whole world—especially to the Egyptians—that He was the only God through whom liberty could be attained, and that all other gods were powerless.

God, through Moses, instructed the children of Israel to rely on Him alone, to walk in His ways, thereby teaching the vitality of faith in Him: "... that he might make thee know man doth not live by bread only, but **by every word** that proceedeth out of the mouth of the LORD doth man live" (Deut. 8:3). In Matthew 4:4 and Luke 4:4, the Messiah confirms that it did not change because of His appearance on the scene—a Torah test proof of Deuteronomy 8:3. Evidently the Ten Commandments also proceeded from the mouth of God. The Messiah testified that He was not about to make any changes to them: "Think **not** that I am come to destroy the law, or the prophets: I am not come to destroy, but to **fulfil <pleroo>**[10]. For verily I say unto you, **Till heaven and earth pass** [yet future], **<u>one jot or one tittle</u> shall in no wise pass from the law, till all be fulfilled <ginomai>**[14]" (Matt. 5:17–18; read also Luke 16:17).

> **Side note:** The word "fulfil" was translated from the Greek word *"pleroo,"* which is #4137 in *Strong's Concordance,* where it is described as "to satisfy, verify, accomplish, complete, fill up, fully preach, perfect, to execute into office"; in other words, the Messiah "put a perfected instruction into full effect." And that effect is testified to by His walk

in God's Word and keeping His commandments perfectly, through which God's sacrificial, charitable <**agape**>[8] love was manifested in Him, thus causing Him to willingly sacrifice His life as a ransom for our sins (John 10:18; Gal. 1:4; 1 John 1:9).

Thus, just as Moses trained God's Torah instructions to Abraham's descendants when God redeemed them from the Egyptian bondage; we will see that those instructions remain in full force and effect in this era in which we live today, and they will be carried over into the world to come when His word and truth, the Torah, will be perpetually inscribed into the hearts and minds of His obedient children (Jer. 31:33; Heb. 8:10). That's why the Messiah testified that He had not come to abolish one jot or tittle of God's laws. People with faith in the God of Abraham through the Messiah will be identified: "... *and his name shall be* ***in their foreheads*** (Rev. 22:4; read also Ex. 13:9, 16; 31:13, 17; Deut. 6:8; 11:18; Ezek. 9:4; 20:12, 20; Gal. 3:28–29; 6:16). His laws of love and mercy will be trained, and thus eternally inscribed into the hearts and minds of His people, perpetually engraved into the thinking process. God commands parents to begin that process with their children in their home (Ex. 13:14; Deut. 6:1–7).

3a. Israelites, Jews, and Gentiles

I'll briefly define a few terms that are essential to understand some of the events as they relate to Israelites, Jews, Pharisees, Sadducees, and Gentiles/heathens. It will help us to understand how the early traditional church fathers, because of their extreme hatred for the Jews, perverted much of God's Word in order to invent church doctrines in a way to make them say that God gave His commandments only to the Jews and that obedience to them is not required by New Testament believers. Many will go as far as to say that God will condemn a person for keeping His commandments, because by keeping them one supposedly has rejected the Messiah's sacrifice and God's grace. And those doctrines are preached as God's divine word. As Paul also acknowledged in Romans chapter 8, we'll see that the root cause of this extreme enmity is actually founded upon man's inherent hatred toward God, whereby any laws coming from Him are inevitably hated. Thus we will see that it's the preaching of God's laws as being Jewish that gives traditional Christianity the audacity to condemn those who keep the Ten Commandments, thereby advocating lawlessness as liberty.

> **Side Note:** The carnal-thinking mind inherently hates God; it's a trait we inherited from Adam and Eve. "It's in the genes" as some would say in modern terms. So, contrariwise, Paul explains in Romans chapter 8 that the spiritually thinking mind will willingly submit to God's laws:
>
> For they that are after the flesh do mind the things of the flesh; but they that are after the Spirit the things of the Spirit. For to be **carnally minded is death**; but to be **spiritually minded is life and peace** [compare with Deuteronomy chapter 30]. Because **the carnal mind is**

> **enmity against God: for it is not subject to the law of God, neither indeed can be**. So then they that are in the flesh cannot please God. But ye are not in the flesh, but in the Spirit, **if so be that the Spirit of God dwell in you**. Now if any man have not the Spirit of Christ, he is none of his. And if Christ be in you, the body is dead because of sin; but the Spirit is life because of righteousness. But **if** the Spirit of him that raised up Jesus from the dead dwell in you, he that raised up Christ from the dead shall also quicken your mortal bodies **by his Spirit that dwelleth in you.** (Rom. 8:5–11)

So we can see that a carnal-thinking mind is hostile toward the creator God because it cannot be subjected to His laws, as His laws are spiritual: "For we know that the **law is spiritual**: but **I am carnal**, sold under sin" (Rom. 7:14). Accordingly, to be able to love God in spirit and please Him, we need to have His Spirit dwelling in our heart, whereby, according to what Paul stated in Romans chapter 8 (cited above), we would then willingly become subjected to His laws. After all, God wants us to love Him and our neighbor: "**God is love <agape>**[8]; and he that dwelleth in love <**agape**>[8] dwelleth in God, and God in him" (1 John 4:16). Contrary to traditional anti-Jew teaching, according to scriptures, God's commandments are that love: "By this we know that we love the children of God, when we love God, and keep his commandments. **For this is the love <agape>**[8] **of God, that we keep his commandments <entole>**[9]: and his commandments are not grievous" (1 John 5:2–3). Since God's laws are spiritual (Rom. 7:14), they deliver life and peace: "For **to be carnally minded is death**; but **to be spiritually minded is life and peace**" (Rom. 8:6).

In Romans 7:14–25, Paul confesses that since the law is spiritual while he is carnal, he will be warring with his carnality as long as he lives. He concludes that the laws and commandments are there to convict him and then correct him while he's in the carnal state, which is why he delights in God's laws (verse 22). In chapter 8 he encourages us to walk after the Spirit and not after the carnal desires of the flesh, because God is working in us to conform us into the image of His Son, the Messiah, who was resurrected into His spiritual image (verse 29). And His followers will be in the Messiah's spiritual and immortal image after the resurrection (1 Cor. 15:42–54), when death, the penalty of sin, will be overcome and thus swallowed up.

This side note may appear to be somewhat off topic. I feel that it's important at this point to show how Paul explains the difference between a carnal-thinking mind and a spiritual-thinking mind. I know that this is extremely controversial to typical traditionally orchestrated theological philosophy in that they teach that our Lord and Savior nailed the Ten Commandments to the tree, thus invalidating them. But as Paul states, a carnal thinking mind inherently hates the creator God, thus inevitably causing one to hate His laws—hence no offence, but accordingly, the traditional theologians automatically fall into that category. On the flip side, a spiritual-thinking mind inherently loves the creator God, thus inevitably causing one to love His laws; after all, God's laws are what liberate a man to his creator God and to one another. (Read Psalms chapter 119 and James 2:8–12.)

It's very important to realize the seriousness of that corrupt philosophy, because you'll see as we progress that the theologians who invented the traditional church doctrines together with their trained ministers were—and still are today—thinking carnally. Of course they argue the opposite to be the case, in order to reason around the need to keep the Ten Commandments. But God's Spirit will *not* work against His commandments. It's vitally important to understand this concept to be able to grasp what follows—namely, how traditional theologians with an inherent anti-God mind-set have successfully indoctrinated potentially billions of people to believe that the Ten Commandments are no longer valid by foisting them off onto the so-labeled condemned Jews.

Furthermore, they claim that the Jews—whom the Messiah (and His apostles) excoriated for keeping traditional commandments **<entalma>**[9a] wherewith God's commandments **<entole>**[9] are inevitably forsaken (Matt. 15:6–9; chapter 23; Mark 7:6–9)—have been condemned for keeping God's commandments. Again that's what's given them the audacity to boldly proclaim that the Messiah abolished the Ten Commandments. Not to offend—because the whole traditional church system has been blinded—but the foundation of today's mainstream traditional church doctrines have been established upon exactly that philosophy. And whether they know it or not—and whether they like it or not—by far, the majority of the people of that church system are descendants of the Israelites. Just as was prophesied would happen—which seems to have come to fruition—for forsaking the God of Creation by breaking His commandments, whereby they have given up their identifying sign (Ex. 31:13–18; Ezek. chapter 20), they've lost their identity (Deut. 32:26), of which we'll learn more as we progress along.

So, with that mind-set, the following statement will be very hard to swallow by mainstream traditional churchgoers. I'll try to explain how the theocracy behind the anti-Jew, anti-Law, and hence anti-Torah foundation—which has been a supreme breeding ground for Satan to successfully establish his anti-God philosophy—has been blindly preached by his ministry in modern-day mainstream traditional churches for many centuries already. As we go through the next portion of this book, we'll learn how Satan used the traditionally accepted anti-Jew philosophy to cunningly grow that philosophy into an anti-God theocracy with which the traditional church system is plagued without knowing it (because, as Paul stated in 2 Corinthians chapter 3 and 4, just like the Pharisees, they've been blinded; their hearts are uncircumcised and are thus veiled from the truth because of their rejection of the true written Torah). Thus we'll see that the anti-Jew philosophy is actually founded upon an inherent hatred for the God of Abraham. Through it we'll see that that hatred comes from the forsaking of God's commandments *through* the teaching of traditional doctrines as commandments—traditions that Satan foisted upon our parents of old, Adam and Eve, establishing a philosophy we still prefer.

To make that philosophy even more effective, these demon-inspired mainstream traditional theologians have based Bible commentaries and Bible courses upon that philosophy. This has a tremendous influence on the average Bible readers and teachers—*especially* the ones that go to the systematically traditionalized and preconditioned Bible schools, Bible colleges, and universities. I say this because the curriculum used in these institutions comes from commentaries, essays, novels, and so on that hinge on the teachings of these evolutionary-based theologians, who have labeled their twisted and perverted theological philosophy as divine Scriptural instructions to suit man's glory-seeking anti-Torah lustful needs and desires. But the God of Abraham is the opposite of evolution; He says He does not change by the slightest degree: "Every good gift and every perfect gift is from above, and cometh down from the Father of lights, **with whom is no variableness, neither shadow of turning**" (James 1:17; read also Mal. 3:6; Heb. 13:8).

Martin Luther, renowned worldwide as one of the church-reforming heroes, flat-out condemned the Jews in the last few years of his life, as revealed in one of his many anti-Jew/anti-Torah books, *Von den Jüden und Iren Lügen* (*On the Jews and Their Lies*), which he wrote in 1543, about four years before his death. In this book he expresses extreme and vicious enmity toward the Jews and repeatedly orders his followers to destroy them, burn their synagogues, homes, schools, and Bibles, and ultimately slay them. He preached to his followers that God would hold them accountable to the Messiah's blood for *not* doing so! And the modern-day traditional church doctrines were established by people such as Constantine, Luther, Hitler, and their followers; no wonder their doctrines are so anti-Law and God-hating.

If you'll study Adolf Hitler's motives for the holocaust that he orchestrated in the 1930s, you'll learn that he used information such as Martin Luther's writings as a mentorship to justify his already-extant enmity with the Jews. The Nazi regime and the socialist-communist system still draw strength from such works as Luther's writings.

I will try to illustrate how these theologians, who are by and large Israelites, have perverted scriptures to suit their lustful anti-God doctrines. Bear in mind that they've lost their identity; wherefore, they *cannot* understand scriptural prophecies, because they are blinded—veiled from the truth. For instance, they have a very foggy understanding, *if any*, as to who is a Jew, or an Israelite, or a Pharisee, or for that matter a Gentile. To them, Pharisees, Sadducees, Jews, and Israelites are all simply condemned Jews. For the same reason, they see the rest of the world as Gentiles or Christians. And they go on to teach that the Messiah came to condemn the Jews in order to save the Gentiles; that's why traditional Christians are so dead-set determined to be Gentiles. With such a mind-set, they *cannot* gain any knowledge about what the scriptures prophesy about the Israelites, Jews, Pharisees, Sadducees, or the Gentiles. Why? They're veiled from the truth. Mankind's inherent desire to live lawlessly—free—is why they want to be Gentiles. It's true; the Gentiles chose to live by Baal's laws instead of God's, just as the traditional Christians have chosen to do. And lawlessness is the very reason God destroyed the Gentiles by the thousands—or millions—in the past. And as free moral agents, we are still free to choose whom we will serve (Judges 10:13–14; 1 Kings 18:21).

Traditional Christians know that the Pharisees are dedicated commandment-keeping Jews because that's what they hear from the pulpit while the ministers preach sermons about how the Jews are going to hell for trying to be justified by keeping God's commandments—which is why they labeled the Ten Commandments as being so horrible and Jewish. And they go on to preach how not keeping the commandments has justified them, the Gentile Christians of the New Testament church. That's why, when they read the accounts where the Messiah, or an apostle, excoriated the Pharisees for keeping traditional commandments that are inevitably contrary to God's commandments, they lump them all together—the Israelites, Jews, Pharisees, and Sadducees—and label them all as condemned commandment-keeping Jews.

As I showed earlier, they do the same with the Pharisaic traditions and God's commandments. Since the Messiah condemned the use of the Judaized commandments <**entalma**>[9a] (the Talmud) that the Pharisees had syncretized with God's commandments <**entole**>[9], the theologians also lump them all together and label them as burdensome, grievous, weak, and beggarly commandments of the condemned Jews. Based on that belief, the claim is made that one will be condemned for keeping the Ten Commandments—particularly the fourth one, which specifically identifies the Jews in today's society because many of them still observe the Lord's Sabbath on the seventh day of the week! Under that same umbrella, they also condemn the Jews for keeping God's holy days and for observing God's dietary and health laws. It has absolutely nothing to do with whether or not what the Jews practice is right or wrong according to the God of Abraham. What matters is simply that they *cannot have anything in common with the Jews!* So, based on that philosophy—**nothing** bearing on Scriptural *right* or *wrong*—whatever the Jews do must be condemned! And they establish their traditional church doctrines based on that philosophy.

This is why, when we mention observing God's commandments, the traditional churchgoer will immediately try to gun us down with phrases like, "Those burdensome and weak and beggarly laws and commandments were for the Jews! Jesus set us free from that bondage and nailed it to the cross, and by keeping them you're trampling on His blood, for which you'll go to hell to burn alive for all eternity," without knowing what they are saying. That's understandable, because that's what they constantly hear from their preachers, who've been trained by the demonized theologians I'm trying to expose. And their faithful followers are convinced by them that they are hearing God's divine word!

The Messiah was nailed to the tree for mankind *breaking* God's commandments, not for *keeping* them. And now we can have those transgressions forgiven by Him if we recognize that truth and repent of the breaking of them and start keeping them: "If we confess our sins, he is faithful and just to forgive us our sins, and to cleanse us from all unrighteousness" (1 John 1:9). That's the very liberty with which He set us free from the penalty of transgressing God's laws, for which we otherwise—if not repented of—deserve to die.

God's commandments are for us in every way. That's why He calls them His royal laws of love and liberty: "If ye fulfil the **royal law** according to the scripture, Thou shalt love thy neighbour as thyself, ye do well: But if ye have respect to persons [elevating man's laws to the same level as or above God's], ye commit sin, and are convinced of the law as transgressors. For whosoever shall keep the whole law, and yet offend in one point, he is guilty of all. For he that said, Do not commit adultery, said also, Do not kill. Now if thou commit no adultery, yet if thou kill, thou art become **a transgressor of the law**. So speak ye, and so do, as they that shall be judged by the **law of liberty**." (James 2:8–12; 1 John 4:16; 5:1–3). Judgment for transgressing the liberating law exacts the death penalty: "Then **when lust hath conceived, it bringeth forth sin: and sin, when it is finished, bringeth forth death"** (James 1:15; read also Gen. 2:17; Rom. 6:23). The penalties against us for the breaking of them (Col. 2:14) are what is, if repented of, nailed to the tree—not God's commandments.

Because of the anti-Jew, anti-Law, and hence anti-Torah doctrines, theologically trained traditional preachers violently denounce everything that the Jews do. That's how people like Constantine the Great and Luther outlawed the Lord's Sabbaths: since the Jews keep them, they must condemn them! Keeping God's commandments, particularly the Lord's Sabbath commandment, is condemned by them because early Church fathers labeled it as Judaizing (Philip Schaff and Henry Wace, eds., *Nicene and Post-Nicene Fathers: Second Series*, vol. 14, [Peabody, MA: Hendrickson Publishers, 1996], 148). Constantine also traded off the Lord's Passover for the pagan Easter using the same reasoning (Ibid., 54–56, 108). Thus, they've traded off the commandments that openly identify one's obedience to the God of Creation—namely the first one (Ex. 20:2–3), and more specifically the fourth one (Ex. 20:8–11). They do to some extent honor the commandments of the second tablet because they are to a large extent enforced by the laws of most countries. Mankind has great fear for the evolutionary gods who make the nation's laws, but not for the eternal non-evolutionary God, who created the laws of the universe and gives us the breath we breathe. That's because of mankind's inherent fear of men—because of the inherent hatred for God (Rom. 8:7). I respect and obey the laws of the land as long as they don't contradict the laws of God. When contested, we're commanded to obey God: "Then Peter and the other apostles answered and said, **We ought to obey God rather than men**" (Acts 5:29; read also 4:19; Ps. 40:4; 62:5–10; 118:8; Jer. 17:5–8).

Notice how the first commandment is usually worded: "Thou shalt have no other gods before me" (Ex. 20:3). The preceding verse—because of anti-Jewism—is left out because it states *which* God we ought to obey and worship. It identifies the God who redeemed the so-called Jews from Egypt: "I am the Lord thy God, which have brought thee out of the land of Egypt, out of the house of bondage" (Ex. 20:2). Since traditional doctrines teach that the fourth commandment was given only for the Jews, they teach that it does not apply to the New Testament church. So the two particular commandments that very specifically identify the creator God of Abraham have been misappropriated and taken out of context to a point where they apply *only* to Jews and *not* to today's Christians—according to the traditional commandments of men—because of the fear or respect of persons (James 2:9).

Throughout the scriptures, the eternal God has revealed the observance of the fourth commandment as an everlasting sign indicating which God we serve—identifying His peculiar treasured children—by keeping the Sabbath holy for God, not for the Jews:

> Speak thou also unto the children of Israel, saying, Verily **my** sabbaths [not the Jews'] ye shall keep: for **it is a sign between me and you** throughout your generations [ongoing]; that ye may know that I am the Lord that doth sanctify you [set you apart]. Ye shall keep the sabbath therefore; for it is holy unto you: every one that defileth it shall surely be put to death: for whosoever doeth any work therein, that soul shall be cut off from among his people. Six days may work be done; but in **the seventh** is the sabbath of rest, **holy to the Lord** [the Messiah as Lord—a Jew]: whosoever doeth any work in the sabbath day, he shall surely be put to death. Wherefore the children of Israel shall keep the sabbath, to observe the sabbath throughout their generations, **for a perpetual <`owlam>**[1] **covenant. It is a sign between me and the children of Israel for ever <`owlam>**[1]: for in six days the Lord made heaven and earth [identifying the non-evolutionary God of Creation], and **on the seventh day he rested**, and was refreshed. And he gave unto Moses, when he had made an end of communing with him upon mount Sinai, two tables

> of testimony, tables of stone, **written with the finger of God.** (Ex. 31:13–18)

God gave the Sabbaths specifically so that the people would know who sanctified them (set them apart from the world): "Moreover also I gave them my sabbaths, to be a sign between me and them, that they might know that **I am the LORD that sanctifieth <qadash>[15] them.** And hallow my sabbaths; and they shall be a sign between me and you, that ye may know that I am the LORD your God" (Ezek. 20:12, 20).

As we can see, the anti-Jew mind-set in modern religion is the major cause for a lot of scriptures to become misconstrued and misappropriated in a serious effort to make them say that the Ten Commandments are abolished. The success—of which the traditional church system is a triumphant testimony—is extremely sobering. Many—or most—of those misrepresentations in question are from Paul's "hard to understand" scriptures, of which Peter gave us a good forewarning (2 Peter 3:15–17). And those doctrines are not about to cease, because they are passed on from generation to generation by ministers who are trained by the theologians who create the curriculum for the conventional Bible schools, colleges, and universities where new ministers are constantly born. Of such is Satan's workshop, through which his ministers indoctrinate the masses through the public education system and the traditional pulpits that are at his disposal. That program covers most of North America (USA and Canada), and also other Israelite nations across the globe—namely the whole Anglo-Saxon population: the Israelites who were scattered about 2,700 years ago.

> **Side note:** Satan has indoctrinated hundreds of millions of people through the traditional pulpits in a cunning way in which the traditional Christians will worship him when he goes to sit upon the throne in the temple in the near future (Isa. 14:13–14; Ezek. 28:2–9; Dan. 7:25; 1 John 2:18; 2 Thess. 2:3–4; Rev. 13). He has them trained to his ways! That's why he has trained them to reject the Torah—they now have nothing to measure his doctrines

> against; his commandments are in complete and total compliance with the traditional church doctrinal system, because he designed it in the first place (John 8:44; 2 Cor. 11:13-15).

The traditional church system has done the same with the perpetual covenants that God made with His Israelites. Throughout the scriptures, the prophecies about the past, present, and future all relate to God's people as Israelites. So whenever theologically trained Christians read a scripture that addresses an Israelite, Jew, or Pharisee, it's immediately labeled with their anti-Jew mind-set, in the sense that whatever the topic at hand may be, it must relate to Judaizing, from which they must refrain at all cost, and condemn it; they can't have anything in common with the Jews! After all, that's why they've labeled the Ten Commandments as Jewish, burdensome, weak, and beggarly elements of the world and preach it as such. For that reason, it's important to define who and what these people are, else the prophecies make very little sense, or no sense at all. Therefore I'll briefly identify them. Knowledge of that will also help to discern between God's commandments and man's, and thus help to differentiate between God's moral laws and the animal sacrificial and ritualistic laws.

> Gentiles are heathen people who did not know the God of Abraham and worshipped pagan gods: Howbeit then, when ye **knew not God**, ye did service unto them which by nature are no gods. (Gal. 4:8)
>
> Wherefore remember, that ye being in **time past Gentiles** in the flesh, who are called Uncircumcision [Gentiles] by that which is called the Circumcision [Jews—Israelites] in the flesh made by hands; That at that time ye were without Christ, being **aliens from the commonwealth of Israel**, and **strangers from the covenants of promise**, **having no hope**, and **without God** in the world. (Eph. 2:11–12)

Side Note: Gentile people did not know the God of Creation, the God of Israel; wherefore, they did not practice the commandments and laws of that God. Nevertheless, God destroyed multitudes of them as if they had known and broken them intentionally, of which we can read very gruesome and colorful testimonies. Accounts in the book of Genesis show that the people were wicked and evil (Gen. 6:5); for this, the death penalty was served (e.g., the Great Flood [Gen. 6–8] and Sodom and Gomorrah [Gen. 19:24–25]). When God delivered His Israelite children from Egypt, He killed all the firstborn of man and beast among the pagan worshippers in Egypt (Ex. 13:15), and drowned the whole Egyptian army together with the Pharaoh (Ex. 14:13-31). He destroyed the heathen nations on the other side of Jordan River because of their lawlessness: "Not for thy righteousness, or for the uprightness of thine heart, dost thou go to possess their land: but **for the wickedness of these nations** [Gentiles—Heathens] the Lord thy God doth drive them out from before thee, and that he may perform the word which the Lord sware unto thy fathers, Abraham, Isaac, and Jacob" (Deut. 9:5).

He destroyed Gentile people for not abiding by His laws: "Defile not ye yourselves in any of these things: for in all these **the nations** [Gentiles] **are defiled** which I cast out before you: And the land is defiled: therefore **I do visit the iniquity thereof upon it**, and the land itself vomiteth out her inhabitants" (Lev. 18:24–25). Whether or not the Gentiles knew that they were breaking the laws of the creator God, He destroyed them, even centuries before He inscribed His commandments into stone tablets at Mount Sinai. Why did He destroy the Gentiles if His laws applied only to the Jews, *and* only after Mount Sinai? And to prove that His laws had not changed, He destroyed the Gentiles again in the same fashion—after Mount Sinai. God confirmed it yet again when Peter confronted Ananias and his wife Sapphira after they lied, breaking the ninth commandment, which was apparently already nailed to the tree with the Messiah (Acts 5:1–10). Paul stated in the New Testament, decades after the Messiah's resurrection, that lawbreakers—like sodomites together with their supporters—still deserve death: "Who knowing the judgment of God, that they which commit such things **are <eisi>**[16]

[not "were" as *past* tense, but "are" as *present* tense] **worthy of death**, not only do the same, but have pleasure in them that do them" (Rom. 1:32). The Greek word <**eisi**>[16] is used well over a hundred times in the KJV New Testament as "are"—present tense, not past tense. Paul states that commandment breakers, and even those who merely take pleasure in those who do so, still deserve death if they do not repent.

A broken law does not go unpunished; else it's not a law. As has been proven over and over in the scriptures, in both the Old and New Testaments, you do not need to know of a specific law to be able to break it and be punished for it. That's what law is! And ignorance is no excuse: "**My people are destroyed for lack of knowledge**: because thou hast rejected knowledge, I will also reject thee, that thou shalt be no priest to me: **seeing thou hast forgotten the law of thy God**, I will also forget thy children" (Hos. 4:6). God's law is the same as a traffic law, except that He does not require a patrolman or a witness in order to punish the transgressor. And when He does punish, He does it out of His sacrificial, charitable <**agape**>[8] love in order to correct that person as well as others who become aware of it, in hopes that it will cause them to repent of their wickedness (commandment-breaking) and go back to obeying His commandments and laws of love and liberty, which causes Him to pour out His blessings. (Read Lev. 26; Deut. 8 and 28; and Ezek. 18 and 33.) Sometimes God's correction method requires the transgressor to be killed in order to rid the camp of certain far-reaching iniquities, for the benefit of the other people.

> Paul states in Ephesians 2:11–12 that the Gentiles had been aliens from the commonwealth of Israel, strangers from the covenants of promise, thus hopeless—without God. Then in verse 19 he brings in the hope for them, in that they now are no longer strangers and aliens, but are now fellow citizens with the saints (Israelites) upon whom the promises were made. According to the philosophy of traditional Christendom, they will have no part of these covenants, because they profess to remain Gentiles and the covenants and promises come from the Old Jewish

Testament; they can't have anything in common with the Jews! They need to seriously reconsider that belief if they want to partake in the promises of Abraham (Gal. 3:26–29). They need to reconcile their line of reasoning so that they may also claim the covenantal promises of Abraham through his children, the Israelites:

> ... the inheritance of the congregation of Jacob [Israel]. (Deut. 33:4)
> ... the Israel of God (Gal. 6:16).

I will give a brief chronology of the tribes of Israel. The information I used to compile this list is what I've collected from a book that the late Herbert W. Armstrong wrote: (*The United States and Britain in Prophecy*) and also from a few other sources. I will list them so you can see where the majority of the so-called lost tribes of Israel are potentially located in the world today, according to these resources together with some Scriptural references.

Reuben = France. This tribe was dignified but troubled. "Reuben, thou art my firstborn, my might, and the beginning of my strength, the excellency of dignity, and the excellency of power: Unstable as water, thou shalt not excel; because thou wentest up to thy father's bed; then defiledst thou it: he went up to my couch" (Gen. 49:3-4; 1 Chron. 5:1-2).

Simeon (and **Levi**—priesthood) = Welsh, Jews, and Scots. Members of this tribe were scattered mostly within Israel, and also among other Israelite nations. "Simeon and Levi are brethren; instruments of cruelty are in their habitations" (Gen. 49:5).

Judah = Sons of Perez (Pharezites) and Zerah (Zarhites), including the royal lineage of Ireland, Scotland, and England. This tribe comprises ethnic Israelis; Occidental (white) Jews, Ashkenazi and Sephardic Jews, and sons of Shelah (Shelamites). (Gen. 46:12; Num. 26:20). They are also scattered among all other tribes—some in the land of Israel. (Ezra 4:12). King David and the Messiah were of this lineage. "The sceptre shall not depart from Judah, nor a lawgiver from between his feet, until **Shiloh**

<Shiyloh>[17] [the Messiah in the Pharez and Zerah line (Gen. 46:12; Matt. 1:3)] come; and unto him shall the gathering of the people be" (Gen. 49:10).

Dan = Republic of Ireland, Denmark. Members of the tribe of Dan mixed with the northern tribes. "Dan shall be a serpent by the way, an adder in the path, that biteth the horse heels, so that his rider shall fall backward" (Gen. 49:17; read also Judges 18:12, 29). Those in Northern Ireland are mainly from Ephraim.

Naphtali = Norway, Sweden, Germany. This tribe is attractively described. "Naphtali is a hind let loose: he giveth goodly words" (Gen. 49:21).

Gad = Switzerland. The tribe of Gad will apparently have to temporarily accept the EU domination. "Gad, a troop shall overcome him: but he shall overcome at the last" (Gen. 49:19).

Asher = Belgium and Luxembourg. The tribe of Asher is known for its wealth. "Out of Asher his bread shall be fat, and he shall yield royal dainties" (Gen. 49:20).

Issachar = Finland, and between Europe and Russia. "Issachar is a strong ass couching down between two burdens" (Gen. 49:14).

Zebulun = Holland (the Netherlands). "Zebulun shall dwell at the haven of the sea; and he shall be for an haven of ships; and his border shall be unto Zidon" (Gen. 49:13).

Joseph: Joseph had two sons, Manasseh and Ephraim. These tribes make up the English-speaking Anglo-Saxon nations. That's why I usually refer to North America as the United States and Canada combined—we have much in common. "Joseph is a fruitful bough, even a fruitful bough by a well; whose branches run over the wall" (Gen. 49:22).

Manasseh = the United States of America. This is Joseph's firstborn and is a blessed nation. "He also shall become a people, and he also shall be great" (Gen. 48:19; 14–22).

Ephraim = The British Commonwealth: Britain, Canada, Australia, New Zealand, and part of South Africa and Zimbabwe. "But truly his younger brother shall be greater than he, and his seed shall become a multitude of nations" (Gen. 48:19; 14–22).

Benjamin = Normans, Icelanders, Quebecois—former Vikings. "Benjamin shall ravin as a wolf: in the morning he shall devour the prey, and at night he shall divide the spoil" (Gen. 49:27). Some of Benjamin's tribe joined the tribes of Judah and Levi when the scattering occurred about 740 BC (2 Kings 16–17). Paul also makes mention of the fact that he was an Israelite, a Hebrew, a Jew, born in Benjamin's lineage. "circumcised the eighth day, of the stock of **Israel,** of the tribe of **Benjamin,** an **Hebrew** of the Hebrews; as touching the law, a **Pharisee** [Jew]" (Phil. 3:5; read also Rom. 11:1).

Israelites: Israelites are the twelve patriarchal Hebrew descendants of Abraham, named after Jacob, whose name God changed to Israel when He transferred the promises of Abraham to him: "And he said, Thy name shall be called no more Jacob, but **Israel"** (Gen. 32:28). Many Gentiles joined the Israelites, who also were redeemed by the same God: "And a **mixed <`ereb>**[18] **multitude** went up also with them" (Ex. 12:38). All who had **faith** and believed that the God of Abraham, Isaac, and Jacob/ Israel—the **God of Israel**—would redeem them from the Egyptian bondage and slavery were counted as Israelites and as such reconciled to Him, thus justified. God calls all people who have faith in Him Israelites, regardless of nationality. He plays no favors and accepts no bribes:

> For the LORD your God is God of gods, and Lord of lords, a great God, a mighty, and a terrible, which **regardeth not persons**, nor taketh **reward <shachad>**[19] [bribes]. (Deut. 10:17)

> Of a truth I perceive that God is **no respecter of persons.** (Acts 10:34)

The Israelites' unfaithfulness to God caused them to profane the LORD's Sabbaths, wherefore God had them first captured and then scattered (Ezek. chapter 20; 2 Kings chapters 15 to 17), through which they lost their identity (Deut. 32:26). The ten so-called lost tribes—the tribes other than Judah and Benjamin—have proven it to be so. As descendants of the twins' father, Joseph, North America (Canada and USA) is largely composed of Joseph's twins, Ephraim and Manasseh. Few modern-day

Israelites know it, and yet *fewer* accept the facts when learning about it; especially traditional Christians, who will accept no information which might associate them with the Israelites (or Jews, as they labeled all Israelites). That gets much too close to the tyrannical law-enforcing God of the Sabbath-keeping Jews, of which they will have no part. They can't have anything in common with the Jews!

Jews: The Jews are named after Judah who is one of the twelve Patriarchs. In Genesis 49:10 God says that the Messiah will be born in this lineage; wherefore, some of their identity has remained, and it will remain until King David takes up his throne again to rule in the millennium. The first time the word "Jew" is mentioned in the KJV Scriptures is 2 Kings 16:6. That's when God had the tribes first taken into captivity by Gentile/heathen nations and then scattered throughout the whole world, just as He warned them He would do to them if they would steer away from His commandments and flirt with the traditional commandments of the pagan societies around them: "And I will scatter you among the heathen, and will draw out a sword after you: and your land shall be desolate, and your cities waste. Then shall the land enjoy her sabbaths, as long as it lieth desolate, and ye be in your enemies' land; even then shall the land rest, and enjoy her Sabbaths" (Lev. 26:33–34; read also Deut. 4:27–28; 28:36, 64). Notice that God is specifically abhorred when His Sabbath laws are broken, because by diligently keeping them His children are identified, and thereby blessed and nourished. And by keeping the land Sabbaths, the land also remains nourished, by God's design—no chemicals or fertilizer required. That scattering occurred about seven hundred years after they left Egypt (2 Kings chapters 15 to 17). At that point most of the people of the tribes of Judah and Benjamin banded together with many of the Levites and formed one tribe, and since then the members of that tribe have been called Jews, named after Judah. Paul states in Romans 3:1–3, as Stephen also does in Acts 7:38, that God entrusted the Jews with His oracles—His word.

Pharisees: The Pharisees are a very religious sect of Jews who, after their captivity—in an effort to prevent another future captivity—invented hundreds of traditional commandments **<entalma>**[9a] that they elevated to the status of God's commandments **<entole>**[9]. They set a higher importance in their traditional oral laws (the Talmud, of which Judaism is born) than on God's written laws. Paul was a highly respected, high ranking member of that sect before his conversion (Rom. 11:1; Acts 23:6; 26:4–6; 2 Cor. 11:22; Gal. 1:13–14; Phil. 3:5). The Pharisees believe in the resurrection of the dead (Acts 23:8), but the majority of them do not believe that the Messiah in the Gospels is the promised Messiah of the prophecies.

Sadducees: The Sadducees are a sect of Pharisees who do not believe in the resurrection of the dead (Matt. 22:23; Mark 12:18; Luke 20:27; Acts 23:8). They accept only the written laws and reject the oral laws.

In John chapters 5–10, the Messiah frequently excoriated the Pharisees while He explained to them why they could not believe or understand Him; it was because they did not believe what the Torah had prophesied of Him, because of their perversion of the Torah by their traditional doctrines (Matt. 15:1–20; Mark 7:1–15; John 5:46–47; 8:29–32; read also 2 Cor. 3:14–4:4). The exact same principles apply to today's traditional Christians, who also cannot understand God's truth because of their unbelief, thus leading to the rejection of the instructions of the Torah. In both cases, it's the keeping of their traditional commandments **<entalma>**[9a] that come from the god of this world, instead of God's commandments **<entole>**[9] that come from the creator God of Abraham, that keeps them veiled/blinded from understanding the true gospel of the kingdom of God (Matt. 4:23; 9:35; Mark 1:14–15), which is the message that the Messiah came to preach (Mark 1:14; Acts 1:3).

Once again, it's important to keep this type of information in mind throughout the rest of this book, and moreover when reading the Holy Scriptures. It will help to comprehend the theologians' motives for inventing such aggressive anti-Jew and thus anti-Torah church doctrines wherewith they also have been blinded, just as the Pharisees were (John 5:46–47; 2 Cor. 3:14–17). It will also help to measure up doctrines in order to differentiate between them and the Holy Scriptures. When you understand this principle, you'll see the apostasy with which that traditional anti-Torah doctrinal system has deceived millions, or perhaps billions, of its faithful followers. And if and when you understand that apostasy, you will have to choose whose commandments you will follow from that moment forward.

4. GOD'S LAWS FOR ALL MANKIND—DESIGNED FOR ETERNITY

For the purpose of what I am focusing on at this point, I will clarify a few principles about what God's instructions are for His people. The first five books of the scriptures, namely Genesis, Exodus, Leviticus, Numbers, and Deuteronomy, are referred to in Hebrew terms as the Towrah, which is known in English as the Torah: "I will put my **law <towrah>**[5] in their inward parts" (Jer. 31:33). Look at *Strong's Concordance* in section 15 and you'll see that the Law/Torah represents what the Old Testament defines as God's instructional laws, which contain the Ten Commandments. There's a general teaching in the traditional church system that the Messiah changed God's requirement for keeping the Ten Commandments to "love thy neighbor," in an effort to support their doctrines that declare the abolishment of the Ten Commandments. As we continue through this book, we'll see that these instructions are the same in the Old and New Testaments, and that they *all*, each and every one of them, focus on the theme of first of all loving God with all our heart and might, which fulfills **<pleroo>**[10] the requirements of the first tablet: "And thou shalt love the LORD thy God **with all thine heart**, and with all thy **soul**, and with all thy **might"** (Deut. 6:5; read also Deut. 10:12; 11:13; 13:3; Josh. 22:5); and likewise, to love thy neighbor as thyself, which fulfills **<pleroo>**[10] the requirements of the second tablet:

> Thou shalt not go up and down as a talebearer among thy people: neither shalt thou stand against the blood of thy neighbour: I am the LORD. **Thou shalt not hate thy brother <u>in thine heart</u>**: thou shalt in any wise rebuke thy neighbour, and not suffer sin upon him. Thou shalt not avenge, nor bear any grudge against the children of thy

> people, but thou shalt **love thy neighbour as thyself**: I am the LORD. ... But the stranger that dwelleth with you shall be unto you as one born among you, and **thou shalt love him as thyself**; for ye were strangers in the land of Egypt: I am the LORD your God." (Lev. 19:16–18, 34; read also Deut 10:19)

The Messiah—by example and witness—attests in the New Testament that the principle of how the keeping of God's commandments produces the **sacrificial charitable <agape>**[8] **love** has not changed, and He cites it directly from the Torah out of the Old Testament scripture—yet another perfect Torah test proof: "Thou shalt love the Lord thy God **with all thy heart**, and with all thy **soul**, and with all thy **strength**, and with all thy **mind**; [fulfills the first tablet] **and thy neighbour as thyself** [fulfills the second tablet] (Luke 10:27; read also Matt. 5:43–48; 22:36–40; Gal. 5:14; James 2:8). He further expounds on the vital moral principle that God designed and started in the beginning (1 John 2:7) to establish a holy and perfect character into man's heart—His temple: "Therefore all things whatsoever ye would that men should do to you, **do ye even so to them**: for **this is the law and the prophets**" (Matt. 7:12; read also Luke 6:31–36). That kind of mind-set is developed by faithfully keeping God's commandments.

He is clearly citing Old Testament Torah scriptures to clarify and amplify their moral values, which God wants to have perpetually trained into the hearts and minds of His children (Jer. 31:33; Heb. 8:10)! The word "law" in Jeremiah 31:33 is transliterated from the Hebrew word **<towrah>**[5], which describes God's laws—particularly the first five books of the scriptures, which contain the Ten Commandments. Paul understood it and preached it accordingly: "Love worketh no ill to his neighbour: **therefore love <agape>**[8] **is the fulfilling <pleroma>**[10b] **of the law**" (Rom. 13:10). Fulfilling a done-away law? The traditional preachers claim that Paul is the one who said that the Torah—especially the Ten Commandments—was done away! And since the traditional demon-driven Pharisees couldn't live up to God's commandments and laws, they claim *that* to be the reason the Messiah started the New Testament church through the Gentiles, without requiring obedience to them. There's no scriptural evidence for that, though there is for the opposite. As we'll see, the New Testament congregation is *not* a new church. Neither is it designed only for Gentiles.

As we can read about in Matthew chapters 15 and 23, Mark chapter 7, John chapters 5–10, and Romans 9:31–10:3; self-righteousness and covetousness come from keeping traditional doctrines, because they come from Satan, the devil, the ruler and prince of this world, and the father of pride, murder, and lies (John 8:44; 14:30; 2 Cor. 11:13–15; Eph. 2:2).

According to the account of Zacharias and Elizabeth, faithful obedience to God's commandments is required to be considered righteous before Him. Abraham, the father of faith, was righteous before God ***because*** he kept God's commandments: "**Because** that Abraham obeyed my voice, and kept my **charge <mishmereth>**[2], **my commandments <mitsvah>**[3], **my statutes <chuqqah>**[4], **and my laws <towrah>**[5]" (Gen. 26:5; read also 22:16–18). It's commonly preached that the ancients were required to keep God's commandments, but that now we're commanded *not* to keep them because we now have faith. Abraham's faith in God *caused* him to *willingly* keep God's commandments; wherefore, God accounted it to him for righteousness: "But wilt thou know, O vain man, that **faith without works is dead? Was not Abraham our father justified by works**, when he had offered Isaac his son upon the altar? Seest thou how faith wrought with his works, and **by works was faith made perfect** [compare Gen. 17:1]? And the scripture was fulfilled **<pleroo>**[10] which saith, Abraham believed God [had FAITH], and **it was imputed unto him for righteousness**: and he was called the Friend of God. **Ye see then how that by works a man is justified, and not by faith only**" (James 2:20–24). David, a man after God's own heart, wrote, "All thy commandments **<mitsvah>**[3] are righteousness" (Ps. 119:172). And John wrote, "All unrighteousness is sin" (1 John 5:17). He also wrote, "Whosoever committeth sin transgresseth also the law: for **sin is the transgression of the law" <anomia>**[12](1 John 3:4).

Sobering food for thought: According to the Messiah's own words in Matthew 5:17–19, He did not change an iota of God's laws. If He had changed God's moral and spiritual laws even by just one jot or tittle, then the Pharisees would have obeyed God's instructions by charging Him as a false prophet, which, again according to his own words, exacts the death sentence (Deut. 13:1–5). By abolishing or changing God's laws, He would have sinned (Matt. 5:17–19; 1 John 3:4; James 1:15), thus disinheriting His Father's kingdom and disqualifying Him to be our sinless and blameless Savior, thereby also disinheriting us! Praise the Eternal, because He did no such thing: "**Think not that I am come to destroy the law**, or the prophets: I am **not** come to destroy, but to **fulfil <pleroo>**[10]. For verily I say unto you, **Till heaven and earth pass, one jot or one tittle shall in no wise pass from the law**, till all be **fulfilled <ginomai>**[14]. **Whosoever therefore shall break one of these least commandments, and shall teach men so, he shall be called the least in the kingdom of heaven**: but whosoever shall do and teach them, the same shall be called great in the kingdom of heaven" (Matt. 5:17–19).

Tragically, as we saw earlier, *traditional* Christendom has been indoctrinated to believe that the Messiah condemned the Jews for keeping God's commandments. As is typical of traditional Christendom, it was exactly the other way around. The Messiah was crucified for keeping *God's* commandments instead of their *traditional* commandments. And the Messiah blatantly condemned the use of traditional commandments because the use of them inevitably forsakes God's commandments (Matt. chapter 15; Mark chapter 7), thus depriving the people of the liberty and blessings God promises for *keeping* them. And we can't serve God and tradition at the same time: "**No servant can serve two masters**: for either he will hate the one, and love the other; or else he will hold to the one, and despise the other. **Ye cannot serve God and mammon**" (Luke 16:13). It's very important to study such truths and to allow them to become well-grounded in our faith. Throughout the Gospels, the Messiah commands people of faith to follow in His footsteps to lighten their load: "Take my yoke upon you, and learn of me; for I am meek and lowly in heart: and ye shall find rest unto your souls. For **my yoke is easy, and my burden is light**" (Matt. 11:28–30;

read also Matt. 8:22; 16:24; 19:21; Mark 8:34; 10:21; Luke 9:23, 59–62; 18:22; John 13:15; Acts 12:8; Phil. 2:5–8; 1 Peter 2:21; 1 John 2:6). That's because He kept God's commandments, through which He attained God's love: "If ye keep **<tereo>**[21] my commandments, ye shall abide in my love **<agape>**[8]; even as I have kept **<tereo>**[21] my Father's commandments, and abide in his love **<agape>**[8]" (John 15:10; read also John 5:19, 30; 6:38).

The Messiah knew that religious leaders were using His name to snare and oppress people while resisting His ways: "And **why call ye me, Lord, Lord, and do not the things which I say**" (Luke 6:46)? And Matthew chapter 23 is a prime example of how the religious leaders used the supremacy of God's laws to enforce their perversion of them to lord authority over the people under their rule, for their gain, which the Messiah blatantly condemned. He called that a Gentile trait (Matt. 20:25; Mark 10:42; Luke 22:25).

Stephen told his audience that the Messiah was already in the congregation of old in the wilderness: "This is **he** [the Messiah], that was in the **church <ekklesia>**[20] [called-out congregational assembly] in the wilderness" (Acts 7:38). Paul called the New Testament congregation by the name that the God of Abraham assigned to it: "And as many as walk according to this rule, peace be on them, and mercy, and upon the **Israel of God**" (Gal. 6:16). It is named after the Old Testament congregation: "Moses commanded us a law, even the inheritance of the **congregation <q@hillah>**[20a] **of Jacob**" (Deut. 33:4; read also Ps. 125:5). Remember, God changed Jacob's name to Israel after He passed Abraham's covenantal promises onto him (Gen. 32:28). Likewise the Old Testament congregation of Jacob became the New Testament Israel of God. Those promises are still being passed on from generation to generation—to all who endure in the faith of the Messiah and the God of Israel.

Paul stated that the congregation is established upon the doctrines of the prophets of the past, the apostles of that present time, with the Messiah as the cornerstone: "And are built upon the foundation of the **apostles** and **prophets, Jesus Christ** himself being the chief corner stone" (Eph. 2:20). Just as in the tabernacle of old, the mercy seat remains the Lord's! Jude exhorted the people to not forget the teachings from the prophets and saints of the past: "Beloved, when I gave all diligence to write unto you of the **common salvation**, it was needful for me to write unto you, and exhort you that ye should earnestly contend for **the faith which was once delivered unto the saints**" (Jude 3). These words came from God; not from Moses or any other man: "For the prophecy came not **in old time** by the will of man: but **holy men of God** spake as they were **moved by the Holy Ghost <pneuma>**[11] [Spirit]" (2 Peter 1:21; read also 2 Tim. 3:16). It's very obvious that the instructions from the Old Testament were not abolished because of the Messiah's First Coming.

To become an eternal member of the family of the God of Israel, we must be conformed into a Spiritual Israelite: "For whom he did foreknow, he also did predestinate **to be conformed to the image of his Son**, that he might be the firstborn among many brethren" (Rom. 8:29; read also Isa. 46:13; Gal. 6:16). You will find, right down to the last pages of the scriptures, that God's plan of salvation has never changed. The new covenant will be made only with people who have been converted to conform to the God of Israel: "But this shall be the covenant that I will make with the **house of Israel"** (Jer. 31:33). And the unchanging, non-evolutionary God states the same in the New Testament: "For this is the covenant that I will make with the **house of Israel"** (Heb. 8:10). They will be His holy priesthood ("Ye shall be unto me a **kingdom of priests**" [Ex. 19:6; read also Deut. 7:6]) *if* they keep His commandments: "The LORD shall **establish thee an holy people** unto himself, as he hath sworn unto thee, **if thou shalt keep the commandments of the LORD thy God**, and walk in his ways" (Deut. 28:9). John confirmed this unchanged non-evolutionary command: "He that saith he abideth in him ought himself also so to walk, even as he walked" (1 John 2:6).

They inherited the **congregation of Jacob** (Deut. 33:4), which in the New Testament is called the **Israel of God** (Gal. 6:16), referring to the same priesthood:

> Ye also, as lively stones, are built up a spiritual house, an **holy priesthood**, to offer up spiritual sacrifices, acceptable to God by Jesus Christ. (1 Peter 2:5)

> They shall be **priests of God**. (Rev. 20:6, read also 1:6 and 5:10).

This is the God of Abraham, Isaac, and Jacob/Israel (Gen. 32:28); the one who has not changed (Mal. 3:6; Heb. 13:8; James 1:17). There is only one God who can save people—Jews and Gentiles alike; one God of Israel: "And Jesus answered him, The first of all the commandments is, **Hear, O Israel; The Lord our God is one Lord**" (Mark 12:29). The God of Abraham is the only god that does not change. All of the other gods are evolutionary gods that are always on the alert to change in order to meet the needs of their followers, as long as doing so will lead them away from the true God of Abraham, thus on to destruction. Satan will even use truth to indoctrinate a lie.

The New Jerusalem has only twelve gates—one for each of the twelve tribes of Israel: "... and had **twelve gates**, and at the gates twelve angels, and names written thereon, which are the names of the **twelve tribes of the children of Israel**" (Rev. 21:12). There is no Gentile covenant, no Gentile gate, and no Gentile tree or root system. Whether you are a flesh-born Israelite, Jew, or Gentile, there is only one way to enter through those gates; you must be adopted and grafted into the original tree. And that tree has only one root system, which is of the God of Abraham, Isaac, and Jacob/Israel—the original Old Testament congregation of Jacob, the New Testament Israel of God! (Deut. 33:4; Gal. 6:16; Psalms 125:5).

The Messiah talked about that tree in John chapter 15. Paul explicitly explained in Romans chapter 11 the process of how all the branches are broken off in order to show mercy to all. And the only way to become a fruit of that tree is to be adopted and grafted into it by God:

> And if some of the branches be broken off, and thou, being a wild olive tree, wert **graffed in among them** [among

the Israelites, not separate from them], and **with them partakest of the root and fatness** of the olive tree [sharing the nourishment of the tree of life]; **Boast not** against the branches. But if thou boast, thou bearest not the root, but the root thee. Thou wilt say then, The branches were broken off, that I might be graffed in. Well; **because of unbelief** they were broken off, and thou standest by faith. Be not highminded, but fear: For if God spared not the natural branches [Israelites—Jews], take heed lest he also spare not thee [Gentiles—unnatural]. Behold therefore the goodness and severity of God: on them which fell, severity [for commandment-breaking]; but toward thee, goodness, if thou **continue** in his goodness [obeying His commandments]: otherwise thou also shalt be cut off [not once saved-always saved]. And they also, if they abide not still in unbelief [keep His commandments again], shall be graffed in: for God is able to graff them in again. For if thou wert cut out of the olive tree which is wild by nature, and wert graffed contrary to nature into a good olive tree: how much more shall these, which be the natural branches, be graffed into **their own** olive tree? For I would not, brethren, that ye should be ignorant of this mystery, lest ye should be wise in your own conceits; that blindness in part is happened to Israel, until the fulness **<pleroma>**[10b] of the Gentiles be come in. And so **all Israel shall be saved**: as it is written, There shall come out of Sion the Deliverer, and shall turn away ungodliness from Jacob: For **this is my covenant unto them** [the Israelites], when I shall take away their sins. (Rom. 11:16–27)

The Israelites got entangled with the paganism of the Gentile nations around them, which inherently caused them to lose their faith in the God of their fathers, thus forsaking His commandments, wherefore God divorced them (Jer. 3:8). A question arises: would God break off the Israelites for breaking His commandments, graft them back in for keeping them, and then graft in Christians for not keeping them, and break them off for keeping them? I know that sounds preposterous, but that's what traditional Christian philosophy would have us believe.

Paul refers to the Israelites as the natural branches. The tree into which God is grafting His faithful people is the tree of life. And the people with faith *in* and *of* the Messiah can be grafted into the tree into which faithful Abraham's descendants were already grafted in and broken off. The Israelites were referred to as the children of Abraham, Isaac, and Jacob/Israel, through which the promises and covenants still flow.

Paul gives us a very strong warning against boasting. Traditional Christianity notoriously boasts about how God supposedly condemned the Jews/Israelites in order to build a New Testament Gentile church to be saved by. And now they are on continual missions to save the Jews (and other lost people—all commandment keepers) by indoctrinating them with traditional commandments about a lawless, anti-God messiah; a messiah who condemns the keeping of God's Commandments.

Inset: Again, I don't understand why the traditional Christians are so determined on being Gentiles. There is nothing good spoken of the ways of the Gentiles anywhere in the scriptures, but rather the opposite. Whenever the Gentiles are mentioned in the scriptures, it's always in the sense that God's people must refrain from all traits of them because they worship only paganism; they don't know God (1 Cor. 12:2; Gal. 4:8; Eph. 2:11; 5:8; Col. 1:21). I suppose the very reason they have such a strong craving to be Gentiles is because pagan worship is what the traditional preachers advocate, and—just as in the days of old—proclaim it in in the name of the Lord. The thought of being associated with the Israelites of the scriptures scares the living daylights out of traditional Christendom because of their belief that the Jews are all going straight to hell because they keep God's commandments, whereby they supposedly reject God's grace. That's why they can have nothing in common with them.

With that philosophy in mind, I will ask you traditionalists a simple question: If you see a Jew stop at a red traffic light, does that mean that from that moment on a Christian must not stop at red traffic lights, because you can have nothing in common with the Jews, wherefore if you obey the law and stop there you will go straight to hell? That seems to be the rationale when God's commandments are being discussed. They say, "That's for the Jews and not for Gentiles—Christians! The Sabbath is for the Jews; Sunday is for Christians! The Jews don't eat scavengers, but Christians must, lest food be wasted, which is sin! God's holy days are Jewish burdens; Christians keep New Year's, Easter, Halloween, and Christmas." And on and on it goes. I hear such responses from local professing Christians frequently, always in a derogatory sense, as if to say, "If you want to please God, you cannot do so with something that the Jews are doing, or professing to be doing."

Another issue comes to mind while on that topic. As Paul explained in Romans chapter 11, the Israelites were broken off of the olive tree for disobeying God's commandments—particularly the Lord's Sabbath commandment, which proved their unbelief, whereby they lost their identifying sign (Exodus 31:13–18). And you cannot break the fourth commandment without first breaking the first commandment, because the fourth commandment identifies the creator God of the first commandment, which is the only God who can save people from bondage. Keeping Sunday in place of the LORD's Sabbath identifies the sun god Mithra, a god that cannot save a person from bondage but is rather the cause of bondage. Each time God punished the Israelites hard enough for breaking His commandments, they went back to keeping them again, and God would again accept them back into His protective care and bless them. That's God's abundant grace, which we receive for obeying Him.

What I hear today from traditional Christendom is that the Israelites/Jews need to stop keeping God's commandments to be accepted by Him again. That's like saying that God punished His children of old for breaking His commandments, and today He punishes them for keeping His commandments. But the God of Abraham is *not* a confused evolutionary god (1 Cor. 14:33)!

The garden of Eden is where God started His plans for mankind, from where He chased the people out for breaking His commandments. As we can see in Revelation 21:12 and 22:14, that's where eternity is headed for those who obey Him and keep His commandments: "**Blessed are they that do his commandments, that they may have right to the tree of life,** and may enter in through the gates into the city" (Rev. 22:14). The flaming sword that is preserving the tree of life (Gen. 3:24) will be removed after it has burned all the wickedness from this earth (Ps. 50:3; Isa. 51:6; Mic. 1:4; Matt. 24:35; Mark 13:31; 2 Peter 3:10; Rev. 20:11). The period of time that God has set aside to change His people from the first mortal Adam into the likeness of the last spiritual Adam—hence the adoption into His Spiritual family—is the sanctification period in which He sets His people apart from the world for His honor and glory by and through His signs and marks that identify who is truthfully serving Him: "Speak thou also unto the children of Israel, saying, Verily **my** sabbaths ye shall keep: for it is a **sign between me and you throughout your generations; that ye may know that I am the LORD that doth sanctify <qadash>[15] you**" (Ex. 31:13).

I take this testimony very seriously. God called them *His* Sabbaths, not the Jews'; and *His* Sabbaths identify Him by reverently acknowledging Him as the unchanging, non-evolutionary Creator of heaven and earth, not the ever-changing evolutionary god of traditional religion. "Keep the sabbath day to **sanctify <qadash>[15] it**, as the LORD thy God hath commanded thee" (Deut. 5:12). Likewise, if we keep God's Sabbaths, we are also sanctified, and as such identified and marked by them as a sign and testimony that we are God's children. If we don't keep them, we are then identified by observing days and times of some ever-changing evolutionary god(s) of this world.

Traditional Christendom dwells on evolutionary gods that change, adopt, and invent commandments according to *their* lusts; they are apt to adapt to people's desires. The God of Abraham is just the opposite; we must adapt to His commandments and adopt His ways. In the analysis, one thing is certain: we will serve one god or another; it's just that simple (Matt. 6:24; Luke 16:13). If the Holy Spirit is not in one's heart, the evil spirit will immediately take up residence; the heart will never be vacant—one or the other it will be: "When the unclean spirit is gone out of a man, he walketh through dry places, seeking rest, and findeth none. Then he saith, I will return into my house from whence I came out; and when he is come, he findeth it empty, swept, and garnished. Then goeth he, and taketh with himself seven other spirits more wicked than himself, and they enter in and dwell there: and **the last state of that man is worse than the first** [Satan has moved in with his army]. Even so shall it be also unto this wicked generation (Matt. 12:43–45; read also Luke 11:24–26; Heb. 6:4–6; 10:26; 2 Peter 2:20–22).

As we saw earlier, there were many Gentiles that left Egypt together with the Israelites. They all observed the Passover together; all were called Israelites of God! This is that original tree that started in the beginning of days, through which all who had the faith *of* Abraham in the creator God would be blessed: "In thy seed shall **all the nations** of the earth be blessed" (Gen. 26:4). The New Testament teaching is completely consistent with the Old Testament. Everything *must* line up from Genesis 1:1 on, right down through Revelation 22:21; else we have a contradiction! And if we find one contradiction, that would render the Scriptures useless. Traditional Christendom has created multitudes of contradictions. According to their beliefs, which they have crafted to support their traditional doctrines, the New Testament contradicts the Old Testament—and also itself.

Paul explained that God has blinded the Israelites in order that His mercy may be shown to all people: "For God hath concluded them **all** in unbelief, **that he might have mercy upon all"** (Rom. 11:32; read also 3:23; Gal. 3:22). Not one person will enter God's kingdom by his own merits and efforts. But that doesn't mean that we shouldn't obey God and keep His commandments. Faith in the Messiah does not grant permission to live a lawless life. Rather, faith in Him provides the means needed to keep God's commandments proper by the Holy Spirit, which God grants those who obey Him (Acts 5:32; Heb. 5:9). Obeying Him is keeping—not breaking—His commandments.

There is much to benefit from the scattering of the Israelites among the Gentile nations. The Israelites lost their knowledge of God (Deut. 32:26; Gal. 4:8) by becoming a secular part of the God-less pagan Gentile communities around them with whom they had frequently flirted before. So when the apostles would go to preach the gospel of the kingdom of God to the Gentiles, the scattered Israelites would also hear the Word and become jealous (Rom. 10:19; 11:11), whereby some would become believers, through which the Gentiles also would obtain mercy: "For as ye [Gentiles] in times past have not believed God, yet have now obtained mercy **through their unbelief**" (Rom. 11:30). That mercy was demonstrated first to the Jews, then also to the Gentiles (John 4:22; Rom. 1:16; 2:9–10). In essence God will again redeem His people—not just from the land of Egypt, but this time from the whole world, where He had them scattered. And again, just as there were many Gentiles who chose to join and become Israelites (Ex. 12:38) when God called them out of the Egyptian bondage, He will again call out His children from the sinful Babylonian system, and again many Gentiles will be given an opportunity to join in on that journey to paradise. They will all together be grafted into the only tree of inheritance that there is—the tree of life, the Messiah, the one and only congregation of Jacob, the Israel of God (Deut. 33:4; Gal. 6:16).

Notice at the start of Romans chapter 11 that God has never given up on the Israelites, let alone condemned them, as is a common Protestant belief. Our compassionate Savior forgave them while He was dying on the tree: "Father, forgive them; for they know not what they do" (Luke 23:34). The disciples were Jews, including Paul (Rom. 11:1–5). The only people that have condemned the Jews since the crucifixion are the early church fathers of the Babylonian system, such as popes, emperors, leaders like Martin Luther and Adolf Hitler—most of whom are Freemasons—and their followers (basically traditional Christendom), and of course the Muslims. I'm not here to judge the Jews, Christians, or Muslims, but all three of these sects are *extremely* opposed to the other two sects, thus causing all of them to create a savior figure to worship who adopts their traditional beliefs, thus inevitably contradicting the creator God / Messiah of the Holy Scriptures.

The Messiah said to the Jews that He came also for to gather His other sheep: "And **other sheep I have**, which are **not of this fold**: them also I must bring, and they shall hear my voice; and there shall be **one fold, and one shepherd**" (John 10:16). One Israel, one Lord God! "I am not sent but **unto the lost sheep of the house of Israel"** (Matt. 15:24). He is speaking to the Jews about the other Israelites that are scattered among the Gentile nations. Around 600 BC Jeremiah prophesied about that regathering: "But, The LORD liveth, that brought up the children of Israel from the land of the north, and from all the lands whither he had driven them: and I will bring them **again** into their land that I gave unto their fathers. Behold, **I will send for many fishers**, saith the LORD, and **they shall fish them**" (Jer. 16:15–16). The Messiah confirmed that prophecy to His disciples: "Follow me, and I will make you **fishers of men**" (Matt. 4:19). That's a Torah test prophecy that is not yet completely fulfilled; it's still ongoing today.

Paul knew the Torah by heart by the time he was a teenager (that's why he constantly cites its prophecies), wherefore he knew that the Israelites were still scattered. This generated in him a tremendous passion to fish for them—his kinsmen in the flesh:

> I say the truth in Christ, I lie not, my conscience also bearing me witness in the Holy Ghost [Spirit], That I have great heaviness and continual sorrow in my heart. For I could wish that myself were accursed from Christ for my brethren, my kinsmen according to the flesh: Who are Israelites [not only Jews]; to whom pertaineth the adoption [into God's Family tree, the tree of life, the Messiah], and the glory [God's glory], and the covenants [*all* the covenants], and the giving of the law [instructions in righteousness], and the service of God [provisions for reconciliation], and the promises [covenantal promises through Abraham's descendants—the Israelites, including

> Jews]; Whose are the fathers [the Israelites, including Jews], and of whom as concerning the flesh Christ came, who is over all, God blessed for ever. Amen. (Rom. 9:1–5)

These Israelites are the other flock of which the Messiah spoke. James was also aware of the scattering: "... to the twelve tribes which are **scattered** abroad, greeting" (James 1:1). The Pharisees acknowledged the scattering: "**will he go unto the dispersed among the Gentiles**, and teach the Gentiles [fish for them] (John 7:35)? The Messiah made no mention of preaching *only* to the Gentiles, but to fish for the house of Israel among them. He commanded His first twelve disciples to preach to the lost sheep of Israel, and not to the Gentiles (Matt. 10:5).

Please note that Paul stated that the adoption, God's glory, the covenants, the law, and the promises—basically all together summed up as the Lord's salvation—all belong to the Israelites. Anyone who wants to have any of that goodness will have to share it with the Israelites, which also includes Jews. The anti-Jew people must overcome the hatred for the Jews if they want to be grafted into the one and same tree of life.

Paul's preaching in the Gentile populations would inevitably be like fishing for his kinsmen. Since the Israelites were blinded, many did not accept the gospel. God is calling out only a remnant in this era; but there is a much greater exodus coming, when all Messianic believers shall be saved (Rom. 11:26). But the blindness will remain until the fullness of the Gentiles is come (when the Israelites will be released from captivity—the scattering—Rom. 11: 25; Ps. 14:7; Isa. 59:20), at which time the Messiah will descend upon the Mount of Olives to rescue Zion, and establish the new covenant with the whole house of Jacob. The house of Jacob consists of Israelites, Jews, and all who've been converted and believe in the promises God made through faithful Abraham, including the converted Gentiles (the mixed multitude), the congregation of Jacob, the Israel of God (Deut. 33:4; Gal. 6:16); salvation will *then* be delivered (Rom. 11:25–27; Rev. 12:10).

That gathering is foreshadowed and depicted by one of God's annual holy day festivals—the Feast of Tabernacles. Without an understanding of the Torah, God's holy days have no meaning to man; and God's awesome plan of salvation for His creation revolves around, is established upon, and is revealed through the observance of His holy days, which I'll briefly cover in section 5a. And once again, since some of the Jews still observe God's holy days, traditional Christianity can have nothing in common with them. That's why traditional Christendom doesn't know what the festivals of the Lord portray, wherefore they've chosen—with a divine zeal—to observe the popular Christianized pagan holidays instead! Therefore, since God's holy days portray God's awesome plan of salvation, traditional Christians cannot attain a true understanding of it. The observance of those festivals is explained in the Torah with some of its true meanings being fulfilled and further revealed in the New Testament scriptures. Thus, since traditional religion—because of its anti-Jew principles—rejects the Torah instructions (it's for the Jews), it's impossible for traditional Christians to understand the meanings of God's holy day festivals, making it rather easy for Satan to foist his pagan festivals upon them.

The Torah teaching and instructions dwell wholly on the theme of developing in man a character of a merciful, godly **<agape>**[8] love toward God and mankind, without which we have no forgiveness of sin: "And forgive us our debts, as we forgive our debtors ... For if ye forgive men their trespasses, your heavenly Father will also forgive you. But if ye forgive not men their trespasses, neither will your Father forgive your trespasses (Matt. 6:12, 14–15). Blessed are the merciful: for they shall obtain mercy" (Matt. 5:7). The Measure of love and mercy that we have for our fellow men is the measure of love and mercy that God will have on us. If you'll study the Torah with an open and unbiased mind, you will be amazed at how perfect God designed His instructions for us in a way that will always aim at bettering our relationship with Him and with our neighbor. And not Moses, but the God of Abraham, ordained them, for all the people who have faith in Him:

> **One law** shall be to him that is **homeborn** [Israelites—Jews]**, and unto the stranger** [adopted Gentiles] ... (Ex. 12:49).

> Ye shall have **one manner of law, as well for the stranger** ... (Lev. 24:22).

> ... for **I am the LORD** your God. **One law and one manner shall be for you, and for the stranger** ... (Num. 15:16).

This is confirmed in the New Testament by the Torah test: "There is **neither Jew nor Greek** ... for **ye are all one** in Christ Jesus. **And if ye be Christ's, then are ye Abraham's seed, and heirs according to the promise**" (Gal. 3:28–29; read also Rom. 2:28–29; 10:12; 1 Cor. 12:13; Eph. 2:14–16; Col. 3:11). All who believe in the God of Abraham become members of His family, the congregation of Jacob / the Israel of God (Deut. 33:4; Gal. 3:28–29; 6:16).

A sacrificial-type charitable **<agape>**[8] love for God and neighbor, which produces liberty with God and mankind, lies at the heart and core, and lays the foundation of each and every aspect of each and every law and commandment God ever created! Obedience to them is the only seedbed there is to obtain the fruits of a merciful, godlike character. That's what develops peace. It's unfathomable how He designed them so perfect in all aspects of it. A true Torah study will give one a fair understanding about how sovereign and merciful a God and Father He truly is. A heartfelt desire for a godly **<agape>**[8] love-like character is what God needs to find in us to be able to conform us into His image (Rom. 8:29).

After the Messiah returns, changes His children to spirit beings, and permanently inscribes His commandments and laws of **<agape>**[8] love into their hearts, they will possess His character, thus being conformed into His image and likeness (Rom. 8:29) from literal flesh to literal spirit:

> That which is born of the **flesh is flesh**; and that which is born of the **Spirit is spirit**" (John 3:6).

They will also be conformed to him from mortality to immortality:

> Now this I say, brethren, that flesh and blood cannot inherit the kingdom of God; neither doth corruption inherit incorruption. Behold, I shew you a mystery; We shall not all sleep, but we shall all be changed, In a moment, in the twinkling of an eye, **at the last trump** [the seventh (Rev. 11:15)]: for the trumpet shall sound, and the dead shall be raised incorruptible, and we shall be changed. For this corruptible must put on incorruption, and **this mortal must put on immortality**. So when this corruptible shall have put on incorruption, and this mortal shall have put on immortality, **then** shall be brought to pass the saying that is written, Death is swallowed up in victory. (1 Cor. 15:50–54)

Death is overcome by the resurrection from literal death to life eternal: "Concerning his Son Jesus Christ our Lord, which was made of the seed of David according to the flesh [the first flesh-born mortal, Adam (Genesis 1:26; 5:1–3)]; And declared to be the Son of God with power, according to the spirit of holiness, **by the resurrection from the dead** [the spirit-born last immortal Adam (1 Corinthians 15:45)]" (Rom. 1:3–4). The Messiah was raised to an eternal spiritual life (reborn to Spirit life, John 3:3–7) because of His perfect obedience to God's commandments and laws while He was mortal.

This may sound simple, but that is God's plan for us. God will inscribe into our heart at the resurrection His laws of love and liberty—His spiritual and moral laws, the Ten Commandments, which He inscribed into stone with His finger—for a benefit to all the people who desire His <**agape**>[8] love and mercy. And He desires to write them into the hearts of such people that love Him and desire to be like Him, thereby obeying Him (Acts 5:32; Heb. 5:9). I will say again that not practicing God's commandments is not obeying the God who instituted them and commanded us to observe them.

4a. The Physical Laws, the Ritual Laws, and the Spiritual Laws

After centuries (more than ten generations) of being under subjection to the Egyptian constitution—of which the latter half of that time span was spent in bondage to extreme slavery—the Israelites had forgotten and thus were no longer keeping God's commandments. So, as Paul acknowledged, when God redeemed them from Egyptian slavery, He added sacrificial and ritualistic laws and duties to constantly remind them of their transgression of the Ten Commandments: "Wherefore then serveth the **law** **<nomos>**[22] [animal sacrificial laws and rituals]? It was added because of **transgressions** **<parabasis>**[23] [commandment breaking], till the seed should come to whom the promise was made; and it was ordained by angels in the hand of a mediator" (Gal. 3:19; read also Hebrews chapters 9–10). And God had Moses write those laws into a book (Josh. 8:31).

Many of these laws were physical and materialistic; designed and ordained by God in a way that would train a habit of obedience into their hearts and minds, in order that they would learn to obey His spiritual laws from their hearts so that they could then love Him from the heart. Some of these laws came with animal sacrificial rites, and food and drink offerings; these could not take away, but reminded them of, their sins. This was to build up their faith in the need of the promised Savior who would take the sins away: "But in those [animal] sacrifices there is a **remembrance** again made of sins every year. For it is **not possible that the blood of bulls and of goats should take away sins** ... And every priest standeth daily ministering and offering **oftentimes** the same sacrifices, **which can never take away sins**" (Heb. 10:3–4, 11). And it did lead them to the promised Savior and Messiah (Gal. 3:24), who, because of His sacrificial-type charitable **<agape>**[8] love for God and for mankind, was able to fulfill—bring to pass, finish, complete—and thus end the need for these animal sacrificial and ritualistic laws, thus nailing them to the tree: "When Jesus therefore had received the vinegar, he said, It is **finished <teleo>**[24]: and he bowed his head, and gave up the ghost [Spirit]" (John 19:30). Now He, as the perfect, unblemished, and sinless sacrificial Lamb of God, became our Passover (1 Cor. 5:7) by willingly taking upon Himself the death penalty of our guilty past (Rom. 3:25; John 10:11, 15, 17–18; Gal. 1:4; 1 John 1:9) and of sins that we commit in life thereafter, if repented of (Acts 13:38; 17:30; Col. 1:20; 1 Tim. 1:15; Heb. 9:15; 1 John 2:2; 4:10); thus He reconciled us to God the Father in heaven, saving us from eternal death by His resurrection: "For if, when we were enemies, we were **reconciled to God by the death of his Son**, much more, being reconciled, **we shall be saved by his life**" (Rom. 5:10).

The end result—the goal and purpose (Rom. 10:4; 13:8–10; Gal. 6:2)—of the laws was to teach mankind how to love the Lord with all their heart, mind, and strength, and to love their neighbors as themselves and to have mercy on them; whereby God's mercy was shown to them. This is what the Messiah demonstrated for us through His nonrebellious suffering while He was being tortured and crucified, which accomplished that goal. As the KJV translators penciled it in Romans 10:4, "Christ is the **end <telos>**[24a] of the law for righteousness." *Strong's Concordance* defines the Greek word "*telos*" as "to set out for a definite point or goal." The Messiah kept God's commandments and laws to their uttermost expectations without breaking a jot or tittle of them (Matt. 5:17–18; John 15:10). That's what developed the sacrificial-type charitable <**agape**>[8] love in Him. And today He commands us to follow in His footsteps in order to develop that sacrificial-type charitable <**agape**>[8] love in us, through which His perfect and holy character is developed, thus conforming us into His image (Rom. 8:29).

That commandment is not something new, because God required the same of Abraham: "And when Abram was ninety years old and nine, the LORD appeared to Abram, and said unto him, I am the Almighty God; **walk before me, and be thou perfect**" (Gen. 17:1; read also Lev. 11:44; 19:2; 20:7). Likewise, as a foreshadowing of the Messiah, Abraham also achieved that character by keeping God's commandments and laws: "Because that Abraham obeyed my voice, and kept my **charge <mishmereth>**[2], **my commandments <mitsvah>**[3], **my statutes <chuqqah>**[4], **and my laws <towrah>**[5]" (Gen. 26:5; read also 18:19). God chose Abraham because he would teach his children His laws (Gen. 18:19). Our God/Messiah has *not* changed: "Jesus Christ the same yesterday, and to day, and for ever" (Heb. 13:8). One Lord, one God; not two, not a trinity, but one unchanging, non-evolutionary Lord God!

It's a common traditional church teaching that we don't need to keep the Ten Commandments because the Messiah kept them for us. That's ludicrous! Although Abraham kept them, this did not exempt his children from the requirement to keep them: "The LORD shall establish thee **an holy people** unto himself, as he hath sworn unto thee, **if thou shalt keep the commandments of the LORD thy God, and walk in his ways**" (Deut. 28:9). John repeated that scripture about sixty years after the resurrection of the Messiah to remind us that to have sins forgiven by the Messiah requires one to walk in the way of the Lord, which includes keeping God's commandments: "And he is the propitiation for our sins: and not for ours only, but also for the sins of the whole world. And hereby we do know that we know him, **if we keep his commandments**. He that saith, I know him, and keepeth not his commandments, is a liar, and the truth is not in him. But whoso keepeth his word, in him verily is the **love <agape>**[8] of God **perfected <teleioo>**[24b]: hereby know we that we are in him. He that saith he abideth in him ought himself also so to walk, even as he walked" (1 John 2:2–6). The New Testament Messiah requires the same of us as the Old Testament God did:

> **Be ye therefore perfect <teleios>**[24c], even as your Father which is in heaven is perfect **<teleios>**[24c]. (Matt. 5:48)
>
> But as he which hath called you is holy, **so be ye holy** in all manner of conversation. **Because it is <u>written</u>** [in the Torah], **Be ye holy; for I am holy.** (1 Peter 1:15–16; read

also Luke 1:74–75; 2 Cor. 7:1; 1 Thess. 4:3–4, 7; Heb. 12:14; 2 Peter 3:11)

Traditional Christianity solemnly states that it's impossible to keep the Ten Commandments and that you'll earn eternal life in hellfire for trying, because you supposedly reject the Messiah's sacrifice and God's grace by living by them. According to their doctrines, we are to deny the Ten Commandments so that God's grace may abound; this is like a license to sin (Jude 4). Paul, who traditional Christians claim commanded that, is strongly opposed to that philosophy: "What shall we say then? **Shall we continue in sin** [breaking the Ten Commandments]**, that grace may abound? God forbid**. How shall we, that are dead to sin [been forgiven], live any longer therein [keep breaking the Ten Commandments]," (Rom. 6:1–2).

Paul condemned a lawless faith. He said that although we are freed from the penalty of sin by the Messiah's sacrifice—which the animal sacrifices couldn't do—we shall not sin while professing to be under God's grace: "What then? **shall we sin, because we are not under the law <nomos>**[22] [animal sacrifices]**, but under grace? God forbid**. Know ye not, that to whom ye yield yourselves servants to obey, his servants ye are to whom ye obey; whether of sin unto death [the penalty for breaking God's commandments], or of obedience unto righteousness?" (Rom. 6:15–16). That's the exact opposite of that lawless grace philosophy, which is only one of many methods Satan has cunningly devised to blaspheme God's Holy Word—by teaching as divine authority that God designed the Ten Commandments in such a way that they couldn't be kept. God does *not* create misery for His people for the purpose that He wants them to fail. Contrariwise, He takes no pleasure that even the wicked should perish, but that they should repent from their sins and live; because that, He is the God of life: "Say unto them, As I live, saith the Lord GOD, **I have no pleasure in the death of the wicked; but that the wicked turn from his way and live: turn ye, turn ye from your evil ways; for why will ye die, O house of Israel**?" (Ezek. 33:11; read also Ezek. 18:32; Lam. 3:33; 1 Tim. 2:4; 2 Peter 3:9).

To make this point clear, God is urging His people to repent for breaking His commandments, not for keeping them! Keeping God's commandments delivers blessings and life; breaking them delivers curses and death:

> See, I have set before thee this day **life and good**, and **death and evil**; In that I command thee this day to love the LORD thy God, to walk in his ways, and to **keep his commandments** and **his statutes** and **his judgments, that thou mayest live** and multiply: and the LORD thy **God shall bless thee** in the land whither thou goest to possess it. But **if thine heart turn away**, so that thou wilt not hear, but shalt be drawn away, and worship other gods, and serve them; **I denounce unto you this day, that ye shall surely perish**, and that ye shall not prolong your days upon the land, whither thou passest over Jordan to go to possess it. I call heaven and earth to record this day against you, that I have set before you **life and death, blessing and cursing: therefore choose life** [He urges His people to live, not to break His commandments and die]**, that both thou and thy seed may live**: [Why?] **That thou mayest love the LORD thy God**, and that thou mayest obey his voice, and that thou mayest cleave unto him: for **he is thy life**, and the length of thy days: that thou mayest dwell in the land which the LORD sware unto thy fathers, to Abraham, to Isaac, and to Jacob, to give them. (Deut. 30:15–20)

God considered Zacharias and Elizabeth righteous for keeping His commandments (Luke 1:6; Matt. 23:35). According to that scripture—which is in the *New* Testament—the Ten Commandments could be kept. That does not suggest that they never sinned, but that they were committed to obey God's commandments, which, when transgressed, convicted them (Rom. 7:7), whereby, through their faith in God as their only Healer, Redeemer, and Savior, and faith in the promised Messiah, would cause them to repent of their trespasses, by which God forgave them by His everlasting mercy and grace. That's how

God forgave many saints and prophets of old. Faith in God and the Messiah causes Him to forgive sins by His mercy and grace; read Leviticus 26:40–42, 1 Kings 8:33–50, 2 Chronicles 7:14, and Ezekiel 18 and 33 as examples of a few scriptures that show how His mercy and grace always have forgiven sins when people humbly repented of them before Him. To preach that God's commandments should not be practiced because you will be damned if you do is *not* Scriptural but is rather a lie from Satan, the devil, the deceiver of the whole world (Rev. 12:9). Incidentally, the whole world includes you and me. But God promises that He will not allow us to be tempted with more than we can bear (1 Cor. 10:13). And if we have enough faith to believe that, God will provide a way out for us when Satan puts into our path the temptation to violate a commandment of His.

I'm not suggesting that keeping commandments forgives sins, because it never has and never will. But keeping them steers us away from breaking them, and breaking them—or not keeping them—is sinning (1 John 3:4; James 1:15; 2:9–10), while practicing them teaches us about God's **<agape>**[8] love. When we slip up and break them, they will convict us (Rom. 3:20; 7:11–12) and cause us to turn away from that sin and turn to God (repent) and ask Him to forgive. God then forgives us by His grace, through our faith in the sacrifice of the Messiah (1 John 1:9). Throughout his epistles, Paul taught of that very liberty wherewith faith in the Messiah's sacrifice has set us free, which is in constant and perfect harmony with the teaching of the Torah—thus another Torah test proof. Nowhere does God say that He would send His Lamb (Himself in flesh) to abolish His eternal laws and commandments. He came to provide a way for us to have our sins forgiven for transgressing them in order to bring us back into alignment with Him, so that we can be conformed to fit His holy kingdom, thus proving to us that His commandments *could* be kept, but not without His holy and righteous spirit.

That's how He transforms us from the first Adam of death to the last Adam of life (Rom. 8:29; 1 Cor. 15:45), thus conforming us into sons and daughters of His Family: "At the same time, saith the LORD, **will I be the God of all the families of Israel**, and they shall be my people" (Jer. 31:1). As another Torah test proof, that end-time prophecy is confirmed in the New Testament: "And what agreement hath the temple of God with idols? for ye are the temple of the living God; as God hath said, **I will dwell in them, and walk in them; and I will be their God, and they shall be my people**" (2 Cor. 6:16).

If the Ten Commandments are abolished, what did the Messiah die for then? And if that be so, what should one repent of now? If the Ten Commandments no longer exist, then accordingly, all the people that have been born after that cannot sin! The purpose of repenting of one's sins and being baptized is all about coming out of sin (stopping violating God's laws), starting a new walk in life in the Messiah's steps (Rom. 6:4), and refraining from sinning (**obeying** God's laws). After repenting for breaking God's commandments, He forgives us. Then, after being baptized and anointed in His name, He gives us His Holy Spirit, which sheds His **<agape>**[8] love (1 John 4:16; 5:2–3) upon our hearts (Rom. 5:5), thereby enabling us to willingly obey His laws and thus love Him from our heart: "Then Peter said unto them, **Repent <metanoeo>**[25], and be **baptized <baptizo>**[26] every one of you in the name of Jesus Christ for the remission of sins [what sins?], and ye shall receive the gift of the Holy Ghost [Spirit]" (Acts 2:38; read also Luke 13:3; Acts 3:19; 8:22; 26:20; Rev. 2:5).

Thus, with the help of God through the Holy Spirit, we can then fulfill His laws: "**Love <agape>**[8] worketh no ill to his neighbour: therefore **love <agape>**[8] is the **fulfilling <pleroma>**[10b] [NOT abolishing] of the law" (Rom. 13:10; read also Gal. 5:14; James 2:8). That's God's whole purpose and goal for His royal laws of love and liberty (James 1:25; 2:8–12) as taught throughout the Torah: "Now the **end <telos>**[24a] [goal; purpose; result] of the commandment is **charity <agape>**[8] [**sacrificial-type love**] out of a pure heart" (1 Tim. 1:5). And the Messiah accomplished that goal for those who believe that He was the righteous Lamb of God: "For Christ is the **end <telos>**[24a] [goal; purpose; result] of the law for righteousness to every one that believeth" (Rom. 10:4). Because of the anti-Law mind-set, common theologians interpret Romans 10:4 in a way to make it say that the Messiah came to make an abolishing end of the Ten Commandments.

Let's read such a perverted interpretation into a couple of other scriptures where that same Greek word "telos" (Strong's Concordance) #5056 is used. We just read one of them in 1 Timothy 1:5, cited above. I'll add a couple more scriptures where the word "telos" is used and translated into English as "end." Read these and see if the intended use of the word "telos" was to indicate an abolishing end or if it perhaps indicated a prophesied goal or purpose:

> Ye have heard of the patience of Job, and have seen the **end <telos>**[24a] of the Lord; that the Lord is very pitiful, and of tender mercy. (James 5:11)

> Receiving the **end <telos>**[24a] of your faith, even the salvation of your souls. (1 Peter 1:9)

Now read Romans 10:4 again with this rendering in mind. All of these passages harmonize with what the Messiah states in Matthew 5:17—that He did not come to destroy God's laws, or fulfill them to an abolishing end, but rather that He came to magnify them to **fulfill <pleroo>**[10] them in order to bring them to fruition—their intended **end <telos>**[24a], their purpose and goal.

How can one stop violating God's laws if they don't exist anymore? How can one repent of a crime that cannot even be committed? To violate a law, there must first be a law to violate, "... for where no law is, there is no transgression" (Rom. 4:15; read also 5:13). What, then, is the purpose of the Messiah pouring out His innocent blood to atone for a sin that cannot even come into existence? Any sane person can see that it cannot be so. But such is the teaching of the anti-Jew, anti-Law, anti-Torah church doctrines. And many there are that believe them, because a carnal mind desires it to be so.

So how can a person become righteous and perfect before the Eternal? According to His Word, His laws play a key role:

> And what nation is there so great, that hath statutes and judgments so righteous as all this law **<towrah>**[5], which I set before you this day? (Deut. 4:8)

> The **law <towrah>**[5] **of the LORD is perfect, converting the soul**: the testimony of the LORD is sure, making wise the simple. The statutes of the LORD are right, rejoicing the heart: the **commandment of the LORD is pure**, enlightening the eyes. The fear of the LORD is clean, enduring for ever: the judgments of the LORD are true and righteous altogether. More to be desired are they than gold, yea, than much fine gold: sweeter also than honey and the honeycomb. Moreover **by them is thy servant warned**: **and in keeping of them there is great reward.** (Ps. 19:7–11; read and study Psalms 111 and 119)

It sounds to me as though it would help to practice God's laws if one desires to become more righteous and less wicked before Him. "My tongue shall speak of thy word: for **all thy commandments are righteousness**" (Ps. 119:172; read also Luke 1:6). Was God just joking here? The God of Abraham, Isaac, and Jacob is not an evolutionary god, which means that He has not changed, and will not change, His views on His laws (Hebrews 13:8). God, in the New Testament, considered Zacharias and Elizabeth righteous before Him for keeping His commandments and laws (Luke 1:6).

Except for God's few chosen prophets and messengers, the people of ancient times did not have the Holy Spirit available to them. Moses was the mediator for the children of Israel. Today we have the Holy Spirit available to us, which makes it possible to fulfill God's commandments and laws. We have the Messiah as our mediator, whose faith and spirit—if it be in us (Rom. 5:5; 8:8)—allows us also to fulfill God's spiritual and moral laws from the heart. And it requires the Holy Spirit in one's heart to be able to keep God's commandments properly, which God gives only to those who obey Him:

> And we are his witnesses of these things; and so is also the Holy Ghost [Spirit], whom God hath given **to them that obey him.** (Acts 5:32)

> And being made perfect, he became the author of eternal salvation **unto all them that obey him.** (Heb. 5:9)

Which indicates obedience to God—*keeping* His commandments, or *not* keeping them? It *must* be one or the other. As we study the scriptures from Adam to Noah, to Abraham, and then to Moses—especially the Israelites' journey from Egypt to Canaan, and also the following 1,400 years—we find that God's commandments cannot be broken without consequences, because no matter which one of them we break, and no matter who breaks it, it breaks the chain of love and mercy. If one's sin was voluntary or intentional—such as murder, adultery, profaning the Lord's Sabbath, or any commandment that requires the death penalty for its violation—it was certain death. Although punishment doesn't always occur instantly, God's laws did not change upon entering into the New Testament era. There is a very solid testimony to that in the account where Ananias and his wife die for no other reason than for lying (Acts 5:1–10). "The wages of sin is death" (Romans 6:23). That account is another very powerful Torah test proof to prove that God's laws did not change after the crucifixion. They died in the New Testament Era - after the crucifixion - for violating the Ten Commandments.

As stated in the Torah, if the sin was out of ignorance, the sentence was not always death, but no sin went unpunished. A broken law automatically exacts a penalty, unless repented of in time. As Paul stated, the commandments are still there to convict us when we fail, in order to correct us:

> What shall we say then? Is the law sin? God forbid. Nay, **I had not known sin, but by the law: for I had not known lust, except the law had said, Thou shalt not covet** [the tenth commandment]. But sin, taking occasion by the commandment, wrought in me all manner of concupiscence. For without the law sin was dead [before his conversion, the commandments couldn't convict him]. For I was alive without the law once: but when the commandment came, sin revived, and I died [upon conviction by the Ten Commandments, Paul repented and got baptized, thus burying the old sinful, lawless man—the first Adam—in the watery grave (Rom. 6:6)]. And the commandment, which was ordained to life [by God],

> I found to be unto death [it convicted him of his sins]. For sin, taking occasion by the commandment, deceived me, and by it slew me. **Wherefore the law is holy, and the commandment holy, and just, and good.** (Rom. 7:7–12)

Read the rest of that chapter and you'll see that upon his conversion, Paul realized that he was worthy of death, which caused him to repent of his lawlessness and get baptized (the watery grave). As he stated, without the commandments to convict him, he would have remained as a dead man walking toward the grave.

When we study the purpose of God's laws and commandments, we find that they all focus on one and the same theme: If we love God with all of our heart, and the neighbor as ourselves, God's mercy and grace are absolutely endless. And the Ten Commandments are God's moral laws that give us the instructions on how to love Him first (the first tablet), as well as the neighbor (the second tablet). Every law that God ever created hinges on the sacrificial charitable <**agape**>[8] love elements of these commandments. Thus, we discover that God is the Creator, and the sustainer of love, mercy, and grace; because that is what each and every one of His laws is instrumentally and divinely designed to accomplish, when obeyed from the heart. And that's the example the Messiah set for us and urges us to imitate (Luke 6:46; 1 Cor. 11:1–2; Gal. 1:11–12). And the eternal God/Messiah commands us to follow His burdenless commandments of love and liberty, *not* man's burdensome traditional commandments of bondage (Matt. 15 and 23; Mark 7; Gal. 1:1; 6–14; Eph. 3:3).

I will try to elaborate a bit on how this affects us. When we abide by God's laws, we are set at liberty with Him and with our brethren, because if we truly obey them from the heart, it is impossible to wish bad even upon our enemies:

> But I say unto you, **Love your enemies**, bless them that curse you, do good to them that hate you, and pray for them which despitefully use you, and persecute you. (Matt. 5:44)

> But **love ye your enemies**, and do good, and lend, hoping for nothing again; and your reward shall be great, and ye shall be the children of the Highest: for **he is kind unto the unthankful and to the evil. Be ye therefore merciful,** as your Father also is merciful. (Luke 6:35–36)

Can you see God's Fatherly love and mercy for His creation? This is what the Messiah practiced and taught on the Sermon on the Mount when He illustrated how the laws apply in the spiritual sense. (Read Matthew 5 through 7.) In the carnal sense you are considered a murderer if you *literally* kill a man, but spiritually you are a murderer for hating another without cause. In the carnal sense you are considered an adulterer if you commit the literal act of adultery, but spiritually, if you look at a woman to lust after her, you have committed adultery with her already in your heart. That's what the Messiah was prophesied to do; He would magnify the law and demonstrate its spiritual intent to mankind, *not* abolish it: "The LORD is well pleased for his righteousness' sake; he will **magnify the law**, and make it honourable" (Isa. 42:21). Again, this commandment—which is another Torah test proof—did not lose any strength at the crucifixion and resurrection, but it brought its spiritual intent to fruition. God has always desired for people to love one another from the heart; that's the whole purpose of His commandments and laws as He instructed throughout the Torah: "**Thou shalt not hate thy brother in thine heart**: thou shalt in any wise rebuke thy neighbour, and not suffer sin upon him. Thou shalt not avenge, nor bear any grudge against the children of thy people, but **thou shalt love thy neighbour as thyself**: I am the LORD" (Lev: 19:17–18).

Let's illustrate what happens when we magnify a few of the other commandments with the same intent as our Messiah did to a couple of them during His sermon on the Mount of Olives. Before the crucifixion and resurrection of the Messiah—the Holy Spirit not yet given to the lay person—God judged them in the physical sense of being, wherefore He considered it a sin for them for bowing down to visible and touchable idols. Spiritually He judges us for merely thinking about it. An idol does not have to be visible. It does not need to carry a god nametag or label. Anything for which we hold a high esteem can be an idol before God: "No servant can serve two masters: for either he will hate the one, and love the other; or else he will hold to the one, and despise the other. **Ye cannot serve God and mammon**" (Luke 16:13). This is so because He looks upon one's heart: "But the LORD said unto Samuel, Look not on his countenance, or on the height of his stature; because I have refused him: for the LORD seeth not as man seeth; for man looketh on the outward appearance, but **the LORD looketh on the heart**" (1 Samuel 16:7; read also 1 Kings 8:39 Acts 15:8).

The two commandments that the children of Israel transgressed the most often, for which God often punished them with death, were worshipping idols and profaning the Lord's Sabbaths. If a man was found doing physical labor or commerce on the Lord's Sabbath day, he was literally stoned to death. It was for breaking the first four commandments, specifically the idolatry and the Sabbath commandments, that God had the Israelites first captured and then scattered: "I lifted up mine hand unto them also in the wilderness, that **I would scatter them among the heathen**, and disperse them through the countries; Because they had not executed my judgments, but had despised my statutes, and **had polluted my sabbaths, and their eyes were after their fathers' idols**" (Ezek. 20:23–24; read all of chapter 20).

You can't break the Lord's Sabbath commandment without first bowing down to another god, such as the sun god idol, which breaks the first and second commandments. And according to the way the Messiah illustrated the murder and adultery commandments in their spiritual intent, one would be spiritually dead for merely *thinking* about work, business, finances, or any personal or servile affairs on God's holy day. This day was made holy and sanctified (set apart) by God, who created it to spend some undivided time in worship and praise with His children. He has an appointment with us on His appointed day. His statutes **<chuqqah>**[4] relate to appointed duties and times that **He** has set and commands His children to keep for Him. That's why He made a special perpetual covenant regarding not the Jews' Sabbaths, but *His* Sabbaths, which sets those who observe it apart from the world:

> Verily **my** sabbaths ye shall keep: for it is a **sign between me and you** throughout your generations; that ye may know that **I** am the LORD that doth sanctify you [sets us apart]. Ye shall keep the sabbath therefore; for it is holy unto you: every one that defileth it shall surely be put to death: for whosoever doeth any work therein, that soul shall be cut off from among his people. Six days may work be done; but in **the seventh is the sabbath of rest, holy to the LORD**: whosoever doeth any work in the sabbath day, he shall surely be put to death. Wherefore the children of Israel shall keep the sabbath, to observe the sabbath throughout their generations, for a **perpetual** <`owlam>[1] covenant. It is a **sign between me and the children of Israel for ever** <`owlam>[1]: for in six days the LORD made heaven and earth, and on **the seventh day** he rested, and was refreshed. And he gave unto Moses, when he had made an end of communing with him upon mount Sinai, two tables of testimony, tables of stone, **written with the finger of God.** (Ex. 31:13–18)

End-time prophecies confirm that *especially* the Sabbath commandment needs to be delightfully kept by everyone—including Gentiles, who claim God as their LORD:

> Thus saith the LORD, Keep ye judgment, and do justice: for my salvation is near to come, and my righteousness to be revealed. **Blessed is the man that doeth this**, and the son of man that layeth hold on it; **that keepeth the sabbath from polluting it**, and keepeth his hand from doing any evil. **Neither let the son of the stranger** [a Gentile], **that hath joined himself to the LORD, speak, saying, The LORD hath utterly separated me from his people:** neither let the eunuch say, Behold, I am a dry tree. For thus saith the LORD unto the eunuchs that keep **my sabbaths**, and choose the things that please **me**, and

> take hold of **my** covenant; Even unto them will I give in mine house and within my walls a place and a name better than of sons and of daughters: **I will give them an everlasting name**, that shall not be cut off. **Also the sons of the stranger, that join themselves to the LORD, to serve him, and to love the name of the LORD, to be his servants, every one that keepeth the sabbath from polluting it, and taketh hold of my covenant; Even them will I bring to my holy mountain, and make them joyful in my house of prayer**. (Isa. 56:1–7; read also 1 Peter 1:1–2)

God does not separate the Jews/Israelites from the Gentiles who claim Him as their Lord. All are justified as one in the Messiah (Gal. 3:28), the mixed multitude (Ex. 12:38).

Isaiah chapter 56 is an end-time prophecy, and its warning goes out to Israelites and Gentiles alike. Look at the blessings God promises for those who will honor and delightfully keep His Sabbath proper:

> And the LORD shall guide thee continually, and satisfy thy soul in drought, and make fat thy bones: and thou shalt be like a watered garden, and like a spring of water, whose waters fail not. And they that shall be of thee shall build the old waste places: thou shalt raise up the foundations of many generations; and thou shalt be called, The repairer of the breach [a definite end-time prophecy], The restorer of paths to dwell in. **If thou turn away thy foot from the sabbath**, from doing thy pleasure on my holy day; and call the sabbath a delight [NOT a burden], the **holy of the LORD** [NOT the Jews], honourable; and shalt honour him, not doing thine own ways, nor finding thine own pleasure, nor speaking thine own words: **Then** shalt thou delight thyself in the LORD; and I will cause thee to ride upon the high places of the earth, and feed thee with the heritage of Jacob thy father: for the mouth of the LORD hath spoken it. (Isa. 58:11–14)

This is an important part of God's plan of how He will use those who show obedience to Him by keeping His Sabbath, to rebuild this world after the Satan-inspired people of this age have destroyed it; thus restoring or regenerating even the desolate places. (We'll learn more about this subject in section 5a). The prophecies and promises in Isaiah 56 and 58 include the Gentiles who have joined themselves to the Lord. Don't the Sunday and pagan holiday worshippers profess to be joined to the Lord? If they do, why then are they not keeping the **Lord's** Sabbaths instead of the pagan Sundays and holidays?

Peter addressed the strangers—Gentiles—with the same instructions as he did the Jews: "Peter, an apostle of Jesus Christ, **to the strangers** throughout Pontus, Galatia ..." (1 Peter 1:1; read also Acts 10:45). There's a common belief in the mainstream traditional Christendom that the Messiah and His apostles kept the Lord's Sabbath, which they've labeled as the Jewish Sabbath because of their fear of the Jews. I find it pathetic to label the Messiah a coward.

A very sobering thought: It might even be considered blasphemy to label the Messiah and His apostles as having gone along with pagan and talmudic customs and traditions in fear of the Jews. Think about it: In Matthew chapters 15 and 23, Mark chapter 7, and John chapters 5–10, the Messiah excoriated—and in some cases flat out condemned—the Pharisees for teaching their traditions as commandments. That doesn't sound like He was afraid of them. Would He turn around and cowardly follow their traditions after condemning their use of them? The Messiah and His apostles were crucified for keeping *God's* commandments instead of their *traditional* commandments. If they had gone along with the traditions of the Pharisees, they would not have been crucified by them. The Messiah and his apostles were not hypocrites.

Furthermore, according to traditional Christian philosophy, I'm earning eternal life in the fires of hell for keeping the Lord's Sabbath. Okay, so be it. But what will happen to the Messiah and His apostles for keeping the Lord's Sabbath? Will I meet up with them in the fires of hell for keeping the Lord's Sabbath, which they kept instead of the Christian Sunday, and for keeping God's holy days instead of the Christianized pagan holidays? Please give that some serious thought.

Paul kept the Lord's Sabbaths *with Gentiles*, even after the unbelieving and disagreeable Jews—of whom he was supposed to have been afraid—rejected him. That presented a perfect opportunity for him to tell the Gentiles—and the believing and agreeable Jews—to come back Sunday if God had changed His Sabbath to Sunday. But he didn't:

> And when the Jews were gone out of the synagogue, **the Gentiles besought that these words might be preached to them the next sabbath**. Now when the congregation was broken up, many of the Jews and religious proselytes followed Paul and Barnabas: who, speaking to them, persuaded them to **continue in the grace of God. And the next sabbath day** came almost the whole city together to hear the word of God. (Acts 13:42–44)

> And he reasoned in the synagogue **every sabbath**, and **persuaded the Jews and the Greeks.** (Acts 18:4)

He preached to the Jews and Gentiles on the Sabbath for eighteen months: "And he continued there **a year and six months**, teaching the word of God among them." (Acts 18:11; read verse 4–11)

Contrary to common teaching, the Ten Commandments were not invented by Moses. God spoke them to His people face-to-face, wrote them in stone with His finger, and delivered them to Moses, who was to teach His special children about their Creator's love, mercy, and grace. "The Lord talked with you **face-to-face** in the mount out of the midst of the fire" (Deut. 5:4). However, did man learn to label God's commandments as the laws of Moses, with the implication that they are bad for us? "These words **the Lord spake** unto all your assembly in the mount out of the midst of the fire, of the cloud, and of the thick darkness, with a great voice: and **he added no more**. And **he** [God] **wrote them in two**

tables of stone, and delivered them unto me [Moses]" (Deut. 5:22). God knew that Moses would later be accused of inventing a bunch of stupid, burdensome commandments for them to keep, so He had Moses make it clear that He—God—wrote them into stone and sealed them. He added no more.

> Nevertheless, traditional Christendom has labeled the Ten Commandments as burdensome Jewish commandments of Moses of the Old Testament that, when observed in the New Testament era, will land one in hellfire. But one covenant cannot disannul another: "And this I say, that the covenant, that was confirmed before of God in Christ, the law, which was four hundred and thirty years after, cannot disannul, that it should make the promise of none effect" (Gal. 3:17). Nothing has been added or deleted from the Ten Commandments: "He added no more." And one covenant does not abolish another. God does not break His promises. Thus the adding of the animal sacrificial laws did not forfeit the promises God made to us through Abraham, Isaac, and Jacob.

We saw earlier that Abraham's keeping of God's commandments did not exempt his children (the heirs) from the obligation of keeping them. The Messiah's followers are Abraham's heirs: "For ye are all the children of God by faith in Christ Jesus. For as many of you as have been baptized into Christ have put on Christ. There is **neither Jew nor Greek**, there is neither bond nor free, there is neither male nor female: for **ye are all one in Christ Jesus**. And **if ye be Christ's, then are ye Abraham's seed, and heirs according to the promise** (Gal. 3:26–29). And the Messiah advises us to continue keeping the commandments if we love Him: "If ye love me, keep my commandments" (John 14:15; read also Ex. 20:6); and desire eternal life: "If thou wilt enter into life, keep the commandments" (Matt. 19:17).

About sixty years after the Messiah's resurrection, John was shown in a vision who would be in God's Kingdom and how they got there:

> Here are they that **keep <tereo>[21] the commandments of God, and the faith of Jesus.** (Rev. 14:12; read also Rev. 12:17)

> Blessed are they that **do his commandments, that they may have right to the tree of life, and may enter in through the gates into the city**. (Rev. 22:14; read also verse 7)

According to traditional Christianity, God's commandments were only for the Jews of the old covenant, and the faith of the Messiah is for the Gentile Christians of the new covenant / New Testament church. John said that the ones who keep (guard; preserve) God's commandments and the faith of the Messiah were seen in God's kingdom! He does not say the Jews that kept God's commandments and the Christians that kept the Messiah's faith were seen, but that those who kept **both** of those moral requirements were seen in God's kingdom!

Faith in and of the Messiah does not void our obligation to keep God's commandments, but rather, His faith in us provides us with what is needed to be able to keep them proper, as He did:

> If ye abide in me, and my words abide in you, ye shall ask what ye will, and it shall be done unto yo (John 15:7)

> Let that therefore abide in you, which ye have heard **from the beginning. If that which ye have heard from the beginning shall remain in you, ye also shall continue in the Son, and in the Father.** And this is the promise that he hath promised us, even eternal life. (1 John 2:24–25)

In other words, he told the listeners that if they would keep that which they heard from the beginning (the Torah), they should also continue in God and His Son. "And whatsoever we ask, we receive of him, **because we keep his commandments**, and do those things that are pleasing in his sight" (1 John 3:22). John did not tell them to deny the Ten Commandments in order to follow the Messiah, but that if they would keep the commandments as heard from the beginning, they should then be equipped to follow—continue—in the Messiah and His Father. The Messiah refreshed the Ten Commandments at Mount Sinai and carved them into stone tablets, and that's what they heard from the beginning. Likewise, as John stated, if we will follow those instructions today, we shall also continue in the Messiah and His Father.

Accordingly, God's laws and commandments did not start at Mount Sinai; neither could they have terminated at the crucifixion. (I explain this on page 122 of my book *The Commandments of God,* based on Rom. 5:12–14). How could Satan be kicked out of heaven if there were no commandments to break? He sinned—transgressed God's laws and commandments (1 John 3:4; Matt. 5:19; James 2:9)—even before he met Adam and Eve. He allowed pride to take hold, which caused him to lie and seduce a number of angels to rebel with him against God's laws, whereby he did not love his fellow servants. This made him a murderer (1 John 3:15). With that same pride, he seduced and deceived Adam and Eve, which caused them to sin, whereby they inherited death, after which we are born (Gen. 5:3). Isaiah chapter 14 and Ezekiel chapter 28 describe Satan's fall. Acknowledging the effects of this fall will help to understand the whole purpose of what God is working out here on this earth. (We'll learn more about this vital topic in sections 5 and 6). If God's laws and commandments didn't exist before Mount Sinai, then Satan, Adam and Eve, the pre-Flood people, Nimrod and his followers after the Flood, the people of Sodom and Gomorrah, and the Egyptians could not have sinned. But God destroyed multitudes of people, including so-called ignorant Gentiles (Lev. 18:24–25), in that time because of their sinning (Gen. 6:5); they transgressed God's laws (Matt. 5:19; 1 John 3:4; 5:17; James 2:8–11), which exacted the death penalty (Gen. 2:17; 3:3, 19; Ex. 31:14–15), just as it still does today (Matt. 15:4; Mark 7:10; Rom. 1:32; 6:23; James 1:15).

When we break a law, we've sinned, for which penalties apply. What is sin? "Sin is the transgression of the law" (1 John 3:4; read also Matt. 5:19; James 2:8–11). If I hate my brother, I have transgressed God's law, which states, "Thou shalt not kill" (Ex. 20:13). For not loving him, I am become a murderer, wherefore I will *not* inherit eternal life: "Whosoever hateth his brother is a murderer: and ye know that **no murderer hath eternal life** abiding in him" (1 John 3:15). In so doing, I inevitably hate God also. We cannot love God if we don't love our brother. And this commandment has not changed from the Old to the New Testament: "If a man say, I love God, and hateth his brother, he is a liar: for he that loveth not his brother whom he hath seen, how can he love God whom he hath not seen? And this commandment have we from him, That he who loveth God love his brother also" (1 John 4:20–21). John cited this from the Old Testament:

> **Thou shalt not hate thy brother in thine heart:** thou shalt in any wise rebuke thy neighbour, and not suffer sin upon him. ... **thou shalt love thy neighbour as thyself: I am the LORD**. (Lev. 19:17–18)

> And thou shalt love the LORD thy God with all thine heart, and with all thy soul, and with all thy might. (Deut. 6:5)

That's another Torah test proof. The Torah teaches that mercy must flow through the whole chain; else *we* cut it off at its source, which is God. We can see that God has always required that we *love the neighbor*. That did *not* change at the crucifixion, as is taught by traditional Christendom, where it's divinely taught that loving the neighbor has replaced the need to keep the Ten Commandments. Keeping the Ten Commandments develops that love.

Because the Israelites were punished more often for profaning the Lord's Sabbaths and for committing idolatry than for breaking any other commandments (read Ezek. chapters 8 and 20), the rabbis and Pharisees invented multiple hundreds of rules and regulations in an effort to prevent the captivity and the persecutions of their past from being repeated. But their proud, glory-seeking hearts (Rom. 9:31–10:3) attempted this by using their traditions as doctrines and commandments (Matt. 15; Mark 7), which delivers bondage *(Matt. 23)*—hence the Talmud. On the contrary, if they had repented and returned to keeping God's commandments and laws, God would have granted them the liberty they were searching for (James 2:8, 12; John 8:31–32; Rom. 7:12), as He has promised for keeping them (Ex. 20:6; 34:7;

Lev. 26:1–13; Deut. 5:10; 7:9; 28:1–14; 30:19; Ps. 89:34). There were many occasions where God did bless them, and each time, the world couldn't help but marvel at His sovereignty and power.

God's endless mercy: Hosea chapter 13 is written like a farewell, or rather an obituary, because God saw the Israelites—who were like children of His Family—as having spiritually died. But in chapter 14 God, again demonstrating His endless mercy, still invites them back. If they would repent, He would again treat them like His children and bless them abundantly. That's the kind of mercy and grace that the creator God teaches throughout the Torah. And once again it goes to show that God's grace did not begin at the crucifixion, as is a common traditional teaching; rather, His grace, which has always been His trademark, was magnified by it (Isa. 42:21).

Because of their control-mongering pride and filthy wealth, the Pharisees utterly regulated the people to death, for which the Messiah abhorrently excoriated them: "Well hath Esaias prophesied of you hypocrites, as it is written, This people honoureth me with their lips, but their heart is far from me. **Howbeit in vain do they worship me, teaching for doctrines the commandments** <entalma>[9a] **of men. For laying aside the commandment** <entole>[9] **of God, ye hold the tradition of men ... Full well ye reject the commandment** <entole>[9] **of God, that ye may keep your own tradition ... Making the word of God of none effect through your tradition**" (Mark 7:6–9, 13; read also Matt. chapters 15 and 23). Through traditional commandments <**entalma**>[9a] God's commandments <**entole**>[9] are automatically and systematically forsaken, from which a hatred for God is inevitably born. That's a strong testimony that a carnal-thinking man's hatred toward the creator God is born by using man's traditions. That's why the Messiah condemned their traditions.

With all their man-made traditions elevated to commandment <**entole**>[9] status as it was, it would likely be impossible to do anything without breaking at least one or more of *their* commandments <**entalma**>[9a]. Thus the love, liberty, mercy, and grace God grants us for keeping His commandments <**entole**>[9], upon which faith in the true Messiah is established, thus developing God's <**agape**>[8] love, is thereby directly opposed and hence suppressed from the people. And that's how they continually convicted the Messiah. He did many miracles, such as liberating people from bondage by rebuking their demons, which He often did on His Sabbath day to show and teach of the liberty for which that commandment was created. But according to the Talmud, the Messiah violated the Ten Commandments because He did that on the Lord's Sabbath day. Ironically, even though traditional Christendom hates the Jews, they agree with the Pharisees on that. If that be so, then the Messiah sinned, thereby disqualifying His position as the unblemished sacrificial Lamb of God. The people who believe that He was the Messiah need to think this theory through thoroughly, because according to that philosophy, the professing Messiah is being accused of sinning.

Thus, just as the Pharisees taught, traditional Christendom is also teaching that liberty is achieved by obedience to their traditional doctrines. They teach that keeping God's commandments is Judaized bondage, and as such is a sinful work whereby God's grace and the Messiah's faith is rejected, and that true liberty and grace come from *not* keeping them. Thus they evangelize people to follow their church traditions, which they profess and preach as coming directly from God's divine Word.

> A few words of encouragement for the oppressed: The book of Amos is not very long, and I want to encourage you to study it. In it, God reveals in very simple terms how He will deal with the oppressors of this world. It really helped me to understand how today's mainstream religions are syncretized and harmonized with the political socialist-communist/Masonic-orchestrated business order of the day. After studying the book of Amos and also reading through the book of Job a couple of times—realizing the hell that Job had to go through—my pity party shamefully ended rather abruptly. That humbled me enough to overcome my shortcomings, in turn aiding me to forgive the people who had oppressed me, and thus teaching me to patiently accept and appreciate the fact that God will take care of such matters, as per His will and not mine.

4b. Works of the Laws

The animal sacrificial and ritualistic duties required ongoing labor for the people, which is why Paul frequently referred to them as the works of the laws: “Knowing that a man is not justified by the **works <ergon>**[27] [physical labor] of the **law <nomos>**[22] [animal sacrifices and rituals], but by the faith of Jesus Christ …” (Gal. 2:16). They were designed to continually occupy their minds to train them to focus on worshipping and praising only their creator God as their ultimate healer from sickness and redeemer from bondage and sin. According to the instructions and examples of the Messiah and His apostles, to enter into God’s kingdom still requires continual sacrifice. Our Messiah and His disciples and apostles were sacrifices, and the animals of the sacrificial and ritualistic system foreshadowed this. His followers are a living sacrifice: “I beseech you therefore, brethren, by the mercies of God, that ye **present your bodies a <u>living sacrifice</u>, holy, acceptable unto God**, which is your reasonable service. And **be not conformed to this world** …” (Rom. 12:1–2; read also 1 Peter 2:5; James 4:4).

If we, as a living sacrifice, continually abide by these instructions, we will not be enticed into the worldly lusts so easily. Our Savior requires of us a much greater sacrifice now than before:

> And if thy right eye offend thee, **pluck it out**, and cast it from thee … And if thy right hand offend thee, **cut it off**. (Matt. 5:29–30)

> For whosoever will save his life shall lose it: and **whosoever will lose his life for my sake shall find it.** (Matt. 16:25; read also Luke 17:33; John 12:25)

> All that will live godly in Christ Jesus **shall suffer persecution**. (2 Tim. 3:12)

> **We must through much tribulation** enter into the kingdom of God. (Acts 14:22)

With the Messiah superseding the animals in the sacrificial system, and then requiring us to follow in His steps, the sacrificial laws are magnified, thus brought to their prophesied and intended purpose and fullness—the end goal thereof (Rom. 10:4; 12:1); they are *not* abolished (Matt. 5:17–18). Thus, we also have replaced the animals of the sacrificial and ritualistic system; that is, if the Messiah's spirit dwells in us. After all, we owe Him our life; He purchased us with His own blood (Luke 1:68; 24:21; Acts 20:28; Gal. 3:13; 4:5), which was foreshadowed by God's purchasing of the Israelites of old time with the blood of the unblemished lamb prior to the Messiah's manifestation (Deut. 32:6; Ex. 12:5; Pss. 74:2; 111:9; Isa. 63:16).

This inspires me to ask the anti-Law Christians a few questions regarding the subject at hand. In mainstream Christendom it's commonly taught that once you accept Jesus into your heart, you are then free to live lawlessly—"Don't become burdened with the keeping of the Jewish Ten Commandments," they preach!

1. Did the Messiah say anywhere during His ministry that following Him according to His new covenant requirements would be any easier than it was for the people under the God of the old agreement? (Read Matt. 10; Luke 14; Acts 14:22; 2 Tim. 3:12.) Even the animal sacrificial and ritual laws—the works of the law—were not as grievous and burdensome as the traditional preachers make them out to be. God never demands anything from His people that is impossible or too hard to do (1 Cor. 10:13). The Messiah confirmed this with a philosophy that is overwhelmingly opposite that which we hear from traditional preachers: "Come unto me, all ye that labour and are heavy laden, and I will give you rest. Take my yoke upon you, and learn of me; for I am meek and lowly in heart: and ye

shall find rest unto your souls. For **my yoke is easy**, and **my burden is light**" (Matt. 11:28–30). He stated this while the animal sacrificial and ritualistic laws were still in full force and effect. According to the Messiah's words, keeping the laws and commandments of God was totally without burden. He kept the Ten Commandments perfectly, rendering Him sinless, thus not requiring Him to do the atoning sacrifices and rituals. That's why He stated that to take His yoke upon us—following Him by keeping God's commandments instead of man's—would be easy and burdenless (Matt. 11:28–30).

It's man's arrogance—a demon-driven control-mongering pride—that has caused man to label obedience to God's laws and commandments a burden, thus continually feeding the carnal mind's inherent enmity toward God. Through that arrogance, man has turned to his own traditions, which—as history has proven over and over—inevitably produces bondage to slavery *of* and *by* men, because it comes directly from Satan. A strong testimony to that can be read in 1 Samuel chapter 8, where we started voting for our first man-appointed ruler; this is virtually the birth of today's democratic-communist religion. And Nehemiah chapter 5, Lamentation chapter 5, and Haggai chapter 1 are parallels to the economic status of the modern-day nations of Israel. It is much the same as it was in Egypt some 3,500 years ago; we've been blindly enslaved back into man's bondage by debt, inspired by a religiously supported government system. But, just as happened then, we've been indoctrinated by the traditional commandments of a political religion, through communist philosophy, to believe that this is liberty! Do we honestly believe that that's liberty?

2. Regarding the Ten Commandments; which one of them required *then*, or *now*, any kind of works <**ergon**>[27] or labor to keep them? Example: Does loving the true God of heaven and earth require works? Or to not use His name in vain? Or loving one's neighbor? Or not to hate

or kill another person? Or not to lie to *or* about them? Or not to steal from them? Or not to be covetous? Or not to commit adultery with his or her spouse? How much <**ergon**>[27] works is required to love, respect, and honor one's parents? Will I be condemned because of the works required to honor and respect my parents, because by doing so I'm practicing the works of one of the ten so-labeled burdensome, thus abolished, commandments?

3. How much more work is needed to rest on God's sanctified (set apart) holy Sabbath days to praise and worship Him as the Creator of heaven and earth, than to keep the Sunday Sabbath, which Constantine adopted and Christianized in honor of the pagan sun god Mithras? How much more works are required to keep God's holy day festivals, than to keep the Christianized Babylonian pagan holidays like Easter and Christmas?

   I'm frequently called a Jew, non-Christian, anti-Christ, and Muslim, among many other names, all expressed in a derogatory sense as pointing to someone that the name-callers know with all certainty is earning eternal life in hellfire for not keeping Sunday and the Christianized pagan holidays, for not coming to their church, and for not eating things like pork and snails; in other words, I am called these things for keeping the commandments of the God of Creation instead of the traditional commandments of their god.

   By the way; can we keep cold water hot? Right, we can't. First it has to be *made* hot. The same applies to God's holy days and His Sabbaths, which He first made holy and then commanded us to keep holy. How can we keep days holy that God never made holy? Can the pope—or any other man—make something holy?

Now take article number 2 above and add all the additional laws from the book of Moses, but without the animal sacrificial rites, because they were fulfilled by the Messiah to the point that they were finished, and thus superseded by the sacrifice of the Messiah (Heb. 9–10): “When Jesus therefore had received the vinegar, he said, It is **finished <teleo>**[24]: and he bowed his head, and gave up the ghost [Spirit]” (John 19:30). See how much works are required to fulfill even them. Each and every one of them is an instruction designed and ordained by God for our benefit. And as a loving Father, He gave them to His children to help them fulfill His spiritual laws so that they would learn to have a sacrificial-type charitable **<agape>**[8] love for Him from their heart. How can we love God when we rebel against the very laws that express and teach of His love: “And we have known and believed the love that God hath to us. **God is love <agape>**[8]**; and he that dwelleth in love <agape>**[8] **dwelleth in God, and God in him**” (1 John 4:16). How can we achieve that **<agape>**[8] love? “By this we know that we love the children of God, **when we love God, and keep his commandments**. For **this is the love <agape>**[8] **of God, that we keep his commandments**: and his commandments are not grievous” (1 John 5:2–3). Man has made the keeping of commandments grievous and burdensome by not living by the commandments.

5. GOD'S LAWS IN TODAY'S CONGREGATION

As we illustrated by using the examples from the Sermon on the Mount, today it's much easier to transgress God's laws than before, because God looks upon our hearts; thus now He is judging even what we're merely thinking. But, thanks be to God, the obedient people now have the Holy Spirit available to them, which sheds God's love upon the hearts to help to fulfill His spiritual laws: "The **love <agape>[8] of God is shed abroad in our hearts** by the Holy Ghost [Spirit] which is given unto us" (Rom. 5:5). Once again, what is God's love?

> For **this is the love <agape>[8] of God, that we keep his commandments**. (1 John 5:3)

> Therefore love **<agape>[8] is the fulfilling <pleroma>[10b] of the law**. (Rom 13:10; read also Gal. 6:2; James 2:8)

> **Obedience** to God is required to obtain the Holy Spirit and salvation:

> ... The Holy Ghost [Spirit], whom **God hath given to them that obey him**. (Acts 5:32)

> And being made perfect, he became the author of eternal salvation unto all **them that obey him**. (Heb. 5:9)

Obedience to God is to live by every word that proceeds out of the mouth of God (Deut. 8:3; Matt. 4:4; Luke 4:4). Incidentally, the Ten Commandments proceeded from the mouth of God!

Believers in the true Messiah know that God's commandments are still as important, binding, and necessary as ever, because we all need His **<agape>**[8] love in our heart to be fit for His kingdom—His family. It's a matter of faith—believing and *trusting* what the Messiah said: "Think **not** that I am come to destroy the law, or the prophets: I am **not come to destroy**, but to **fulfil <pleroo>**[10]. For verily I say unto you, **Till heaven and earth pass**, one **jot** or one **tittle** shall in no wise pass from the law, till **all** be **fulfilled <ginomai>**[14]" (Matt. 5:17–18). The Messiah came to fulfill **<pleroo>**[10] God's laws by magnifying them, which brought them to their full potential and purpose, making them honorable and thereby glorifying God. And He says that they will remain in full force and effect until *all* prophecies have been fulfilled **<ginomai>**[14]—brought to pass. We will see in the next section what has been fulfilled so far and what yet remains to be fulfilled.

Traditional Christendom—indoctrinated by religious forefathers like Constantine the Great and Martin Luther—preach that everything has *already* been fulfilled. I've heard that line hundreds upon hundreds of times. If that be so, then the hope of the resurrection to eternal life in God's kingdom diminishes. According to 1 Corinthians chapter 15, the resurrection is the only hope of life eternal. If everything is already fulfilled, then the resurrections are already past—a philosophy which Paul condemned: "And their word will eat as doth a canker: of whom is Hymenaeus and Philetus; Who concerning the truth have erred, **saying that the resurrection is past already**; and **overthrow the faith of some**. Nevertheless **the foundation of God standeth sure**, having this seal, The Lord knoweth them that are his. And, **Let every one that nameth the name of Christ depart from iniquity**" (2 Tim. 2:17–19; read also 1 Tim. 1:20; Ps 102:25; John 17:24; 1 Cor. 3:11; Eph. 1:4; Heb. 1:10; 4:3; Rev. 13:8). God's foundation stands sure; it has not changed, and it will not.

In the following section, we'll explore what the Messiah has fulfilled, what He yet will come to fulfill, and in what order he will fulfill it. We'll see how the God of Abraham unveils His awesome plan of salvation by the way in which He portrays the layout of His holy day festivals. Then you'll see why it is that man cannot understand the fullness of God's awesome plan in any other way than through the understanding of His holy day festivities as they portray His plan. I hope that you'll see the awesomeness of God's plan for His creation, and how traditional doctrines—because of the early church fathers' anti-Jew philosophy, from which an anti-God philosophy is borne, have perverted that plan by and through the rejection of the so-labeled Jewish Old Testament Torah scriptures. This will also help to understand why traditional Christianity, because of their hatred for the Jews, has adopted and accepted the pagan holiday festivals to worship God instead of His holy day festivals.

Oh, by the way, you have just become a witness that heaven and earth have not yet passed. So, according to the words of the Messiah, not one jot or tittle has passed from God's laws. Yes, heaven and earth will pass, but not until *all* is fulfilled. And even after that, His Word will still continue: "Heaven and earth shall pass away, but my words [Deut. 8:3; Matt. 4:4; Luke 4:4] shall not pass away" (Matt. 24:35; read also Mark 13:31). We are commanded to live by Every Word of God: "But he answered and said, It is **written**, Man shall not live by bread alone, but by **every word that proceedeth out of the mouth of God**" (Matt. 4:4; read also Luke 4:4—cited by the Messiah from Deut. 8:3). The Ten Commandments are God's Words. Whom will you believe—the Messiah or the anti-Law preachers? As a free moral agent, you must choose for yourself.

At this point I need to add a section to briefly explain the Messiah's return to fulfill God's *greater* fall harvest, which will be set in motion on the scriptural Lord's Day. That's when the Messiah returns to begin the fulfillment (Matt. 5:18) of God's greater harvest of humans.

5a. God's Holy Day Plans—Man's Awesome Promise of Hope

A brief summary of the book of Exodus: I will briefly go through the chronology of events that took place in Egypt in the few centuries in which Abraham's descendants—the Hebrew children of promise known as the Israelites—were enslaved by the Egyptian constitution; these events are described throughout the book of Exodus. It will help to understand many of the aspects of God's purpose for His annual and weekly Sabbaths, because that is where the Israelites started to keep them; I will briefly cover this in this section. It's vitally important to realize that the Israelites kept God's holy days *before* they got to Mount Sinai, *before* the old covenant was ratified, and *before* Moses wrote any laws into the book. I make mention of this to rule out a common traditional argument that is used to falsely gun down God's command to keep His holy days, because of a claim that they were a part of the old covenant and the Old Testament commandments. And since the proponents of that argument preach that the Old Testament, together with all of its old covenants, was given only to the Jews at Mount Sinai, they make the claim that God's holy day festivals were abolished and nailed to the tree by the Messiah. Although that line of reasoning is totally unscriptural, this ought to rule out that reasoning altogether.

Exodus chapters 1 to 11 shows how Abraham's Hebrew/ Israelite descendants were held in extremely hard slavery in Egypt by the ruling Pharaoh. It also shows how God prepared Moses and his Levite brother Aaron to redeem those enslaved Israelites from that Egyptian bondage. Chapter 12 describes how the Israelites—including many Gentiles (verse 38)—were saved from death by observing the Lord's Passover, and how the Lord Himself killed the firstborn of every family and the livestock of all the households that did not observe it (verse 29). Chapter 12 has the instructions on how to keep the Lord's Passover, which foreshadowed the promised Messiah, who would come and sacrifice His life, thus shedding His innocent blood to pay for the sins of mankind. Chapter 12 also has the instructions for the Days of Unleavened Bread, which is a symbol of God redeeming His people from sin's bondage, thus reconciling them to Him while they practice ruling out sin. In scripture, leaven symbolizes sin, and eating unleavened bread while keeping the feast reminds His people to reject sin and put it out of their lives, whereof Paul reminds us (1 Cor. 5:7–8). The Messiah also warned us to be cautious of the leaven/sin of false religion (Matt. 16:6, 12; Mark 8:15 and Luke 12:1), thus implying that advocating man's traditions is as leaven.

Chapters 13 through 15 describe the Israelites leaving Egypt and crossing through the Red Sea on dry soil, and the drowning of the great Egyptian army in the same path while giving the Israelites chase. In chapter 16 God reminds the Israelites of the proper day for keeping His weekly Sabbath, by giving them enough manna on the sixth day of the week to last them through the seventh-day Sabbath. God, in order to prove His appointed seventh-day Sabbath, caused worms to breed in any manna that they tried to preserve for any day other than His Sabbath, while He preserved the manna they saved for His appointed seventh-day Sabbath. Chapters 17 through 20 show their journey up to Mount Sinai, from where God / the Messiah personally spoke His eternal Ten Commandments to the people face-to-face (Deut. 5:4) and then wrote them into two stone tablets with His own finger. (Ex. 31:18; Deut. 9:10).

Chapters 21 to 24 contain the civil laws with which they were to conduct their lives as God's nation of people on earth. In chapter 24 they make a covenant—a binding agreement—that they ratify by blood. In chapters 25 to 30, God gives Moses the blueprint for the tabernacle, with its very unique furniture—an arrangement that intrinsically depicts our hearts as His temple. In chapters 29 to 30, God ordains His priesthood, where He sanctifies and consecrates Aaron as the high priest, and Aaron's two sons as ministers for His congregation. In chapter 31 God makes a special perpetual Sabbath covenant with His people in order to identify His people from the rest of the world henceforth. In chapter 32, while Moses is up on the mountain, receiving more instructions from God, the Israelites make a golden calf to worship as their redeeming god, whom they profess to worship in the name of God—a feast to the Lord (verse 5). The remaining book of Exodus describes the continuing journey as more instructions are given regarding the animal sacrificial and ritualistic ordinances and what they entail. The book of Leviticus provides a fuller description of those ordinances.

The book of Leviticus also holds full accounts of God's dietary laws, health laws, clean and unclean animals, witchcraft condemnations, morality and marriage laws, and many more laws regarding the health and welfare of mankind. God created every law with man's health and welfare in mind. Chapter 23 (and Deuteronomy chapter 16) describes God's holy day festivals. Chapter 26 (and Deuteronomy chapter 28) gives detailed ongoing prophesies about the blessings for keeping God's commandments, and likewise curses for not keeping them.

Before going into details of God's holy day festivals, I will clarify that they are GOD's annual feasts and Sabbath days—*not* the Jews': "Speak unto the children of Israel, and say unto them, Concerning the **feasts of the LORD** [*not* the Jews'], which ye shall proclaim to be holy convocations, even **these are my feasts**. Six days shall work be done: but **the seventh day is the sabbath** of rest, **an holy convocation**; ye shall do no work therein: it is the **sabbath of the LORD** [*not* the Jews'] in all your dwellings. These are the **feasts of the LORD**, even holy convocations, which ye shall proclaim in their **seasons <mow'ed>**[7]" (Lev. 23:2–4). That should put the argument of whose holy days they are out of the way. We can see that God bound the seventh-day Sabbath together with His annual Sabbaths; they stand or fall together, and they all include holy convocations in which He commands His people to assemble for fellowship and to worship Him, in order to learn about Him and His plans for mankind, while feasting and rejoicing in Him (Lev. 23:2–4; Deut. 14:23–26; Neh. 8:1–12). He sanctified them (set them apart) for His holy purpose, and He commands us to teach them to our children, together with His commandments, statutes, and laws (Ex. 13:14; Deut. 4:10; 6:1–7).

The first three holy day festivals foreshadow and depict the Messiah's First Coming, while the last four foreshadow and depict His Second Coming. The Messiah observed them with His disciples, and He commands us to continue keeping them in remembrance of Him at the appointed time:

> And he took bread, and gave thanks, and brake it, and gave unto them, saying, This is my body which is given for you: **this do in remembrance of me.** (Luke 22:19)

> And this day shall be unto you for a memorial; and ye shall keep it a feast to the LORD throughout your generations; ye shall keep it a feast by an ordinance **for ever <'owlam>**[1]. (Ex. 12:14; read verses 14–20)

> Thou shalt therefore keep this ordinance **in his season <mow'ed>**[7] **from year to year** [annually]. (Ex. 13:10).

When He returns, He will keep them with us again in His Father's kingdom: "But I say unto you, I will not drink henceforth of this fruit of the vine, **until that day <u>when I drink it new with you</u> in my Father's kingdom** (Matt. 26:29; read also Mark 14:25; Luke 22:14–20). They will be kept annually by His people when He returns: "And it shall come to pass, that every one that is left of all the nations which came against Jerusalem shall even go up **from year to year** to worship the King, the LORD of hosts, and to **keep the feast of tabernacles"** (Zech. 14:16). Followers of Him are to imitate Him (John 7:8–14; 13:15; 15:4; 1 Peter 2:21; 1 John 2:3–6). His new covenant church era began on one of His annual festivals—the day of Pentecost—when He delivered the Holy Spirit to His followers (Acts 2:1–4).

God commanded that His holy days be observed forever by His people (Ex. 12 and Lev. 23; Deut. 16). The Messiah's followers continued to observe God's holy days long after the resurrection (Acts 2:1; 18:21; 20:6, 16; 27:9; 1 Cor. 5:7–8; 11:23–27; 16:8). Paul refers to them as continuing/remaining shadows of the marvelous events in God's plan of salvation, which haven't yet all been fulfilled. He stated that they *are* (continue/remain) a shadow of things to come, because they reveal God's true plan of salvation: "Let no man therefore judge you in meat, or in drink, or in respect of an **holyday**, or of the new moon, or of the **sabbath days**: Which **are <esti>**[28] a shadow of things to come" (Col. 2:16–17; read also 1 Cor. 11:24). He instructed even Gentile people to keep them (1 Cor. 5:8; 11:23–26; Col. 2:16–17).

Observing God's holy days throughout the year reminds His people of the miraculous role that the Messiah plays in His awesome plan of salvation. By studying the true Gospel of the kingdom of God and the divine calling to a new way of life (John 6:44, 65; Rom. 6:4), we see the establishment of the Messiah's congregation as a resemblance of God's family. Thus, by focusing on the important role that the Messiah plays in these festivals, we begin to understand that the true meaning behind God's holy day festivals reveals His awesome plan of saving mankind from itself.

During the course of God's festivals are seven annual high-day Sabbaths—holy convocations in which no work is to be done. The first and second annual high Sabbath days are the first and last (seventh) days of the Feast of Unleavened Bread, the third annual high Sabbath day is the Feast of Pentecost, the fourth annual high Sabbath day is the Day of Trumpets, the fifth annual high Sabbath day is the Day of Atonement, the sixth annual high Sabbath day is the first day of the Feast of Tabernacles, and the seventh annual high Sabbath day is the Eighth Day, which is commonly called the Last Great Day.

The gathering of the firstfruits as depicted by Pentecost, and the gathering of His greater fall harvest as depicted by the Feast of Tabernacles, are foreshadowed in the Torah: "And the feast of harvest, the firstfruits of thy labours [Pentecost], which thou hast sown in the field: and the feast of ingathering [Feast of Tabernacles], which is in the end of the year, when thou hast gathered in thy labours out of the field" (Ex. 23:16; read also 34:22).

The first three holy days of the year occur in late spring and early summer, as they relate to God's early harvest of His firstfruits. The Messiah has already fulfilled the first two feasts—the Passover and the Days of Unleavened Bread. Pentecost is being fulfilled in the present era—the gathering and sanctifying (setting apart) of His firstfruits—the remnant.

The Lord's Passover is the first annual festival of the year (Exodus chapter 12; Lev. 23:5). It teaches us that the Messiah was absolutely sinless and blameless: "And he made his grave with the wicked, and with the rich in his death; because **he had done no violence, neither was any deceit in his mouth**" (Isa. 53:9; read also Luke 23:41; Heb. 4:15; 1 Peter 2:22; 1 John 3:5). Paul mentioned another Torah test proof of that prophecy: "For he hath made him to be sin for us, **who knew no sin**; that we might be made the righteousness of God in him" (2 Cor. 5:21; read also Luke 23:41; 1 Peter 2:22; 1 John 3:5; Heb. 4:15). The Messiah's sinlessness qualified Him to be the unblemished Passover Lamb of God (John 1:29; 1 Cor. 5:7; 1 Peter 1:19; Rev. 5:6–12; 7:14; 12:11; 13:8; 14:4), who willingly shed His blood and gave His life (John 10:11–18) as a ransom to forgive the sin of mankind in order to remove it's penalty—death: "Even as the Son of man came not to be ministered unto, but to minister, and **to give his life a ransom for many**" (Matt. 20:28; read also Isa. chapter 53; Mark 10:45; John 1:29; Acts 13:38; 20:28; Rom. 3:25; 5:8–10; 1 Cor. 5:7; 15:3; Gal. 1:4; Eph. 1:7; Col. 2:13; 1 Tim. 2:6; Titus 2:14; Heb. 1:3; 2:17; 9:26–28; 1 Peter 1:18–19; 2:24; 3:18; 1 John 2:2; 4:10; Rev. 1:5). While observing His last Passover together with His disciples, He humbly washed their feet and commanded His followers to do the same if they wanted to have part in Him: "If I then, your Lord and Master, have washed your feet; ye also ought to wash one another's feet" (John 13:14; read verses 5–17).

The second of God's Festivals is the Feast of Unleavened Bread (Exodus chapter 12; 13:6; 23:15; 34:18; Lev. 23:6). This festival reminds us that God took us out of Egyptian bondage—redeemed us from this world's sin:

> Seven days thou shalt eat unleavened bread, and in the seventh day shall be a feast to the LORD. Unleavened bread shall be eaten seven days; and there shall no leavened bread be seen with thee, neither shall there be

> leaven seen with thee in all thy **quarters <g@buwl>**[29]. And thou shalt shew thy son in that day, saying, **This is done because of that which the Lord did unto me when I came forth out of Egypt** [redeemed from sin's bondage]**. And it shall be for a sign unto thee upon thine hand, and for a memorial between thine eyes, that the Lord's law may be in thy mouth: for with a strong hand hath the Lord brought thee out of Egypt.** Thou shalt therefore keep this ordinance **in his season <mow'ed>**[7] from year to year. (Ex. 13:6–10; read also Ex. 12:8; Lev. 23:6; Deut. 16:3)

The Messiah fulfilled the wave sheaf offering during the Days of Unleavened Bread, which was His Father's acceptance of Him as His sinless (unleavened) wave sheaf offering and Passover Lamb, which glorified God. Thus it reminds us today that we've been called to reject lawlessness and repent of sin: "Purge out therefore the old leaven [reject lawlessness], that ye may be a new lump [repent of sin], as ye are unleavened [been forgiven; redeemed]. For even Christ our passover is sacrificed for us: Therefore **let us keep the feast**, not with old leaven, neither with the leaven of malice and wickedness; but **with the unleavened bread of sincerity and truth**" (1 Cor. 5:7–8; read also 11:27–29; Luke 13:3; Acts 2:38; 3:19). Observing this feast in that context reminds us that we are to live by every word of God and according to the Messiah's teaching and examples (Deut. 8:3; Matt. 4:4; Luke 4:4; 1 Cor. 10; James 5:10; 1 Peter 2:21).

Leaven symbolizes sin, and as such, it is to be removed from our dwelling place for the duration of the seven days of this feast: "Seven days shall there be no leaven found in your houses: for whosoever eateth that which is leavened, even that soul shall be cut off from the congregation of Israel [removed from God's Family], whether he be a stranger [Gentile], or born in the land [Israelite]" (Ex. 12:19; read also 13:7; 1 Cor. 5:7–8). Leaven is to be removed from one's property: "Unleavened bread shall be eaten seven days; and there shall no leavened bread be seen with thee, neither shall there be leaven seen with thee in all thy **quarters <g@buwl>**[29]" (Ex. 13:7). Eating unleavened bread and removing leaven from within one's borders symbolizes practicing a life of sincerity and truth by rejecting lawlessness, thus putting out sin.

Pentecost is the third of God's festivals; it is called the Feast of Weeks in the Old Testament (Ex. 23:16; 34:22; Deut. 16:10). It is the festival of the early harvest of firstfruits. This feast depicts the Messiah's confirmation of the continuation of His congregation, now with believers who were filled with the Holy Spirit. During its observance by His early followers—the firstfruits—the Messiah delivered the Holy Spirit to them: "And when the day of Pentecost was fully come, they were all with one accord in one place. And suddenly there came a sound from heaven as of a rushing mighty wind, and it filled all the house where they were sitting. And there appeared unto them cloven tongues like as of fire, and it sat upon each of them. And **they were all filled with the Holy Ghost <pneuma>**[11] [Spirit], and began to speak with other tongues, as the **Spirit <pneuma>**[11] gave them utterance" (Acts 2:1–4; read also Rom. 5:5; Gal. 4:6; James 1:18). That ceremony circumcised—unveiled—their hearts, thus giving them spiritual understanding: "For he is not a Jew, which is one outwardly; neither is that circumcision, which is outward in the flesh: But he is a Jew, which is one inwardly; and **circumcision is that of the heart, in the spirit <pneuma>**[11], and not in the letter [circumcised in the flesh]; whose praise is not of men, but of God" (Rom. 2:28–29; read also Deut. 10:16; 30:6; Jer. 4:4; Col. 2:11). By the unveiling—circumcision of the heart—an obedient nature is thus borne to live by the commandments of God: "Circumcision [being Jew-born] is nothing, and uncircumcision [being Gentile-born] is nothing, **but the keeping of the commandments of God**" (1 Cor. 7:19; read also Ex. 23:16; John 14:14–26; Acts 5:32; Rom. 5:5; 7:7–12; Heb. 5:9; Rev. 14:4–5, 12). The Messiah, as God's firstborn Son and firstfruit, fulfilled the Pentecost (Feast of Weeks) when He delivered the promised comforter and helper, the Holy Spirit, in order to continue His congregation, now with His newly Holy Spirit–inspired apostles and believing followers (Acts 2:1–4).

We've now briefly covered the first three holy day festivals—the harvest of firstfruits. The firstfruits will be given salvation upon the Messiah's return: "Marvel not at this: for the hour is coming, in the which all that are in the graves shall hear his voice, And shall come forth; they that have done good, unto the resurrection of life; and they that have done evil, unto the resurrection of damnation" (John 5:28–29; read also verses 24–29; Rev. 11:15–18; 12:10; 14:4, 12; 22:14). That will occur at His Second Coming: "For as in Adam all die, even so in Christ shall all be made alive. But **every man in his own order**: Christ the firstfruits; **afterward they that are Christ's at his coming**" (1 Cor. 15:22–23). And that's when He brings our rewards: "And, behold, I come quickly; and **my reward is with me**, to give every man according as his work shall be" (Rev, 22:12).

The Messiah Himself confirmed that His return will occur after the Great Tribulation:

> Immediately **after the tribulation** of those days shall the sun be darkened, and the moon shall not give her light, and the stars shall fall from heaven, and the powers of the heavens shall be shaken: And **then shall appear the sign of the Son of man** in heaven: and then shall all the tribes of the earth mourn, and **they shall see the Son of man coming in the clouds of heaven with power and great glory**. And he shall send his angels with a great sound of a **trumpet <salpigx>**[30], and they shall gather together his elect from the four winds, from one end of heaven to the other. (Matt. 24:29–31; read also 1 Cor. 15:52; 1 Thess. 4:16)

There are four more of God's holy days that have yet to be fulfilled; we'll briefly cover these next. As we will see later, the Messiah's followers observed all the holy days even decades after the resurrection.

The next four holy day festivals—the late-summer / early fall harvest of people—remain yet to be fulfilled. The early harvest of firstfruits we just covered depicts the remnant He is harvesting and preparing to help Him rule and reign on this earth in the millennium after He returns to put an end to the Great Tribulation: "And hast made us unto our God kings and priests: and **we shall reign on the earth**" (Rev. 5:10; read also 20:4–6; Dan. 7:27). The millennium depicts the greater harvest of humans, when God will again gather His people from all over the world in a much greater exodus than the first one from Egypt. That's when He will gather them from where they have been since He had them scattered around 700 BC.

The Day of Trumpets is the first of God's four late-summer / early fall festivals that has not yet been fulfilled (Lev. 23:24; Num. 29:1). It points to the Messiah's glorious visible and audible return to earth at the end of this age; events likened to when He spoke the Ten Commandments from Mount Sinai in a thundering and earth-shaking voice: "And the seventh angel **sounded <salpizo>**[31]; and there were **great voices** in heaven, saying, **The kingdoms of this world are become the kingdoms of our Lord, and of his Christ; and he shall reign for ever and ever**" (Rev. 11:15; read also verses 15–19; Rev. 12:10; 16:17; Matt. 24:29–31; 1 Cor. 15:52; 1 Thess. 4:16; Ex. 19:16–19; Isa. 27:13; Dan. 2:44; 7:11–27). Upon His return He will resurrect His saints who have died and instantly change His saints who are yet alive into immortal spirit beings: "Behold, I shew you a mystery; We shall not all sleep, but we shall all be changed, In a moment, in the twinkling of an eye, at the **last** [seventh] **trump <salpigx>**[30]: for the **trumpet shall sound <salpizo>**[31], and the dead shall be raised incorruptible, and we shall be changed. For this corruptible must put on incorruption, and this mortal must put on immortality" (1 Corinthians 15:51-53; read also Matt. 24:31, 40-41; 25:1-13; Luke 17:34-36; John 5:25-29; 1 Thess. 4:13-17; Rev. 7:9). This speaks of the first resurrection (Rev. 20:4-5).

NOTE: 1 day is to God as 1000 years (Ps. 90:4; 2 Peter 3:8). God commands man to work for his necessities the first six days of the week, resembling six Scriptural days - 6000 years since Adam started tilling the ground (Gen. 3:23). God's seventh-day Sabbath (the 7th millennium), pictures the following 1000 years in which His resurrected saints will spiritually rest (Heb. 4:1-11) during their rule and reign on this earth together with the Messiah, without Satan's influences (Rev. 20:4). The mortal survivors of the great tribulation (Matt.24:40-41; 25:1-13; Luke 17:34-36; Rev. 7:9) will also experience a tremendous rest from

Satan's influences, while they will prosper in peace and harmony under God/Messiah's governance. These people are the ones who will survive and endure to the end (Matt. 24:13; Mark 13:13). Those **taken** - like in Matthew 24:40-41, 25:1-13, and Luke 17:34-36 - are the ones that will be changed/resurrected upon the Messiah's return (1 Cor. 15:50-54; 1 Thess. 4:13-18), and those **left** are the ones that will continue to dwell on this earth, thus entering and welcoming the Satan-free millennium. This speaks of the first resurrection (Rev. 20:4–5).

This festival commemorates the blowing of trumpets that marks a sequence of major apocalyptic end-time events. There are seven trumpets described in the book of Revelation, the last (the seventh) of which will announce the Messiah's glorious return to earth (Matt. 24:29–31; 1 Cor. 15:52; 1 Thess. 4:16; Rev. 11:15). Numbers chapter 10 describes the significant meanings of a series of different trumpet blasts and alarms, after which the Feast of Trumpets is named: "And in the seventh month, on the first day of the month, ye shall have an holy convocation; ye shall do no servile work: it is a day of blowing the **trumpets <t@ ruw'ah>**[32] unto you" (Num. 29:1).

The apostle John was shown about the fulfillment of the late-summer / early fall harvest festivals. The Messiah caused him to spiritually envision the events of a horrendous apocalypse, and subsequently His glorious return to rule this earth, which He gave to Satan about six thousand years ago to govern as he sees fit (Luke 4:6). The event of His return is called the Lord's Day throughout the scriptures: "Alas for the day! for the **day of the LORD** is at hand, and **as a destruction from the Almighty** shall it come" (Joel 1:15; read also Joel 2:1; Isa. 2:12; 13:6, 9; Zech. 14:1; Mal. 4:5; Acts 2:20; 1 Cor. 1:7–8; 5:5; 2 Cor. 1:13–14; 1 Thess. 5:2–3; Rev. 1:10). Peter preached about it: "The sun shall be turned into darkness, and the moon into blood, before that great and notable **day of the Lord** come" (Acts 2:20). Paul also tells us about that event: "For yourselves know perfectly that the **day of the Lord** so cometh as a thief in the night. For when they shall say, Peace and safety; then **sudden destruction** cometh upon them, as travail upon a woman with child; and they shall not escape" (1 Thess. 5:2–3). These scriptures refer to a time when the Lord will return to earth to prove to Satan and his followers (mankind) that He remains the sovereign God of the universe and thus will take over the rule of this earth.

In Matthew 24:21 the Messiah emphasized the fact that the great and terrible events—first in horror from Satan's wrath and then ultimately from God's wrath, and likewise also salvation—will be much greater than the judgments that He executed when He redeemed the Israelites from Egyptian bondage, of which Exodus chapters 3 through 14 hold a very colorful and sobering account.

The book of Revelation is the account of the prophesied apocalyptic events that will lead up to the Messiah's return and how He will take control of this planet. It starts off by confirming the importance of keeping God's word that is in it: "The Revelation of Jesus Christ, which God gave unto him, to shew unto his servants things which must shortly **come to pass <ginomai>**[14]; and he sent and signified it by his angel unto his servant John: **Who bare record of the word of God, and of the testimony of Jesus Christ**, and of all things that he saw. **Blessed is he that readeth, and they that hear the words of this prophecy**, and **keep <tereo>**[21] **those things which are written therein**" (Rev. 1:1–3). The people continuing in the keeping (guarding; preserving) of God's commandments through faith *in* and *of* the Messiah will attain access to God's kingdom at His coming: "Here is the **patience** of the saints: here are they that **keep <tereo>**[21] the **commandments <entole>**[9] of God, **and** the faith of Jesus" (Rev. 14:12; read also Rev. 6:9; 12:17; 22:14).

That's how God's grace will abide in us if we keep His commandments: "If ye keep my commandments, ye shall abide in my **love <agape>**[8]; even as I have kept my Father's commandments, and abide in his **love <agape>**[8]" (John 15:10; read also 1 John 3:24; 4:7). Contrary to Protestant teaching, keeping God's commandments and laws does not disconnect one from His grace (Rom. 6:1–16). Rather, it establishes it: "Do we then make void the law through faith? God forbid: yea, we **establish <histemi>**[72] the law" (Rom. 3:31). And not keeping just one of them is breaking them (James 2:10–11), which is sin (Matt. 5:19; 1 John 3:4; James 2:8–11). And *no* sin (commandment breakers) will enter God's kingdom (1 Cor. 6:9–10; Gal. 5:19–21; Eph. 5:5; Heb. 12:14; Rev. 20:14–15; 21:8; 22:15).

First we'll take a brief look at Revelation 1:10, and then I'll explain how the vision that John was taken into of the prophetic Lord's Day reveals a display of panoramic events that will take place in the future, just as God prophesied through the prophets of old (Isa. chapter 46; Ezek. 37:14; Heb. 6:17–18) that He would fulfill His awesome plans. John is shown the events that will be fulfilled on God's late-summer / early fall harvest of God's people, as depicted by God's holy days: "I was **in the Spirit** on the **Lord's day**, and heard behind me a great voice, as of a **trumpet <salpigx>**[30]" (Rev. 1:10; read also Rev. 14:12; 21:10).

The book of Revelation reveals a series of seven trumpet blasts, of which the last one will announce the return of the Messiah at a time that the prophets and the apostles referred to as the Lord's Day. This event is quite certainly to occur on a day known in scripture as the Day of Trumpets (Lev. 23:24; Num. 29:1), which depicts the first of God's four late-summer / early fall holy days that mark the beginning of His great harvest of people. Paul wrote of this marvelous event:

> For this we say unto you by the word of the Lord, that we which are alive and remain unto the coming of the Lord shall not prevent [precede] them which are asleep. For the Lord himself shall descend from heaven with a **shout**, with the **voice of the archangel**, and with the **trump <salpigx>**[30] of God: and the dead in Christ shall rise first: Then we which are alive and remain shall be caught up together with them in the clouds, to meet the Lord in the air: and so shall we ever be with the Lord. (1 Thess. 4:15–17; read also Matt. 24:29–31; John 14:3; 1 Cor. 15:51–53; 2 Thess. 1:5–7)

In the resurrection chapter (1 Cor. 15), while Paul explains the sequential order of events that are to take place in the coming resurrection, he identifies a particular trumpet that will announce that event as the last one: "Now this I say, brethren, that flesh and blood cannot inherit the kingdom of God; neither doth corruption inherit incorruption. Behold, I shew you a mystery; We shall not all sleep, but we shall all be changed, In a moment, in the twinkling of an eye, at the **last <eschatos>**[33] **trump <salpigx>**[30]: for the **trumpet <salpizo>**[31] shall sound, and the dead shall be raised incorruptible, and we [the Messiah's followers yet alive who endured to the end (Matt. 24:13; Mark 13:13)] shall be changed. For this corruptible must put on incorruption, and this mortal must put on immortality" (1 Cor. 15:50–53). This is the same theme that the Messiah explained to Nicodemus when He explained to him the fact that we must be changed into non-fleshly spirit beings before we can enter God's kingdom (John chapter 3). And as these scriptures show, this will happen at the Messiah's return to earth (1 Cor. 15:23) after the tribulation period (Matt. 24:29–31; Mark 13:22–27; Luke 21:25–28), when He comes to resurrect His Saints to immortal and incorruptible spirit beings, just as He was later raised up from literal death unto spiritual eternal life.

Joel prophesied of the events which were shown to John in his vision. His whole book speaks mostly of the terrible events of the Great Tribulation: "Blow ye the **trumpet <showphar>**[34] in Zion, and sound an **alarm <ruwa'>**[32a] in my holy mountain: let all the inhabitants of the land tremble: for the **day of the Lord** cometh, for it is nigh at hand" (Joel 2:1). The short book of Zephaniah also paints a very vivid picture about the pouring out of God's wrath upon the wickedness on this Babylonian, Satan-inspired earth on that prophetic Lord's Day, causing indescribable destruction and desolation. And the book of Revelation portrays a very vivid, thus horrifying, picture of those events in more modern terms.

This world, or this present age, has been governed by Satan through his demonic army of religious and political control-mongering men for about six thousand years, or six scriptural days. One day is to the Lord as a thousand years: "But, beloved, be not ignorant of this one thing, that **one day** is with the Lord as a **thousand years"** (2 Peter 3:8; read also Ps. 90:4).

The apocalyptic outgoing of the sixth millennium, thus the onset of the seventh millennium, is foreshadowed throughout the scriptures as the Lord's Day, as we read in the scriptures. During the Great Tribulation, Satan, through religious and political governing societies, will cause the whole world to become furiously enraged and entangled in the worst war in the history of mankind. Just before the horrific events of that war annihilates all human life from the face of this earth, the Messiah, ruling with a rod of iron (an authoritative staff or scepter of correction), will intervene and put an end to that war by totally disabling Satan and annihilating his army (Ps. 2:9; 49:14; 89:23; Dan. 7:22; Rev. 2:26–27; 12:5; 19:15).

Over three thousand years ago, God warned the Israelites with a tremendous prophecy before they crossed the Jordan River, which was forty years after they left Egypt. He told them that they would be scattered and put into bondage again because of their unfaithfulness to Him. He specifically warned them that they would serve foreign gods from the surrounding nations who would entice them to flirt with them (committing adultery), thereby forsaking Him:

> And it shall come to pass, that as the LORD rejoiced over you to do you good, and to multiply you; so the LORD will rejoice over you to destroy you, and to bring you to nought; and ye shall be plucked from off the land whither thou goest to possess it. And **the LORD shall scatter thee among all people, from the one end of the earth even unto the other; and there thou shalt serve other gods**, which neither thou nor thy fathers have known, even wood and stone. And **among these nations shalt thou find no ease**, neither shall the sole of thy foot have rest [will be enslaved]: but the LORD shall give thee there a trembling heart, and failing of eyes, and sorrow of mind [can't see any way out]: And **thy life shall hang in doubt** before thee; and thou shalt fear day and night, and shalt have none assurance of thy life. (Deut. 28:63–66)

That scattering did occur about seven hundred years later (2 Kings 17), which enslaved them again into the bondage of this world. They/we are still scattered, and the identity is almost 100 percent lost: "I said, I would scatter them into corners, I would make the remembrance of them to cease from among men" (Deut. 32:26).

God's greater fall harvest festivals (Lev. 23:24–44) depict the time when God will again, the second time, gather His people from all nations in a much greater exodus than the previous one from Egypt: "And it shall come to pass in that day, that the Lord shall set his hand **again the second time** **to recover the remnant of his people**, which shall be left, from Assyria, and from Egypt, and from Pathros, and from Cush, and from Elam, and from Shinar, and from Hamath, and from the islands of the sea" (Isa. 11:11; read also Jer. 16:14–15 [cited below]; 29:14; 32:37; Zech. 10:10). After this, God's commandments will be kept:

> And it shall come to pass, when all these things are come upon thee, the blessing and the curse [the scattering, Deut. 28:64], which I have set before thee, and **thou shalt call them to mind among all the nations** [they will remember], whither the LORD thy God hath driven thee, And shalt return unto the LORD thy God, and **shalt obey his voice according to all that I command thee this day**, thou and thy children, **with all thine heart, and with all thy soul**; That **then the LORD thy God will turn thy captivity**, and have compassion upon thee, **and will return and gather thee from all the nations, whither the LORD thy God hath scattered thee**. If any of thine be driven out unto the outmost parts of heaven, from thence will the LORD thy God gather thee, and from thence will he fetch thee: And the LORD thy God will bring thee into the land which thy fathers possessed, and thou shalt possess it; and he will do thee good, and multiply thee above thy fathers. And **the LORD thy God will circumcise thine heart, and the heart of thy seed, to love the LORD thy God with all thine heart, and with all thy soul, that thou mayest live**. And the LORD thy God will put all these curses upon thine enemies, and on them that hate thee, which persecuted thee. **And thou shalt return and obey the voice of the LORD, and do all his commandments which I command thee this day**. (Deut. 30:1–8)

God is calling His remnant out from all over this world by bringing His commandments to our memory. He says that we will remember His commandments that He commanded ***that day***. There's no mention of a change from the commandments that He commanded *that day* into something different in the New Testament era, as is preached from the mainstream pulpits. The conviction always seems to begin with His Sabbaths, because as we can read in Ezekiel chapter 20 (and other scriptures) the profaning of it was the main cause for first having us taken captive, then scattering us: "I lifted up mine hand unto them also in the wilderness, that **I would scatter them among the heathen, and disperse them through the countries**; Because they had not executed my judgments, but had **despised my statutes**, and had **polluted my sabbaths**, and their eyes were after their fathers' idols [pagan sun god worship]" (Ezek. 20:23–24; read also chapter 8).

God will gather His people again from all the nations where He had them scattered: "Therefore, behold, the days come, saith the LORD, that it shall no more be said, The LORD liveth, that brought up the children of Israel out of the land of Egypt; But, The LORD liveth, that brought up the children of Israel from the land of the north, and **from all the lands whither he had driven them**: and I will bring them **again** into their land that I gave unto their fathers (Jer. 16:14–15; read also Deut. 30:3–6 [cited above]; Isa. 11:11; Jer. 23:3–8; 29:13–14; 30:3; 32:37–44; Ezek. 20:33–38; 28:25–26; 34:16; 36:24; Hos. 3:5; Amos 9:14–15; Matt. 24:31; Rom. 11:26–27).

Ezekiel prophesied about the spiritual aspect of the change that will take place in people's hearts at that time—the circumcision of the heart:

> For I will take you from among the heathen, and **gather you out of all countries**, and will bring you into your own land. Then will I sprinkle clean **water** upon you, and ye shall be clean: from all your filthiness, and from all your idols, will I cleanse you. A **new heart** also will I give you, and a **new spirit** will I put within you: and I will take away the stony heart out of your flesh, and I will give you

> an heart of flesh. And **I will put my spirit within you**, and **cause you to walk in my statutes, and ye shall keep my judgments, and do** them. (Ezek. 36:24–27)

This explains the glorious power that the Messiah will use to establish His Father's kingdom. He, together with His resurrected firstfruits, will set up God's government to rule this earth for one thousand years (Ps. 37:11; Matt. 5:5; 1 Peter 2:9; Rev. 5:10; 20:4–6), making it possible for all who dwell on the earth at that time to observe God's Commandments, because Satan and his influences will be removed from the scene (Rev. 20:1–3).

While the Messiah explained the end-time events to His disciples, He specifically stated that His return to earth would most assuredly be *after* the Great Tribulation and *not* before it:

> Immediately **after the tribulation** of those days shall the sun be darkened, and the moon shall not give her light, and the stars shall fall from heaven, and the powers of the heavens shall be shaken: And **then** shall appear the sign of the Son of man in heaven: and **then** shall all the tribes of the earth mourn, **and they shall see the Son of man coming in the clouds of heaven with power and great glory**. And he shall send his angels with a great sound of a **trumpet <salpigx>**[30] [signifying Feast of Trumpets], and they shall **gather together his elect from the four winds**, from one end of heaven to the other. (Matt. 24:29–31; read also Mark 13:24–27; Luke 21:25–28; Acts 2:20; 1 Cor. 15:52; 1 Thess. 4:16; Rev. 1:7; 6:12; 10:7; 11:15; 12:10; 16:17; 19:6; Isa. 27:13; Dan. 2:44; 7:14, 18, 27)

The Day of Atonement is the second of God's late-summer / early fall harvest festivals (Lev. 16:29–31; 23:27–32; 25:9; Num. 29:7). Its observance reminds us that the Messiah shed His blood and gave His life as a ransom to atone for the sins of mankind. This day also points to a one-thousand-year period when Satan and his influences will be locked away (Lev. 16:20–22; 29–31; Rev. 20:1–3). This holy day depicts the Messiah (our High Priest) making atonement for our sins, reconciling us to God, and thus allowing us access through the veil into the "Holiest of all" (Matt. 27:51; Mark 15:38; Eph. 2:18; Heb. 9:8–14; 10:19–20). By fasting on this day, we draw closer to God while meditating on the reconciliation of us to our Creator as our merciful Healer and Redeemer. The Messiah is essential in this process as our High Priest (Gen. 14:18; Heb. 3:1; 4:14–16; 5:4–6, 10; 6:20; 7:26; 8:1; 9:11), and as our eternal sacrifice for sin (Heb. 9:12, 26–28; 10:10–12).

The Feast of Tabernacles depicts the Messiah's return as King of Kings and Lord of Lords (Ex. 23:16; Lev. 23:34–44; Num. 29:12; Deut. 16:13–15). That's when the Messiah will put an end to the worst war to ever have been invented by Satan, together with his army of religious and political governing bodies, which are his servants (Ps. 2:9; 49:14; 89:23; Dan. 7:22; Rev. 2:26–27; 12:5; 19:15). The Messiah will gather His people again (the second time), this time from all nations (Matt. 24:31; Isa. 11:11; Jer. 16:14–15; 23:3–8; 29:14; 30:3; 32:37–44; Ezek. 28:25–26; 34:11–16; 36:24; Amos 9:14–15), in order to establish His Father's kingdom on earth. He, together with His resurrected firstfruits, will set up God's government to rule this earth for one thousand years (Ps. 37:11; Matt. 5:5; 1 Peter 2:9; Rev. 5:10; 20:4–6). Rule under His laws and commandments will extend from Jerusalem throughout the whole world to usher in and confirm the new covenant (Jer. 31:31–34; 50:5; Ezek. 37:26; Mic. 4:2; Heb. 8:8–13), while ushering in a period of unprecedented peace and prosperity (Isa. 2:2–4; 9:7; 11:1–16; 35:1–10; 65:17–25; Jer. 31:34; 50:5; Ezek. 34:8–31; 36:8–38; Dan. 2:35, 44; 7:13–14; Hab. 2:14; Rom. 8:18–23; Heb. 8:11).

This feast was also called the Feast of Ingathering (Ex. 23:16; 34:22; Deut. 16:13), named appropriately after the gathering of grain into storage and safety in the late-summer / early fall harvest. And the Feast of Tabernacles—or the Feast of Booths, as it is called in some scriptures—also depicts the time when the patriarchs of old temporarily dwelled in booths made with palm branches during the seven days of that awesome feast (Lev. 23:40–43; Neh. 8:14–18; John 12:12–13; Rev. 7:9). As such, it also depicts and foreshadows God's dwelling place in our hearts (Ex.

25:8; 29:45; 1 Kings 6:13; John 1:14; 1 Cor. 3:16; 2 Cor. 6:16; Heb. 3:6; Rev. 21:1–3), after His laws and commandments are written into it for eternity (Jer. 31:33; Heb. 8:10). Our hearts will be circumcised by God: "And **the LORD thy God will circumcise thine heart, and the heart of thy seed, to love the LORD thy God with all thine heart, and with all thy soul, that thou mayest live**" (Deut. 30:6; read also Deut. 10:16; Jer. 4:4; Rom. 2:28–29; Phil. 3:3; Col. 2:11). Thus, He will dwell in our hearts after they have been cleansed of earthly idols and prepared *by* and *through* the Messiah's sacrifice to become fit and suitable to be His temple: "And what agreement hath the temple of God with idols? **for ye are the temple of the living God**; as God hath said, **I will dwell in them**, and walk in them; and I will be their God, and they shall be my people. **Wherefore come out from among them, and be ye separate, saith the Lord, and touch not the unclean <akathartos>**[35a] **thing**; and I will receive you" (2 Cor. 6:16–17; read also Eph. 2:21–22; Heb. 3:6).

In the spiritual vision, John was shown how God's people will rejoice when they realize that salvation has been delivered to them on that great extraordinary event that will take place during the Feast of Tabernacles, which will be held in the presence of the Messiah and His Father:

> After this I beheld, and, lo, a great multitude, which no man could number, of all nations, and kindreds, and people, and tongues, stood before the throne, and before the Lamb, clothed with white robes, and **palms in their hands** [preparing for the Feast of Tabernacles]; And cried with a loud voice, saying, Salvation to our God which sitteth upon the throne, and unto the Lamb. And all the angels stood round about the throne, and about the elders and the four beasts, and fell before the throne on their faces, and worshipped God, Saying, Amen: Blessing, and glory, and wisdom, and thanksgiving, and honour, and power, and might, be unto our God for ever and ever. Amen. (Rev. 7:9–12)

The Messiah foretold the disciples that He would again keep the holy days with them when He returned: "For I say unto you, I will not drink of the fruit of the vine, until the kingdom of God shall come" (Luke 22:18). What a glorious feast that will be. *Allelujah to the Lamb of God!*

Side Note: John used the Greek word **<skenoo>**[36] to describe the Messiah's desire and purpose for dwelling on this earth. That word was translated into English as "dwelt": "And the Word was made flesh, and **dwelt <skenoo>**[36] among us, (and we beheld his glory, the glory as of the only begotten of the Father,) **full <pleres>**[10a] of grace and truth" (John 1:14). The word **<skenoo>**[36] is a symbolic expression of God's temple, resembling the tabernacle of old, where God dwelled in the mercy seat inside the Holy of Holies. God frequently states in the Old and New Testaments that He desires His people to circumcise their hearts (Deut. 10:16; 30:6; Jer. 4:4; Rom. 2:28–29; Col. 2:11) so that they may love Him from their hearts, because He wants to dwell in them (Ex. 25:8; 29:45; Lev. 26:12; Jer. 31:33; Heb. 8:10).

The word **<skenoo>**[36] is also used with the same implication in Rev. 7:15; 12:12; 13:6; 21:3. In other words, since a believer's heart is God's temple (John 14:17, 23; 1 Cor. 3:16; 6:19; 2 Cor. 6:16; Eph. 2:21; 1 Peter 2:5), He wants to tabernacle in it: "And I heard a great voice out of heaven saying, Behold, the **tabernacle <skene>**[36a] of God is with men, and he will **dwell <skenoo>**[36] with them, and they shall be his people, and God himself shall be with them, and be their God" (Rev. 21:3; read also Ex. 29:45; Lev. 26:12; Jer. 31:33; 32:38; Ezek. 11:20; 36:28; 37:26–27; Zech. 8:8; 13:9 1 Cor. 3:16; Eph. 2:21–22; 2 Cor. 6:14–18). Paul called his body a temporary residence for the spirit: "For we know that if our earthly house of this **tabernacle <skenos>**[36b] were dissolved, we have a building of God, an house not made with hands, eternal in the heavens" (2 Cor. 5:1). Peter used the word "skenoma" while describing his mortal body as a temporary residence through which God works here on earth: "Yea, I think it meet, as long as I am in this tabernacle **<skenoma>**[36c], to stir you up by putting you in remembrance; Knowing that shortly I must put off this my **tabernacle <skenoma>**[36c], even as our Lord Jesus Christ hath shewed me" (2 Peter 1:13–14).

End-time prophecies state that all nations will be required to keep God's weekly and annual Sabbaths when the Messiah returns: "Thus saith the LORD, Keep ye judgment, and do justice: for my salvation is near to come, and my righteousness to be revealed. Blessed is the man that doeth this, and the son of man that layeth hold on it; **that keepeth the sabbath from polluting it**, and keepeth his hand from doing any evil. **Neither let the son of the stranger, that hath joined himself to the LORD**, speak, saying, The LORD hath utterly separated me from his people" (Isa. 56:1–3). *All* people, including the Gentiles who lay claim onto the Lord's name, are *required to keep His Sabbaths*: "**Also the sons of the stranger** [Gentile]**, that join themselves to the LORD, to serve him,** and to love the name of the LORD, to be his servants, **every one that keepeth the sabbath from polluting it, and taketh hold of my covenant**; Even them will I bring to my holy mountain, and make them joyful in my house of prayer: their burnt offerings and their sacrifices shall be accepted upon mine altar; for mine house shall be called an house of prayer **for all people**" (Isa. 56:6–7).

For the people who love God, His Sabbaths are a delight: "If thou turn away thy foot from the sabbath, from doing thy pleasure on my holy day; and call the sabbath a delight, the holy of the LORD, honourable; and shalt honour him, not doing thine own ways, nor finding thine own pleasure, nor speaking thine own words: Then shalt thou delight thyself in the LORD; and I will cause thee to ride upon the high places of the earth, and feed thee with the heritage of Jacob thy father: for the mouth of the LORD hath spoken it" (Isa. 58:13–14). Those that aren't keeping the Lord's weekly and annual Sabbaths will experience the plagues of Egypt, and worse:

> And this shall be the plague wherewith the LORD will smite all the people that have fought against Jerusalem; **Their flesh shall consume away while they stand upon their feet, and their eyes shall consume away in their holes, and their tongue shall consume away in their mouth.** And it shall come to pass in that day, that a great tumult from the LORD shall be among them; and they

> shall lay hold every one on the hand of his neighbour, and his hand shall rise up against the hand of his neighbour. And Judah also shall fight at Jerusalem; and the wealth of all the heathen round about shall be gathered together, gold, and silver, and apparel, in great abundance. And so shall be the plague of the horse, of the mule, of the camel, and of the ass, and of all the beasts that shall be in these tents, as this plague. (Zech. 14:12–15)

Zechariah made this prophecy particularly clear, and he specifically emphasized that it applied to people of all races:

> And it shall come to pass, **that every one that is left of <u>all the nations</u>** which came against Jerusalem **shall even go up from year to year to worship the King, the LORD of hosts, and <u>to keep the feast of tabernacles</u>**. And it shall be, that **whoso will not come up of all the families of the earth** unto Jerusalem to worship the King, the LORD of hosts, even upon them shall be no rain. And if the family of Egypt go not up, and come not, that have no rain; there shall be the plague, wherewith **<u>the LORD will smite the heathen</u>** [mainstream traditional Christendom - professing to be Gentiles] **<u>that come not up to keep the feast of tabernacles</u>. This shall be the punishment of Egypt, and the punishment of <u>all nations</u> that come not up to keep the feast of tabernacles**. (Zech. 14:16–19; read also Deut. 28:61)

These are undoubtedly end-time prophecies, speaking unmistakably to **people of all nations**—which includes Gentiles whether they're Christians or not—***all who call Him Lord!*** God says what He means, and He means what He says! Which will *you* believe—the scriptures, or the anti-Jew/anti-Law Sabbath-hating ministers? It's a choice *you* must make for yourself.

The Messiah is the Lord of the Sabbath (Matt: 12:8; Mark 2:28). The seventh-day Sabbath depicts the scriptural one-thousand-year Satan-free period in which the Messiah will usher in and establish the new covenant, thus delivering salvation and peace to this earth: "And I heard a loud voice saying in heaven, **Now is come salvation**, and strength, and the kingdom of our God, and the power of his Christ: for the accuser of our brethren [Satan's ministry] is cast down, which accused them before our God day and night" (Rev. 12:10; read also 1 Peter 1:5). In that one-thousand-year period with Satan locked away (Rev. 20:1–3), all of God's creatures (including animals) will know the eternal God and obey His royal laws of love and liberty, because they will be inscribed into the hearts just as He inscribed them into stone at Mount Sinai (Jer. 31:31–34; Heb. 8:11–12; Isa. 11:7–9; Ezek. 36:26–27; Hab. 2:14; Rom. 8:22; 2 Cor. 3:3; Rev 5:13). That's when He brings our rewards: "And, behold, I come quickly; and **my reward is with me**, to give every man according as his **work <ergon>**[27] shall be" (Rev. 22:12; read also 11:18). Thus the Messiah and His resurrected firstfruits will rule and reign on this earth for one thousand years without Satan's influences (Rev. 5:10; 20:1–6). It's hard to imagine what it will be like to have Satan and his wicked and evil influences cast out of the way. Man and beast will once again live in total harmony, as it was in the garden of Eden before Adam and Eve rejected God. Of such is the salvation of the Lord, which will be nothing short of **awesome**!

The last festival, but far from the least, the Eighth Day (Lev. 23:39; Num. 29:35)—commonly called the Last Great Day—is stacked back-to-back with the seventh day of the Feast of Tabernacles. That day depicts the Messiah's completion (fulfillment—Matt. 5:18) of His great Fall harvest of humans by resurrecting to mortal life (the second resurrection, Rev. 20:5–6) all people who've died without having been called to know the truth about salvation in the Messiah and the truth about the Gospel of the kingdom of God (Ezek. 37:1–14; Luke 11:31–32; Rom. 11:7–27). Please note that this is *not* a second chance for salvation, but as a fair and just God, He gives every person to whom He's given breath (potentially multiple billions of people) one opportunity to choose between His ways and Satan's.

In Revelation 20:4–6 we read that the *first* resurrection is followed by the thousand years of rule and reign of the Messiah and His saints, and chapter 5 states that it will be *on this earth*:

"... And hast made us unto our God kings and priests: and **we shall reign on the earth**" (Rev. 5:10). After that period comes the second resurrection, at which time people like those from Sodom and Gomorrah will be resurrected: "Verily I say unto you, It **shall be** more tolerable for the land of Sodom and Gomorrah in the day of judgment, than for that city" (Matt. 10:15; read also 11:21-24; 12:42; Mark 6:11; Luke 10:12-14; 11:31).

The dry bones mentioned in Ezekiel chapter 37 will be resurrected to mortal life; God will give them the breath of life:

> The hand of the LORD was upon me, and carried me out in the **spirit <ruwach>**[37c] of the LORD, and set me down in the midst of the valley which was full of bones, And caused me to pass by them round about: and, behold, there were very many in the open valley; and, lo, they were very dry. And he said unto me, Son of man, can these bones live? And I answered, O Lord GOD, thou knowest. Again he said unto me, Prophesy upon these bones, and say unto them, O ye dry bones, hear the word of the LORD. Thus saith the Lord GOD unto these bones; **Behold, I will cause breath <ruwach>**[37c] **to enter into you, and ye shall live: And I will lay sinews upon you, and will bring up flesh upon you, and cover you with skin, and put breath <ruwach>**[37c] **in you, and ye shall live; and ye shall know that I am the LORD**. So I prophesied as I was commanded: and as I prophesied, there was a noise, and behold a shaking, and the bones came together, **bone to his bone**. And when I beheld, lo, the **sinews and the flesh came up upon them**, and the **skin covered them** above: but there was no **breath <ruwach>**[37c] in them. Then said he unto me, Prophesy unto the **wind <ruwach>**[37c], prophesy, son of man, and say to the **wind <ruwach>**[37c], Thus saith the Lord GOD; Come from the four **winds <ruwach>**[37c], O **breath <ruwach>**[37c], and **breathe <naphash>**[37a] **upon these slain, that they may live** [only mortals need breath to live]. So I prophesied as he commanded me, and the breath **<ruwach>**[37c] came into them, and they lived, and stood up upon their feet, an

> exceeding great army. Then he said unto me, Son of man, these bones are the whole house of Israel: behold, they say, Our bones are dried, and our hope is lost: we are cut off for our parts [God divorced them (Jer. 3:8)]. Therefore prophesy and say unto them, Thus saith the Lord GOD; **Behold, O my people, I will open your graves, and cause you to come up out of your graves, and bring you into the land of Israel. And ye shall know that I am the LORD, when I have opened your graves, O my people, and brought you up out of your graves, And shall put my spirit <ruwach>[37c] in you, and ye shall live, and I shall place you in your own land: then shall ye know that I the LORD have spoken it, and performed it, saith the LORD.** (Ezek. 37:1–14)

Just like Adam, these people will be brought back to mortal life; they will become living souls: "And the LORD God formed man of the dust of the ground, and **breathed <naphach>**[37a] into his nostrils the **breath <n@shamah>**[37b] of life; and man became a living **soul <nephesh>**[37]" (Gen. 2:7). (We'll learn more about what the breath of life of a living soul really is in section 6b). It's very obvious that those people described in Ezekiel chapter 37 will breathe; they'll have sinews to work and function with, they will be covered with flesh and skin, and God will put His spirit into them and give them the land He promised them over three thousand years ago, and they will prosper in it. This is the promise that God made to Abraham over four hundred years before the Israelites left Egypt (Gen. 12:3; 22:18; 26:4–5; Ex. 32:13; Gal. 3:8), because Abraham had faith in God, which caused him to keep His commandments (Gen. 22:18; 26:1–5).

The Messiah's role in God's plan of salvation is His theme in John chapters 4 through 9, particularly from chapter 7–9, where He was teaching at a Feast of Tabernacles. He cited numerous Torah scriptures that revolve around the fact that many people will come to be saved by being cleansed, purified, and nourished by faith in the bread of life and the living water, which are spiritual symbols of Him as the merciful Lord who cleanses, heals, and forgives sins, thereby redeeming our death sentence and thus extending God's promised gift of eternal life (John 6:33–58: 7:37–39; Rom. 6:23; 1 John 2:25; Isa. chapter 11). He also demonstrated this theme with His disciples while He instituted the new Passover symbols, in which He ordained the broken bread as His body, broken for us, and the wine as His atoning blood, which heals us from our past sins (Isa. 53:5; Rom. 3:25; 1 Peter 2:24), which also included Him taking water and humbly washing His disciples' feet (Matt. 26:26–30; Mark 14:22–26; Luke 22:14–20; John 13:1–15). And He commanded His followers to do the same if they wanted part in Him: "Peter saith unto him, Thou shalt never wash my feet. Jesus answered him, **If I wash thee not, thou hast no part with me. If I then, your Lord and Master, have washed your feet; ye also ought to wash one another's feet. For I have given you an example, that ye should do as I have done to you**" (John 13:8, 14–15).

It's amazing how even the New Testament scriptures reveal that sickness comes from broken laws. When the Messiah healed a person of a sickness He would often straightly tell them to *sin no more* (John 5:14), *thy sins are forgiven thee* (Luke 5:20). God promised healing for keeping His commandments: And said, If thou wilt diligently hearken to the voice of the LORD thy God, and wilt do that which is right in his sight, and wilt **give ear to his commandments, and keep all his statutes**, I will put none of these diseases upon thee, which I have brought upon the Egyptians: for **I am the LORD that healeth thee** (Exod. 15:26; read also Lev. 26:1–13; Deut. 28:1–14). Likewise, He promised curses, sickness, pestilence, and plagues for not keeping His Commandments (Lev. 26:14–39; Deut. 28:15–68).

In John chapter 9 He healed a blind man to confirm the miraculous and awesome power of that spiritual living water of which He was preaching. The living water like the "pool of Siloam" has always played a very significant role in the ritualistic ceremonies of the temple services, with which the Jews of that day were familiar. His overall theme shows that the spiritual hunger and thirst of mankind can be satisfied only *by* and *through* faith in Him and in His Father (John 6:44, 65; 14:6)—the only saving and life-giving Messiah through whom one may be saved (Matt. 1:21; Acts 4:12; 10:43; 1 Tim. 2:5–6). And those who believe and have faith to endure to the end will be given to drink of the living water (Joel 3:18; Zech. 13:1; Rev. 7:17; 21:6).

Point to ponder: John chapter 9 closes with an eye-opening epilogue. He tells the Pharisees that in the latter days, the blind (those who honestly never have known the truth) would be made to see, and those that see (those who heard the truth but perverted or denied it, such as the rabbis and Pharisees of that day, or the religious leaders and rulers of today) would be made blind! I believe that mainstream traditional Christendom is a living testimony that what He said there has come to pass, because they talk a lot about the God of the scriptures while professing a messiah who has literally scrapped and condemned practically everything that God ever commanded His children to do. They are spiritually blind; their hearts are veiled—uncircumcised (2 Cor. 3:14 to 4:4). Since they reject the commandments of the Old Testament, they inevitably reject the God of the Old Testament, wherefore they cannot understand the God/Messiah of the New Testament, who actually came to confirm and reveal His Torah prophecies of the Old Testament.

Satan will be loosed again for the duration of the prophetic eighth day; according to Isaiah, this period will last about one hundred years (Isa. 65:20), in order to give those resurrected mortal beings an opportunity to choose between God's ways and Satan's. God does this in order to give all the people who have never had the opportunity to hear of God's true plan of salvation in the Messiah, and about the true Gospel of the kingdom of God, an opportunity to choose between life (the ways of the God of heaven and earth) and death (the ways of the god or gods of this world). That's the purpose for the second resurrection, which occurs *after* the thousand years of the Messiah's rule on this earth (Rev. 20:4–7). It's important to realize that this event is *not* a second chance for salvation. The merciful God of righteousness and justice gives every person to whom He has given the breath of life (potentially many billions of people) one opportunity, each by his own free will (Deut. 30:1, 15, 19; Josh. 24:15; 1 Kings 18:21), to choose to become a citizen of God's kingdom, which is life, or of Satan's kingdom—this world—which is death (Deut. 30:15–20; John 11:25; Rom. 6:16). That's why Satan is loosed for that time period—to give the recipients of the second resurrection also an opportunity to choose, just like the remnant He is calling out today, in this era. This ties in with what appears to be the final event, the "great white throne judgment" of Revelation 20:5–15. All those not written into the book of life by the time of the great white throne judgment will experience the second death, which is the final, total, and eternal death (Rom. 6:23), and absolute destruction by fire (Rev. 20:6, 14–15).

That's when the third resurrection appears, when the incorrigibly wicked will be awakened to be judged and thrown into the lake of fire to be destroyed for eternity, together with those from the second resurrection who have not repented. As the prophets penned it, they will be ashes under the feet of the righteous: "And ye shall tread down the wicked; for they shall be **ashes under the soles of your feet** in the day that I shall do this, saith the LORD of hosts" (Mal. 4:3; read also Ezek. 28:19).

So all the people—potentially multiple billions—who have never had the Messiah's salvation plan and the true gospel of the kingdom of God revealed to them during their lifetime, will be resurrected to mortal life in that era, which occurs immediately after the thousand Satan-free years on earth:

> And I saw thrones, and they sat upon them, and judgment was given unto them: and I saw the souls of them that were beheaded for the witness of Jesus, and for the word of God, and which had not worshipped the beast, neither his image, neither had received his mark upon their foreheads, or in their hands; and they lived and reigned with Christ a thousand years [the first resurrection]. **But the rest of the dead lived not again until the thousand years were finished** [the second resurrection]**. This is the first resurrection**. Blessed and holy is he that hath part in the first resurrection: on such the second death hath no power, but they shall be priests of God

> and of Christ, and shall reign with him a thousand years. (Rev. 20:4-6; Ezek. 37:1-14; Matt. 25:31-46).

Thus He will be "bringing many sons unto glory" (Heb. 2:10; Rom. 11:26; 1 Tim. 2:4).

The observance of God's annual and weekly Sabbaths and festivals reminds His people that He's working out His plan of extending salvation from sin and death to all of mankind—past, present, and future—thereby offering the gift of eternal life into His family. The Messiah told us to pray for the time when earth would be as heaven: "Thy kingdom come. Thy will be done **in earth, as it is in heaven**" (Matt. 6:10). What an **awesome** plan!

Think about this: There is a huge movement in mainstream Christendom of preaching that the Messiah will rapture them away to train them to help Him rule during the Great Tribulation period. The above scriptural texts refer directly to that time, and they unmistakably state that the people will be keeping God's commandments. How can the Messiah use traditional Christians to teach people about and with God's commandments and laws, when they are divinely trained to not keep them and they teach that keepers of them will be condemned to hell?

The Messiah's followers surely kept God's holy days decades after the resurrection of our Messiah:

> Purge out therefore the old leaven, that ye may be a new lump, as ye are unleavened. For even Christ our **passover** is sacrificed for us: Therefore **let us keep the feast** [Passover and Days of Unleavened Bread], not with old leaven, neither with the leaven of malice and wickedness; but with the unleavened bread of sincerity and truth [days of unleavened bread]. (1 Cor. 5:7–8)

> And we sailed away from Philippi after the **days of unleavened bread**, and came unto them to Troas in five days; where we abode seven days. (Acts 20:6)

And because he saw it pleased the Jews, he proceeded further to take Peter also. (Then were the **days of unleavened bread**.) (Acts 12:3)

But I will tarry at Ephesus until **Pentecost.** (1 Cor. 16:8)

And when the day of **Pentecost** was fully come, they were all with one accord in one place. (Acts 2:1)

For Paul had determined to sail by Ephesus, because he would not spend the time in Asia: for he hasted, if it were possible for him, to be at Jerusalem the day of **Pentecost.** (Acts 20:16; read also 16:13). Code pleading Acts 16:13 in the original Greek text indicates that the Sabbath mentioned there is in the plural: And on the sabbath **<sabbaton>**[45a] **<hemera>**[45b] we went out of the city by a river side... (Acts 16:13). The Jay P. Green Interlinear Greek/English Bible coded with Strong's Concordance renders it clearly in that way: And on the **day <hemera>**[45b] of the **sabbaths <sabbaton>**[45a],... (Acts 16:13) (Jay P. Green *Interlinear Bible, Greek-English*, Volume IV—New Testament, by JP Green Sr. translator, ISBN 978-1-56563-979-9, [Peabody, MA: Hendrickson Publishers, 2007]). Pentecost is often referred to as the Feast of Weeks (Deut. 16:10), wherefore the text in Acts 16:13 appears to refer to Pentecost.

Now when much time was spent, and when sailing was now dangerous, because the fast was now already past, Paul admonished them. (Acts 27:9). Verse 12 states that the time was in the fall of the year (the onset of winter), indicating that the fast would have been the **Day of Atonement**, which is observed in the fall.

...But bade them farewell, saying, **I must by all means keep this feast** [the **Feast Of Tabernacles**] that cometh in Jerusalem: but I will return again unto you, if God will. And he sailed from Ephesus (Acts 18:21). A chronological study of the events that took place between Acts 16:13 and 18:21 lands the time of this event in the fall of the year, thus revealing that this feast would have been the **Feast of Tabernacles**.

Paul passed on the Messiah's command to keep the Passover as a yearly remembrance:

For I have received of the Lord that which also I delivered unto you, That the Lord Jesus the same night in which he was betrayed took bread: And when he had given thanks, he brake it, and said, Take, eat: this is my body, which is broken for you: **this do in remembrance of me**. After the same manner also he took the cup, when he had supped, saying, This cup is the new testament in my blood: this do ye, as oft as ye drink it, **in remembrance of me**. For as often as ye eat this bread, and drink this cup, ye do shew the Lord's death till he come. Wherefore whosoever shall eat this bread, and drink this cup of the Lord, unworthily, shall be guilty of the body and blood of the Lord. (1 Cor. 11:23–27; read also Matt. 26:26–29; Mark 14:22–26)

The Passover instructions come from Exodus chapter 12:

And this day shall be unto you for a **memorial**; and ye shall keep it **a feast to the LORD** throughout your generations; ye shall keep it a feast by an ordinance for **ever <`owlam>**[1]. Seven days shall ye eat unleavened bread; even the first day ye shall put away leaven out of your houses: for whosoever eateth leavened bread from the first day until the seventh day, that soul shall be cut off from Israel [God's congregation]. (Ex. 12:14-15; read the whole chapter).

The whole chapter holds the instructions for the Lord's Passover and Days of Unleavened Bread. God Himself set the specific appointed times at which He wants His people to congregate with Him: "Thou shalt therefore **keep <shamar>**[38]

this **ordinance <chuqqah>**[4] in his **season <mow'ed>**[7] from **year to year** [annually]" (Ex. 13:10).

If God's holy day festivals had been abolished at the stake, the apostles would have known it. And if it were so, they would not have been gathered to keep the Pentecost (Acts 2:1), which they were still keeping in accordance with the Old Testament commandments. Had they not done so, they would have missed out on the Messiah's giving of the Holy Spirit on God's appointed day (Ex. 34:22; Lev. 23:15; Deut. 16:9–10). And so it is with each of God's holy day festivals and His weekly Sabbaths as they pertain to His awesome plan of salvation. God set the days, and He made them holy, for His purpose and, for our benefit!

Paul commanded us to let no one but the Messiah judge us regarding the observance of the LORD's Sabbaths and holy days, and what we allow or forbid to eat and drink, because they are, or remain, a shadow of things to come: "Let no man therefore judge you in **meat, <brosis>**[39] [food] or in **drink, <posis>**[39a] [drinking] or in respect of an holyday, or of the new moon, or of the sabbath days [weekly and annual Sabbaths]: Which **are <esti>**[28] [not 'was'] a shadow of things **to come <mello>**[40] [between now and future tense—*not* past]; but the body **<u>is</u>** of Christ" (Col. 2:16–17). The Greek manuscript does not contain the word "is". These much-misunderstood verses become clear, thus noncontradictory to Torah scripture, when we understand God's true salvation plan and the awesome hope for mankind as designed by Him, which He reveals through the observance of His holy day festivities. These verses undoubtedly withstand the Torah test when read in proper context.

Theologians typically interpret these verses in a way to try to make it say that Paul here stated that God's holy day Sabbaths, His weekly Sabbaths, and His dietary and health laws have been abolished, and that one will be condemned (judged) for observing them today. Because of their law-done-away mind-set, they make a great effort to try to make Colossians 2:17 say that God's laws *were* (past tense) merely a shadow of the good things to come, and as such have all been fulfilled by the Messiah's First Coming, in a way that abolishes them henceforth. Let's put some weight onto that line of reasoning to see which way the scale tips.

The Greek word **<esti>**[28] is used in the Greek New Testament texts over eight hundred times, and a search of its use in the KJV scriptures clearly shows that it's not termed as past tense, but as present or future tense, as in "And lo a voice from heaven, saying, This **is <esti>**[28] [not "was"] my beloved Son, in whom I am well pleased" (Matt. 3:17). There's another Greek word that is used in Colossians 2:17; it also clearly indicates a future tense and not a past tense, and it's found at the end of the sentence as "to come" **<mello>**[40]. The Greek word **<mello>**[40] is used in the Greek New Testament texts over one hundred times, and a search of its use in the KJV scriptures shows that it is used in a few instances to explain events as a present tense, and it is by far used the most as a future tense, but not as a past tense. There's an excellent example in the letter Paul wrote to Timothy, where he speaks about present events and future events: "For bodily exercise profiteth little: but godliness is profitable unto all things, having promise of the life that **now is <nun>**[40a] [now—present tense—immediate], and of that which is **to come <mello>**[40] [between now and the future—not the past]" (1 Tim. 4:8). In Matthew 2:13 the Greek word **<mello>**[40] refers to the fact that Herod **will <mello>**[40] seek the child —future tense. Also in Matthew 3:7: Who hath warned you to flee from the wrath **to come <mello>**[40]? Nevertheless, we'll give the believers of that philosophy the benefit of the doubt and assume for this exercise that it is as they proclaim it to be.

The Messiah already came to fulfill the first four holy day festivals, which depict and foreshadow the events of the Messiah's First Coming—the late-spring / early summer harvest festivals. The first three festivals involving the Passover and Days of Unleavened Bread truly have been fulfilled, and the third Festival, Pentecost, is in the process of being fulfilled while we're being sanctified—set apart for Him.

The last four holy day festivals, which depict and foreshadow the events of the Messiah's Second Coming—the late-summer / early fall festivals—have not yet been fulfilled. Paul reminded us that those Sabbaths and Festivals are—remain; continue—shadows of good things to come. If the fulfilling of them abolishes them, as is commonly advocated, why don't the believers of that philosophy—at least according to their own doctrinal reasoning—then keep the ones which have not yet been fulfilled? Instead, contrary to their own line of reasoning, they do keep *pagan* holidays in lieu of the late-spring / early summer holy days that have been fulfilled, but not the holy days that have not yet been fulfilled. And when asked why they don't keep the fall festivals, they claim that "they've been fulfilled; wherefore, they're abolished and nailed to the cross with Jesus." Ponder that self-contradictory doctrine honestly, and see if that reasoning makes any sense. If they would do according to their own line of reasoning, they would not keep the holidays that they keep in lieu of the fulfilled late-spring / early summer festivals, but instead keep the unfulfilled late-summer / early fall festivals.

Point to ponder: In today's mainstream traditional church system, precepts having no roots in the Messiah are preached as divinely coming from Him; thus, for the same thing the Messiah excoriated the Pharisees for (as recorded in Mark chapter 7 and Matthew chapters 15 and 23), He's being worshipped in vain. As I clarified earlier, the weekly and annual Sabbaths are God's, *not* the Jews' or anyone else's. But since the early church fathers have labeled them as belonging to the Jews, and since it has been canonized that Constantine's followers (Catholic and Protestant) can have nothing in common with the Jews, the followers of those doctrines must condemn the observance of God's holy days. That's why they have chosen to observe the Christianized pagan holidays, such as Easter, Christmas, Sunday, and so on, instead of God's weekly and annual Sabbaths. They tag these pagan holidays with the name of the Lord and preach them as divine commandments of God.

Through study and observance of God's holy days, one gains an understanding of His awesome plan of salvation for mankind such as is not possible in any other way. They portray God's sacrificial-type charitable love in a very unique and efficient way—the way He planned it from the beginning: "Brethren, I write no new commandment unto you, but an old commandment which ye had from the beginning. The old commandment is the word which ye have heard from the beginning" (1 John 2:7; read also Titus 1:2; 1 Peter 1:18–20). What Word had they heard from the beginning? Throughout all his letters, including the book of Revelation, John stressed the fact that we can obtain God's <**agape**>[8] love by keeping His commandments, as they had heard from God the Father *from the beginning*:

> I rejoiced greatly that I found of thy children walking in truth, as we have received **a commandment from the Father**. And now I beseech thee, lady, **not as though I wrote a new commandment unto thee, but that which we had from the beginning, that we love one another. And this is love <agape>[8], that we walk after his commandments** <**entole**>[9]**. This is the commandment, That, as ye have heard from the beginning, ye should walk in it.** (2 John 4–6)

> For this is the message that ye heard **from the beginning, that we should love one another.** (1 John 3:11)

There is absolutely no hint that the Messiah of the New Testament came to change as much as an iota of the commandments that the God and Father of the Old Testament had ordained from the beginning. To preach that the Messiah did any such thing is teaching an anti-God messiah. John puts an extra emphasis on the fact that to love one another requires walking after God's commandments, because they are God's <**agape**>[8] love. And it's not something that changed at the First Coming of the Messiah. He cited these scriptures from the Torah (Lev. 19:18; 26:1–13; Deut. 28:1–14), where the principles of love, mercy, and grace are taught as an everlasting trait of the creator God of Abraham.

As with all deceiver-inspired plans, the traditional salvation plan has just enough truth in it to flavor the theological ear-tickling corruption with which Satan has mixed it: "But I fear, lest by any means, **as the serpent beguiled Eve through**

his subtilty <panourgia>[41] [craftiness—Gen. 3:1–5], so your minds should be corrupted from the **simplicity <haplotes>**[42] [singleness] that is in Christ. For if he that cometh preacheth **another Jesus**, whom we have not preached, or if ye receive **another spirit**, which ye have not received, or **another gospel**, which ye have not accepted, ye might well bear with him" (2 Cor. 11:3–4; read also verses 13–15; Gen. 3:1–5; John 8:44; Col. 2:4, 8, 18; 1 Tim. 4:1–3; 2 Peter 3:17). In order to abrogate God's commandments, His holy days, and His dietary and health laws, the deceiving god of this world (2 Cor. 4:3–4; Eph. 2:2; Rev. 12:9), through theological philosophers, and hence traditionally trained ministers (Jer. 23; 50:6; 2 Cor. 11:13–15; Gal. 1:6–9; Eph. 6:12; 2 Peter 2:1; 1 John 4:1; Rev. 2:2), has convinced traditional Christendom that everything was already fulfilled by the Messiah on the tree, and in a sense that abolishes them. This is done very subtly in a cunning effort to make God's commandments go away, because of their anti-Jewism, in order to reason around the need to keep the Lord's Sabbath. That's the commandment that sticks out like a sore thumb because it gets noticed by the religious Babylonian society, whose teaching is to worship the creator God on the sun god's Sunday and pagan holiday festivals. That's what Paul meant when he spoke about preaching another Messiah, another spirit, and another gospel in 2 Corinthians 11:3–4. Even when a traditional Christian admits (it happens occasionally) that God's Laws and Commandments should be kept, they reason around it by telling us that they keep Sunday and the pagan holidays in order to not be a stumbling block. If the Messiah and His disciples and apostles had taught and lived by such doctrines, they would not have been executed. God's word strictly commands His people to come out of paganism (2 Cor. 6:14–17; Rev. 18:2–4).

That evolutionary philosophy does not bode well with a non-evolutionary God who has an unmovable foundation and agenda. These philosophers are trying to make the word "fulfilled" mean "abolished," which I will illustrate in section 6.

Yes, the Messiah fulfilled—finished (John 19:30)—His role as the unblemished sacrificial Lamb of God when He willingly shed His blood and gave His life as a ransom to forgive the sin of mankind, to remove its penalty: "Even as the Son of man came not to be ministered unto, but to minister, and to **give** his life a ransom for many" (Matt. 20:28; Isa. 53; Mark 10:45; John 1:29; Acts 13:38; 20:28; Rom. 3:25; 5:8; 1 Cor. 5:7; 15:3; Gal. 1:4; Eph. 1:7; 1 Tim. 2:6; Titus 2:14; Heb. 1:3; 2:17; 9:28; 1 Peter 1:18–19; 2:24; 3:18; 1 John 2:2; 4:10; Rev. 1:5). That portion of the Old Testament prophecies was what the Messiah truly fulfilled on the tree. And that's the point that Paul stressed to King Agrippa while he explained to him during his trial—as a Torah test proof—which prophecies the Messiah had fulfilled thus far (Acts 26:22–23). The crucifixion and resurrection did not fulfill all that the Messiah has taken on to fulfill. God's mystery will be finished after the Messiah returns to fulfill the rest of the prophecies: "But in the days of the voice of the **seventh** angel, when he shall begin to sound, **the mystery of God should be finished, as he hath declared to his servants the prophets** [a Torah test proof yet to be fulfilled]" (Rev. 10:7; read also 11:15; 1 Cor. 15: 51–56; Phil. 3:21; 1 Thess. 4:15–17).

Isaiah prophesied of that time in the future when the Messiah will bring our rewards: "Behold, the Lord God will come with strong hand, and his arm shall rule for him: behold, **his reward is with him**, and his work before him" (Isa. 40:10). That's another Torah test that will be proven when that occurs in the future after the Messiah returns: "And, behold, I come quickly; and **my reward is with me**, to give every man **according as his work shall be**" (Rev. 22:12; read also 11:18). That will be a magnificent part of the accomplishment and completion (fulfilling—Matt. 5:18) of His prophesied end-time restoration program: "And Jesus said unto them, Verily I say unto you, That ye which have followed me, **in the regeneration** when the Son of man shall sit in the throne of his glory, ye also shall sit upon twelve thrones, **judging the twelve tribes of Israel**" (Matt. 19:28; read also Luke 22:30; Acts 1:6; 3:18–21; Rev. 2:26–29; 20:4; 21:14). The regeneration, the restoration, and the restitution clearly refer to the future, when the final judgment will take place.

According to Isaiah 1:26 and Amos 9:11, God's kingdom will be restored to its original state, as it was before Satan messed it up and defiled it and convinced our ancient parents, Adam and

Eve, to do the same (Isa. 51:3; Ezek. 36:35). It's confirmed in both the Old and New Testaments that the heavens *and* the earth will be restored:

> For, behold, I create new heavens **and a <u>new earth</u>**: and the former shall not be remembered, nor come into mind. (Isa. 65:17; read also 66:22; Rev. 20:11; 21:1–2)

> Nevertheless we, according to his promise, **look for new heavens and a <u>new earth</u>** [a Torah test yet future]**, wherein dwelleth righteousness.** (2 Peter 3:13; Rev. 21:1)

That's why God refers to it as a regeneration and restoration process; He will restore the heaven and the earth. This runs contrary to traditional teaching, where it is taught that the saved will go to heaven, because the earth will be no more.

Likewise, the conforming regeneration and restoration process from the first Adam to the last Adam is likened in a similar fashion (Rom. 8:29; 1 Cor. 15:45–54). That process, as defined in prophecy, applies synonymously to humans, animals, the earth, and the heavens. all of God's creation (Isa. 51:6–7; Matt. 24:35; Mark 13:31; Heb. 1:10–11; 2 Peter 3:10–14; Rev. 20:11; 21:1) shall be renewed, regenerated, and restored to its original state (2 Peter 3:13; Rev 21:1). The Messiah's supernatural change from a corruptible fleshly being (the first Adam) to a glorified spirit being (the last Adam) (1 Cor. 15:45), was His restoration: "And now, O Father, glorify thou me with thine own self with **the glory which I had with thee before the world was**" (John 17:5; read also 1:1–4; Eph. 3:9). He is our forerunner, a pattern we must duplicate and follow to the end. As the firstborn of many brethren (Rom. 8:29; Eph. 1:5; Col. 1:15–18), He's bringing many sons to glory (Heb. 2:10).

The traditional salvation plan portrays a wrestling match going on between God and Satan to win souls, whereby they have esteemed today as the only day for salvation. In the religiously confused world in which we live today (most Christians agree this is the case), Godlessness and lawlessness are worsening by the hour. So, according to this philosophy, Satan is obviously winning the battle, which actually portrays the almighty God as a weakling and loser. If that were so, and if salvation is to be over and done with by the time He returns, why, then, would the Messiah return to rule and reign on this earth for a thousand years together with thousands of His selected Saints? Why is He bringing the valley of dry bones back to mortal life together with Satan back on the scene if they have already been judged and placed into their eternal destination, possibly thousands of years ago? These questions are answered by God when we learn of the awesome role that His Son the Messiah plays in His salvation plan, as revealed *by* and *through* the observance of His holy day festivals.

Some will be awakened from their graves in the first resurrection and receive eternal spiritual life. Many will be awakened to mortal life in the second resurrection. We don't hear the traditional preachers teaching of a second resurrection. They teach that whoever is not saved in the era we're in today will go straight to hell to burn alive for all eternity. Accordingly, there is eternal life either way—in heaven or in hell. The Messiah spoke in parables for that very purpose; this is not the only time for salvation:

> And the disciples came, and said unto him, **Why speakest thou unto them in parables?** He answered and said unto them, **Because it is given unto you to know the mysteries of the kingdom of heaven, but to them it is not given.** For whosoever hath, to him shall be given, and he shall have more abundance: but whosoever hath not, from him shall be taken away even that he hath. **Therefore speak I to them in parables: because they seeing see not; and hearing they hear not, neither do they understand.** And in them is fulfilled the prophecy of Esaias, which saith, By hearing ye shall hear, and shall not understand; and seeing ye shall see, and shall not perceive: For this people's heart is waxed gross, and their ears are dull of hearing, and their eyes they have closed; **lest at any time they should see with their eyes, and**

> **hear with their ears, and should understand with their heart, and should be converted, and I should heal them.** (Matt. 13:10–15)

This is not *their* time of salvation, by which He means the majority. He revealed frequently that in this era, only a remnant will be saved.

In today's era He is preparing only the late-spring / early summer harvest of firstfruits for the first resurrection. God's plan of salvation and the gospel of His kingdom will be revealed to the vast majority of people during the millennial reign, and even more so after the second resurrection—the Eighth Day.

As we can see, there are three resurrections required to fulfill the end-time prophecies. The typical Protestant-traditional salvation plan requires only one resurrection, or rather none. Their doctrines claim that we possess an immortal soul that immediately upon death goes to either eternal life in heaven or eternal life in hellfire, which does not require any future resurrections at all. Remember, according to traditional doctrines, all has already been fulfilled! This was Paul's argument in 1 Corinthians chapter 15, and other places, to get them to understand that true followers of the Messiah will be resurrected in like manner as He was, but not before the last trumpet (1 Cor. 15:52; Rev. 11:15). Each will be resurrected in his or her own order, not before His coming: "But **every man in his own order** [some in the first resurrection, others in a later resurrection]: Christ the firstfruits; afterward they that are Christ's **at his coming** (1 Cor. 15:23). He plainly taught that no one will have immortality until that has occurred (1 Cor. 15:42–54). The only one who has immortality is the Lord (1 Tim. 6:16). Paul wrote this to Timothy about three decades after the Messiah's resurrection. If people were able to gain immortality after the Messiah's resurrection, as is commonly reasoned, Paul would have known it (John 14:26; 16:13). He explained in the resurrection chronology in 1 Corinthians chapter 15 and 1 Thessalonians 4:13–18 in plain detail that humans will attain immortality *after* the resurrection. I will cover that in more detail in section 6b.

The Messiah confirmed that no man had gone to heaven before His resurrection: "And **no man hath ascended up to heaven**, but he that came down from heaven, even the Son of man which is in heaven" (John 3:13). Peter confirmed that no man had gone to heaven after the resurrection: "... David, that he is both dead and buried, and his sepulchre is with us unto this day ... For David is **not** ascended into the heavens ..." (Acts 2:29, 34). The Saints of ancient times are still awaiting the coming resurrection to receive their promises: "These all died in faith, **not having received the promises**, but having seen them afar off, and were persuaded of them, and embraced them, and confessed that they were strangers and pilgrims on the earth ... **And these all, having obtained a good report <u>through faith</u>, received <u>not</u> the promise**: God having provided some better thing for us, **that they without us should not be made perfect**" (Heb. 11:13, 39–40). The phrase "These all died in faith" doesn't bode well with traditional preachers, because they teach that those people of old had works (*had* to keep the Ten Commandments), and now we have faith (are forbidden to keep the Ten Commandments).

That traditional plan is not designed by the creator God of heaven and earth, the One who wills all people to repent and be saved (Ezek. 18:23, 31–32; 33:11; 1 Tim. 2:4; 2 Peter 3:9) and who will save all Israel, His people, the congregation of Jacob / the Israel of God: (Deut. 33:4; Ps. 14:7; Ezek. 34:30; Jer. 23:6; 31:31–34; Rom. 11:26; Gal. 6:16; Heb. 8:10–12). Please give this some serious thought and study, and see for yourself which plan aligns with the Word of the merciful and gracious God, as found in His Word and promises. Only after studying God's *true* salvation plan as depicted *by* and *through* His holy days can we see the deceit in the traditional salvation plan and thus start to understand His miraculously awesome plan of how He, as the Creator and sustainer of all creation, will save mankind from self-destruction and thus deliver salvation to His creation (Isa. 11:6–11; 65:24–25; Ezek. 34:25; 36:24–35; Hos. 2:18; Rom. 8:20–22; 11:25–27).

The instructions and revelations of God's salvation plan as pictured through His holy days is scattered throughout the scriptures, from Genesis 1:1 to Revelation 22:21: "For precept must be upon precept, precept upon precept; line upon line, line upon line; here a little, and there a little" (Isa. 28:10; read also 6:9; Matt. 13:14–16). And by studying God's Word on that platform while applying the Torah test, one will never be left with any contradictions (John 10:35), or confusion (1 Cor. 14:33). God tells us whom He will give understanding: "The fear of the LORD is the beginning of wisdom: **a good understanding have all they that do his commandments.**" (Ps. 111:10; read also Deut. 4:2–6). Contrariwise, according to God's Word, those that don't keep His commandments will not understand Him. That's the very reason traditional Christendom can't understand God's true salvation plan; they boastfully reject the Ten Commandments, thereby hard-heartedly choosing to be blinded to the truth of the non-evolutionary God of creation, thus waxing their hearts gross.

God created the first six days of the week for man to labor for his necessities (resembling six thousand scriptural years). Then He created the seventh day and sanctified it—set it apart—for His holy purpose. He perpetually set apart His weekly and annual Sabbaths from all other days in order that it would also set the observers of them apart from the rest of the world, thus creating for Himself a peculiar people to be His saints and priests: "Now therefore, if ye will obey my voice indeed, and **keep my covenant**, then ye shall be a **peculiar treasure <c@gullah>**[43] unto me above all people: for all the earth is mine: And ye shall be unto me a **kingdom of priests**, and an holy nation" (Ex. 19:5–6; read also Deut. 14:2; 26:18; Ps. 135:4). That plan has not changed in the New Testament: "But ye are a chosen generation, **a royal priesthood**, an holy nation, a **peculiar <peripoiesis>**[44] people; that ye should shew forth the praises of him who hath called you out of darkness into his marvellous light" (1 Peter 2:9; read also Titus 2:14). He created and ordained His Sabbaths and made them holy to be a sign between Him and His peculiar people forever, however long that may be (Ex. 20:8–11; 31:13–17).

I will stress again that these are not Jewish Sabbaths, but the Lord's! The Pharisees boasted that God had created them (as Jews) for His Sabbaths, but the Messiah set them straight in that He had created the Sabbaths for mankind, and not man for the Sabbaths (Mark 2:28) - not just for the Jews. God claims them as His. As we saw earlier, Paul kept the Lord's Sabbaths with the Gentiles, decades after they were apparently abolished and nailed to the tree with the Messiah: "And when the Jews were gone out of the synagogue, **the Gentiles besought that these words might be preached to them the next sabbath**. Now when the congregation was broken up, many of the Jews and religious proselytes followed Paul and Barnabas: who, speaking to them, persuaded them to **continue in the grace of God. And the next sabbath day** came almost the whole city together to hear the word of God" (Acts 13:42–44; read also verses 14, 27; 16:13; 17:2; 18:4, 1 Cor. 5:7–8). This was a perfect opportunity for Paul to correct his followers (the believing Jews and Gentiles), that since the nonbelievers (Sabbath-observing commandment-keepers—according to traditional Christianity) had shunned them, they should do it on the proper day, Sunday, if the Messiah had changed it. But he didn't, because he believed the Sabbath-keeping Messiah when He stated that He had not come to change a jot or tittle of God's laws and commandments. Paul preached about God's grace on God's Sabbath days.

For God's people, there still is a Sabbath day of rest: "There remaineth therefore a **rest <sabbatismos>**[45] to the people of God" (Heb. 4:9). And the Messiah confirmed that we are still set apart from the world by keeping God's commandments, for which people, especially those close to us, will persecute us: "And a man's foes shall be they of his own household" (Matt. 10:36; read also John 4:44; 13:18; 16:1–3; Deut. 13:6; Ps. 41:9; Mic. 7:5–6). This will potentially get us executed by the religious leaders of the day (Matt. 24:9; Mark 13:9; Luke 21:12; John 15:20; 16:2); just as they did to Him and His early followers for keeping His Father's commandments **<entole>**[9] (John 5:19, 30; 8:28; 15:10) instead of the traditional commandments **<entalma>**[9a] of the religious system of that day (Matt. 15; Mark 7). When contested, God's laws must always overrule man's (Ps. 40:4; 62:7–9; 118:8; Prov. 3:5; Jer. 17:5; Acts 4:19; 5:29; Gal. 1:10). If the Messiah had compromised by giving in to the traditions of the religious rulers of His day—in order to not be a stumbling block—they would not have needed to crucify Him. He was ordained to be a stumbling block to people (Ps. 118:22; Isa. 8:14; 28:16; Matt. 21:42; Rom. 9:32–33; 1 Peter 2:8). He did not stray an iota from God's commandments (John 15:10), else He would not have qualified to be the sinless, unblemished Savior for mankind. Paul specifically stated that if his mission was to please men (paganism), then he could not serve the Messiah: "For do I now persuade men, or God? or do I seek to please men? for **if I yet pleased men, I should not be the servant of Christ**" (Gal. 1:10). According to traditional teaching, Paul must have been a stumbling block.

The onset of the events of the Lord's Day will terminate the six-thousand-year period (the first six scriptural days of the week) in which Satan has governed this earth together with mankind, thus beginning the next thousand years (the Lord's scriptural seventh-day Sabbath), in which the Messiah will rule and reign without Satan's influences. The Lord's seventh-day Sabbath foreshadows and depicts the spiritual rest (Heb. 4:1–11) that His resurrected saints from the first resurrection will experience during those thousand Satan-free years of unprecedented peace and prosperity while they rule and reign on this earth together with the Messiah. The mortal people who will be on earth will also enjoy that Sabbath rest during the millennium. It is unimaginable what it will be like to be able to dwell and prosper here on this earth without Satan to influence dictators, oppressors, and suppressors, wherefore there will be no greed, no corruption in government or religion, and no jealousy, with everybody always more willing to give than to receive (Acts 20:35), which is what God's sacrificial-type charitable <**agape**>[8] love teaches throughout the Old and New Testaments. God's <**agape**>[8] love, which will be experienced during the millennium, is a kind of sacrificial love that is not selfish, which makes it practically impossible for a carnal mind to fully understand, because a sacrificial-type charitable <**agape**>[8] love cannot be bribed or tempted. God is not a respecter of persons (Deut. 10:17; Acts 10:34; Rom. 2:11), but the carnal mind thrives on favors.

Mankind is familiar with an emotional-social love between friends, which is an <**agapao**>[8a] love. The character of an <**agape**>[8] love is what the Eternal teaches throughout the

Torah, which is an endless and unconditional and unchanging love and mercy for one another. That kind of love is the apostle Paul's theme in Romans chapters 9 through 11 as he goes on to explain the attributes of God's endless and unfathomable, undeserved mercy and grace for His creation because of His **<agape>**[8] love. And in chapter 8 he explains how God prepares His people spiritually to conform them into the image of His Son and Messiah (Rom. 8:29), which is in progress now for His chosen—set apart—people of His late-spring / early summer harvest of firstfruits, which is our sanctification period.

Side Note: 1 Corinthians chapter 13 is a good place to study about the degree of charity and sacrifice that an **<agage>**[8] love prescribes to. Paul used the Greek word **<agape>**[8] nine times in that chapter: "And though I bestow all my goods to feed the poor, **and though I give my body to be burned**, and have not **charity <agape>**[8], it profiteth me nothing. **Charity <agape>**[8] suffereth long, and is kind; **charity <agape>**[8] envieth not; **charity <agape>**[8] vaunteth not itself, is not puffed up" (1 Cor. 13:3–4). And he told Timothy that God's goal for His commandments is to develop such a sacrificial-type charitable love in our hearts: "Now the **end <telos>**[24a] [goal; purpose; result] of the **commandment <entole>**[9] **is <esti>**[28] [present and future tense] **charity <agape>**[8] out of a pure heart, and of a good conscience, and of faith unfeigned" (1 Tim. 1:5). Read the entirety of 1 Corinthians chapter 13, where the word **<agape>**[8] is translated nine times as "charity," with the intent to show the Godly type of sacrifice-inspired love that opens the gateway to God's mercy and grace. That's the kind of love that caused the Messiah to willingly sacrifice Himself for a ransom for your death penalty and mine (John 10:18; Gal. 1:4; 1 John 1:9). And He acquired that sacrificial-type charitable **<agape>**[8] love by strictly adhering to God's commandments **<entole>**[9], whereby Baal's commandments **<entalma>**[9a] are inevitably rejected—thus defeating Satan.

There is a lot more very exciting information to learn about God's holy days, and I want to encourage you to study it to the full, which you will never regret if you do. I won't go into much more detail here regarding this topic, but it seemed appropriate to break some ice here, partly because I needed to show that the Lord's Day of Revelation 1:10 is not what the traditional church doctrines make it out to be. Common Bible commentators and theologians cunningly interpret and explain it in a way to make it justify Sunday keeping and Easter Sunday, which are just a couple of a host of other pagan holidays like Christmas, Halloween, etc. Interestingly, there is absolutely *no* scriptural evidence to connect this event to either Sunday, Easter, Easter sunrise service, or the first day of the week. But this goes to show that we ought to be very cautious how, if at all, we use the commentaries, because they are thought up and written by men who are potentially inspired and trained by the same demon-driven theological monsters I'm trying to expose in my books, on my website, and in my tracts.

Another point to ponder: Think about this: if the Lord's Day of Revelation1:10 resembles Sunday or Easter Sunday / the first day of the week, that would mean that, according to the scriptures which we went over in this section, those days should be filled with the Lord's apocalyptic wrath. Are they? The book of Revelation vividly reveals the prophesied horrifying events that will transpire on this earth when the Messiah returns on the Lord's Day with a rod of iron to end Satan's rule on this earth while passing judgment, and then takes control of earth. The Messiah revealed the liberating aspects of the Lord's Sabbath by healing people from sickness and from demons on that/His day. That's what the Lord's Sabbaths portray throughout the scriptures, when understood from God's perspective. But the Lord's Day is not referred to as His Sabbaths anywhere in the Scripture.

5b. A Pretribulation Rapture—Satan's Babylonian Bypass Theory

Since we covered a few Scriptures in section 5a that are also used by many of the traditional theologians—thus also their trained ministers—in an effort to validate and justify their so-called pretribulation Rapture theory, I want to clarify a few items before we leave this topic. For the traditional Christians who rely on the pretribulation Rapture (commonly called the pretrib Rapture) to save them from the wrath of the prophesied apocalyptic events of the Great Tribulation, please study these scriptures very carefully together with other related scriptures to see if its purpose and chronology aligns with God's plans. For your own sake, put the Torah test to work for you.

As we have clearly and unmistakably confirmed, the Messiah will return to earth to first resurrect His saints who have died, and to next instantly change His saints who are still alive at that time ("have endured to the end" [Matt. 24:13; Mark 13:13]) *after* the tribulation, at the last (seventh) trumpet, which will announce His return (Matt. 24 29–30; 1 Cor. 15:51–53; 1 Thess. 4:16–17; Rev. 11:15). His return *after* the tribulation is the first resurrection (Rev. 20:4–6). A pretribulation Rapture would require a resurrection *before* that first resurrection.

Who are the innumerable multitudes described in Revelation 7:9? These are multitudes of people from all over the world:

> After this I beheld, and, lo, a **great multitude, which no man could number, of all nations, and kindreds, and people, and tongues**, stood before the throne, and before the Lamb, clothed with white robes, and palms in their hands [palm branches for the Feast of Tabernacles]; And cried with a loud voice, saying, **Salvation to our God** which sitteth upon the throne, and unto the Lamb.

> And all the angels stood round about the throne, and about the elders and the four beasts, and fell before the throne on their faces, and worshipped God, Saying, Amen: Blessing, and glory, and wisdom, and thanksgiving, and honour, and power, and might, be unto our God for ever and ever. Amen. And one of the elders answered, saying unto me, What are these which are arrayed in white robes? and whence came they? And I said unto him, Sir, thou knowest. And he said to me, **These are they which came out of great tribulation**, and have washed their robes, and made them white in the blood of the Lamb. Therefore are they before the throne of God, and serve him day and night in his temple: and he that sitteth on the throne shall dwell among them. They shall hunger no more, neither thirst any more; neither shall the sun light on them, nor any heat. For the Lamb which is in the midst of the throne shall feed them, and shall lead them unto living fountains of waters: and God shall wipe away all tears from their eyes. (Rev. 7:9–17)

Those are the Messiah's followers who endured the tribulations to their end (Matt. 10:22; 24:13; Mark 13:13; Dan. 12:11–13). There is no Rapture mentioned. These are those who trusted (had faith) in God / the Messiah to take them through their trials without a Rapture.

The Messiah and His disciples and apostles set an example for us by showing us that to become worthy of Him requires that we go through much tribulation: "Confirming the souls of the disciples, and exhorting them to **continue in the faith**, and that **we must through much tribulation enter into the kingdom of God**" (Acts 14:22; read also 2 Tim. 3:12; Phil. 1:29). The scriptural scene of how His faithful saints will enter into God's kingdom is quite different from the faithless traditional pretrib Rapture theory. The Messiah will bring the rewards for the prophets and Saints when He returns to this earth *after* the Great Tribulation, and no sooner: "And, behold, I come quickly; and **my reward is with me**, to give every man according as his work shall be" (Rev. 22:12; read also 11:18; Isa. 35:4; 40:10).

Why did He specifically state that He would return to put an end to those terrible events "for the elect's sake" if He was to already have raptured His elect away before the Tribulation began?

> When ye therefore shall see the abomination of desolation, spoken of by Daniel the prophet, stand in the holy place, (whoso readeth, let him understand:) Then let them which be in Judaea **flee into the mountains**: Let him which is on the housetop not come down to take any thing out of his house: Neither let him which is in the field return back to take his clothes. And woe unto them that are with child, and to them that give suck in those days! But pray ye that your flight be not in the winter, **neither on the sabbath day**: For then shall be great tribulation, such as was not since the beginning of the world to this time, no, nor ever shall be. And except those days should be shortened, there should no flesh be saved: but **for the elect's sake** those days shall be shortened. (Matt. 24:15–22; read also Dan. 12:11; Mark 13; Luke 21)

Why would He shorten those days for the elect's sake if they were already with Him in glory?

If a pretrib Rapture is in the offering, then many of the Messiah's warnings that He gave to His followers about enduring through the tribulations of this age were in vain. According to scriptures, the Messiah's followers must endure the earthly tribulations to the end to be saved: "But he that shall endure unto the end, the same shall be saved" (Matt. 24:13; read also Dan. 12:12; Matt. 10:22; Mark 13:13; James 1:12). He specifically encouraged His faithful followers—those to whom He's going to give the crown of life—to hang on even unto death if need be. Why would He do this if they were to be raptured away beforehand? "Fear none of those things which thou shalt suffer: behold, the devil shall cast some of you into prison, that ye may be tried; and ye shall have tribulation ten days: **be thou faithful unto death, and I will give thee a crown of life**" (Rev. 2:10). He forewarned us throughout the Gospels that those who follow Him will go through much tribulation, to which all of His faithful disciples are a testimony; they endured to the end—unto death—without relying on a Rapture.

Another question arises: did our Savior make a mistake? According to traditional church doctrine, He apparently abolished the Ten Commandments, particularly the Lord's Sabbath commandment, when He was nailed to the tree. Why, then, would He add yet more confusion concerning a Sabbath day? Especially since He is unmistakably referring to a time a couple thousands of years after He would have already abolished God's commandments? God does *not* confuse matters (1 Cor. 14:33).

I know that many will argue that the events of Matthew chapter 24 (and likewise Mark 13 and Luke 21) had already come to pass when the Romans destroyed the Temple in AD 70, thus meaning that those events had been fulfilled. True enough, that was a fair warning to the people who worshipped in that temple at that time to take heed—because it did occur a few decades later (after the Ten Commandments were supposedly abolished)—but the context of the Messiah's testimony goes much farther. He is unmistakably referring to the Great Tribulation period followed by His glorious return to put an end to the most horrific events of Satan's/man's war on earth. Did the Messiah come down in AD 70 (verse 30) and take over the rule of earth to stop the destruction of the temple, as He prophesied that He would when that tribulation of which He spoke in Matthew chapter 24, Mark chapter 13, and Luke chapter 21 occurred?

His instructions do not suggest getting ready to get hoisted away in any sense; rather they urge the reader to be prepared to "flee to the mountains" without delay. Please note that verse 3 clearly states that He is giving these instructions to His disciples. He tells them to not even get anything from out of their house when that happens. In other words, they are to 'get down and run for safety.' Were they not supposed to be raptured away by now? He is warning His disciples to be prepared to do what it takes to avoid as many of those events as possible by watching world events while praying to Him that He may guard and keep them while they flee from those events: "Watch ye therefore, and pray always, that ye may be accounted worthy to **escape** all these things that shall **come to pass <ginomai>**[14], and to stand before the Son of man" (Luke 21:36; read also Mark 13:33). He provides this warning so that they may endure to the end, until He returns. Only those with total faith in the Messiah and His Father will be able to endure those times. He specifically prayed to His Father to keep His disciples on this earth: "**I pray not that thou shouldest take them out of the world**, but that thou shouldest **keep <tereo>**[21] them from the evil" (John 17:15). He does not speak of rapturing them away from it: "And now I am no more in the world, but **these are in the world**, and I come to thee. Holy Father, **keep <tereo>**[21] [guard and protect] through thine own name those whom thou hast given me, that they may be one, as we are. While I was with them in the world, I **kept <tereo>**[21] them in thy name: those that thou gavest me I have **kept <phulasso>**[46] [watched; preserved], and none of them is lost, but the son of perdition; that the scripture might be **fulfilled <pleroo>**[10]" (John 17:11–12).

Looking back through history, one can see that people like Abel, Noah, Abraham, Joseph, Moses, Enoch, Elijah, David, Daniel and his three friends (Shadrach, Meshach, and Abednego), and other saints of old had total unwavering faith in the eternal God. They did not expect to be raptured away from this world. Their unwavering faith allowed them to know that their God did not need to remove them from this earth to protect them from wicked commandment-hating men, as long as they obeyed Him; the Messiah confirmed that He would preserve His own in this era (John 15:19; 17:14–20; 1 John 4:4–6). And the saints of old were kept—guarded and preserved—from the Flood, from burning sulfur, pestilences, famines, the fiery furnace, army giants, hungry lions, prison chains, poisonous snakebites, and the like, by keeping God's commandments. That's the liberty with which He rewards, blesses, and compensates the people who faithfully keep His commandments, because His commandments constitute His **<agape>**[8] love and liberty (Lev. 26; Deut. 28).

All nations will be blessed through faithful Abraham *because* he kept God's commandments: "... **Because <`eqeb>**[47] that Abraham obeyed my voice, and **kept <shamar>**[38] my charge, my

commandments <mitsvah>[3], my **statutes <chuqqah>**[4], and my **laws <towrah>**[5]" (Gen. 26:5). That did not exempt Abraham's descendants from the obligations to keep God's commandments, because they also needed the **<agape>**[8] love that the keeping of them produces. So it is today; because our Savior and Messiah kept God's commandments, His righteousness is extended to us. That does not exempt us from needing to obey God and keep His commandments. We need to keep them because they teach us about God's **<agape>**[8] love, which is required to become a member of His family.

The faith that the patriarchs of old had in God is the kind of faith that He expects all believers to have in Him, so that He can demonstrate His sovereignty and almighty power through them. Consider Moses and the children of Israel at the Red Sea. The Israelites, because of their loss of faith, could see no way other than that they would be taken by the Egyptians— Satan's army. Faithful Moses said to them, "Fear ye not, stand still, and **see the salvation of the Lord**" (Ex. 14:13). That's real faith in God as a Savior, not a cowardly Rapture-escape bypass!

Noah, a righteous (commandment-keeping) man, was mocked by the world for 120 years while he built the ark. He continued—endured to the end—in trusting God alone, obeying His commandments and not man's, whereby he had to condemn the world, which made him righteous before God (Gen. 7:1; Ps. 119:172; Heb. 11:7; 2 Peter 2:5–9). That's faith in the Creator, without which that boat would not have floated. Without absolute faith in God, Noah would not even have considered building that boat in the first place. Without faith in God there never was, nor would there ever be, any salvation. And the Messiah specifically tells us to take heed and learn from the past testimonies like those of Noah and Lot, because it will happen in the same way:

> But as the days of Noe were, so shall also the coming of the Son of man be. For as in the days that were before the flood they were eating and drinking, marrying and giving in marriage, until the day that Noe entered into the ark, **And knew not until the flood came, and took them all**

> **away; so shall also the coming of the Son of man be.** (Matt. 24:37–39; read verses 37–51)
>
> In that day, he which shall be upon the housetop, and his stuff in the house, let him not come down to take it away: and he that is in the field, let him likewise not return back. **Remember Lot's wife**. Whosoever shall seek to save his life shall lose it; and whosoever shall lose his life [for His sake—Luke 9:24] shall preserve it. (Luke 17:31–33; read also 9:24; Matt. 16:25; Mark 8:35)

When the Messiah returns and starts gathering His people, there shall be no looking back. We are to have our lamps filled with oil ahead of time so that when He comes, we will be ready. There will be no filling lamps at that point in time; it will be too late for deathbed repentance, just as was the case during Noah's Flood and the fires at Sodom. Lot's wife did not have her spiritual lamp filled with oil; she was not prepared to leave the luxuries and carnal comforts of city life behind. She loved the city upon which she relied for her daily oil. That made her spiritually dead; wherefore, although she physically escaped for a very short season, she was not saved from destruction!

I encourage you to study this and decide for yourself which scenario harmonizes with God's Word and which contradicts it—the traditional plan or the one we just reviewed. Which plan is the truest test of faith according to scriptures? God has an awesome plan that He openly reveals to "them which have ears to hear" and keep His commandments. God tells us who will be able to understand Him (Ps. 111:10). According to God's Word, He will not reveal His plans to lawless, commandment-hating theologians and ministers, as the Messiah also confirmed in the New Testament (Matt. 11:25; Luke 10:21).

The pretrib Rapture—a Babylonian bypass theory—was invented by Satan in the garden of Eden and passed on through his commandment-hating ministers, to whom God, *according to His Word*, does not reveal His plan of salvation (1 Cor. 1:26; Ps. 111:10). Paul confirmed that the Messiah's followers will gather unto Him at His return, and not before: "Now we beseech you, brethren, **by the coming of our Lord Jesus Christ** [His return], and by **our gathering together unto him**" (2 Thess. 2:1). We now know with certainty that the Messiah will return after the Great Tribulation, at the last trumpet blast, when we will gather unto Him; the 'ingathering' at a future Feast of Tabernacles (Ex. 23:16; 34:22; Deut. 16:13; Matt. 24:31).

Ever since he was dethroned, Satan has continually worked on crafty ways to deceive people into believing that there is a way other than the eternal God's way to enter into God's kingdom (family). He actually goes further by teaching that there is a way to get to heaven and right onto God's throne (Isa. 14:12–15; Ezek. 28). One example is when he convinced Nimrod, a servant of his who had many followers, to build the tower of Babel as a bypass to heaven, and become like God: "And they said, Go to, let us build us a city and a tower, **whose top may reach unto heaven**; and let us make us a name, lest we be scattered abroad upon the face of the whole earth ... Therefore is the name of it called **Babel** **<Babel>**[48] [confusion]; because the LORD did there confound the language of all the earth: and from thence did the LORD scatter them abroad upon the face of all the earth" (Gen. 11:4, 9). That's the foundation of the powerful religious Babylon the great, the mother of harlots, through which Satan has deceived multiple billions of people by confusing truth with lies, of which the Rapture-bypass theory is just one prime example of many. A carnal-thinking mind is ever seeking such comforts because it inherently hates God and His commandments (Rom. 8:7), wherefore it ever seeks justification to avoid His ways.

We now have some background and have thus unveiled some of the foundational structure upon which the church traditions have been established, and we have briefly compared it with the Creator's true plan of salvation for His creation. And we'll continue from there.

6. GOD'S COMMANDMENTS AND LAWS IN THE NEW COVENANT

In section 5, I touched briefly on the fact that the new covenant will be fully established after the Messiah returns to take over the rule of this Satan-inspired world; I will clarify this more in this section. Much of what I will cover in this section pertains to the aspects of the events of God's fall harvest festivals: the Feast of Trumpets, the Day of Atonement, and, most of all, the Feast of Tabernacles and the Eighth Day. As we've learned from the scriptures, these late fall harvest festivals depict and foreshadow the return of our Messiah followed by a thousand-year era when there will be no sinning because Satan will be locked away together with his wicked and evil influences. But we know that as long as we are in this carnal body and in this present Satan-governed era (John 14:30; Eph. 2:2; 6:12), we are able to, and occasionally will, sin. According to John, whoever says otherwise sins yet again by calling God a liar:

> If we say that we have no sin, we deceive ourselves, and the truth is not in us. (1 John 1:8)
>
> If we say that we have not sinned, we **make him a liar**, and his word is not in us. (1 John 1:10)

The Messiah was tempted by Satan and his ministers the entire time He was in a mortal state of being. After He was resurrected into a spirit being, He could no longer be tempted. And a time is coming when His faithful followers, after also being resurrected into spirit beings and moved on to life eternal, also will not be able to sin: "Whosoever is born of God doth not commit sin; for his seed remaineth in him: and he **cannot** sin, because he is born of God [resurrected; born into God's family]"

(1 John 3:9). That sounds too good to be true, right? With Satan and his wicked and evil influences removed, there will be real **<agape>**[8] love and peace instead of greed and covetous hatred for one another, which for six thousand years has been the recipe for ongoing wars between people and between nations.

Theologians hold that the book of Hebrews, particularly chapter 8, proves that the old covenant and the Old Testament have been abolished, and that only the new covenant and the New Testament are valid and binding on the Messiah's followers today. They read that philosophy into it in an effort to invalidate the Ten Commandments. We will see, according to the *very same* scriptures that they use to advocate that belief, that it cannot be so. And we'll allow those scriptures to interpret themselves: "In that he saith, A new covenant, he hath made the first old. Now that which decayeth and waxeth old is **ready <eggus>**[49] to vanish away" (Heb. 8:13). Note that the word "covenant" is not in the Greek manuscript. Following is the Jay P. Green Sr. transliteration of that verse: "In the saying, New, He has made old the first; the thing and being made old and growing aged (is) **near <eggus>**[49] disappearing" (Heb. 8:13) (Jay P. Green *Interlinear Bible, Greek-English*, Volume IV—New Testament, by JP Green Sr. translator, ISBN 978-1-56563-979-9, [Peabody, MA: Hendrickson Publishers, 2007]).

Theologians will typically interpret that verse in a way to make it say that the new covenant is the only one binding on the Messiah's New Testament believers. That's why the traditional church system teaches that the prophecies that are written about in the Old Testament regarding what the Messiah would come to do were already all fulfilled at His crucifixion, and in such a sense that God's laws and commandments were hence abolished by the fulfillment of the prophecies. That philosophy creates a need to invent a convenient interpretation to make the word "fulfill" in Matthew 5:17 say that it was fulfilled to an abolishing or destructive end, as it is preached. The Messiah strictly disagrees, when He states: "Think **not** that I am come to **destroy <kataluo>**[50] the law, or the prophets: I am **not** come to destroy, but to **fulfil <pleroo>**[10]. For verily I say unto you, Till heaven and earth pass, one jot or one tittle shall in no wise pass from the law, till all be **fulfilled <ginomai>**[14]" (Matt. 5:17–18). He specifically stated that He did not come to destroy the law but to fulfill it, bringing it to its absolute utmost expectation and potential (Isa. 42:21).

I will cite a few scriptures where the same Greek words, **<pleroo>**[10] and **<ginomai>**[14], are used, and we will see that those words do not convey the slightest hint of an abolishing end. The Greek word **<pleroo>**[10] in *Strong's Concordance* explains it to mean "fulfil, replete, filled up, top off, fully preach, complete, perfected, etc."

There are over ninety instances in the KJV New Testament where the Greek word #4137 **<pleroo>**[10] is used, and #1096 **<ginomai>**[14] is used over six hundred times. Read the following scriptures and apply the word "abolish" or "destroy" wherever those words are used, and see if it makes sense that it should mean that any of the events described in these scriptures should have come to an abolishing fulfillment or destructive end, a rendering upon which the traditional anticommandment ministry has established many doctrines, and which it has preached as having divinely come from God:

1. "And Jesus answering said unto him, Suffer it to be so now: for thus it becometh us **to fulfil <pleroo>**[10] all righteousness" (Matt. 3:15).
2. "Thy kingdom come. Thy will **be done <ginomai>**[14] in earth, as it is in heaven" (Matt. 6:10).
3. "Then touched he their eyes, saying, According to your faith **be it <ginomai>**[14] unto you" (Matt. 9:29).
4. "And the child [the Messiah] grew, and waxed strong in spirit, **filled <pleroo>**[10] with wisdom: and the grace of God was upon him" (Luke 2:40).
5. "And he began to say unto them, This day is this scripture **fulfilled <pleroo>**[10] in your ears" (Luke 4:21).
6. "And the Word was made flesh, and dwelt among us, (and we beheld his glory, the glory as of the only begotten of the Father,) **full <pleres>**[10a] of grace and truth" (John 1:14).
7. "Then took Mary a pound of ointment of spikenard, very costly, and anointed the feet of Jesus, and wiped his feet

with her hair: and the house **was filled <pleroo>**[10] with the odour of the ointment" (John 12:3).

8. "Hitherto have ye asked nothing in my name: ask, and ye shall receive, that your joy may be **full <pleroo>**[10]" (John 16:24).
9. "Thou hast made known to me the ways of life; thou shalt make me **full <pleroo>**[10] of joy with thy countenance" (Acts 2:28).
10. "Saying, Did not we straitly command you that ye should not teach in this name? and, behold, **ye have filled <pleroo>**[10] Jerusalem with your doctrine, and intend to bring this man's blood upon us" (Acts 5:28).
11. "Owe no man any thing, but to love one another: for he that loveth another **hath fulfilled <pleroo>**[10] the law. For this, Thou shalt not commit adultery, Thou shalt not kill, Thou shalt not steal, Thou shalt not bear false witness, Thou shalt not covet; and if there be any other commandment, it is briefly comprehended in this saying, namely, Thou shalt love thy neighbour as thyself. Love worketh no ill to his neighbour: therefore love is **the fulfilling <pleroma>**[10b] of the law" (Rom. 13:8–10).
12. Through mighty signs and wonders, by the power of the Spirit of God; so that from Jerusalem, and round about unto Illyricum, I have **fully preached <pleroo>**10 the gospel of Christ (Rom. 15:19).
13. "Whereof I am made a minister, according to the dispensation of God which is given to me for you, **to fulfil <pleroo>**[10] the word of God" (Col. 1:25). (This verse would describe the traditional antilaw preachers if the word "fulfill" could mean "abolished", because they have abolished almost 100 percent of the truth from God's Word in their philosophy.)
14. "Greatly desiring to see thee, being mindful of thy tears, that **I may be filled <pleroo>**[10] with joy" (2 Tim. 1:4).
15. "And these things write we unto you, that your joy may be **full <pleroo>**[10]" (1 John 1:4).
16. "And I heard a loud voice saying in heaven, Now **is come <ginomai>**[14] salvation ... (Rev. 12:10).

17. "The Revelation of Jesus Christ, which God gave unto him, to shew unto his servants things which must shortly **come to pass <ginomai>**[14]; and he sent and signified it by his angel unto his servant John" (Rev. 1:1).

This little exercise ought to settle the issue once and for all that the words **<pleroo>**[10], **<pleres>**[10a], **<pleroma>**[10b], and **<ginomai>**[14], which are usually translated into English as "fulfil," do not mean an abolishing fulfillment, such as traditional Christendom needs it to portray in Matthew 5:17–18 in order to justify their commandment-hating/God-despising doctrines. In every case, these words describe filling up, bringing to a full potential, bringing to perfection, fully preach, to supply, topping off, and the like. None of these Greek words indicate any hint in the scriptures that they mean "abolished" or "done away." On the contrary, Matthew 5:17–18 holds one of the most powerful Torah tests to prove that the Messiah was the Promised One of the Old Testament God, by PROVING that He made NO changes to His Father's instructions; thus harmonizing by another Torah test proof between Deut. 18:18-19 and John 12:49-50.

Continuing Hebrews chapter 8: We will use a few prior verses that lead to what is actually being said in Hebrews 8:13. We will also use the Old Testament prophecies from which these verses are directly cited in order to help put it into proper perspective by its intent and chronology: "For this is the covenant that I will make with the house of Israel after those days, saith the Lord; I will put **my laws** into their mind, and write them in their hearts: and **I will be <esomai>**[16b] [future tense] **to them a God,** and they shall be **<esomai>**[16b] [future tense] to me a people: And they shall not teach every man his neighbour, and every man his brother, saying, Know the Lord: for **all shall know me, from the least to the greatest**. For I will be merciful to their unrighteousness, and their sins and their iniquities will I remember no more" (Heb. 8:10–12). This is cited directly from what God prophesied through Jeremiah around 600 BC, thus another Torah test. We find it in Jeremiah 31:31–34, and I will quote verse 33 to show which laws God had in mind to install into our hearts and minds when He returns to establish the new covenant with His faithful followers, and when that will transpire: "But this shall be the covenant that I will make with the house of Israel; After those days, saith the LORD, I will put my **law <towrah>**[5] in their inward parts, and write it in their hearts; and will be their God, and they shall be my people" (Jer. 31:33).

First off, God is surely referring to the new covenant here, because this was written about 600 BC, which was around seven hundred years after He made the old covenant with the Israelites. This law sounds to me like something I would like for God to inscribe into my heart and mind, especially since that makes Him my literal Father who will forget my wrongs! The word "law" here is translated from the Hebrew word "towrah," commonly known in English as "Torah." The Torah is the first five books of the scriptures, and "towrah" means "directing instructions, teaching." The definition in *Strong's Concordance* states that it refers *especially* to the Decalogue and Pentateuch. The Pentateuch is the first five books of the scriptures, and it contains the Decalogue—the Ten Commandments.

That is the very package of laws that, according to traditional church doctrine, the Messiah abolished and nailed to the tree. And according to God's Word, He will not give these laws of love and liberty to anyone who harbors such a belief:

> And we are his witnesses of these things; and so is also the Holy Ghost [Spirit], **whom God hath given to them that obey him.** (Acts 5:32)

> And being made perfect, he became **the author of eternal salvation unto all them that obey him.** (Heb. 5:9)

And for people that dwell on that belief, I suppose they have their victory, because to them lawlessness has come to mean liberty as it is preached from the pope's traditionally indoctrinated global network of pulpits, Roman Catholic and Protestant alike, namely traditional Christendom.

Side Note: The traditional Christians are convinced that they are Gentiles, and they refuse to have it any other way. God states in the Old and New Testaments that He will make a new covenant with the Israelites. There is no indication anywhere that He will make a covenant with the Gentiles. But Paul explained in Romans chapter 11 how the Gentile people who believe in God can be grafted into the tree of life together with the Israelites, which inevitably includes the Jews. The Gentile people who have faith in the God of Abraham will have much in common with the Jews after all.

As we saw in section 5a, the prophetic theme as portrayed by Jeremiah, Isaiah, and Ezekiel points to a future exodus that will be much greater than the previous one, when God will *again*, the *second* time (Isa. 11:11) out of His **<agape>**[8] love and mercy for His creation, gather together His children from not only Egypt, but this time also from all other nations where they were scattered about 2,600 years ago, to give them their promised inheritance (Jer. 16:14–15), because God keeps and fulfills His promises. The Feast of Tabernacles portrays this awesome theme of the fulfilling of the marvelous late-summer / early fall harvest of people, thus bringing that part of God's plan to fruition during the Messiah's millennial reign. At that point, the Messiah will *cause* people to respect God's laws: "And out of his mouth goeth a sharp sword, that with it he should smite the nations: and he shall rule them with a rod of iron [God's Word enforced by and through His laws; the scepter]" (Rev. 19:15; read also Ps. 2:9; Isa. 11:4; 2 Thess. 2:8; Rev. 1:16; 2:27; 12:5; 19:21). When all of God's creation, *including animals*, are living in accordance with God's commandments, then the laws will be truly fulfilled **<ginomai>**[14] (Matt. 5:18). Even after that, His Word will still be in full effect: "Heaven and earth shall pass away: but **my words shall not pass away**" (Luke 21:33). Incidentally, the Ten Commandments are vital parts of His Words, seeing that the Messiah is His Word: "**In the beginning was the Word** [the Messiah]**, and the Word** [the Messiah] **was with God, and the Word** [the Messiah] **was God"** (John 1:1). The Messiah was God's Word - including the Ten Commandments - in the flesh (John 1:14). So, in essence, the Ten Commandments are the God/Messiah of Creation, who is life eternal: "And I know that his **commandment <entole>**[9] is life everlasting: whatsoever I speak therefore, even as the Father said unto me, so I speak" (John 12:50).

Many of these scriptures prophecy about the time and events when God will gather the Messianic believers in the greater exodus, which will happen in the future, after which God will inscribe His laws/Torah into their hearts **for eternity**, just as He inscribed them in stone at Mount Sinai some 3,500 years ago. And most of these prophecies are based on what Moses already prophesied when they reached the Jordan River around 1300 BC—that God would bring plagues upon them, have them taken captive, and then have them scattered all over the world, because of their unfaithfulness to Him:

> **If thou wilt not observe** to do all the words of this **law <towrah>**[5] that are written in this book, that thou mayest fear this glorious and fearful name, THE LORD THY GOD; Then the LORD will make thy plagues wonderful, and the plagues of thy seed, even great plagues, and of long continuance, and sore sicknesses, and of long continuance. (Deut. 28:58–59)

> And I will scatter you among the heathen, and will draw out a sword after you: and your land shall be desolate, and your cities waste. (Lev. 26:33; read also Deut. 4:27–28)

God said that He will rejoice in the laying on of plagues, just as He at first rejoiced in blessing them. That's because humans, as free moral agents, typically choose curses by serving other gods instead of blessings, which God promises if they would serve Him, and Him alone by keeping His commandments: "And it shall come to pass, that **as the LORD rejoiced over you to do you good**, and to multiply you; **so the LORD will rejoice over you to destroy you**, and to bring you to nought" (Deut. 28:63). Then He will regather them in a greater exodus in the end of days, after they remember Him, repent, and return to Him:

> And it shall come to pass, when all these things are come upon thee, **the blessing and the curse**, which I have set before thee, and **thou shalt call them to mind** [they/we will remember] among all the nations, whither the LORD

> thy God hath driven thee, **And shalt return unto the LORD thy God, and shalt obey his voice according to all that I command thee this day,** thou and thy children, with all thine heart, and with all thy soul; That then the LORD thy God will turn thy captivity, and have compassion upon thee, **and will return** and **gather thee from all the nations, whither the LORD thy God hath scattered thee.** If any of thine be driven out unto the outmost parts of heaven, from thence will the LORD thy God gather thee, and from thence will he fetch thee: And the LORD thy God will bring thee into the land which thy fathers possessed, and thou shalt possess it; and he will do thee good, and multiply thee above thy fathers. **And the LORD thy God will circumcise thine heart, and the heart of thy seed, to love the LORD thy God with all thine heart, and with all thy soul, <u>that thou mayest live.</u>** (Deut. 30:1–6)

Thus, after remembering God's blessings for keeping His commandments, and the curses for not keeping them, their hearts will be circumcised (unveiled) (2 Cor. 3:14 to 4:4). Then they will be able to understand the whole scriptures as God's divine Word, as it also applies to us today.

Read Leviticus chapter 26, Deuteronomy chapter 28, and also chapters 30 through 32, where Moses makes great ongoing living prophecies (which are likely of the greatest prophecies ever made) about what will happen to the future generations—us—and beyond. That's where God promises great blessings for obedience to His commandments, and great and terrible curses, plagues, and diseases for disobedience to them. And this second exodus will occur when He gathers His people—the congregation of Jacob / the Israel of God—from all nations when they/we turn back to Him and obey His commandments. That gathering has not yet occurred since He had them scattered about 700 BC. As we saw in section 1, the Messiah will come and regather His people, thus setting them free from the captivity, and be their Ruler and their King of peace. This is the very event that the Jews hoped for (and still do), and it is the one they expected the Messiah had come to fulfill at his First Coming.

When the new covenant will be fully established and fulfilled, all people will know God, from the least to the greatest (Jer. 31:34; Heb. 8:11). The earth will be full of God's knowledge (Isa. 11:9; Hab. 2:14; Heb. 8:11), and sinning will not be (1 John 3:9). This is a very strong and sure testimony that it cannot be referring to the past or present era, but to the future, because

1. the Israelites are still scattered across the world;
2. the Israelites have not returned to truly obey God's commandments;
3. many people—including most religious groups—don't know the true God of Abraham; and
4. Satan can still tempt us, wherefore
5. we are still able to sin.

If, as according to Protestant teaching, these prophecies were already all fulfilled at the crucifixion, why then did the Messiah commission the disciples to "go ye into all the world, and **preach the gospel** to every creature" (Mark 16:15)? It doesn't harmonize well that He would commission His disciples to preach His gospel, if everyone already knew Him since He was resurrected, does it? This also sets up a contradiction within the traditional church's doctrinal system itself. They claim to be obligated to deliver God's Word to the people that don't know God, at home and abroad; to teach them to not sin. In the same breath they preach that the new covenant is already fully established and delivered (that all is fulfilled), wherefore the people, according to scripture, would already all know God (Jer. 31:34; Heb. 8:11) and would not be able to sin (1 John 3:9)! If all is fulfilled, what, then, is the need of a congregation? What gospel is there to be preached to people who already know it and are not able to sin anymore? According to the scriptures, *after* all is fulfilled, then, everyone will know God, after which there will be no unrighteousness (Jer. 31:34; Heb. 8:11).

Side Note: If God's commandments and laws are fulfilled to an abolishing end, then, according to scriptures, preaching about sin after the crucifixion has been totally in vain. Think about it; that same minister who is commanding the people to not sin is virtually telling them to not break God's commandments and laws, which according to his own divinely preached doctrine don't even exist. And he's urging them to not sin; in other words he is saying "Don't break God's commandments, which are done away!" What an oxymoron if there ever was one!

That would be similar to a highway patrolman telling you that since a friend paid your fine for violating the speed law, the speed laws are fulfilled, thus abolished, wherefore there are no more speed limits; they've now been taken out of the way for your liberty's sake. But if you drive too fast, he'll give you a speeding ticket. Again, that's a perfect example of an oxymoron.

As a child I sometimes misbehaved, which caused my dad to discipline me—often with a belt on my behind. He did that for only one purpose: he loved me, which gave him a heartfelt desire to correct me of my rebellious character: "He that spareth his rod hateth his son: but **he that loveth him chasteneth him** betimes" (Prov. 13:24; read also 19:18; 22:15; 23:13; 29:15, 17; Deut. 8:5; Heb. 12:6–7). This is a teaching from our Creator: "For **whom the Lord loveth he chasteneth**, and scourgeth every son whom he receiveth" (Heb. 12:6). Discipline for my violation of my dad's rules or laws did not permit me to repeat that offence without *more* repercussions; neither did it abolish that law, but rather it was to remind me to quit violating it, for my own good. That's exactly what Paul loved about God's commandments—they convicted him in order to correct him: "**I had not known sin, but by the law: for I had not known lust, except the law had said, Thou shalt not covet** [the tenth commandment] ... For sin, taking occasion by the commandment, deceived me, and by it slew me [convicted him]. **Wherefore the law is holy, and the commandment holy, and just, and good** [it corrected him by causing him to repent]" (Rom. 7:7, 11–12).

About three decades after the crucifixion, the writer of Hebrews stated clearly that the old is ready to vanish. It has not happened yet. The writer used the Greek word **<eggus>**[49], meaning "near to the point"; the same word is used about thirty times in the KJV New Testament as "near; nigh; at hand." John used that word in end-time prophecies that have not yet come to pass:

> Blessed is he that readeth, and they that hear the words of this prophecy, and keep those things which are written therein: for the time is **at hand <eggus>**[49]. (Rev. 1:3)

> And he saith unto me, Seal not the sayings of the prophecy of this book: for the time is **at hand <eggus>**[49]. (Rev. 22:10)

We may be at the onset of some of these prophecies, but for the most part they are still before us. John recorded those prophecies about nineteen centuries ago, and they are still not fulfilled to the full. The word **<eggus>**[49] is used numerous times, referring to proximity (near to, but not there): "Now Bethany was **nigh <eggus>**[49] unto Jerusalem, about fifteen furlongs off" (John 11:18).

Reading Hebrews chapter 8 in this context while also applying the Torah test allows it to harmonize with scriptural prophecies without contradicting them. But it seriously contradicts such doctrines as those that require all to be already fulfilled, *especially* when "fulfilled" is used in a sense to mean "abolished." And such lies are taught to multiple millions, or perhaps billions, of people in order to justify their abrogating of the Ten Commandments, in order to reason around the obligation to obey the ones that mark which god or gods they serve—namely the first tablet (Ex. 20:2–11), and yet even more specifically the LORD's Sabbath commandment of the God of Abraham. But as we now know, all is not yet fulfilled! And even the laws which *are* fulfilled are not abolished but are perfected by the Messiah and brought to fruition.

One of the first things that the Messiah will do when He returns is usher in the new covenant, into which His called-out ones are currently growing and being trained (sanctified; set apart), conforming them into His image (Rom. 8:29). When He returns to earth at the sound of the last (seventh) trumpet, God's temple will be revealed in a similar manner as when He originally spoke the Ten Commandments from Mount Sinai: "And the temple of God was opened in heaven, and there was seen in his temple the ark of his testament [covenant]: and there were **lightnings**, and **voices**, and **thunderings**, and an **earthquake**, and great hail" (Rev. 11:19). The Greek text uses the word "covenant" and not "testament" in this scripture. The ark of the covenant bears the Ten Commandments: "**There was nothing in the ark save the two tables of stone**, which Moses put there at Horeb, when the LORD made a covenant with the children of Israel, when they came out of the land of Egypt" (1 Kings 8:9). Looks like the Ten Commandments will be displayed for all to see when He comes back and reveals Himself. Read the last half of Revelation chapter 11 and the first half of chapter 12, and you'll see that the delivery of the new covenant will come with some major earth-shaking and knee-buckling events. The people will be terrified when He displays His power and great glory. (Read Ex. 19:16 to 20:22; Matt. 24:30–31; Heb. 12:21; Rev 11:18; 16:18–19.)

That knee-buckling feeling is sometimes evident in our daily lives. When we hear a sobering and convicting scriptural truth, does it not sometimes send shivers up our spines, and cause the hairs on the backs of our necks to rise? We may even get a fuzzy feeling and weakness, making us feel as though we have rubbery joints from the waist down. All knees shall bow to Him (Isa. 45:23; Rom. 14:11). That feeling, which I believe most of us have experienced, is just a tiny foreshadowing of what we'll feel when the Messiah delivers the new covenant: "And then shall appear the sign of the Son of man in heaven: and **then shall all the tribes of the earth mourn <kopto>**[51], and they shall see the Son of man coming in the clouds of heaven with **power <dunamis>**[52] [violent strength] **and great glory"** (Matt. 24:30; read also Exod. 20:18-19).

> **Side Note:** The Greek word <**kopto**>[51], translated as "mourn," is described in *Strong's Concordance* as "to beat the breast in grief—cut down." That's what people will feel when they see the redeeming Messiah coming back down to earth. And the Greek word <**dunamis**>[52], translated as "power" is described as "force, a miracle itself—violence—mighty (wonderful) work." As He says in verse 21, the world will be in an unimaginable time with unimaginable events transpiring: "For then shall be great tribulation, such as was not since the beginning of the world to this time, no, nor ever shall be" (Matt. 24:21; read also Zech. 14:2–3; Joel 3:2; Dan. 12:1–2). His intervening to stop that ferocious violence will be nothing short of an absolutely unimaginably awe-inspiring power. Allelujah to the Lamb of God!

As prophesied, God is training (inscribing, conforming—Rom. 8:29) His laws of love and liberty (Rom. 5:5; James 1:25; 2:8) into the hearts and minds (circumcising, unveiling the foreskin of the hearts—Deut. 10:16; 30:6; Jer. 4:4; 2 Cor. 3:14–16; Rom. 2:29; Col. 2:11) of His obedient followers (Acts 5:32; Heb. 5:9), so that when He comes back to first resurrect those that died in His faith, and immediately after that to change those who remained alive (survived, endured to the end) in His faith (1 Cor. 15:51–54; 1 Thess. 4:15–17); will be taken by force (raptured?) and delivered into His presence, to Mount Zion, from where He and His Saints will rule this earth for a thousand years. If there is to be a Rapture, this would be it. His plan of salvation will then, in the last time, be revealed and delivered: "And I heard a loud voice saying in heaven, **<u>Now</u> is come salvation**, and strength, and the kingdom of our God, and the power of his Christ ... [for those] who are **kept** <**phroureo**>[53] by the power of God through faith unto salvation ready to be revealed in the **last** <**eschatos**>[33] time" (Rev. 12:10; 1 Peter 1:5). These prophecies refer to the very end time, when the Messiah returns to earth.

Just like the children of Israel in the ancient of days were kept under the law (Gal. 3:23), wherewith God "hemmed them in" to guard, protect, and preserve them from the wickedness and evils of the pagan gods of the surrounding nations, Peter says we also are now kept by the awesome power of that same God through faith unto salvation, which is in the Messiah's sacrifice. That faith which is required to be able to keep His commandments proper can be obtained only through the Holy Spirit, which sheds God's <**agape**>[8] love upon our hearts: "... because the **love** <**agape**>[8] of God is shed abroad in our hearts by the Holy Ghost [Spirit] which is given unto us." (Rom. 5:5). And it's given *only* to those who obey God (Acts 5:32; Heb. 5:9), whereby, through the Messiah's faith in us (Rom. 8:9), we can fulfill God's moral, loyal, and spiritual laws, the Ten Commandments (Rom. 13:10; James 2:8; 1 Tim. 1:5), from the heart. John explains in simple and unmistakable terms what that <**agape**>[8] love is and how to obtain it: "By this we know that we love the children of God, when we love God, and keep his commandments. For **this is the love** <**agape**>[8] **of God, that we keep his commandments**: and his commandments are not grievous" (1 John 5:2–3). This theme of love and liberty as taught in the Gospels and by the apostles comes directly from the Torah. And by the Messiah's perfect and wholehearted obedience to God's commandments, exactly as taught throughout the Torah, He truly obtained God's sacrificial-type charitable <**agape**>[8] love, thereby revealing the Torah's purpose and the end goal of God's commandments and laws (Rom. 10:4; Gal. 6:2; 1 Tim. 1:5), thus a very powerful Torah test.

I will try to show how these scriptures portray God's keeping of His children as a Father who truly and sincerely loves his children. It is typical for the traditional anti-Law ministers to interpret "kept under the law" in such a way as to portray God as a harsh and cruel tyrannical slave driver who used His so-labeled burdensome, grievous, and hard-to-be-borne laws and commandments to punish His children (beat them up) purely for His pleasure. Accordingly, with that mind-set, they preach that the Messiah finally came to do away with these terrible and burdensome Jewish laws and commandments altogether. And they profess that the liberty wherewith He set us free was His abolishing of the Ten Commandments, thereby creating a license to live as we please without needing to be concerned about any consequences, as long as we do whatever it may be that we do, in the name of the Lord. Always remember that the **<agape>**[8] love which the Messiah obtained ***through*** His perfect obedience to God's commandments is what caused Him to willingly and charitably **<agape>**[8] sacrifice His life for His brethren (John 10:18; Gal. 1:4; 1 John 1:9). God designed the Ten Commandments in such a way that obedience to the first tablet will always point us in the direction that will cause us to give absolute reverence and awe to Him, and obedience to the second tablet will likewise always cause us to inherently desire the best for the neighbor. That's the true description of the **<agape>**[8] love of God. So let's see what Paul really said in a few of the Scriptures upon which traditional theology has built a host of contradictory doctrines in order to try to make God's commandments go away: "But before faith came, we were **kept <phroureo>**[53] under the **law <nomos>**[22], shut up unto the faith which should afterward be revealed" (Gal. 3:23).

In the days of old, God kept (protected, guarded, preserved) His children with His laws in the material and physical manner—hemmed them in to guard them—until the faith of the Messiah was revealed, thus the Holy Spirit made available to man. And He keeps His children with His laws now in the spiritual manner, by the **<agape>**[8] love that He sheds upon the hearts of faithful and obedient people (Acts 5:32; Heb. 5:9). Now He holds us accountable for what we do not only physically but also spiritually—even regarding what we merely think.

Misconception about Salvation in the Messiah of the New Covenant: A common belief is that once we accept the Messiah as our personal Lord and Savior through faith, from then on we don't need to keep God's commandments and laws, because He supposedly kept them for us and then abolished them. In what is commonly called the Sermon on the Mount (Matthew chapters 5 through 7), the Messiah explained the true spiritual intent of God's commandments and laws as they apply to the adherents of the new covenant. He explained that in the days of old (when the Holy Spirit was given only to His selected prophets and servants), the people were not convicted of violating a commandment until the physical act had been accomplished, and the violation had to be witnessed by at least two people (Deut. 17:6; John 8:17; 2 Cor.

13:1; Heb. 10:28–29). The two-witness principle still applies, and now that the Holy Spirit is available to everyone who believes Him, if we have the Holy Spirit in us, we become personally accountable before God for what we merely think.

The Messiah started the Sermon on the Mount off by reassuring the audience—including you and me—that He did not abolish one single law:

> Think **not** that I am come to destroy the law, or the prophets: I am not come to destroy, but to **fulfil <pleroo>**[10]. For verily I say unto you, **Till heaven and earth pass, one jot or one tittle shall in no wise pass from the law, till all be fulfilled <ginomai>[14]. Whosoever therefore shall break one of these least commandments, and shall teach men so, he shall be called the least in the kingdom of heaven: but whosoever shall do and teach them, the same shall be called great in the kingdom of heaven**. For I say unto you, That except your righteousness shall exceed the righteousness of the scribes and Pharisees [proselytizers—theologically trained ministers?], **ye shall in no case enter into the kingdom of heaven**. Ye have heard that it was said by them of old time, **Thou shalt not kill**; and whosoever shall kill shall be in danger of the judgment [the literal act committed—violation of the sixth commandment (Ex. 20:13)]: But I say unto you, That **whosoever is angry with his brother without a cause** [the Spiritual act of hatred committed in the mind (1 John 3:15; 4:20)—violation of the sixth commandment (Exodus 20:13; Rom. 6:23; James 2:8–11)] shall be in danger of the judgment" (Matt. 5:17–22).

According to these scriptures, the pharisaical people—the clergy—who do not keep and teach God's commandments will not be in God's kingdom.

He compared the physical aspects with the spiritual intent of God's laws: "Ye have heard that it was said by them of old time, **Thou shalt not commit adultery** [the literal act—violation of the seventh commandment (Ex. 20:14)]: But I say unto you,

That **whosoever <u>looketh</u> on a woman to lust after her hath committed adultery with her already in his heart** [the spiritual act—committed in the mind—violation of the seventh commandment]" (Matt. 5:27–28). He meant what He said; "not one jot or tittle" is abolished from God's laws, but rather, as Isaiah prophesied (Isa. 42:21), He came to magnify God's laws, which brought about their spiritual intent. Paul also confirmed that aspect very aggressively: "Do we then **make void the law through faith**? God forbid: yea, **we establish the law**" (Rom. 3:31). In other words, Paul is saying that keeping God's laws in the new light of faith—through the Holy Spirit—upholds, reinforces, and establishes them, thus confirming the Torah's intent of them, and that withstands the Torah test prophecies by a high degree.

The Messiah explained by symbolic examples that the laws are spiritually magnified: "And **if thy right eye offend thee, pluck it out, and cast it from thee**: for it is profitable for thee that one of thy members should perish, and not that thy whole body should be cast into hell. And **if thy right hand offend thee, cut it off, and cast it from thee**: for it is profitable for thee that one of thy members should perish, and not that thy whole body should be cast into hell" (Matt. 5:29–30). It doesn't sound as though the Ten Commandments are abolished, or the sacrifices, except that we don't sacrifice animals today. According to His words, it is now much easier to violate God's laws than before. If we believe Him, we then—instead of animals—become a living sacrifice for the Messiah, as He Himself—through His Father's mercy for us—set an example for us:

> I beseech you therefore, brethren, by the mercies of God, that **ye present your bodies a living sacrifice, holy, acceptable unto God**, which is your reasonable service. And be not conformed to this world [the lusts thereof]: but be ye transformed by the renewing of your mind [the spiritual aspect of God's laws], that ye may prove what is that good, and acceptable, and perfect, will of God (Rom. 12:1–2). Ye also, as lively stones, are built up a spiritual house, an holy priesthood, **to offer**

> **up spiritual sacrifices, acceptable to God by Jesus Christ**. Wherefore also **it is contained in the scripture** [the Torah test confirmation], Behold, I lay in Sion a chief corner stone, elect, precious: and he that believeth on him shall not be confounded. (1 Peter 2:5–6; read also verse 9; Isa. 28:16; 61:6; Eph. 2:21–22; Phil. 4:18; Heb. 13:15–16)

While expounding upon the spiritual aspects of God's laws, the Messiah explained the importance of quickly reconciling any differences we may have with another in order to avoid wrath:

> Therefore if thou bring thy gift to the altar, and there rememberest that thy brother hath ought against thee; Leave there thy gift before the altar, and go thy way; **<u>first</u> be reconciled to thy brother**, and **then** come and offer thy gift. **Agree with thine adversary quickly, whiles thou art in the way with him**; lest at any time the adversary deliver thee to the judge, and the judge deliver thee to the officer, and thou be cast into prison. Verily I say unto thee, **Thou shalt by no means come out thence, till thou hast paid the uttermost farthing.** (Matt. 5:23–26)

That is the proper rendering of the scriptural eye-for-eye principal as it is designed to be used by the judicial system; it is *not* to be used as a means to exact personal revenge, as was the typical situation of the pharisaic and Roman societies of that time, and as still is the carnal desire. Paul also advised to settle the matter in a proper fashion so as not to provide a place for Satan to play his enticing game of revenge: "Be ye angry, and sin not: **let not the sun go down upon your wrath**: Neither give place to the devil [revenge]" (Eph. 4:26–27; read also Ps. 4:4; James 4:7). Committing acts that cause adversarial conflicts opens the door for Satan to enter, and not reconciling it quickly opens the door yet farther for him to entice us with carnal revengeful thoughts, which was his goal in the first place.

The Messiah explained how that works—that Satan will not miss an opportunity to fill one's heart with his army if the door is left open even only briefly:

> **He that is not with me is against me: and he that gathereth not with me scattereth** [it's one or the other]. When the unclean spirit is gone out of a man, he walketh through dry places, seeking rest; and finding none, he saith, I will return unto my house whence I came out. And when he cometh, he findeth it swept and garnished [the wicked spirit obviously not yet replaced with the Holy Spirit]. Then goeth he, and taketh to him seven other spirits more wicked than himself; and they enter in, and dwell there: and the last state of that man is worse than the first. (Luke 11:23–26)

The moral to this is that a person will serve one god or another. It cannot be two; neither can it be none—one or the other it will be!

God, with His fatherly **<agape>**[8] love, uses His laws to protect and guard His children from worldly lusts, literally as a father cares for his children. Fortunately we now have the Holy Spirit available to us to make it possible to obey God's commandments from the heart, thus enabling us to also grow in His **<agape>**[8] love. That's Paul's theme in Romans chapter 7, where he explains how the practicing of God's commandments and laws will convict us in order to correct us when we fail. And by practicing God's commandments **<entole>**[9] instead of Satan's traditional commandments **<entalma>**[9a], we have the Eternal's power on our side: "Ye are of God, little children, and have overcome them: because **greater is he that is in you** [the Holy Spirit]**, than he that is in the world** [the wicked spirit]" (1 John 4:4).

The traditional teaching has God's guarding weapons pointing the opposite way, *toward* His children, to make God, together with His laws and commandments look like a tyrannical and oppressive god! Contrariwise, God has His guarding weapons pointing exactly the opposite way than is required to suit the traditional anticommandment church doctrines. God protects us and hems us in to guard us against the pagan customs of the heathen and Gentile Babylonian world around us. By design, when a commandment is violated, it will convict us, and if not repented of, God may drop His guard, wherefore we lose the liberty and protection that He promises for obeying His commandments, thus causing us to end up back in man's bondage. That's exactly what's happened in mainstream traditional Christian society. Not keeping God's commandments but divinely obeying their traditions is what they teach as the liberty wherewith the Messiah set us free, wherefore the liberty God promises for keeping His commandments is being withheld from them by God.

His people are now in the sanctification, or consecration, period. God sanctifies (sets apart) His children to conform them to His ways (Rom. 8:29) in the wilderness journey from Egypt (the Babylonian system of this Satan-inspired world) to Canaan (God's congregational assembly; His family of faithful believers)—the congregation of Jacob (Deut. 33:4), the Israel of God (Gal. 6:16). This process is being not only ignored but also rather violently denounced in the common salvation plan as presented in today's traditional church system. They have labeled the sanctification process as Jewish works; as trying to earn one's salvation by one's own merits. Sanctification is the act of preparing, purifying, and setting apart for God: "And God blessed the seventh day, and **sanctified <qadash>**[15] it because that in it he had rested from all his work which God created and made" (Gen. 2:3). The word **<qadash>**[15] is synonymous with the word "consecrate" as used in the following passage: "And thou shalt speak unto all that are wise hearted, whom I have filled with the spirit of wisdom, that they may make Aaron's garments to **consecrate <qadash>**[15] [set apart for a special purpose--for God's purpose] him, that he may minister unto me in the priest's office ... Thus shall ye **separate <nazar>**[15a] [set apart for God's holy purpose] the children of Israel from their uncleanness" (Ex. 28:3; Lev. 15:31).

The sanctification period is the time in which God sets us apart for His holy purpose while we, as a living sacrifice (Matt. 16:24; Rom. 12:1–2; 1 Peter 2:5), temporarily dwell here on this

Satan-inspired earth, where Satan and his ministers continually try to conform us by Christianizing his pagan customs and traditions. God allows this in order to try us and see if we will actually count the cost and follow Him (Matt. 10; Luke 14) to the bitter end (Matt. 24:13; Mark 13:13; Heb. 3:6; Deuteronomy chapter 13). This is our preparation period; the time in which we fill our lamps with oil (Matt. 25) so that we will be ready when the Bridegroom comes to marry us into God's kingdom, His family; this will occur at the marriage supper of the Lamb (Rev. 19). Allelujah to the Lamb of God.

When the new covenant is fully established, God's commandments and laws of love, liberty, mercy, and grace will be inscribed into the hearts and minds of His people, who will then no longer be able to sin (1 John 3:9). This is why the Messiah said that not one jot or tittle will pass from the law until all is fulfilled—in other words, until all creation, including animals (Isa. 11:6–8; 65:25; Ezek. 34:25; Hos. 2:18) live by His laws, which will allow unimaginable and awesome never-before-experienced peace and prosperity on earth. Life will be like it was in the garden of Eden before Satan defiled it through man (Ezek. 36:35; Rev. 22:14)! God's laws of love, liberty, and mercy will be inscribed, or programmed, into the hearts and minds of all of His chosen creation to make everlasting love, peace, and liberty possible for eternity! Paul states in Romans 10:4 that this is the whole teaching, purpose, and goal (**end <telos>**[24a]) of the law (Torah). That's why God always used the Hebrew word #5739 **<`owlam>**[1], meaning "without beginning or end," whenever He described time factors of anything pertaining to His laws and commandments, statutes, and holy days—in other words, His Torah instructions, and all such terms that describe His merciful and fatherly attributes for His special treasured and peculiar children (Ex. 19:5; Titus 2:14; 1 Peter 2:9).

The word **<`owlam>**[1] is used in the Hebrew text over four hundred times and is translated into English using words like "forever," "evermore," "perpetual," "eternal," "everlasting," and "always." Forever is a very long time, except for traditional Christendom, for whom it ended at the cross. Everything that God prophesied in the Old Testament has been fulfilled to an abolishing end at the cross, according to the doctrines of traditional Christendom.

After God's laws are inscribed into our hearts and minds, His mercy will flow endlessly; thus unrighteousness will be a thing of the past and our sins will be forgotten (Jer. 31:34; Heb. 8:12). For then will we be in the true image of the last life-giving Adam (1 Cor. 15:45; Rom. 1:4), just as the resurrected Messiah is now, into which figure we will then have been conformed (Rom. 8:29; 1:3–4), literally died, and literally been resurrected—reborn into His image. Thus, salvation will be delivered. As John said, "**<u>When</u> he shall appear, we shall be like him**; for we shall see him as he is" (1 John 3:2). Paul says in Romans 8:21–23 that all creation is waiting for that redemption. The change from carnal to spiritual, from mortal to immortal, and from corruptible to incorruptible is the resurrection (1 Corinthians 15:50–54)—the literal rebirth to spirit being for which the saints of old are still waiting (Hebrews chapter 11). After the resurrection, the wages of sin—death (Gen. 2:17; Rom. 6:23; James 1:15)—will lose its power (1 Cor. 15:54–56), just as it did for the Messiah when He was resurrected from literal physical death to eternal spiritual life: "That which is born of the **flesh is flesh** [can die]; and that which is born of the **Spirit is spirit** [cannot die]" (John 3:6; Luke 20:36).

Death maintains its power as long as the deceiver and ruler of this world—Satan, the devil—can influence us to transgress God's law (1 John 3–4). After God circumcises man's heart and inscribes His laws of love and liberty into it for eternity, His commandments will be fulfilled and thus kept perfectly, as the Messiah did and commanded us to imitate (John 14:15; 15:10; Matt. 19:17). That's the righteousness of the life-giving redeeming and healing Messiah. Praise His holy and righteous name!

Side Note: At this point I need to ask the anti-Law Christians a few more questions: If God's laws and commandments are abolished, why, then, do the preachers of these law-done-away doctrines erect big, expensive church buildings into which they entice hordes of people to gather whom they feel obligated—by God, they say—to teach not to sin? Humans love to hear that they are not required, or rather even forbidden, to keep God's commandments to be saved. Typical mainstream traditional Christians will flat out condemn you if you dare try to keep them. "Just come to our church every Sunday and on all the yearly festivals," they will imply, "and keep following and supporting this church, and you'll be saved!" After all, it's likely *your* money that built that church, and also maintained it, which you willfully work for and then fork over for this good cause, lest you sin, right? By the way, don't forget the large salaries and expenses of the holy crew that you hired to tickle your ears through their business, which you and others like you are paying for! So now he had better speak in your favor, right? That whole system revolves around money, and to keep it flowing, they must tickle the ears in the pews so that members keep coming back, and also entice more people to join their fold. It makes perfect business sense.

Now, why would I support such a money-gobbling business only to have one of the pope's pulpit parrots preach to me about how and why not to sin *after* he has already preached sermon upon sermon to me explaining how the Messiah came to abolish the Ten Commandments by keeping them for us? Then he'll preach fire-and-brimstone sermons explaining how I'm committing sin and earning a ticket to eternal life in the blazing fires of hell because of all the works required to keep God's commandments, which he portrays as a hateful set of burdensome Jewish laws! How can I sin by keeping a commandment that apparently doesn't exist? After all, the scriptural definition of sin is the breaking of the Ten Commandments (1 John 3:4). If, as the preacher teaches from the pulpit, the Ten Commandments are done away, then sinning has become impossible! I know this sounds crazy and confusing. And it is, by design of the theological Babylonian <**Babel**>[48] doctrines, which are not supposed to be understood by their listeners; their followers are to come to *them* for understanding of *their traditions*. That's the purpose for seminaries and other institutes where traditional preachers go to get trained to preach their philosophy. Can you see how Satan uses the traditional pulpits to indoctrinate the masses with his lies? Our Messiah never went to a seminary (John 7:15).

What warrants the need of a preacher who is systematically trained to brainwash people with such blatant self-contradicting, confusing Babylonian traditional lies? My advice to the traditional ministers is to stop preaching that vain philosophy. It will save a lot time and money for the followers of that program. After all, you don't need to worry anymore about people burning alive forever in the fires of hell because of sinning, because, according to your own doctrines, the potential for mankind to sin ended at the crucifixion, remember? So, with that concern and burden out of the way, go ahead and do something productive for yourself *and* for others if you will—like maybe teaching God's truth as found in His scriptures.

According to traditional Christianity, a lot of works are required to obey God and keep His commandments. That's what apparently condemns you, because you are then supposedly trying to earn your ticket to heaven, they say, as if heaven is the reward of the saved: "Blessed are the meek: for they shall inherit the **earth**" (Matt. 5:5). Is it bad to be meek, because the meek will not go to heaven but inherit the earth? (That's a topic for another time, because it deserves a book of its own. But it's worth the time and effort to study it. I mention it here because it's just another example of how vain traditional doctrines are. That's why the Messiah condemned traditions of men—they don't rest on scriptures).

All the commandment keepers that I know are well aware of the fact that no man ever has earned his salvation, nor will any man ever do so, but for the sake of this argument I'll give traditional Christendom the benefit of the doubt. Let's say that it's so. Is not the traditional church system then also trying to earn their salvation (their ticket to heaven) by their traditional works, such as building churches and furniture; preparing and preaching sermons; preparing and teaching lessons for Sunday school, Bible schools, and colleges; preparing and operating the functions at Bible camps; doing all the work to accomplish the duties in the mission fields (proselytizing) home and abroad

(Matt. 23:15); preparing for and celebrating pagan holidays' festivities for families and church activities; and many more very time-consuming, labor-intensive programs that all have an endless appetite for literal works and for money? And to top it off, to achieve the intended goals of these ceremonial rituals requires a lot of very dedicated physical *works?* Why are you doing all these works to save people if works will earn one eternal life in hellfire? Why try to save people from sin if the laws are done away, thus having abolished all potential for man to transgress them? Accordingly, trying to save people from hellfire is totally in vain, except for the fact that it does revolve around a tremendous amount of money obtained by hard works! I agree that it's good for business, but that's where the buck stops–it' bad law.

I'm not suggesting that you stop doing those things, because after all, it is good business. But I will ask again, what are works, and what is so bad about work? After all, God gave just as much commandment for mankind to work the first six days of the week as He did to not work on the seventh day (Ex. 20:8–11). I oblige the traditional anti-Law Christians to answer these questions, at least for themselves.

I will submit another scenario toward traditional anti-Law Christians that revolves around the same topic. I know that traditional Christians are not supposed to read the Old Testament, or at least not use any of its instructions if they do read it. But if you ever have pried it open and read its contents, you will have noticed that the Israelites were frequently punished for breaking God's commandments—particularly the commandments regarding idolatry and the Sabbath; namely the first tablet, which identifies the creator God of heaven and earth. The early traditional church fathers must have read the Old Testament, because their anticommandment philosophy, which has been passed down through the generations, is established upon an extreme hatred for the Ten Commandments, which came directly from the mouth of the God of the Old Testament (Deut. 8:3; Matt. 4:4; Luke 4:4).

According to traditional anti-Law teaching, there must be millions upon millions of Jews (as traditional Christendom relates to all Israelite and Hebrew people and all who believe in the God of the Old Testament as a non-evolutionary/unchanging God and keep His commandments) that have burned alive in the tormenting hellfire for thousands of years already for breaking those commandments. It's true; the creator God promised wrath and destruction by death (not eternal life) for breaking His commandments, and He keeps His Word and promises.

Consider this: Let's say that there are millions, or perhaps billions, of the so-called Jews who have burned alive in hell already for a few millennia for breaking God's commandments. (My argument is not that God hasn't punished them). Now, according to what traditional Christians are warning me about, the instant I die, I will also get eternal life in hellfire for *keeping* God's commandments—especially the first tablet, which contains the commandments regarding idolatry and the Lord's Sabbath. If that be so, then, in hell I might go up to an ever-burning Jew and ask him why he is there, to which he would respond by saying something like, "I'm here for keeping the Babylonian Sunday instead of the Lord's Sabbaths, for keeping the Babylonian pagan holidays instead of God's appointed holy days, for rejecting the God of Abraham by voting for national kings (1 Sam. 8), for eating the flesh of scavengers," etc.

Now, in turn, he might ask me why I am there, to which I would then have to answer, "I'm here for keeping the Lord's Sabbaths instead of the Christian Sunday, for keeping God's holy days instead of the Christian holidays, for not voting for national kings, for not eating the flesh of scavengers," etc. So, in accordance with this teaching, the people of old were condemned by the God of the Old Testament for breaking His commandments and laws, while the people of today are condemned by the Messiah of the New Testament for keeping God's commandments and laws! "God is **not** the author of confusion" (1 Cor. 14:33); He is one with His Son: "I and my Father are one" (John 10:30). And they are not divided: "And Jesus knew their thoughts, and said unto them, **Every kingdom divided against itself is brought to desolation**" (Matt. 12:25; read also Mark 3:24–25; Luke 11:17). The Lord God of the Old Testament was one: "Hear, O Israel: The LORD our God is one LORD" (Deut. 6:4). And the Lord God of the

New Testament still *is* one: "And Jesus answered him, The first of all the commandments is, **Hear, O Israel; The Lord our God is one Lord**" (Mark 12:29).

Think about it; that Jew and I were judged by the same eternal God, who does not change or waver (Malachi 3:6; Hebrews 13:8; James 1:17) and cannot lie (Titus 1:2; Heb. 6:18). I'm not telling you to change your religion because of what *I* believe. But I must ask you to think soberly and in an unbiased fashion about what that sort of philosophy makes our unchanging, non-evolutionary Lord and Savior out to be. The Messiah did not change God's laws (Matthew 5:17–19; Luke 16:17), and there cannot and will not be any division between Him and His Father (Matthew 12:25; Mark 3:24; John 10:30, 35).

Such teachings come from the traditional Babylonian evolutionary (ever-changing) god of the traditional church system, from which the non-evolutionary God of Abraham, Isaac, and Jacob/Israel is calling His children out (Jer. 50: 1–8; 2 Cor. 6:14–18; Rev. 18:1–4). And by severing from it, we expect to be saved from (or at least punished to a lesser degree—maybe a few fewer stripes) the certain wrath and plagues that *will* befall the deceiving teachers of that system together with their followers; that's a promise from the creator God of the scriptures.

The Messiah did not overcome the sting of death while He was being tortured. His Father, who is the God of life, had to turn His back on Him because He cannot look at sin (Isa. 59:2). Not that the Messiah had sinned, but because He had taken ownership of the penalty of our sins (which is death, over which Satan is god), God had to turn His back on His own Son: "My God, my God, why hast thou forsaken me?" (Matt. 27:46; read also Ps. 22:1). That's why He became so exceedingly grieved in Gethsemane, wherefore He needed comforting and asked His disciples to tarry with Him: "My soul is **exceeding sorrowful**, even unto death: tarry ye here, and watch with me." (Matt. 26:38; read also Luke 22:44; John 12:27; Heb. 5:7). As a mortal human being, the available source of comfort at that moment was the disciples there with Him, who shortly after also forsook Him because of their fear of the traditional religious rulers of their day. These things had to come to pass so that the Messiah would be tempted in every situation in which we could possibly be tempted, including being tortured to death—without a cause: "For we have not an high priest which cannot be touched with the feeling of our infirmities; **but was in <u>all</u> points tempted like as we are, yet without sin**" (Heb. 4:15).

Death, which we inherited from the first Adam, who received it through worshipping Satan, was defeated by the Messiah when God raised Him back to life. Death has to run its course in this Satan-inspired world, as it did even on the sinless and blameless Messiah. Not until the literal death of the first mortal Adam (the bare grain, the seed; 1 Cor. 15:37) could the Messiah be resurrected to the last eternal-immortal Adam:

> Verily, verily, I say unto you, Except a corn of wheat [the bare grain, the seed] fall into the ground and die, it abideth alone: but if it die, it bringeth forth much fruit. (John 12:24; read also Rom. 1:3)

> So also is the resurrection of the dead. It is sown in corruption [the first Adam]; it is raised in incorruption [the last Adam]. (1 Cor. 15:42; read also verse 43–49; Rom. 1:4)

> Concerning his Son Jesus Christ our Lord, which was **made of the seed of David according to the flesh** [the first Adam—the bare grain]; And declared to be the Son of God with power, according to the spirit of holiness [the last Adam-the life quickening fruit], **by the resurrection from the dead.** (Rom. 1:3–4)

That is Paul's highlight in the resurrection chapter (1 Cor. chapter 15). At that point, death—the penalty of sin from the first Adam—is swallowed up in victory (1 Cor. 15:54), whereby sinning becomes a thing of the past: "Whosoever is born of God doth not commit sin; for his seed remaineth in him: and he **<u>cannot</u>** sin, because he is **<u>born of God</u>** [literally reborn of God's spirit]" (1 John 3:9). And as Paul explained in Romans 1:3–4, that change took place in the Messiah by the resurrection from the dead.

The Messiah could be tempted by Satan only while He was in the carnal state of the first Adam. But Satan was totally defeated by Him after He was literally resurrected to life from literal death! Therefore, we are not saved by His death, but it reconciled (justified) us to God, whereby we shall be saved by His resurrection: "For if, when we were enemies, **we were reconciled to God by the death of his Son**, much more, **being reconciled, we shall be saved by his life**" (Rom. 5:10). Death is Satan's victory, and many cheered him on as the Messiah was tortured to death—they were his followers. But the god of death was defeated when the Messiah was resurrected to Spiritual—eternal life. Eternal life is his enemy. This may seem to be a minor issue, but the belief that we are saved by His death has a stronghold on some very serious witchcraft doctrines. For example, the belief that we are saved by His death promotes the belief that all was fulfilled by His crucifixion; on which hinges the belief that salvation has already fully come—and thus *already* saved—which leaves no need for a future resurrection! I will illustrate from an old example that justification alone is not salvation, but that it leads to it if endured to the end. That's the sanctification period—the journey from Babylon (Egypt—Satan's world) to God's kingdom (Canaan—the Promised Land).

The children of Israel were justified—reconciled to God—after they believed and trusted the God of their fathers to redeem them from sin (bondage to slavery in Egypt). Not works of laws, but faith, justified them. Did that save them? Was salvation then delivered because God justified them by their faith and belief in Him as their Savior? They believed in Him, but their faith wavered: "But Israel, which followed after the law of righteousness, hath not attained to the law of righteousness. Wherefore? Because **they sought it not by faith**, but as it were by the works of the law" (Rom. 9:31–32; read also Heb. 4:2). Their following after traditional doctrines of men, which they received from pagan gods, caused them to lose their faith in the God of Abraham.

From the time they left Egypt until they reached the Promised Land was their **s**anctification period, in which God set them apart from the whole world for His holy purpose. God desired the world to marvel at Him because of what He was doing for them through their obedience to His commandments and laws. But they kept following after the customs and traditions of the pagan gods, which caused God to destroy them in the desert: "But with many of them God was not well pleased: for **they were overthrown in the wilderness**" (1 Cor. 10:5; read and study verses 1–11; Num. 14:29–35; 26:64–65; Ps. 106:26; Heb. 3:17; Jude 5). Why were they overthrown? They lost their faith in the non-evolutionary God of Abraham: "For unto us was the gospel preached, as well as unto them: but **the word preached did not profit them, not being mixed with faith** in them that heard it" (Heb. 4:2; read also Rom. 9:31).

God will do such marvels only if His commandments are obeyed and His words are not added to or taken away from:

> Now therefore hearken, O Israel, unto the statutes and unto the judgments, which I teach you, for to do them, that ye may live, and go in and possess the land which the LORD God of your fathers giveth you. **Ye shall not add unto the word which I command you, neither shall ye diminish ought from it** [Why?]**, that ye may keep the commandments of the LORD your God which I command you**. Your eyes have seen what the LORD did because of Baalpeor: for **all the men that followed Baalpeor, the LORD thy God hath destroyed them from among you. But ye that did cleave unto the LORD your God are alive every one of you this day**. Behold, I have taught you statutes and judgments, even as the LORD my God commanded me, that ye should do so in the land whither ye go to possess it. **Keep therefore and do them** [Why?]**; for this is your wisdom and your understanding in the sight of the nations, which shall hear all these statutes, and say, Surely this great nation is a wise and understanding people. For what nation is there so great, who hath God so nigh unto**

> **them, as the Lord our God is in all things that we call upon him for? And what nation is there so great, that hath statutes and judgments so righteous as all this law** [not burdensome]**, which I set before you this day** (Deut. 4:1–8)? According to Balak, God did get exactly that message across to the people, in a way that the people could understand: And Balak the son of Zippor **saw all that Israel had done to the Amorites**. And **Moab was sore afraid** of the people … (Num. 22:2–3). (We'll learn more about the Balaam/Balak account in section 9).

But because of their flirting with the paganism of this world, they lost their faith in God. They did not endure to the end, which caused their bodies to be overthrown and scattered in the wilderness for our example, from which we are to take warning. They were led by the Messiah's Spirit, but because of disobedience to God's commandments and laws, idolatry got the best of them. We cannot serve two gods at once (Matt. 6:24; Luke 16:13), which is idolatry and adultery to God. Paul warns us about that in 1 Corinthians 10:14: "Wherefore, my dearly beloved, **flee from idolatry** [refers to Ex. 20:2–6]". Idolatry is a root cause of sin: "Mortify therefore your members which are upon the earth; fornication, **uncleanness <akatharsia>**[35], inordinate affection, evil concupiscence, and covetousness, **which is idolatry**" (Col. 3:5). According to these scriptures, idolatry violates the first four commandments (Ex. 20:2–11) and God's dietary laws. Let's take a look at how that occurs:

The First Commandment: "I am the Lord thy God, which have brought thee out of the land of Egypt, out of the house of bondage. Thou shalt have no other gods before me" (Exodus 20:2–3).

Mainstream Christianity refuses to worship the God who brought the Israelites out of Egypt. That's why verse 2 is usually not included in the common Ten Commandment displays and in most doctrinal articles. Since they cannot have anything in common with the Jews, Satan has devised doctrines by which his servants serve him to be saved by, professing him in the name of the God of Abraham. For traditional Christendom, their god cannot be the one who redeemed Israel from Egypt (sin)—that's much too *Jewish*.

The Second Commandment: "Thou shalt not make unto thee any graven image, or any likeness of any thing that is in heaven above, or that is in the earth beneath, or that is in the water under the earth: Thou shalt not bow down thyself to them, nor serve them: for I the LORD thy God am a jealous God, visiting the iniquity of the fathers upon the children unto the third and fourth generation of them that hate me; And shewing mercy unto thousands of them that love me, and keep my commandments" (Ex. 20:4–6).

God commands His people to make no images or likenesses of anything in heaven or on earth. We see many displays of the Messiah on a cross. Is that not an image of the Messiah who is in now alive in heaven, not dead on a cross? In addition to that, in the pagan festive seasons—Easter, Christmas, Halloween, birthdays, etc.—we also see much imagery displayed as decorations of the symbols and signs of the heaven above, and of things of the earth (Jer. 10:1–5; 44:17–25; Acts 19:23–35). This commandment clearly states that God will show mercy to those who *keep* His commandments.

The Third Commandment: "Thou shalt not take the name of the LORD thy God in vain; for the LORD will not hold him guiltless that taketh his name in vain" (Ex. 20:7).

A typical understanding of the violation of this commandment takes the view that using the literal names of the Deity, such as God, Jesus, and Christ, as slang words to be the main focus of this commandment. Although that also holds true, God was warning against a much-farther-reaching ideology when He established that commandment. I believe He had doctrines like those of traditional Christendom and the Jewish Talmud in mind when He carved that commandment into the first tablet. Here's why: just like the Israelites of old who frequently worshiped strange gods in the name of the Lord, today's traditional Christendom is snaring people into a circle of religiously fanatic evangelists to worship pagan gods by Christianizing a host of pagan customs and traditions in the name of the Lord. This is akin to the account of the golden calf (Ex. 32:5), in which Aaron proclaims their worship of it as "a feast to the LORD"; the traditional ministers also proclaim the pagan doctrines, customs, and festivities in the name of the Lord! That is one of the most cunning ways to take the Lord's name in vain, which, according to the Torah test prophecy, is a capital felony that will not go unpunished.

The Fourth Commandment: "Remember the sabbath day, to keep it holy. Six days shalt thou labour, and do all thy work: But the seventh day is the sabbath of the LORD thy God: in it thou shalt not do any work, thou, nor thy son, nor thy daughter, thy manservant, nor thy maidservant, nor thy cattle, nor thy stranger that is within thy gates: For in six days the LORD made heaven and earth, the sea, and all that in them is, and rested the seventh day: wherefore the LORD blessed the sabbath day, and hallowed it" (Ex. 20:8–11).

Traditional Christendom has wholesaled this so-labeled burdensome, weak, and beggarly commandment as being specifically handed down for only the Jews, wherefore they've adopted Sunday from the sun god as their day on which to worship. The fourth commandment begins with "remember," not "forget" or "ignore"; "the seventh day," not "the first day"; "the sabbath of the LORD thy God," not "the Sabbath of the Jews." The Messiah confirmed the purpose for the Sabbath in the New Testament: "The sabbath was made for man [not for the Jews only], and not man for the sabbath: Therefore the Son of man is Lord also of the Sabbath" (Mark 2:27–28). It's the extreme anti-Jew mind-set that has caused traditional Christendom to trade off the Lord's Sabbath (which they've falsely labeled as the Jewish Sabbath) for the sun god's Sunday, for which Constantine the Great gets most of the credit.

6a. God's Dietary Laws in the New Covenant

God created certain animals for food, and certain animals He commanded for His people not to eat:

> For **thou art an holy people** unto the LORD thy God, and the LORD hath chosen thee to be a **peculiar <c@gullah>**[43] people unto himself, above all the nations that are upon the earth. **Thou shalt not eat any abominable thing** ... And every beast that parteth the hoof, and cleaveth the cleft into two claws, and cheweth the cud among the beasts, that ye shall eat ... And **the swine**, because it divideth the hoof, yet cheweth not the cud, **it is unclean <tame'>**[54] **unto you: ye shall not eat of their flesh, nor touch their dead carcase.** These ye shall eat of all that are in the waters: all that have fins and scales shall ye eat: And **whatsoever hath not fins and scales ye may not eat; it is unclean <tame'>**[54] **unto you.** (Deut. 14:2–3, 6, 8–10)

God also forbids His people to eat fat and blood:

> But flesh with the **life <nephesh>**[37] thereof, which is **the blood thereof, shall ye not eat.** (Gen. 9:4)

> It shall be a **perpetual <`owlam>**[1] **statute <chuqqah>**[4] for your generations throughout all your dwellings, that ye eat neither fat nor blood. (Lev. 3:17; read also 7:23, 26; chapter 11; Deut. chapter 14)

For the record, this law did not merely come into effect when God took His children out of Egypt. Neither was its beginning at Mount Sinai. As with His other laws, God commanded His people to discern between the clean and unclean before the Great Flood: "Of every **clean beast thou shalt take to thee by sevens**, the male and his female: and of beasts that are **not clean by two**, the male and his female" (Gen. 7:2). God commanded Noah to save a male and a female of each species so that its kind would continue after the Flood. We can assume that Noah's family would need food to endure the journey and also some extra because there would not be food for them to eat until sometime after the water receded, so God commanded Noah to take a few extra of the clean animals aboard. The clean animals were also for sacrificing to God (Gen. 8:20). As we read in the above scripture (Gen. 9:4), blood was also forbidden to be used as food at the time of the Flood.

Noah's account occurred at least seven centuries before God spoke the Ten Commandments to the Israelites. And that law did not end at the crucifixion either. End-time prophecies have very strong warnings concerning the food that we will be eating upon the Messiah's return to earth: "They that sanctify themselves, and purify themselves in the gardens behind one tree in the midst, **eating swine's flesh, and the abomination, and the mouse, shall be consumed together**, saith the LORD" (Isa. 66:17; read also Isa. 65:1–7; Acts 10:14, 28; 11:8; 2 Cor. 6:17; Rev. 18:2). According to God's Word, the consumers of unclean meat—swine and mice—will meet the same fate together with evildoers. And these laws were not instituted only for the Jews. Nobody was called a Jew until about seven centuries after the Israelites left Egypt (2 Kings 16:6), which was about fifteen centuries after the Great Flood, or eleven centuries after God made the covenants with Abraham.

I want to elaborate a little bit on Isaiah 66:17, because there is a very important message inside of it that is seldom recognized for what it says. It's without a doubt an end-time prophecy, wherefore it speaks to us today. I will cite it with a few of the Hebrew words in it from which it was translated, to help reveal its full message: "They that **sanctify <qadash>**[15] themselves, and **purify <taher>**[55] themselves in the **gardens <gannah>**[56] behind one tree in the midst, eating **swine's** flesh, and the **abomination**, and the mouse, shall be **consumed** together, saith the LORD" (Isa. 66:17). I will paraphrase that verse in hopes to clarify its intent yet more: "They who set themselves apart and hedge themselves in the midst of the fenced garden (court) as though they are morally cleansed and purified, while polluting and defiling themselves by eating unclean meat such as pork and mice, will utterly perish," says the LORD. I urge you to study this verse in your Holy Scriptures to your own satisfaction; then choose whether you'll believe it or the traditional clergy (Acts 5:29).

On page 198 I cited Colossians 3:5, where the Greek word **<akatharsia>**[35] is translated as "uncleanness," a derivative of the word **<akathartos>**[35a], which refers directly to the aspects of the unclean animals that God forbids His people from eating. The same rendering is used in the end-time book of Revelation, translated as "foul" and "unclean":

> And he cried mightily with a strong voice, saying, Babylon the great is fallen, is fallen, and is become the habitation of devils, and the hold of every **foul <akathartos>**[35a] spirit, and a cage of every **unclean <akathartos>**[35a] and hateful [detestable] bird. For all nations have drunk of the wine of the wrath of her fornication, and the kings of the earth have committed fornication with her, and the merchants of the earth are waxed rich through the abundance of her delicacies. And I heard another voice from heaven, saying, **Come out of her, my people**, that ye be not partakers of her sins, and that ye receive not of her plagues. (Rev. 18:2–4)

Such scriptures make it clear that eating unclean meat will still be an abomination to God in the future. And the Babylonian whore clearly gets her share of credit for indoctrinating people with the belief that there is nothing unclean any more. Nevertheless, that will not exempt its followers from the wrath that will come down for it. God calls His people out of that system because punishment will be exacted to each and every one of its partakers individually (Ezekiel chapter 18 and 33).

Paul used the same rendering in his letter to the people at Corinth while he cautioned them about ungodly doctrines, and he adds the "unclean issue" to a list of some specific abominations from which he says one must abstain in order to become a child of God:

> Be ye not unequally yoked together with unbelievers: for what fellowship hath righteousness with unrighteousness? and what communion hath light with darkness? And what concord hath Christ with Belial? or what part hath he that believeth with an infidel? And **what agreement hath the temple of God with idols? for ye are the temple of the living God**; as God hath said, **I will dwell in them**, and walk in them; and I will be their God, and they shall be my people. Wherefore **come out from among them, and be ye separate**, saith the Lord, and **touch not the unclean <akathartos>**[35a] **thing**; and I will receive you, And will be a Father unto you, and ye shall be my sons and daughters, saith the Lord Almighty. (2 Cor. 6:14–18)

This scripture is in perfect harmony with Revelation 18 and Isaiah 66, in that God will not accept people in His kingdom who remain in the Babylonian system, defiling themselves with things unclean, such as eating unclean meat. The book of Acts also confirms that word's usage as pertaining to unclean animals: "But Peter said, Not so, Lord; for I have never eaten any thing that is **common <koinos>**[35b] or **unclean <akathartos>**[35a]" (Acts 10:14). These scriptures are perfect Torah test proofs; Peter knew that God does not change!

The Greek word **<akathartos>**[35a] refers to things which are of and by themselves unclean, such as the unclean animals described in Leviticus chapter 11 and Deuteronomy chapter 14. On the other hand, the Greek word **<koinos>**[35b] refers to things that may have been made unclean by some act, such as sacrificing clean animals to foreign gods, thus rendering them polluted and defiled according to God's laws. The secular—heathen/Gentile—people of that day were called common **<koinos>**[35b] and were as such considered unclean **<akathartos>**[35a], because they ate unclean food, were not circumcised, and didn't live according to the laws of the God of Abraham: "Awake, awake; put on thy strength, O Zion; put on thy beautiful garments, O Jerusalem, the holy city: for henceforth there shall no more come into thee the **uncircumcised** [Gentiles, and likely also uncircumcised Israelites] and the **unclean <tame'>**[54]" (Isa. 52:1).

Because of Constantine's anti-Jew decree, wherefore his followers refuse to be anything other than Gentiles, for today's mainstream traditional Christendom nothing is unclean, just as it was for the heathen/Gentile people of old who sacrificed any beasts and critters to their ever-accepting evolutionary gods. Thus they were classified throughout ancient times as unclean people. That's why Peter used the words **<koinos>**[35b] ("common") and **<akathartos>**[35a] ("unclean") the way he did:

1. **Common** = he had never eaten anything that might have been sacrificed to idols.
2. **Unclean** = he had never eaten any unclean animals.

After the vision was revealed, Peter explained to the people that God symbolically showed him by that analogy that He had granted repentance also to the Gentiles, who in the past had been considered common **<koinos>**[35b]—unclean by having been defiled. Thus they were considered unclean. We can see in Isaiah 52:1 that the uncircumcised (Gentiles) were termed unclean by the same definition **<tame'>**[54] with which God termed swine to be unclean: "And the swine, though he divide the hoof, and be clovenfooted, yet he cheweth not the cud; he is **unclean <tame'>**[54] to you" (Lev. 11:7).

In the New Testament they translated the Greek word **<koinos>**[35b] as "common" and also as "unclean," by which they referred to the Gentiles as people who were considered unclean because they had made themselves unclean by defilement. By these terms they also referred to animal meat and other foods such as are considered as clean by God but may have become defiled—made unclean—by having been sacrificed to idols: "I know, and am persuaded by the Lord Jesus, that there is nothing

unclean <koinos>[35b] of itself: but to him that esteemeth any thing to be **unclean <koinos>**[35b], to him it is **unclean <koinos>**[35b]" (Rom. 14:14). Paul explained that process in more detail in 1 Corinthians chapter 8, and 10:16–33, namely how by sacrificing clean meat to Baal defiles it: "But I say, that **the things which the Gentiles sacrifice, they sacrifice to devils, and not to God: and I would not that ye should have fellowship with devils. Ye cannot drink the cup of the Lord, and the cup of devils: ye cannot be partakers of the Lord's table, and of the table of devils**" (1 Cor. 10:20–21). That's why God forbade His children to have anything in common with the Gentiles: "Depart ye, depart ye, go ye out from thence, touch no **unclean <tame'>**[54] **thing; go ye out of the midst of her; be ye clean, that bear the vessels of the LORD**" (Isa. 52:11; read also 2 Cor. 6:14–18; Rev. 18:2–4). And that's what Paul referred to in 2 Corinthians 6:18 when he commanded God's people to abstain from unclean **<akathartos>**[35a] things wherewith one's temple/vessel—symbolically the heart, where God wants to tabernacle/dwell—becomes defiled because of the violation of God's dietary and health laws.

Traditional preachers would have us believe that the Messiah abolished the dietary laws (compare Matt. 4:4; 5:17–19; Luke 4:4; 16:17). In Matthew chapter 15 and Mark chapter 7, the Pharisees viciously charged the Messiah and His disciples of defilement by eating with unwashed hands. Mark's account holds a perfect example of the rendering of the word **<koinos>**[35b] as it applies to the act of **being made** unclean, in this case by not washing one's hands: "And when they saw some of his disciples eat bread with **defiled <koinos>**[35b], that is to say, with **unwashen, hands**, they found fault" (Mark 7:2). The Messiah excoriated them for using their commandments wherewith God's commandments are forsaken, thus **defiling <koinoo>**[35c] their hearts (Matt. 15:18). Peter had trouble understanding this, so the Messiah clarified it: "To eat with unwashen hands **defileth <koinoo>**[35c] not a man" (Matt. 15:20).

Some scriptural translators have titled this account as "Clean and Unclean," and they conclude that account by adding "Thus the Messiah declared all foods clean," with the implication that the animals God declared as unclean are now clean. That's understandable, because these scriptures were translated, and titled, centuries after that belief was already indoctrinated into the traditional church program, of which these translators were obviously diligent followers. But we will see that it—and also what traditional ministers conveniently read into it—cannot be inspired by the eternal God of heaven and earth! It's true; God made all food clean (Gen. 2:9; 9:3; 1 Tim. 4); but nowhere does He call anything food that He previously deemed unclean. In 1 Timothy 4:3 God specifically speaks to "them which believe and know the truth." A believer of the truth will understand it from God's point of view and apply the Torah test, which inherently disallows any contradictions, and there aren't any. Think about it; can the eternally unchanging/non-evolutionary God contradict His own word (John 10:35)?

Interestingly, traditional Christendom is advocating abominable practices, such as what Paul tells us in 2 Corinthians 6:14–18 regarding unclean **<akathartos>**[35a] things from which to refrain. They reason around it by advocating that that is why we are to pray over it. By advocating that, they actually admit that what they're eating is unclean, thus praying in vain. Doing something which is knowingly wrong and expecting God to send His angel of mercy (Ps. 91) is tempting God! The Messiah knew that God would save Him if He was to be thrown off of the pinnacle upon which Satan had taken Him. But voluntarily throwing oneself down in order to prove that God will save one from harm would be tempting Him. That's why the Messiah refused to throw Himself down: " ... And saith unto him, **If thou be the Son of God** [to prove Himself], **cast thyself down** [voluntarily]**: for it is written** [Ps. 91], **He shall give his angels charge concerning thee: and in their hands they shall bear thee up, lest at any time thou dash thy foot against a stone**. Jesus said unto him, **It is written again** [Deut. 6:16—another Torah test]**, Thou shalt not tempt the Lord thy God** (Matt. 4:6–7). Satan literally uses scriptures to deceive us. He cunningly referred to Psalms chapter 91 in his tempting of the Messiah.

In Acts chapter 28 Paul gets bitten by a poisonous snake. The barbarians there with him were instantly convinced that Paul must be a murder who escaped the shipwreck only to be killed on land by vengeance. But, since the venom had no ill effect on Paul, the bystanders changed their thoughts and referred to him as a god. Whatever the reason for the snake to be there and to bite Paul without any consequences, God obviously sent Paul's guardian angel (Ps. 91) to protect him from harm. If Paul had toyed with the snake and provoked it to bite him in order to prove to the bystanders that the eternal God was on his side, God would likely not have sent the guardian angel, because Paul would then have tempted Him.

So, if we pray to the eternal God for His blessing in order that we can willingly commit an abomination, we are then tempting Him. That was a big problem with the Israelites while they journeyed through the wilderness; they kept tempting God—for which they paid dearly: "Neither let us tempt Christ, as some of them also tempted, and were destroyed of serpents" (1 Cor. 10:9; read also Ex. 17:2, 7; Num. 21:5–6). Such sins will be dealt with in fiery indignation: "For if we sin **wilfully after** that we have received the knowledge of the truth [knowing that it's wrong before the act is committed], there remaineth no more sacrifice for sins, But a certain fearful looking for of judgment and fiery indignation, which shall devour the adversaries (Heb. 10:26–27; read also 6:4; Num. 15:30; Zeph. 1:18; Luke 11:26; 2 Peter 2:20–22). That almost sounds like an unforgivable sin.

As strictly as the Pharisees held to God's dietary laws—as they still do—if they had understood that the Messiah had changed God's food law, they would have immediately condemned Him, probably to the point of stoning Him for breaching the Torah test. Those Pharisees would not miss any opportunity to condemn Him. So if there had been just the slightest hint of that being what the Messiah meant by what He said—even if it would mean perverting it for the sole purpose of condemning Him (Mark 12:13; Luke 11:53–54)—they would have, without a shadow of a doubt, taken full advantage of the situation. But there's no indication of such a dispute. They couldn't, because the Messiah made it too plain; they understood Him. The issue was eating with unwashed hands, which was a tradition of their elders invented by the rabbis and Pharisees, and not a commandment of God. So the Messiah *used* that opportunity to show them that their use of traditional doctrines as commandments was what defiled their hearts, because it did not come from God but from their glory-seeking, prideful, lustful, adulterous, and covetous hearts (Matt. 15:18–20). That's why He called them a generation of vipers (Matt. 3:7; 12:34; 23:33; Luke 3:7): their traditions came directly from the serpent of old—their father, Satan, the devil (John 8:44)—because they followed after his traditional commandments wherewith God's commandments are inevitably forsaken (Matt. 15; Mark 7). That's what the issue at hand was in that account.

Side Note: God did command the priests who performed the temple services, such as the sacrificial rituals and ordinances, to wash their hands, because performing those services required approaching God's altar and the Holy of Holies (Ex. 30:17–20). For the reason of disease prevention, He also commands us to wash our hands and clothes if we come in contact with the carcass of a dead man or beast (Lev. 11:18; Num. 5:2; 9:6). Although God endorses good sanitation, He made no commandment regarding hand washing for the purpose of eating, providing the person is otherwise morally clean.

As Peter was napping while food was being prepared, God displayed to him a spiritual vision of clean and unclean animals that he was told to kill and eat (Acts chapters 10–11). He rebelled and stated that he had never eaten anything common **<koinos>**[35b] or unclean **<akathartos>**[35a]. Theologians have misconstrued and misappropriated that account in an effort to make that account say that God's dietary and health laws had been abolished. If the Messiah had purposed the account in Matthew chapter 15 and Mark chapter 7 to show that to be the case—thus violating His own commandments of Leviticus 3:17 and chapter 11, Deuteronomy chapter 14, and Genesis 7:2 and 9:4—Peter would have already been aware of it at this point, because he questioned the Messiah after that argument, and the Messiah answered that the issue was about eating with unwashed hands. The account in Acts 10 occurred about ten years after that argument in Matthew 15. So Peter, by now surely knowing (John 14:26; 16:13), explained that God showed him *through that* *vision* that he was not to call any *man* common or unclean: "And he said unto them, Ye know how that it is an unlawful thing for a man that is a Jew to keep company, or come unto one of another nation; but God hath shewed me that **I should not call any <u>man</u> common <koinos>**[35b] **or unclean <akathartos>**[35a]" (Acts 10:28; read also Acts 11:15–18). If God had meant for Peter to literally eat unclean food and Peter had refused as he did, there would have been repercussions. But there's no indication of such. But the apostles did from that point forward include the Gentiles in their ministry, because that it was prophesied of in the Old Testament—another Torah test prophecy that came to Peter's remembrance:

> And the apostles and brethren that were in Judaea heard that the **Gentiles had also received the word of God**. And when Peter was come up to Jerusalem, they that were of the circumcision contended with him, Saying, Thou wentest in to men uncircumcised [Gentiles], and didst eat with them [Gentiles were common/unclean **<koinos>**[35b]]. But Peter rehearsed the matter from the beginning, and expounded it by order unto them, saying, I was in the city of Joppa praying: and in a trance I saw a vision, A certain vessel descend, as it had been a great sheet, let down from heaven by four corners [proclaim this message to the whole world - another Torah test proof]; and it came even to me: Upon the which when I had fastened mine eyes, I considered, and saw fourfooted beasts of the earth, and wild beasts, and creeping things, and fowls of the air. And I heard a voice saying unto me, Arise, Peter; slay and eat. But I said, Not so, Lord: for nothing **common <koinos>**[35b] or **unclean <akathartos>**[35a] hath at any time entered into my mouth. But the voice answered me again from heaven, **What God hath cleansed, that call not thou common <koinoo>**[35c]. [There are many prophecies in the Old Testament about bringing the Gentiles into His fold.] And this was done three times: and all were drawn up again into heaven. And, behold, immediately there were three men [common **<koinos>**[35b] Gentiles] already come

> unto the house where I was, sent from Caesarea unto me. And the Spirit [which Peter received at Pentecost] bade me go with them, nothing doubting. Moreover these six brethren accompanied me, and we entered into the man's house: And he shewed us how he had seen an angel in his house, which stood and said unto him, Send men to Joppa, and call for Simon, whose surname is Peter; Who shall tell thee words, whereby thou and all thy house shall be saved. [God used Peter, an already converted Jew, to reveal the Holy Spirit to the Gentiles—common/unclean **<koinos>**[35b] people.] And as I began to speak, the Holy Spirit **<pneuma>**[11] fell on them, **as on us at the beginning** [upon their conversion at Pentecost]. **Then remembered I the word of the Lord** [Acts 1:5; 2:16–17]**, how that he said, John indeed baptized with water; but ye shall be baptized with the Holy Ghost** [Spirit]. Forasmuch then as God gave them the like gift as he did unto us, who believed on the Lord Jesus Christ; what was I, that I could withstand God? When they heard these things, they held their peace, and glorified God, saying, **Then hath God also to the Gentiles granted repentance unto life** (Acts 11:1–18; read also Acts 1:5; Joel 2:28–29).

There is no mention in scriptural prophecies that God would ever change His dietary laws. That's why Peter blatantly rebelled and refused to eat the unclean animals. Thus, in accordance with the Torah test, the Messiah's changing of God's dietary laws would have systematically made Him an imposter, by His own commandment. But God *did* declare in numerous scriptures throughout the Torah that He would at some point in the future reveal His Spirit to the Gentiles—to all four corners of the world (Deut. 32:21; Isa. 9:2; 42:6; 49:6; 55:5; 60:1–3; Joel 2:28–29; Luke 2:32)—of which the people that walked with the Messiah were aware (Matt. 4:15–16; 21:43; Luke 2:32; Acts 1:5–8). And as we just read in Acts 11:1–18 above, Peter confirmed that it was exactly as God had prophesied in the Old Testament, and as the Messiah also had reminded them of in Acts 1:5 just prior to His ascension to heaven. Earlier Peter preached about how God had prophesied that He would at some point reveal His Spirit to the Gentiles: "But this is that which was spoken by the prophet Joel; And **it shall come to pass in the last days, saith God, I will pour out of my Spirit upon all flesh** [Jew and Gentile]" (Acts 2:16–17). After Peter finished explaining to the other apostles about how God had used that vision to reveal the fulfillment of an Old Testament prophecy—thus another Torah test proof—they understood him and held their peace (Acts 11:17–18).

Paul also clarified that fact while defending his case in the court, because he was falsely accused of making changes to God's/Moses's laws: "Having therefore obtained help of God, I continue unto this day, witnessing both to small and great, **saying none other things than those which the prophets and Moses** [God's Torah writers] **did say should come: That Christ should suffer** [the crucifixion]**, and that he should be the first that should rise from the dead** [the resurrection to spiritual eternal life]**, and should shew light unto the people** [Israelites—Jews], **and to the Gentiles** [those who were before considered common/unclean **<koinos>**[35b]]" (Acts 26:22–23). Paul stated very specifically which prophecies God had fulfilled through the Messiah, with absolutely no mention of any changes to God's dietary laws. If he had mentioned changes, the Pharisees would immediately have set out to stone him. But they didn't, because Paul made no mention of any laws having been changed or abolished; he stressed only what God had brought to fulfillment **as was prophesied in the Torah**. What he had preached to both the Jews and Gentiles was in perfect and absolute compliance with the Torah; else he would have been a false minister according to the Torah test.

If the dietary laws pertained only to the Jews of the Old Testament, as is taught by the traditional ministry, why are unclean things condemned centuries before Jews existed, and in the New Testament? Why did Paul tell the Gentile people at Corinth not to touch the unclean things (2 Cor. 6:17–18)? Why is God warning His people about the plagues that will befall those who indulge in the Babylonian foul **<akathartos>**[35a] and unclean **<akathartos>**[35a] trappings in the end-time (Rev. 18:2–4)? The answer is right there. God (the God of the Jews and of the

Gentiles, Rom. 3:29) wants to dwell in the hearts of His people, wherefore He demands our vessels to be clean (Isa. 52:11; 2 Cor. 6:17). The non-evolutionary holy God of Abraham *cannot* share a dwelling-place/tabernacle with abominable things.

Point to Ponder: As with the Lord's Sabbath commandment, keeping God's dietary and health laws also sanctifies a person–setting one apart from the rest of the world. That's an extremely scary thought to traditional Christendom.

So God had opened the way for the Gentiles also to have access to the Holy Spirit, which allowed them to also walk in His ways and keep His commandments of love and liberty instead of the commandments of the pagan gods of bondage. And Paul spent a lot of time—by the hand of God—teaching the Gentiles about the ways of the God of Abraham by preaching to them about God's true plan of salvation and about the gospel of the kingdom of God (Acts 19:8; 20:25; 28:23–31). Paul preached to them on the Lord's Sabbath days (Acts 13:14, 27, 42, 44; 15:21; 16:13; 17:2; 18:4); in perfect compliance with the Torah test - he preached about salvation in the Messiah from the Torah (Acts 28:23-31).

Peter made an interesting statement in a letter in which he started off by addressing mainly Gentiles. He emphasized to them the purpose of the Messiah's atoning blood and reminded them to refrain from their previous abominable lusts, and thus instructed them to do those things that are required by God in order to come holy before Him: "As obedient children, not fashioning yourselves according to the **former lusts in your ignorance**: But as he which hath called you is holy, so be ye holy in all manner of conversation; Because it is written, **Be ye holy; for I am holy**" (1 Peter 1:14–16). He cited that directly from the book of Leviticus—the "clean/unclean" chapter:

> **Ye shall not make yourselves abominable** with any creeping thing that creepeth, neither shall ye make

> yourselves **unclean <tamah>**[54a] with them, that ye should be **defiled <tame'>**[54] thereby. For I am the LORD your God: ye shall therefore **sanctify <qadash>**[15] yourselves, and **ye shall be holy; for I am holy**: neither shall ye defile yourselves with any manner of creeping thing that creepeth upon the earth. For I am the LORD that bringeth you up out of the land of Egypt [delivered us from sin], to be your God: **ye shall therefore be holy, for I am holy**. This is the law of the beasts, and of the fowl, and of every living creature that moveth in the waters, and of every creature that creepeth upon the earth: **To make a difference between the unclean <tame'>**[54] **and the clean, and between the beast that may be eaten and the beast that may not be eaten**. (Lev. 11:43–47)

The holy God does not want His children to eat meat from beasts that He specifically created to help keep the earth clean for us. They are scavengers designed by Him so that they can eat things that are very toxic to humans. I want to elaborate a bit on that very topic while adding some science alongside it.

God designed the clean animals with about 6–10 percent fat, with the fat situated in such a way that it can be trimmed off of the meat. He knew that fat was not good for us, so He warned us about that (Leviticus 7:23). He even forbade us to eat the fat of the *clean* animals (Leviticus 7:24), so He designed them so that the fat that they naturally have can be trimmed off of the meat. The animals that are specifically raised for the food market today have been crossbred—against God's will (Leviticus 19:19)—thus modified from its original state. These animals are also fed a whole plethora of hormones, chemicals, and chemically grown feed which also helps to fatten them in a shorter period of time, thus adding fat to all of its body tissues. That fat is in the meat–called marbling–, meaning that it can't be removed or cut off. If we eat that meat, we also eat the fat, together with the chemicals used to achieve that whole process.

If a living creature has a disease caused by a virus, toxins, or any other unhealthy organisms or pathogens in the body, the pathogens typically travel in the bloodstream. God designed it that way so that the unwarranted microorganisms are carried to the right place in one's body so that the immune system can deal with them by destroying them and removing them from the body. Any toxins that the body can't get rid of are stored away in the fatty tissues. Could that be the reason God commanded us not to eat fat and blood? I believe so—among a few other reasons—because they can be loaded with toxins and pathogens. God cares for our health and welfare.

Most people are aware that some fish have fins and scales, while others don't. God allowed only fish with both fins *and* scales to be eaten by His people. The fish and other sea animals without fins or scales are scavengers—typically called bottom feeders. They thrive on whatever lies on the floors of the bodies of water, and that's where most toxins usually end up. Many studies have shown that if the scavengers are removed from a body of water, the fish with fins and scales get sick and die because of the toxins, which are then no longer being removed from the water. So in eating fish—and other seafood—that don't have fins and scales, one is eating animals that thrive on toxins, which then end up in our bodies. Is that what we want in our bodies? It's the same with pork. Just like bears and vultures, swine are also scavengers. And the swine has most of its 40 percent body fat content incorporated into its flesh—by God's design. That fat is practically unavoidable when eating pork. Again, that's probably why God commanded us to not eat the flesh of scavengers—it's loaded with fat and toxins.

Consider This: After miraculously feeding the multitudes, the Messiah commanded that the leftover fragments of food be gathered up (Matt. 14:20, 15:37, Mark 6:43, John 6:13) so no food would be lost (John 6:12). Then, as documented in Mark 5:13, He sent unclean <**akathartos**>[35a] spirits into a herd of two thousand swine, which destroyed them. Think about this: would the Messiah destroy a big herd of swine if He had considered them food, and then, a few days later, command the people to gather up the fragments of bread for the sole purpose of not wasting food? To think so is rather preposterous.

There is nothing recorded in the New Testament that would indicate that the Gentiles rebelled against keeping the laws of God, including the Lord's Sabbaths and His dietary laws. That rebellion plagued early Christendom in the first quarter of the fourth century, when the Roman emperor Constantine the Great—a worshipper of the sun god Mithras—took full advantage of the tremendous power the Roman Empire possessed at that time and made a decree to condemn the so-labeled Jewish seventh-day Sabbath. As a Mithras worshipper, he Christianized the first day of the week as Sunday in honor of his sun god, Mithras. He's also the man to be credited for trading off the Lord's Passover for the pagan Easter, and the LORD's Feast of Tabernacles for Christmas. Since he accused the Jews *alone* as being the murderers of the Lord, he literally labeled those of God's commandments that the Jews observed as being Jewish, therefore condemning as Judaizers all who would likewise dare to keep any such commandments. Thus, commandment keepers—or Judaizers, as he labeled them—were severely persecuted under his rule, to the point of execution for those who would not recant; especially regarding the Sabbath Commandment.

Constantine decreed that all religions should join the Roman system and pay homage to its empire, in exchange for an appeasing promise to put an end to the certain persecutions that were prevalent because of all the different religious beliefs among them. All religious doctrines were accepted and adopted into the fold, as long as they had nothing in common with the Jews. Thus, Christianity did not stamp out paganism, but rather adopted it.

Since the Roman Empire's biggest enemies were the Jews—whom they had already condemned along with other observers of the Ten Commandments—it served the new universally Babylonianized Roman Catholic Church philosophy extremely well to invent doctrines with which to label God's dietary laws, His holy day festivals, and His Ten Commandments as Jewish in order to conveniently condemn them along with the Jews; hence the creed "**CAN'T HAVE ANYTHING IN COMMON WITH THE JEWS, THE MURDERERS OF THE LORD**" (Emphasis added). (Philip Schaff D.D., LL.D. and Henry Wace, D.D., *Nicene and Post-Nicene Fathers: Second Series*, vol. 14, ISBN 1-56563-130-7 [Hendrickson Publishers Inc., P.O. Box 3473, Peabody, MA, 01961-3473], page 54–56, 108). And today's mainstream traditional church system is still establishing doctrines upon that foundation, and zealously advocating them as being most essential for salvation, thus preaching them **in the name of the Lord**. Many scripture commentators also have labeled God's commandments and laws as such, which many of today's traditional Christians use to justify their law-done-away philosophy. But these doctrines are all—each and every one of them—traditional commandments **<entalma>**[9a] of men.

Side Note: It's ironic that the root cause of all wars tends to hinge on religion. For instance, Constantine promised to end the persecution between the religious sects of the day, but he grossly persecuted anyone who would keep the fourth commandment. There are many history books written about the religious wars through which multiple millions upon millions of people have been slaughtered in cold blood solely because of doctrinal differences between the different religious sects. The biggest irony of all is that the sects involved in those wars all claimed to be preaching love in the name of whatever god or gods they served. National wars and even world wars are typically triggered by religious discrepancies between people and nations of people. The bottom line is that religion—just like politics—is extremely dangerous, because its doctrines come from men, the gods of this world, rather than from the creator God.

The writers of the Old and New Testaments took a totally different view, because they believed, and were thus inspired by, the unchanging and always reliable commandments of the God of Abraham:

> It is better to trust in the LORD than to put confidence in man. It is better to trust in the LORD than to put confidence in princes. (Ps. 118:8–9)

> Thus saith the LORD; **Cursed be the man that trusteth in man ... Blessed is the man that trusteth in the LORD,** and whose hope the LORD is. (Jer. 17:5, 7)

> But Peter and John answered and said unto them, **Whether it be right in the sight of God to hearken unto you more than unto God, judge ye.** (Acts 4:19)

> Then Peter and the other apostles answered and said, **We ought to obey God rather than men.** (Acts 5:29)

By the way, the Messiah and His apostles were also Jews who kept and advocated the Ten Commandments, God's holy day festivals, and the dietary laws. If you're a traditional church supporter, what are you going to do about that? Can your minister make that go away? Will you choose to serve Constantine's anti-Jew/anti-commandment philosophy by partaking of the traditional church system, or will you choose to serve the God of Abraham? Having myself also been a dedicated brainwashed follower of the Babylonian system for almost five decades, I know that it's a tough choice to make, because the roots go so very deep.

Satan is the father of murder and lies—darkness and death: "Ye are of your father the devil, and the lusts of your father ye will do. **He was a murderer from the beginning**, and abode not in the truth, because there is no truth in him. When he speaketh a lie, he speaketh of his own: for **he is a liar, and the father of it**" (John 8:44). He causes his followers to focus on the opposite of love, mercy, light, and life: "And this is the condemnation, that light is come into the world, and **men loved darkness rather than light, because their deeds were evil**" (John 3:19). That makes Satan the god, prince, and ruler of darkness, war, and death (John 3:19; Rom. 13:12; 2 Cor. 6:14; Eph. 2:2; 6:12; Col 1:13; 2 Peter 2:4, 17; Jude 1:6, 13; Rev. 16:10). This world is his kingdom to do with as he pleases: "And the devil said unto him,

All this power will I give thee, and the glory of them: for that is delivered unto me; and to whomsoever I will give it" (Luke 4:6). Satan—through the followers of his servants, such as Constantine and Luther—has many well-trained ministers to advocate his lawless messiah: "For such are false apostles, deceitful workers, transforming themselves into the apostles of Christ. And no marvel; for **Satan himself is transformed into an angel of light. Therefore it is no great thing if his ministers also be transformed as the ministers of righteousness**; whose end shall be according to their works" (2 Cor. 11:13–15). He has blinded his ministers and their followers: "In whom the **god of this world** hath blinded the minds of them which believe not" (2 Cor. 4:4; read again 2 Cor. 3:14 to 4:4).

Such is the means of power that Satan has at his disposal to govern this world through societies like the traditional church system, which possess the powerful support of powermongers such as the pope, kings, presidents, prime ministers, traditional preachers, and such lording and control-mongering authoritative people together with their many faithfully trained mobster-type servants. Such philosophy is the inevitable result of using man's commandments **<entalma>**[9a] instead of God's commandments **<entole>**[9] (Matt. 15; Mark 7). But that will change when the true Messiah takes control of this world to fully restore it *by* and *through* the use of only His Father's laws and commandments of sacrificial-type charitable **<agape>**[8] love and liberty, which will replace the **<entalma>**[9a]-borne covetousness, hatred, greed, and discontent of this world's demon-driven and war-inspired traditional and political burdensome religions of bondage!

As scriptures clearly reveal, God's takeover of this earth's government will commence *after* the Great Tribulation. Currently, the kingdom on this earth is not the Messiah's: "My kingdom is not of this world" (John 18:36). Soon, upon His return, it will *become* His Kingdom: "And the seventh angel sounded; and there were great voices in heaven, saying, **The kingdoms of this world are become the kingdoms of our Lord, and of his Christ; and he shall reign for ever and ever**" (Rev. 11:15).

Through pride, Satan seduces mankind to sin (to submit to his many ever-enticing, lustful ways), which warrants death

(Gen. 2:17; Rom. 6:23; James 1:15). He has inspired, deceived, and devoured the people's minds for about six thousand years, which is drawing to its close, and he knows it: "Be sober, be vigilant; because your adversary the devil, as a roaring lion, walketh about, seeking whom he may devour" (1 Peter 5:8; read also Rev. 12:9, 12). He still has that seducing power over mortal beings. That's why all the writers of the New Testament, when talking to people—even those they knew were converted—always encouraged them to refrain from sinning. It doesn't make any sense that they would teach people to refrain from sinning if they were already born again and saved, and thus not able to sin anymore, as is taught by the lawless traditional ministers. It's a common teaching that we are *already* in a born-again saved state, wherefore the supposed immortal soul of believers goes to enjoy eternal life in heaven immediately upon death and likewise the unsaved to eternal life in the fires of hell. But there's no scriptural support for those doctrines, thus it's pure theological tradition, the commandments **<entalma>**[9a] of men, a philosophy that systematically forsakes God's commandments **<entole>**[9] while tragically removing the need for a resurrection.

6b. Does Man Have an Immortal Soul?

Almost all of the modern-day religions in the world teach that God gave man an immortal soul that, when one dies, keeps on living in heaven, hell, purgatory, or perhaps reincarnated in some happy hunting ground or somewhere with seventy virgins. But according to the Holy Scriptures, man does not have an immortal soul. The scriptures state that a soul—whatever that is—can die: "The **soul** that sinneth, it shall **die**" (Ezek. 18:4; read also verse 20 and chapter 33). While the Messiah explained the importance of whom we are to fear and why, He also confirmed in the New Testament that a soul can die: "And fear not them [Satan's ministry] which **kill <apokteino>**[57] the **body <soma>**[58], but are not able to kill the **soul <psuche>**[59]: but rather fear him [the creator God] which is able to **destroy <apollumi>**[60] both soul and body in **hell <geenna>**[61]" (Matt. 10:28). This phrase is commonly used by traditional Christendom in an effort to prove the immortal soul philosophy, but it does not prove that point but rather confirms the Ezekiel statement that the soul can die—hence another Torah test proof.

I will also cite Luke's version of that same account, which clarifies a bit more the point that the Messiah emphasized—that is, the fact that we are to fear God and not Satan, because Satan can kill only the mortal body but God can destroy the mortal body, and also all record of us, in the lake of fire by the second death:

> For there is nothing covered, that shall not be revealed; neither hid, that shall not be known. Therefore whatsoever ye have spoken in darkness shall be heard in the light; and that which ye have spoken in the ear in closets shall be proclaimed upon the housetops. And I say unto you my friends, **Be not afraid of them** [Satan's ministry] **that**

> **kill the body, and after that have no more that they can do. But I will forewarn you whom ye shall fear: Fear him** [the creator God], **which after he hath killed hath power to cast into hell <geenna>**[61] [the lake of fire]; **yea, I say unto you, Fear him.** (Luke 12:2–5)

The Messiah told us to not fear Satan's ministry, which can destroy only one's carnal body, but to fearfully revere the eternal creator God, who knows our thoughts (which are also written down in the book of life) and has the power to totally destroy (cause to die and perish) both one's body (carnal substance) and soul (life; mind; heart; what we think, as is recorded in God's book of life) by the second death in the lake of fire:

> And I saw the dead, small and great, stand before God; and the books were opened [*all* scriptures]: and another book was opened, which is the **book of life <zoe>**[62] [the record of one's soul—life]: **and the dead were judged out of those things which were written in the books** [scriptures and the book of life], **according to their works** [Torah test]. And **death <thanatos>**[63] and **hell <hades>**[64] [the grave] were cast into the lake of fire. **This is the second death <thanatos>**[63]**. And whosoever was not found written in the book of life <zoe>**[62] **was cast into the lake of fire.** (Rev. 20:12–15)

So we can see that our Creator knows all our deeds and thoughts, nothing is hidden, and they're written down in the book of life, which will be measured against the books of the scriptures—a real *personal* Torah test (Rev. 20:12–15, cited above). The book of life is a symbolic storage for our thinking process. That's why we are to fear God and not Satan. Of course Satan, through traditional indoctrination, causes man to fear him. And he teaches that man has an immortal soul that cannot die but will continue to live forever, as he told Eve: "Ye shall not surely die" (Gen 3:4). So in essence, it's the creator God who has the power to destroy—kill—both the carnal body and that which is recorded of us, bad and good, in the fires of hell

<**geenna**>[61], which is the name of the fire pit where they used to burn garbage and also where they sacrificed children to Molech. The Messiah used the term for hell <**geenna**>[61] to show to them that whoever ended up in that place would be burnt to ashes in the lake of fire, where the people who will taste the second death will be cast into. Satan—through his ministers—teaches a fear tactic to the effect that, if we don't take heed and listen to his instructions—as it comes from his traditional pulpits—that we will then burn alive in the fires of hell forever and ever. It is of no concern to Satan that there are thousands of different Church denominations, as long as they teach those certain of his doctrines which identify him as their god, while at the same time preaching against the keeping of the Ten Commandments—specifically his so-labeled 'Jewish' Sabbath Commandment.

Note: The meaning for the Greek word <**zoe**>[62] relates to another Greek word, <**psuche**>[59], which is translated into English as "soul" in the Matthew and Luke scriptures above. The word <**psuche**>[59] is connected to the Hebrew word <**nephesh**>[37], which is also translated into English in many Old Testament scriptures as "soul," and in many instances as "creature," "life," and in some as "breath" or "air"—typically referring to a breath requiring creature. The word <**nephesh**>[37] relates to the Hebrew word <**ruwach**>[37c], which is translated in most places as "breath," "air," "mind," or "spirit." So it seems logical that the book of life, with its recording of our thoughts and deeds, would be referred to as <**psuche**>[59] as used in these scriptures, as it relates directly to the works of a person while yet alive by which he or she will be judged: "And the dead were judged out of those things which were written in the books, according to their works" (Rev. 20:12). None of these terms give any indication that God gave man an immortal soul as a continuation of life immediately upon death.

Nevertheless, death and destruction by fire is not eternal life, but death, as in no more life. This is just as God told Adam and Eve: "For in the day that thou eatest thereof **thou shalt surely die** <**muwth**>[65] (Gen. 2:17; read also Gen. 3:3). For the wages of sin is

death <thanatos>[63]" (Rom. 6:23; read also 5:12). James used the same analogy to explain the consequences of sin: "Then when lust hath conceived [an evil thought committed], it bringeth forth sin [a commandment is broken]: and sin, when it is finished, bringeth forth **death <thanatos>**[63]" (James 1:15). Mortal substance, like the flesh and blood of humans, is corruptible and must die: "In the sweat of thy face shalt thou eat bread, **till thou return unto the ground**; for out of it wast thou taken: **for dust thou art, and unto dust shalt thou return**" (Gen. 3:19; read also Eccl. 3:20). Even God Himself, when He came to dwell on this earth as the Messiah in a carnal mortal state, did not leave this world before first having to die. As a mortal man, He did not have an immortal soul. He was dead in the grave for three days and three nights, until God resurrected Him into a spiritual being, after which He was incorruptible and immortal: "He [David] seeing this before spake of the resurrection of Christ, that his **soul <psuche>**[59] was not left in **hell <hades>**[64] [the grave]" (Acts 2:31).

Acts 2:31 is cited directly from the Old Testament, where it is made clearer in regards to what is meant by the word "soul" as used here: "For thou wilt not leave my **soul <nephesh>**[37] [a breath requiring body or creature] in **hell <sh@'owl>**[66] [grave]; neither wilt thou suffer thine Holy One to see corruption" (Ps. 16:10). That's because he was raised back to life after three days and three nights. If He had an immortal soul, then He was not dead. If He was not dead, then He did not need to be resurrected "and declared to be the Son of God with power, according to the spirit of holiness, **by the resurrection <anastasis>**[67] **from the dead <nekros>**[68]" (Rom. 1:4). He was resurrected (reborn) from death to life eternal, but He did not see the *second* death, which is eternal death by fire. He said Himself that He had been dead: "I am he that liveth, **and was dead <nekros>**[68]; and, behold, I am alive for evermore, Amen; and have the keys of **hell <hades>**[64] [the grave] and of **death <thanatos>**[63]" (Rev. 1:18). He was the first to be reborn from death into a spirit being: "... the first begotten of the **dead <nekros>**[68] ..." (Rev 1:5). The fact that the Messiah's mortal body did not see corruption is yet another fulfilled prophecy (Ps. 16:10), and thus another powerful Torah test proof for the believers to see that He truly was the Messiah of whom the Old Testament prophets had written.

Side Note: The translators used the word "hell" to translate three different Greek words in the KJV New Testament, and I will clarify the different meanings of each of the words. A common belief is that whenever the word "hell" is used in the scriptures, it refers to the lake of fire where all unsaved people supposedly go to burn alive for all eternity. As you will see, that is not at all the true scriptural intent.

1. #86 **<hades>**[64] designates a grave or a place of burial:
    - "He seeing this before spake of the resurrection of Christ, that his soul was not left in **hell <hades>**[64] [grave], neither his flesh did see corruption" (Acts 2:31).
    - "O death, where is thy sting? O **grave <hades>**[64], where is thy victory?" (1 Cor. 15:55).
    - "And the sea gave up the dead which were in it; and **death <thanatos>**[63] and **hell <hades>**[64] [the grave] delivered up the dead which were in them: and they were judged every man according to their works. And death **<thanatos>**[63] and **hell <hades>**[64] were cast into the lake of fire. This is the second death" (Rev. 20:13–14).

It's very clear in this scripture that the word **<hades>**[64] translated as "hell" does not refer to the lake of fire, else it would be cast into itself. Death—the second and final death—will be cast into the lake of fire to be destroyed for eternity, wherefore the grave **<hades>**[64] will no longer be needed and will thus also be destroyed for eternity.

2. #1067 **<geenna>**[61] refers to a valley near Jerusalem where they used to burn garbage. That's also where many Baal worshippers sacrificed their children to Molech. *Strong's Concordance* shows that it originated from the Hebrew word **<Hinnom>**[69]:

- "And if thine eye offend thee, pluck it out, and cast it from thee: it is better for thee to enter into life with one eye, rather than having two eyes to be cast into **hell <geenna>**[61] fire" (Matt. 18:9).
- "Moreover he burnt incense in the valley of the son of **Hinnom <Hinnom>**[69], and **burnt his children in the fire**, after the abominations of the heathen whom the LORD had cast out before the children of Israel" (2 Chron. 28:3).

It's obvious that, although it involves a valley with fire into which they have thrown living people to burn them to death as a punishment, and in which they also burnt children as a sacrifice to Satan, <**geenna**>[61] does not refer directly to the lake of fire, but in some scriptures it symbolizes it, to show that whatever ends up there burns up and turns to ashes.

3. #5020 <**tartaroo**>[70] refers directly to the lake of fire:
   - "For if God spared not the angels that sinned, but cast them down to **hell <tartaroo>**[70], and delivered them into chains of darkness, to be reserved unto judgment" (2 Peter 2:4).

The word <**tartaroo**>[70] is used only once in the KJV Scriptures (2 Peter 2:4), and it relates directly to the lake of fire into which Satan and his demons will be cast. They are already spirit beings, wherefore they cannot die (Luke 20:36; Rom. 6:9; Rev. 21:4) and will thus likely be cast into the lake of fire to burn alive for eternity. Satan and his demons will be joined by his servant the Beast and the False Prophet of the end time: "And the devil that deceived them was cast into the lake of fire and brimstone, where the beast and the false prophet *are*, and shall be tormented day and night for ever and ever" (Rev. 20:10). Those people whose names are not written in the book of life will be burnt to death in that same fire: "And **death <thanatos>**[63] [the second death] and **hell** <**hades**>[64] [the grave] **were cast into the lake of fire. This is the second death <thanatos>**[63]**. And whosoever was not found written in the book of life was cast into the lake of fire**"

(Rev. 20:14–15). The second death is eternal death, not eternal life. Praise the Eternal for chasing Adam and Eve out of the garden of Eden and closing the gate before they took of the tree of life *after* they rejected God, else they would also—as spirit beings that can't die (Luke 20:36)—have been doomed to live forever in the lake of fire together with Satan (Gen. 3:22–24). (More on this in the next section).

Numerous times throughout the Gospels, the Messiah mentions that whoever will follow Him and keep the commandments will never die:

> If thou wilt **enter into life**, keep the commandments. (Matt. 19:17)
>
> Verily, verily, I say unto you, If a man keep my saying, **he shall never see death.** (John 8:51)
>
> Verily, verily, I say unto you, He that heareth my word, and believeth on him that sent me, **hath everlasting life**, and shall not come into condemnation; but is **passed from death unto life.** (John 5:24)
>
> And whosoever liveth and believeth in me **shall never die.** (John 11:26)

But scriptures say that all must die:

> And as **it is appointed unto men once to die** ... (Heb 9:27; read also Gen. 3:19; Eccl. 3:20)

There is no contradiction here. Since all must die at least once (a choice made in the garden of Eden), when these scriptures speak of death, they refer to the second death, which is final and eternal. That's why those who die and get resurrected to eternal life in the first resurrection are symbolically considered not to have died, because every person ever born will die at least once and be resurrected only once: "Blessed and holy is he that hath part in the **first resurrection**: on such the **<u>second</u> death hath no power**" (Rev. 20:6). Those resurrected to *mortal* life in the second resurrection, in the time scriptures describe as the eighth day, will also obtain eternal life, thereby overcoming the second death, *if* they choose to follow and obey the God of Abraham. Those also will not be considered to have died; they will die no more: "And God shall wipe away all tears from their eyes; and there shall be **no more death**" (Rev. 21:4).

The rest of the people will taste the second death by being cast alive into the lake of fire to be destroyed for all eternity. The incorrigibly wicked of all time will be brought back to mortal life in the great-white-throne-judgment period only to also be cast into the lake of fire to be destroyed for eternity. That is the sting (1 Cor. 15:55–56) of the second death (Rev. 20:14–15), which those who attain eternal life through the first and second resurrection will not experience, because the Messiah overcame that for them by the resurrection from the first death, to eternal life—no second death: "But the fearful, and unbelieving, and the abominable, and murderers, and whoremongers, and sorcerers, and idolaters, and all liars, **shall have their part in the lake which burneth with fire and brimstone: which is the <u>second</u> death** (Rev. 21:8). That perfectly describes the destruction of both body and soul, of which the Messiah spoke in Matthew 10:28 and in other scriptures in reference to death, which is the total eternal destruction by death, where they will be turned into ashes, never more to live. So we can see that death is not eternal life but rather death! As mentioned earlier, everybody will die at least once. Likewise, everyone will be resurrected only once—some to eternal life, others to mortal life followed by the judgment as depicted by the Eighth Day Festival. And during the time period of that festival, many will find and accept the salvation of the Lord, while others will remain rebellious and unrepentant and will thus be cast alive into the lake of fire to be burnt up, never to live again. That's death according to the Scriptures!

Even the Messiah had to first literally die to shed the first *mortal* Adam so that He could be resurrected—born again—to obtain eternal life, the last *spiritual* Adam. Just the same, those of us who believe Him, and on the One who sent Him, and keep His commandments will not see the second death, but life everlasting (Matt. 19:17; John 5:24–29). In essence, the first Adam must literally die to be literally resurrected, thus born into the state of the last Adam in order to be able to enter into God's family: "That which is born of the **flesh is flesh** [the first *fleshly* Adam]; and that which is born of the **Spirit is spirit** [the last *spiritual* Adam]" (John 3:6).

I do not believe that this change occurs at the water baptism. The water baptism is a witness and testimony that one has acknowledged the sinful lawless state of the first Adam, of whom we are, and hence accepted the Messiah as the only Lord and Savior by whom to be saved (Acts 4:12), who sacrificed Himself to redeem us from that sinful state. Thereby we commit to follow Him by keeping the Creator's commandments of love henceforth, as He did to set an example for us. After the baptism and laying on of hands, God pours His Holy Spirit upon the heart, which helps to keep His commandments proper because of His **<agape>**[8] love, which He imparts to the repentant believer's heart: "... because the love of God is shed abroad in our hearts by the Holy Ghost [Spirit] which is given unto us" (Rom. 5:5). Being baptized into the Messiah symbolizes the first Adam being put to death and thus beginning a new walk of life after the Messiah, the last Adam: "Therefore we are **buried with him by baptism into death**: that like as Christ was raised up from the dead by the glory of the Father, even so **we also should walk in newness of life**" (Rom. 6:4). But we still remain mortal, which leaves us still able to sin: "**Let not sin therefore reign in your mortal body**, that ye should obey it in the lusts thereof" (Rom. 6:12).

The Messiah was born of the first Adam: "... Concerning his Son Jesus Christ our Lord, which was **made of the seed of David according to the flesh ...**" (Rom. 1:3). As a mortal being already having been baptized with the Holy Spirit abiding in Him (Matt. 3:13–17), Satan was still able to tempt Him to sin (Matt. 4:1–11; Luke 4:1–13). He rebuked Satan by strictly rehearsing

God's commandments from the Old Testament. Even though He was baptized and filled with the Holy Spirit (which symbolically resembles the death of the old Adam) and thus symbolically resurrected into the new Adam, He was still a mortal being, thus still capable of sinning. And He was tempted to the extreme (Heb. 4:15).

But His state of affairs changed dramatically after He was resurrected from a literal death and changed to a literal immortal Spirit being, after which Satan could no longer tempt Him, thus having gained victory over death: "So **when** this corruptible shall have put on incorruption, and this mortal shall have put on immortality [after being resurrected], **then** shall be brought to pass the saying that is written, **Death is swallowed up in victory**" (1 Cor. 15:54; read also Isa. 25:8—another Torah test proof). That victory was obtained by the literal resurrection from His literal death: "... And **declared to be the Son of God** with power, according to the spirit of holiness, **by the resurrection from the dead ...**" (Rom. 1:4). It's very obvious that no one will have immortality until after the literal resurrection from the literal death after the Messiah—the firstborn of all: "And he is the head of the body, the church: who is the beginning, **the firstborn from the dead**; that **in all things he might have the preeminence**" (Col. 1:18). People have been resurrected before the Messiah was resurrected, but to mortal life only—not to immortal life, of which the Messiah is the true Firstborn.

Point to Ponder: If a person is born again upon the water baptism, then all those who were baptized before the Messiah was baptized would have been born again before Him. He would then not be the *first* in all things, would He?

That which is immortal and incorruptible is spiritual and is thus no longer flesh and blood, wherefore it has literally overcome death and literally cannot die (Luke 20:36). That's how Paul explained it:

> Now this I say, brethren, that **flesh and blood cannot inherit the kingdom of God; neither doth corruption**

> **inherit incorruption**. Behold, I shew you a mystery; We shall not all sleep, but we shall all be changed, In a moment, in the twinkling of an eye, **at the last trump** [the seventh trumpet, Rev. 11:15; 12:10; 16:17–18]: for the trumpet shall sound, and **the dead shall be raised incorruptible**, and we [the Messiah's yet alive] shall be changed. For **this corruptible must put on incorruption**, and **this mortal must put on immortality. So when this corruptible shall have put on incorruption, and this mortal shall have put on immortality** [the resurrection]**, then** shall be brought to pass the saying that is written, Death is swallowed up in victory [no second death]. (1 Cor. 15:50–54; read also 1 Thess. 4:15–17)

The saved that have died will be resurrected to eternal life (raised to life again; born again). These events cannot occur until after the resurrections. The Messiah testified that He had been dead (Rev. 1:18). He became an immortal Spirit being through the resurrection from His literal death, not through the baptism. The scriptures make it clear that no one will have immortality until the Messiah returns to resurrect His followers to eternal life, after the last (the seventh) trumpet (Rev. 11:15). Until then, no man has immortality: "Who [the Messiah] **only** hath immortality ..." (1 Tim. 6:16).

Side Note: Paul explained the symbolic death and resurrection:

> And you hath he quickened, **who were dead in trespasses and sins** [before the baptism and the receipt of the Holy Spirit]; Wherein in time past ye walked according to the course of this world [after the commandments of men—Satan], according to the prince of the power of the air, the spirit that now worketh in the children of disobedience: Among whom also we all had our conversation in times past in the lusts of our flesh, fulfilling the desires of the flesh and of the mind; and were by nature the children of wrath, even as others. But God, who is rich in mercy, for

his great love wherewith he loved us, Even when we were dead in sins [walking as dead men], hath quickened us together with Christ [symbolically quickened the mortal man, (Rom. 8:11)], (by grace ye are saved;). (Eph. 2:1–5)

The Messiah made a statement that helps to clarify what Paul meant by his reference to those walking as dead men: "But Jesus said unto him, Follow me; and **let the dead bury their dead"** (Matt. 8:22; read also Luke 9:60). The disciples who were committed to follow Him were considered to be alive; they wanted eternal life, which their Messiah offered them. The one who wanted to go and bury his dead father was considered just as dead as his father, if he cared more about burying him than about following in close step with Him; because He had life to give. Paul explained how that dead state of man symbolically changes to a lively state when he described the baptism process: "Likewise reckon ye also yourselves to be dead indeed unto sin, but alive unto God through Jesus Christ our Lord" (Rom. 6:11; read also Rom. 7:14).

The Messiah explained to Nicodemus that one must be born into a Spiritual (immortal) state to enter God's Kingdom: "Jesus answered, Verily, verily, I say unto thee, Except a man be born of **water** [baptism] and of the **Spirit** [resurrection], he cannot enter into the kingdom of God. That which is born of the **flesh is flesh** [mortal; corruptible flesh]; and that which is born of the **Spirit is spirit** [resurrected to immortality]" (John 3:5–6).

As explained in 1 Corinthians chapter 15, only after the death of the first Adam can one be resurrected (born again) into the state of the last Adam, who has eternal life inherent. Just like our elder brother Messiah, after the resurrection one becomes an immortal, incorruptible Spirit being; no more death occurs (Rev. 21:4), because spirits can't die (Luke 20:35–36). The people become His spiritual children *after* the resurrection.

Note: Man will not have immortality until after the resurrection, which clearly occurs after the last trumpet is blown, which occurs after the Great Tribulation.

Conclusion: God did not give mankind a soul. After He made Adam, He breathed into his nostrils and Adam **became** a mortal living soul: "And the LORD God formed man of the dust of the ground, and breathed into his nostrils the breath of life; and man **became** a living **soul <nephesh>**[37]" (Gen. 2:7). Adam became a living soul/creature after God put the breath of life into him. When a living soul dies, the breath of life **<nephesh>**[37] departs and goes back to God, who gave it: "And it came to pass, as her **soul <nephesh>**[37] was in departing, (for she died) …" (Gen. 35:18). An air-breathing creation—man or beast—is a soul in scripture: "And out of the ground the LORD God formed every beast of the field, and every fowl of the air; and brought them unto Adam to see what he would call them: and whatsoever Adam called every living **creature <nephesh>**[37], that was the name thereof" (Gen. 2:19).

A creature which requires air to live is called a **<nephesh>**[37] in the Hebrew scripture, and in most of the KJV scriptures it is translated into English as "soul," or in some instances as "life," "person," "living creature," "beast," or "mortally": "But flesh with the **life <nephesh>**[37] thereof, which is the blood thereof, shall ye not eat. And surely your blood of your **lives <nephesh>**[37] will I require; at the hand of every **beast** will I require it, and at the hand of **man**; at the hand of every man's brother will I require the **life <nephesh>**[37] of man" (Gen. 9:4–5). In some instances the word "nephesh" is even translated as "dead": "Ye shall not make any cuttings in your flesh for the **dead <nephesh>**[37]" (Lev. 19:28; see also Lev. 21:1; Num. 5:2; 6:11; 9:6, 7, 10). With scriptures such as these at their disposal, I can't see how theologians can establish doctrines that teach that a mortal man has an immortal soul—meaning that the soul continues to live after death. But then again, the Holy Scriptures are not what the traditional preachers go by to establish their doctrines.

Since we don't possess an immortal soul, we'll have to wait until God gives us immortality, which He will when the Messiah returns to resurrect His followers into spiritual beings. Paul stated unmistakably in 1 Corinthians 15:50–54 that we will not obtain immortality until after the resurrection, after which death will be swallowed up—the second death, that is. Just as all must die at least once, the Messiah also had to die once, but He overcame the second death by His resurrection to immortal life as a forerunner and example for us as the firstborn (Rom. 8:29; Col. 1:15, 18) of God's firstfruits (1 Cor. 15:20, 23). And His true followers will go through the same process as He did (Rom. 8:23; 1 Cor. 16:15; James 1:18) to enter into God's kingdom by becoming virtually reborn into His family through a literal resurrection into a literal spirit being (Rom. 11:16; Rev. 14:4).

6c. The Two Adams

I will summarize an issue in hopes to shed some light on the subject of the two states of Adam of which Paul wrote in the resurrection chapter. Understanding the two Adams helps to provide some insight into what God is working out here on this earth today.

The first man was made in the image of God: "And God said, Let us make **man in our image, after our likeness**" (Gen. 1:26). Adam and Eve chose to obey Satan's commands rather than God's. Satan seduced them to believe that the tree of the knowledge of good and evil had immortality and that they did not need the nourishment from the tree of life to live forever:

> Now the serpent was more subtil than any beast of the field which the LORD God had made. And he said unto the woman, Yea, hath God said, Ye shall not eat of every tree of the garden? And the woman said unto the serpent, We may eat of the fruit of the trees of the garden: But of the fruit of the tree which is in the midst of the garden, God hath said, Ye shall not eat of it, neither shall ye touch it, **lest ye die**. And the serpent said unto the woman, **Ye shall <u>not</u> surely die.** (Gen. 3:1–4)

Sure enough, they didn't die immediately. But, using the one day for thousand years, they died in their first day. The tree of life contains God's truth, which is the only way to eternal life:

> I am the vine, ye are the branches: He that abideth in me, and I in him, the same bringeth forth much fruit: for without me ye can do nothing. (John 15:5)

> Jesus saith unto him, **I am the way, the truth, and the life: no man cometh unto the Father, but by me.** (John 14:6)

The Messiah truly is the tree of life, which Paul explicitly describes in Romans chapter 11.

Adam and Eve had the opportunity to take of the tree of life and live forever: "… lest he put forth his hand, and **take also of the tree of life**, and eat, **and live for ever**" (Gen. 3:22). But they sinned (… sin is the transgression of the law [1 John 3:4; read also Matt. 5:19; James 2:9–10]), which exacts the death penalty: "But of the tree of the knowledge of good and evil, thou shalt not eat of it: for in the day that thou eatest thereof **thou shalt surely die**" (Gen. 2:17; read also 3:3; Rom. 6:23; James 1:15). Thereby they rejected God, which caused Him to remove them from the garden, because if they had taken of the tree of life, they would have become Spirit beings and lived for ever in the sinful state in which they were. Then they would have been—as an immortal Spirit being that cannot die (Luke 20:35–36)—cursed for eternity, which is the state Satan the deceiver already was in at that time. So to prevent that from occurring to Adam and Eve (mankind), God chased them out of the garden and closed the gate (Gen. 3:22–24, cited below).

Since then God has been working out His plan to conform mankind back into His image through His Son and Messiah (Rom. 8:29). And it's still man's choice whether he will obey God, keep His commandments, and be conformed to His Son's image; or obey Satan (the god of this world) and perish. It is a choice between life and death; blessings and curses:

> See, I have set before thee this day **life and good**, and **death and evil**; In that I command thee this day to love the LORD thy God, to walk in his ways, and to **keep his commandments** and his statutes and his judgments, **that thou mayest live** and multiply: and the LORD thy God shall bless thee in the land whither thou goest to possess it. But **if thine heart turn away**, so that thou wilt not hear, but shalt be drawn away, **and worship other**

> **gods, and serve them**; I denounce unto you this day, that **ye shall surely perish**, and that ye shall not prolong your days upon the land, whither thou passest over Jordan to go to possess it. I call heaven and earth to record this day against you, that **I have set before you life and death, blessing and cursing: therefore choose life**, [Why?] **that both thou and thy seed may live.** (Deut. 30:15–19; read also 4:26; 11:26–28)

Obedience to the commandments of the creator God promises blessings and life! Obedience to the commandments of man's gods promises curses and death! Just like our parents of old Adam and Eve, we must choose—life or death!

Adam and Eve produced children: "This is the book of the generations of **Adam**. In the day that God created man, in the **likeness of God** made he him" (Gen. 5:1). Genesis chapter 5 reveals that, after Adam sinned, mankind's state of affairs changed. We are now born after the image and likeness of Adam: "And Adam lived an hundred and thirty years, and begat a son **in his own likeness, after his image**" (Gen. 5:3). Now we need to be reborn (conformed—Rom. 8:29) into the image and likeness of God, as Adam would have been if he had accepted the tree of life instead of the tree of the knowledge of good and evil. That process requires man to take nourishment only from the tree of life, which means every word of God (Deut. 8:3; Matt. 4:4; Luke 4:4). And God has preserved that way: "So he drove out the man; and he placed at the east of the garden of Eden Cherubims, and a flaming sword which turned every way, to **keep <shamar>**[38] [hem in; guard; protect; preserve] **the way of the tree of life**" (Gen. 3:24). He has done this for the people who choose to obey Him and keep His commandments: "Blessed are they that do **his** commandments, that they may have **right to the tree of life** [the garden of Eden—God's paradise], and may enter in through the gates into the city [the New Jerusalem (Rev. 21:2)]" (Rev. 22:14; read also verse 2; Ezekiel 47:12; Rev. 2:7). Thus it will have come full circle. Adam got removed from the garden of Eden for breaking God's commandments, and according to these scriptures, those who keep God's commandments will regain access to it.

The Messiah marveled that Nicodemus, who was a ruler and teacher of Israel (John 3:1, 10), didn't know that as an image and likeness of a mortal man (the first Adam), he was not fit for God's kingdom. As we saw in the previous section, to be able to enter into God's kingdom, he needed to be conformed into the image of God, the last spiritual Adam, which is the resurrected and hence spiritual Messiah (John 3:6). And to enter God's kingdom, we must first be changed from fleshly beings to spiritual beings, just like the Messiah now is (Rom. 1:3–4; 1 Cor. 15:50–53). The resurrection from the dead is the event that declared and confirmed the Messiah as the true firstborn Son of God (Rom. 1:3–4). And that's the purpose God is working out on this earth today. He's re-creating Himself in humans (Rom. 8:29) via a rebirth through the righteousness of His holy Son and Messiah—the last Adam.

So, according to scripture, we are now born of, and thus taking after, the image and likeness of what Paul refers to as the first Adam, who was destined to die for obeying Satan's commandments **<entalma>**[9a] instead of God's commandments **<entole>**[9] (Gen. 2:17). Therefore, as descendants of the first Adam we also must die:

> For all have sinned, and come short of the glory of God. (Rom. 3:23)

> For the **wages of sin is death**. (Rom. 6:23; read also Gen. 2:17)

> Then **when lust hath conceived, it bringeth forth sin: and sin, when it is finished, bringeth forth death.** (James 1:15)

> And as it is **appointed** unto men once to die, but after this the judgment. (Heb. 9:27)

Thus, God has purposed to *conform* His people into the image of His resurrected Son (Rom. 8:29); the life-giving Messiah, who overcame sin and death for us, through which He became the life-giving last Adam—a spiritual being: "And so it is written, The first man Adam was made a living **soul <psuche>**[59] [mortal, air-breathing man]; the last Adam was made a **quickening <zoopoieo>**[71] **spirit <pneuma>**[11] [the life-giving spiritual being]. Howbeit that was not first which is spiritual, but that which is natural [the first carnal man—Adam]; and afterward that which is spiritual [the resurrected spiritual being—the Messiah]" (1 Cor. 15:45–46; read 45–55). In Revelation chapters 2 and 3 the Messiah speaks specifically about overcoming this world's religious corruption, sin, by repenting of sins and turning back to His ways. And in chapter 18 He commands His people to sever from the Babylonian system by which we've been corrupted: "Come out of her, my people, that ye be not partakers of her sins, and that ye receive not of her plagues" (Rev. 18:4). Paul, who was constantly at loggerheads with that Babylonian system, also commands us to sever from it (2 Cor. 6:17).

This is very exciting news. God's people must come out of that Babylonian bondage to be liberated and adopted into His family. And that has been His plan for saving mankind from Satan's/man's bondage since the beginning, which He is revealing in the end time:

> Peter, an apostle of Jesus Christ, to the **strangers** scattered throughout Pontus, Galatia, Cappadocia, Asia, and Bithynia, Elect according to the foreknowledge of God the Father, through sanctification of the Spirit, unto obedience and sprinkling of the blood of Jesus Christ: Grace unto you, and peace, be multiplied. Blessed be the God and Father of our Lord Jesus Christ, which according to his abundant mercy hath begotten us again unto a lively hope by the resurrection of Jesus Christ from the dead, To an inheritance incorruptible, and undefiled, and that fadeth not away, reserved in heaven for you, Who are kept by the power of God through faith unto salvation ready to be revealed in the **last <eschatos>**[33] time. (1 Peter 1:1–5)

What an encouraging statement of hope.

7. PAUL KEEPING LAWS?

The apostle Peter gives us a fair warning about how people are twisting ambiguous scriptures to suit man's doctrines, even when their interpretation will contradict unambiguous scriptures:

> And account that the longsuffering of our Lord is salvation; even as our beloved brother Paul also according to the wisdom given unto him hath written unto you; As also in **all his epistles**, speaking in them of these things; in which are **some things hard to be understood**, which they that are unlearned and unstable **wrest, as they do also the other scriptures**, unto their own destruction. **Ye therefore, beloved, seeing ye know these things before, beware lest ye also, being led away with the error of the wicked**, fall from your own stedfastness. (2 Peter 3:15–17)

By twisting scriptures, the crafty man of such effort must also twist other scriptures in an effort to avoid some of the all-too-obvious contradictions as much as possible. But if we study the scriptures with an unbiased mind, bearing in mind that they cannot and will not contradict one another (John 10:35; 1 Cor. 14:33), then the scriptures can be understood. We should thank God for inspiring His scripture writers to give us such plain and valuable warnings. This scripture really opened my eyes and provoked me to deal with the scriptures that seemed to be controversial; thus I learned to allow them to harmonize with each other; which they do if we let them. (I cover this topic in section 4 of my first book, *The Commandments of God*).

After his conversion, Paul learned to love the true liberties of God's laws and commandments as revealed to Him by the

Messiah, instead of the burdens of the traditions of his fathers: "But I certify you, brethren, that the gospel which was preached of me is not after man. For I neither received it of man, neither was I taught it, but by the revelation of Jesus Christ. For ye have heard of my conversation in time past in the Jews' religion, how that beyond measure I persecuted the church of God, and wasted it: And profited in the Jews' religion above many my equals in mine own nation, being more exceedingly zealous of the traditions of my fathers" (Gal. 1:11–14; read also Phil. 3:1–6; Col. 2:8; Matt. 15:6–9; Mark 7:6–9). Peter and other apostles also gave similar testimonies: "Forasmuch as ye know that ye were not redeemed with corruptible things, as silver and gold, **from your vain conversation received by tradition from your fathers**" (1 Peter 1:18; Acts 4:19; 5:29).

Decades after the crucifixion, Luke recorded that Paul lived by and advocated the Torah, which the Messiah's followers considered as "walking orderly": "Them take, and purify thyself with them, and be at charges with them, that they may shave their heads: and all may know that those things, whereof they were informed concerning thee, **are nothing** [not true]; but that thou thyself also **walkest orderly, and keepest the law**" (Acts 21:24).

Paul testified the same of himself: "But this I confess unto thee, that **after the way which they call heresy, so worship I the God of my fathers, believing all things which are written in the law and in the prophets**" (Acts 24:14). The religious leaders labeled Paul as a heretic for following in the Messiah's steps. But he testified that he preached nothing that had not been prophesied of in the Old Testament - a very powerful Torah proof test: "Having therefore obtained help of God, I continue unto this day, witnessing both to small and great, **saying none other things than those which the prophets and Moses did say should come**" (Acts 26:22). He specifically testified what the Messiah came to fulfill at His First Coming: "That [1] **Christ should suffer**, and that he should be the first that should [2] **rise from the dead**, and should [3] **shew light unto the people**, [4] **and to the Gentiles**" (Acts 26:23; read also Deut. 18:15–18; 32:21; Isa. 9:2; 42:6; 49:6; 55:5; 60:1–3; Joel 2:28–29; Luke 2:32).

Paul mentioned four specific events that the Messiah had come to fulfill at His First Coming. He did that in order to prove to his accusers that he professed no changes to the laws and commandments of the Torah. Although the Pharisees were well aware of those prophecies, what he preached ran extremely contrary to their traditional doctrines for the same reason that they hated the Messiah—because the commandments of God that He kept did not align with their Judaized versions of them.

Paul's teachings did not contradict, but rather harmonized perfectly with, the Torah teaching and prophecies. The things he stated that the Messiah came to fulfill were all prophesied in the Old Testament, and they harmonize perfectly with what the Messiah Himself stated about His purpose for the First Coming: "And he said unto them, **These are the words which I spake unto you, while I was yet with you, that all things must be fulfilled, which were written in the law of Moses, and in the prophets, and in the psalms, concerning me**" (Luke 24:44; read also 18:31–34; 24:6–9; Matt. 17:22–23; John 5:46–47). Earlier on, He specified to His disciples which things He would shortly fulfill: "And he began to teach them, that the Son of man must suffer many things, and be rejected of the elders, and of the chief priests, and scribes, and be killed, and after three days rise again" (Mark 8:31; read also Matt. 16:21; 20:18–19; Luke 9:22).

Paul states very clearly that he taught only those things that Moses and the prophets had spoken of. Accordingly, he did not teach that any of God's laws and commandments had changed, because nowhere have any prophets said that God would abolish His commandments, but that they are God's love, wherefore they are eternal; as the Messiah Himself vividly testified: "**Think not that I am come to destroy the law**, or the prophets: I am not come to destroy, but to fulfil. For verily I say unto you, **Till heaven and earth pass, one jot or one tittle shall in no wise pass from the law**, till all be fulfilled. Whosoever therefore shall break one of these least commandments, and shall teach men so, he shall be called the least in the kingdom of heaven: but whosoever shall do and teach them, the same shall be called great in the kingdom of heaven" (Matt. 5:17–19). This unambiguous scripture clearly speaks for itself. And it goes further, to say that even after the heavens and earth have passed, God's words, which incidentally include the Ten Commandments, will remain eternal: "Heaven and earth shall pass away, but **my words** [including the Ten Commandments] **shall not pass away**" (Matt. 24:35). These are very powerful and solid testimonies that confirm the test prophecies of the Torah.

Nowhere in his epistles did Paul state that the crucifixion and the resurrection of the Messiah did away with any of God's laws or commandments. He explained that the Messiah, as the true and unblemished Lamb of God, out of His Godly <**agape**>[8] love for us, willingly sacrificed Himself for us (Gal. 1:4; John 10:18; 1 John 1:9), wherefore the animal sacrifices and rituals are no longer required. As he stated in Acts 26:22, like God's prophets of old prophesied things to come, the Messiah fulfilled that part of the prophecies when He, as the Lamb of God became our Passover (1 Cor. 5:7; Eph. 2:15; Heb. chapters 9–10). Peter also confirmed it: "But those things, **which God before had shewed by the mouth of all his prophets, that Christ should suffer, he hath so fulfilled**" (Acts 3:18). The Israelites knew from the laws of old that the Messiah would come to die for the sins of mankind: "And one of them, named Caiaphas, being the high priest that same year, said unto them, Ye know nothing at all, Nor consider that it is expedient for us, that **one man should die for the people, and that the whole nation perish not. And this spake he not of himself**: but being high priest that year, **he prophesied that Jesus should die for that nation**; And not for that nation only, but that **also he should gather together in one the children of God that were scattered abroad**" (John 11:49–52; read also 12:34; Isa. 53; Ps. 22; Isa. 49:6; 50:6). These same prophecies are what Paul referred to in Acts 26:22 as Torah test proofs.

The Jews knew that a Redeemer was promised to come and suffer for them. Since the professing Messiah came and fulfilled that prophecy without changing a jot or tittle of God's commandments and laws—which was in complete harmony with the Torah test prophecy—the true believers among them acknowledged and accepted Him as the Redeemer of Israel, because what He did aligned perfectly with what God had promised throughout the Old Testament Torah scriptures: "For I delivered unto you first of all that which I also received, how that **Christ died for our sins according to the scriptures; And that he was buried, and that he rose again the third day according to the scriptures"** (1 Cor. 15:3–4; read also Jonah 1:17; Matt. 12:40; John 2:17–22; 12:16–17; Luke 24: 6–8). These fulfilled prophecies were proof that He was the promised Messiah of the Torah prophecies, which thus encouraged them to steer away from the traditions of their fathers and turn to keeping God's commandments, which—as the Messiah forewarned them of—got them killed by the religious rulers of their day.

Paul preached about faith in the Messiah and the coming kingdom of God from the Torah: "he expounded and testified the **kingdom of God**, persuading them **concerning Jesus**, both out of the **law of Moses, and out of the prophets**" (Acts 28:23, read to verse 31). He tells Timothy to hang on to and build upon the things he had learned from the Torah in his childhood: "But **continue thou in the things which thou hast learned and hast been assured of**, knowing of whom thou hast learned them; And that **from a child** thou hast known the holy scriptures, which are able to make thee wise unto salvation **through faith** which is in Christ Jesus. **All scripture is given by inspiration of God**, and is profitable for doctrine, for reproof, for correction, for instruction in righteousness: That the man of God may be perfect, thoroughly furnished unto all good works" (2 Tim. 3:14–17).

In Timothy's childhood, he was taught about salvation through faith in the Messiah—the typical grace teaching from the Torah. When Timothy was a child, there were no New Testament scriptures. Why didn't Paul tell Timothy to make sure that he would discard at all cost what he had been taught from the Old Testament and hang on to what traditional Christianity calls the new commandment-free doctrines of faith and grace if he wanted to be saved? Contrariwise, Paul instructs Timothy to hang on to what he had been taught from the Torah for his faith in the salvation of the Messiah because the works of the Messiah were an assurance that He was the true Messiah of whom the Old Testament scriptures—with which Timothy was familiar—had prophesied. I constantly hear traditional Christians proclaim that Paul preached *against* the Torah! They say that Paul preached that God's laws and commandments were nailed to the tree with the Messiah, wherefore we are condemned for trying to keep them. Paul supposedly preached that the New Testament church should not be using that old and burdensome Jewish Bible, as they have labeled it. That's preposterous, because Paul knew that God's Word had not changed by one jot or tittle, and he preached from it concerning the Messiah and the coming kingdom of God. Paul instructed Timothy to hang on to what he had learned about salvation from the Old Testament scriptures, because now it had been revealed through those Torah prophecies that this was the true Messiah.

The New Testament writers worked off of the Torah scrolls (Old Testament scriptures) and compared the Gospels with them, as Paul encouraged others to do (1 Thess. 5:21). And the Bereans did just that: "These were more noble than those in Thessalonica, in that they received the word with all readiness of mind, and **searched the scriptures daily, whether those things were so"** (Acts 17:11). They compared what they heard from the apostles of the New Testament church, who were labeled as heretics, against the Old Testament scriptures, as we are commanded by God to do (Deut. 12:28–13:5—the Torah test). If any of the apostles' doctrines had not perfectly harmonized with the Old Testament scriptures, the Bereans would rightfully have been required to reject them, and flee from them. And if Paul himself had not diligently studied *and believed* the teachings and prophecies of the Torah, he himself could not have known that the Messiah was the true Lamb of God Passover.

Since the Messiah did not change a jot or tittle of God's laws, Paul knew with absolute certainty that this professing Messiah, without a shadow of a doubt, was the Passover Lamb of God of whom the Old Testament scriptures had prophesied and written. As he stated in Acts 26:22–23, he taught only what God had prophesied throughout the Torah. None of God's prophets ever hinted with even a single word that the God of Abraham, Isaac, and Jacob—namely the God of Israel—would destroy one jot or tittle of His commandments. And since the Messiah specifically testified to that by living it, Paul knew that He was the promised Messiah. The Messiah surely confirmed the Torah test of all time!

> Paul has only good words for God's commandments and laws:
>
> Circumcision [Jew] is nothing, and uncircumcision [Gentile] is nothing, but the **keeping of the commandments of God.** (1 Cor. 7:19)
>
> For not the hearers of the law are just before God, but the **doers of the law shall be justified.** (Rom. 2:13)
>
> Wherefore the **law is holy**, and the **commandment holy**, and **just**, and **good.** (Rom. 7:12)

Paul never gave any hint that God's commandments were abolished, or weakened by any degree. His struggle with the people—Jews, Israelites, and Gentiles—that he preached to was to get them to understand and believe that animal sacrifices and ritualistic works of laws could not justify a man from his sins, let alone reconcile one to God (Heb. 10:4, 11). Only faith in the Messiah's sacrifice can justify one from past sins (Romans 3:25). And this has always been the only way that God justified a man—through faith in Him, by His mercy and grace. It never was any other way. Paul said that faith does not do away with God's laws, but rather that it reinforces, upholds, strengthens, and establishes the continuance of them: "Do we then make void the law through faith? God forbid: yea, **we establish <histemi>**[72] **the law**" (Rom. 3:31). The manifestation of the Messiah—who proved without a shadow of doubt to be the true One of the prophecies—helped them to faithfully confirm and establish the verity of God's laws.

Paul preached that the faith of the Messiah is extended to everyone who believes in His sacrifice and claims the promises of faithful Abraham: "For ye are all the children of God **by faith in Christ Jesus**. For as many of you as have been baptized into Christ have put on Christ. There is neither Jew nor Greek [circumcised nor uncircumcised], there is neither bond nor free, there is neither male nor female: for ye are all one in Christ Jesus. And if ye be Christ's, then are ye Abraham's seed, and **heirs according to the promise**" (Gal. 3:26–29). Abraham kept God's commandments (Gen. 26:4–5). Did that nullify his faith in God, thereby causing him to reject and lose God's grace? No! It pleased God, thereby strengthening His relationship with God, thus increasing His grace. Just like today's traditional Christians, the Israelites—through pagan practices—forsook God's commandments, whereby their faith was focused on traditional pagan gods, thus meaning that they were worshipping God in vain (2 Kings 17; Matt. 15; Mark 7; Rom. 9:32; Heb. 4:2). Those are the same traditions that Paul had advocated earlier in his life and had thus severed from upon his conversion (Gal. 1:13–14; Col. 2:8; 1 Peter 1:18).

The religion of the Pharisees did not come from God or Moses. It was invented by the Rabbis and Pharisees, and is called the Talmud, which is the religion of putting the oral commandments <**entalma**>[9a] of men above the written commandments <**entole**>[9] of God. Paul referred to those doctrines as "the traditions of their fathers" because they came from the fathers who followed after Satan the devil—the Babylonian gods of this world (2 Cor. 3:14 to 4:4) —, as confirmed by the Messiah Himself:

> **Ye are of your father the devil, and the lusts of your father ye will do.** He was a murderer from the beginning, and abode not in the truth, because there is no truth in him. When he speaketh a lie, he speaketh of his own: for he is a liar, and the father of it. And **because I tell you the truth, ye believe me not.** Which of you convinceth me of sin? And if I say the truth, why do ye not believe me? **He that is of God heareth God's words** [Torah test]**: ye therefore hear them not, because ye are not of God.** (John 8:44–47)

That really sums up the fact that traditional doctrines come from Baal and that serving him hides the truth from man, thus making man veiled, or blinded. Paul knew exactly what that talmudic religion was all about, because he used to be a highly respected minister and an extremely aggressive and murderous advocator of it.

As we touched on slightly before, the works that Paul refers to are the traditional doctrines of the Pharisees, which they had mixed with Gnosticism; witchcraft; asceticism; works of penance; animal sacrifices and rituals of the heathen people of Colossi, Galatia, and Corinth; and many other Babylonian pagan philosophies from heathen and pagan nations. And they mixed all those demon-driven/anti-God pagan philosophies with the animal sacrifices, carnal rituals and ordinances, circumcision, and so on (the works of the law) from the old covenant, to be justified by them; however, these things never have justified a man from sin, nor will they ever (Heb. 4:3–4, 11). And they syncretized those philosophies with God's laws and elevated them all together to a status higher than that of the Ten Commandments, through their traditional church system, and preached them as God's divine commandments—a philosophy that the Messiah strictly condemned straight to their face (Matt. 15 and 23; Mark 7).

Traditional preachers teach that in the days of old the people *earned* their salvation by doing those works of the laws but that now we are saved by grace, and grace alone. And they teach that the keeping of the Ten Commandments is the works of the laws. That philosophy was invented in an effort to make it say that by practicing the Ten Commandments you automatically reject the faith of the Messiah and God's grace by trying to earn your salvation by works. But, contrariwise, a study of God's laws vividly reveals that His mercy and grace have always existed, whereby He always has forgiven every sin ever committed by any man who had faith in Him, and Him alone, and repented of his lawlessness. That means one must turn away from religious commandments, turn and follow God's commandments.

God *is* the law, upon which the Ten Commandments are designed. When kept, those commandments produce love, mercy, and grace in His children. That is the <**agape**>[8] love of God, through which He extends to us His grace to forgive our transgressions. The Torah explicitly teaches about how God's mercy never fails. He always has been merciful, and He still is today (Heb. 13:8). This is not something that began after the crucifixion and resurrection of the Messiah. Keeping God's commandments produces the <**agape**>[8] love that is required to love God and neighbor as the Messiah did. The Messiah was able to sacrifice His life for us commandment-breakers because of the <**agape**>[8] love that He acquired by keeping God's commandments. And now, with His Holy Spirit available to us, God sheds His <**agape**>[8] love unto our hearts, whereby we can also keep His commandments so that we can learn to have the <**agape**>[8] love required to love Him and our neighbor from the heart, just as the Messiah set as an example and commands us to imitate:

> This is my commandment, That ye love one another, as I have loved you. Greater **love** <**agape**>[8] hath no man than this, that a man lay down his life for his friends. (John 15:12–13)

> Hereby perceive we the **love** <**agape**>[8] of God, because he laid down his life for us: and we ought to lay down our lives for the brethren. (1 John 3:16)

Side Note: Martin Luther took the liberty to add, delete, and manipulate words in the scriptures while he was translating them into German. He did this in numerous areas in order to suit his Roman Catholic–inspired anti-Jew beliefs. Although he severed from the papacy, his heart remained indoctrinated with the main traditional Babylonian doctrines of the Catholic system to his very end. His strong support for the anti-commandment philosophy that he preached because of his extreme hatred for the Jews is a very strong example.

In the book of Romans he added the word "*allein*" (alone):

Therefore we conclude that a man is justified by faith without the **deeds <ergon>**[27] of the **law <nomos>**[22]. (Rom. 3:28, KJV)

So halten wir nun dafür, daß der Mensch gerecht werde ohne des **Gesetzes <nomos>**[22] **Werke <ergon>**[27], **allein** durch den Glauben. (Römer 3:28, LGB).

In Acts 12:4 Luther translated *Passover* **<pascha>**[74] as *Easter*, as the KJV translaters also did. Luther translated *Passover* as *Ostern* (Easter) fifteen times in the New Testament. It's understandable that he did that in order to support the pagan Easter tradition with which he was indocrinated by the Roman Catholic clergy of his past of which he never did let go; because of the extreme ant-Jew philosophy which he still had in common with them. Since the Jews were still observing the Passover, Luther made absolutely certain that his doctrines would have *nothing* in common with the Jews—in honor of Constantine the Great. So hanging on to the pagan holidays took care of that problem. He abrogated God's holy day Feasts by labeling them as *fulfilled* and *Jewish*—wherefore he had no use, and saw no need for the book of Revelation—it speaks of many things yet to be fulfilled which are depicted by the observance of the Feast days.

With Sunday and pagan holiday worship so deeply ingrained in Luther by the Catholic system from which he separated, his hatred for the obligation to keep God's commandments—which he also considered as Jewish *works*—explains why he labeled James's epistle a *Book of Straw* in one of his earlier prefaces to the Scriptures while he was translating it into German. James believed and appreciated the example where God used our faithful father Abraham to prove what true, honest, and unwavering faith is. James knew and believed that our faith, just like Abraham's, was also being tested: "Ye see then how that **by works a man is justified**, and **not by faith only**. Likewise also was not Rahab the harlot **justified by works**, when she had received the messengers, and had sent them out another way? For **as the body without the spirit is dead, so faith without works is dead also**" (James 2:24–26). Abraham believed **<'aman>**[73]

(trusted; had faith) in God (Gen. 15:6; 22:9–12; Rom. 4:3; Gal. 3:6; Heb. 11:17). If Abraham had merely professed *alone* that he would sacrifice Isaac yet had not actually done any works—such as climbing up the mountain with Isaac and the firewood, building an altar upon which he bound up Isaac, and finally drawing his knife for to slay him—would God have counted his faith for righteousness as He did? God inspired James to write these words for our admonition and instructions to encourage us to carry on in the faith of Abraham, whose promises we desire.

As James quoted, the same principle applies to Rahab (Josh. 2–6; Heb. 11:31). Like Abraham, she did the literal *works* required to prove and satisfy God's calling; and that's what pleased God. And Paul—who according to traditionalists condemned the keeping of commandments—agrees with James:

For **not the hearers** of the law are just before God, **but the doers of the law shall be justified.** (Rom. 2:13)

But be ye **doers of the word**, and **not hearers only, deceiving** your own selves. (James 1:22; read also Matt. 7:21; Luke 6:46)

But this people who knoweth not the law are cursed. (John 7:49)

That was cited directly from the Torah:

Cursed be he that confirmeth not all the words of this law to do them. (Deut. 27:26)

Was God confused when he had His apostles pen these scriptures? You judge that for yourself (1 Cor. 14:33).

Point to Ponder—Faith and Works: If a man has total faith in GMC/Chevrolet, he will typically drive a GMC vehicle because he believes and trusts in that product. If his faith is in Ford, he will drive a Ford vehicle, because he has faith in it. The Messiah and His apostles had total faith in the God of Abraham, wherefore they trusted in and kept and lived by His commandments, even unto death. The Muslim people have total faith in Muhammad, wherefore they trust and obey his laws, also unto death. Traditional Christians profess to have total faith in the God of Abraham, but they totally reject His commandments and laws. And that's a similar argument that the Messiah had

> with the ever-so-proud Pharisees, who also professed to have faith in the God of Abraham but totally rejected His commandments by the use of their traditions (Matthew chapters 15 and 23, Mark chapter 7; John chapters 5—10). So the Messiah is asking the professing followers of Him, "And why call ye me, Lord, Lord, and do not the things which I say?" (Luke 6:46).

After conversion, Paul spent most of his time trying to get the point across, contrary as it was to Judaism *and* to Heathenism, that man never was justified by any other means than through faith in the eternal God of Abraham: "Be it known unto you therefore, men and brethren, that through this man [God/Messiah] is preached unto you the forgiveness of sins: And by him **all that believe** [having faith] **are justified** from all things, from which ye could **not be justified by the law <nomos>**[22] **of Moses**" (Acts 13:38–39). It's the exact opposite of what the traditional church teaches, where it is preached—based on Paul's commands, they say—that we *used* to have sins forgiven by the works of the law (in which they include the Ten Commandments) but now we have faith to be justified by, without needing to be obedient to God's commandments. They claim that we reject God's grace by obeying His commandments. How ironic! As we can see in the above scripture, and in other scriptures, the works of the law never did justify us from sin. Thus, that traditional philosophy has created an obvious contradiction between the teaching of the creator God of the Old Testament and that of the Messiah of the New Testament; hence, an anti-God messiah has been borne.

All blood will be required by God (Gen. 4:10–11; 9:4–6), wherefore He designed the animal sacrificial system as a reminder of sins, in order to establish their faith in the need of a Redeemer who was promised to come and shed His blood and give His life a ransom for the penalty for their sins, thus overcoming death (1 Cor. 15:22–25, 50–58), which is that penalty (Gen. 2:17; Rom. 6:23; James 1:15). God did not design the animal sacrifices and rituals to take away sins: "But in those sacrifices there is a **remembrance** again made of sins every year. For **it is not possible that the blood of bulls and of goats should take away sins ...** And every priest standeth daily ministering and offering oftentimes the same sacrifices, **which can never take away sins**" (Heb. 10:3–4, 11). In all of his epistles, particularly in the book of Galatians—which parallels with Romans—Paul explains that sins *cannot* be forgiven by *any* works or deeds of *any* laws, and that it **never** was that way. He plainly states that justification had **always** come only through **faith**, and not by the animal sacrificial laws. Paul goes on to prove that very point: "But that no man is justified by the **law <nomos>**[22] in the sight of God, it is evident: for, **The just shall live by faith**. And the law is not of faith: but, The man that doeth them shall live in them." (Gal. 3:11–12). Contrary to mainstream traditional doctrine, that is not something that changed at the stake. A couple of decades after it had supposedly changed, Paul cited that directly from the Old Testament:

> Behold, his soul which is lifted up is not upright in him: but **the just shall live by his faith.** (Hab. 2:4)

> Ye shall therefore keep my statutes, and my judgments: which if a man do, he shall live in them: **I** am the LORD. (Lev. 18:5)

Faith in God has been a requirement since the beginning. But just like our parents of old, Adam and Eve, man is still misappropriating faith in God's grace as a license to obey Satan rather than God, without expecting any consequences.

The animal sacrificial laws served their purpose. They reminded the people of their sins and built up their faith in the urgent need of a Redeemer who would be able to take away the penalty of their sins (Rom. 3:25), thus reconciling them to God (Rom. 5:10). And such a Redeemer was promised (Gen. 3:15; 49:10; Isa. 7:14; 8:8; 9:6; chapter 53). And the animal sacrificial and ritualistic laws delivered them all guilty before God (Rom

3:23; Gal. 3:22), thus taking them to the promised Messiah, who replaced and superseded the animal sacrifices and rituals:

> Wherefore then serveth the **law <nomos>**[22] [animal sacrifices and rituals]? It was added because of transgressions [breaking the Ten Commandments], till the seed should come to whom the promise was made. (Gal. 3:19)

> Wherefore the **law <nomos>**[22] [animal sacrifices and rituals] was our schoolmaster to bring us unto Christ, that we might be justified by faith. (Gal. 3:24)

Traditional preachers, indoctrinated by their god Satan, bind the words "law" **<nomos>**[22], "traditional commandment" **<entalma>**[9a], and "God's commandment" **<entole>**[9] together as relating directly to the Ten Commandments. Hence, that interpretation portrays the meaning that the laws **<nomos>**[22] Paul states we are no longer under (Rom. 6:14), by which he clearly refers to the animal sacrificial laws and rituals that were superseded by the Messiah's sacrifice, are the Ten Commandments. Whenever they read any words or phrases in the scriptures that refer to Judaism, traditions of the fathers and elders, traditional doctrines and commandments, laws, ordinances, works of laws, weak and beggarly elements of the world, and the like, they systematically—without fail—apply them directly to the Ten Commandments and label them as such. Satan's reasoning behind this philosophy is not all that complicated; I'll try to explain it.

The traditional church system, which increased in numbers and influence after the reign of Constantine the Great, is extremely anti-Jew, anti-Law, and anti-commandment; hence it is anti-God, because they will not have anyone—including the God of the Old Testament—tell them what to do and how to do it. That philosophy summons a dire need for the Ten Commandments to go away, because God is not tolerant or not flexible enough. God condemns traditional doctrines because they systematically forsake His commandments. So by portraying the Ten Commandments as being the laws we are no longer under (law <**nomos**>[22] [animal sacrifices and rituals]) and divinely teaching them as such, a need is born to divinely teach that if you keep the laws of God, you reject His grace. Thus a need is developed to indoctrinate traditional Christians to avoid keeping God's laws at all cost. And that's what gives them the audacity to preach that Paul, a true man of God who joyfully observed His commandments, condemned the keeping of the Ten Commandments.

To help understand the content of the laws <**nomos**>[22] Paul is referring to, I'll cite Galatians 3:19 first as it is. Next I'll write it out in the way the traditional anti-Law ministry *needs* it to be portrayed, in that it will suppose to make the Ten Commandments go away by a command of God through Paul. Then I'll paraphrase it to help express what Paul really meant for it to read, which will not contradict any other scriptures in the entire book of scriptures. I'll let it speak for itself, and it will—as it always should—meet the needed criteria of the Torah test: "Wherefore then serveth the law? It was added because of transgressions, till the seed should come to whom the promise was made" (Gal. 3:19).

In the traditional Christian vernacular—where law-done-away doctrines are established upon the reasoning that the word "law" in Galatians 3:19 relates directly to the Ten Commandments—it would read something like this: "What is then the purpose of the **Ten Commandments**? They were added because the Israelites kept transgressing them (the Ten Commandments) to bring them unto the faith of the promised Messiah!"

That's what it would read if Paul had meant for the word "law" <**nomos**>[22] to refer to the Ten Commandments <**entole**>[9] in this application. Doesn't make any sense, does it? A transgression is the violation of a principle of the Ten Commandments. So, in essence, Paul would be saying that since the people kept violating the Ten Commandments, God went and added the Ten Commandments. But such is the rendering of it by traditional anti-Law theology.

An easy-to-understand rendering in a noncontradictory, scriptural modern-day vernacular could read something like this: "Because of the Israelites' transgressing of the Ten **Commandments <entole>**[9]—for which they needed forgiveness, and since forgiveness of sins requires blood—God added the **animal** sacrifice and ritual **laws <nomos>**[22] to bring them unto the faith of the future sacrifice of the promised Messiah.

Thus the animal sacrificial and ritualistic laws **<nomos>**[22] constantly reminded them of their sinning (commandment-breaking), for the sole purpose of establishing their faith in the need of a redeemer who would forgive their sins, thus paying their debt by purchasing their death penalty with His innocent blood. That in no way voids the need to obey the Ten Commandments, which were violated in the first place because of unfaithfulness to the God who ordained them.

It's important to bear in mind that the Messiah was crucified because He did not keep God's commandments in accordance with the Judaized/talmudic version of them, wherefore—in accordance with the Torah test commandment—they felt compelled by God to kill Him. Thus, the Messiah's obedience to God's commandments constantly ran at loggerheads with the laws of the Pharisees (and the Romans), and it did get Him crucified for heresy. His early followers—the disciples and apostles—also got executed for the same reason: for obeying God's laws instead of the religious laws of the Pharisees and the Romans:

> Then went the captain with the officers, and brought them without violence: for **they feared the people, lest they should have been stoned**. And when they had brought them, they set them before the council: and **the high priest asked them, Saying, Did not we straitly command you that ye should not teach in this** [the Messiah's] **name?** and, behold, **ye have filled Jerusalem with your** [virtually the Messiah's] **doctrine, and intend to bring this man's blood upon us.** Then Peter and the other apostles answered and said, **We ought to obey God rather than men**. The God of our fathers raised up Jesus, whom ye slew and hanged on a tree. Him hath God exalted with his right hand to be a Prince and a Saviour,

> for to give repentance to Israel, and forgiveness of sins. And **we are his witnesses of these things; and so is also the Holy Ghost** [Spirit]**, whom God hath given to them that obey him**. When they heard that, they were cut to the heart, and **took counsel to slay them.** (Acts 5:26–33; read also 4:19)

This sobering testimony goes to show how big a threat the commandment-keeping Messiah and His followers were to the religious leaders and rulers of that day. And that has not gotten any better in today's traditional religious society, where it's acceptable—and advocated—to keep all pagan customs and traditions, but keeping the Ten Commandments of the God of Abraham is a violent threat. That's much to Jewish! They can't have anything in common with the Jews.

Acts chapters 3 through 7 lays out how the religious rulers and leaders of that day viciously despised the disciples and apostles who were teaching and healing people in the name of the true Messiah. They particularly excoriated and persecuted the apostles for healing by miracles in the Messiah's name. Those people, who were afflicted with all sorts of sicknesses and demon possession, were healed for real—without doctors or prescriptions, with no money or insurance required. That was absolutely unacceptable to the Pharisees and Sadducees, who were controlling the religious people of the day. Their witchcraft profits were now likely in jeopardy, as is acknowledged in Acts 19:23–35.

Acts chapter 8 reveals that Saul gave the orders to have followers of the Messiah persecuted unto death:

> And **Saul** [later called Paul] **was consenting unto his** [Stephen's] **death**. And at that time there was a **great persecution against the church** which was at Jerusalem; and they were all scattered abroad throughout the regions of Judaea and Samaria, except the apostles. And devout men carried Stephen to his burial, and made great lamentation over him. **As for Saul, he made havock of the church, entering into <u>every</u> house, and haling men**

> **and women committed them to prison**. Therefore they that were scattered abroad went every where preaching the word. (Acts 8:1–4)
>
> And Saul, yet **breathing out threatenings and slaughter against the disciples of the Lord, went unto the high priest** [his demon-inspired boss, whom he pleased]. (Acts 9:1; read also John 8:44)

After the stoning of Stephen, while Saul was on his way to Damascus to continue the persecution and slaughter of the Messiah's followers, the Messiah confronted him (Acts 9:3–6). That's when he became converted, and shortly after that his name was changed to Paul. Now that Paul believed in the Messiah, his former gangster members started hunting him down for to kill him for heresy. And that hunt went on for a couple of decades, until they eventually did kill him for following the commandments of God instead of the commandments of men (the Talmud, in this case)—the same reason he had slaughtered many people.

Paul testified to the people at Galatia how he had persecuted the Messiah's followers in the past before his conversion, in the name of tradition: "For ye have heard of my conversation in time past in the **<u>Jews' religion</u>, how that beyond measure I persecuted the church of God, and wasted it: And profited in the <u>Jews' religion</u>** above many my equals in mine own nation, **being more exceedingly zealous of the <u>traditions of my fathers</u>**" (Gal. 1:13–14). His fathers were of the traditional Pharisees, whom the Messiah excoriated for the use of their traditions as doctrines: "But when Paul perceived that the one part were Sadducees, and the other Pharisees, he cried out in the council, Men and brethren, **I am a Pharisee, the son of a Pharisee**: of the hope and resurrection of the dead I am called in question" (Acts 23:6; read also Matt. 15:6–9, chapter 23; Mark 7:6–9, 13; Phil. 3:5). He was of the strictest sect of Pharisees: "Which knew me from the beginning, if they would testify, that **after the most <u>straitest</u> sect of our religion I lived a Pharisee**" (Acts 26:5).

Paul's testimonies clearly show that the religion of the Jews (Judaism), the Pharisees, and the Sadducees, as well as the traditions of the fathers and elders, and so on, are all traditional commandments **<entalma>**[9a] of men, and as such are all condemned by the creator God. They are not in any shape or form commandments of Moses, or of God, but rather of men. Paul made sure that we wouldn't mistake the traditions of men with the commandments of Moses or God: "But I certify you, brethren, that the gospel which was preached of me is **not after man** [not from tradition]. For I **neither received it of man, neither was I taught it** [not from seminary], **but by the revelation of Jesus Christ**" (Gal. 1:11–12). Paul received his training straight from the non-evolutionary creator God / Messiah Himself.

A time is prophesied to come when those who keep God's commandments will again be persecuted, and in many cases executed, by the religious people of the day. Those who keep God's commandments today are already labeled as heretics by traditional Christendom for not following the customs and traditions of their church. They despise commandment keepers for the same reason the Pharisees did—for keeping God's commandments instead of theirs, which is just a reformed talmudic style of the Babylonian/Roman Catholic system. I believe that if it wasn't for the traditional Christians' fear of—and high regard for—the enforcers of the civil laws, commandment-keepers would already get persecuted and possibly executed. Given the evangelistic zeal that the traditional Christians have for their god, they would also be doing it to please their god. Yes, Satan must be really enthralled at how effective and efficient his traditional church system has actually become at fulfilling his wicked and evil scheme.

Sin brings about the curse of the law, which exacts the death penalty for violating God's commandments, from which the animal sacrificial laws (works of the law) cannot free us: "Christ hath redeemed us from the curse of the **law <nomos>**[22], being made a curse for us: for it is written, Cursed is every one that hangeth on a tree" (Gal. 3:13; read also Deut. 21:23). The Messiah redeemed us from that curse, not from the law. Forgiveness of sin through faith in His sacrifice is the liberty wherewith He set us free from that curse. He overcame death (the curse) for us by the resurrection (1 Cor. 15:54–57) after He exchanged His life for our death sentence (Rom. 8:2).

That doesn't mean that God didn't forgive sins before the crucifixion, because He did. How? Just like the example we briefly went over in section 4, the account of Zacharias and Elizabeth. They had faith in God as their only Healer, Redeemer, and Savior. By God's grace through their faith in the promised Messiah yet to come, who would take away the penalty of their sins, He forgave their sins. They looked forward to the Messiah in faith (Hebrews chapter 11), while we look back on it in faith. And as we will see in the following verses, they that had faith in God, believed in His promises, and repented of their transgressions had their sins forgiven by Him, and even their land was healed. People like David, Noah, Abel, Abraham, Zacharias and Elizabeth, and many others—all those who obeyed God's commandments and laws and believed in His promises because of their total faith in Him—were forgiven through their faith by His grace. Paul confirmed the principle of that matter: "Knowing that a man is not justified by the **works <ergon>**[27] of the **law <nomos>**[22], but by the **faith** of Jesus Christ" (Gal. 2:16). Paul cited this from the Old Testament (Hab. 2:4). God's mercy and grace forgave them when they faithfully and humbly came before Him and repented of their commandment-breaking:

> If my people, which are **called by my name**, shall **humble** themselves, and **pray**, and **seek my face**, and **turn from their wicked ways** [repenting]; then will I hear from heaven, **and will forgive their sin, and will heal their land.** (2 Chron. 7:14)

> But **ye that did cleave unto the LORD your God are alive** every one of you this day. (Deut. 4:4)

This doesn't bode well with the traditional preachers, who profess that people used to have their sins forgiven by works of law, wherewith they've labeled the Ten Commandments.

God is the same yesterday, today, and forever (Heb. 13:8). He has always had mercy and grace to forgive sins, for which there are many examples in scripture: Abel, Enoch, Elijah, Noah, Abraham, Isaac, Jacob, Moses, and many more patriarchs of ancient. The whole Torah teaching is all about God's mercy and grace toward repentant people. And God does not change (Mal. 3:6; Heb. 13:8; James 1:17). The message about God's mercy and grace is not something new that began in the New Testament; rather, it is continued in it:

> Take heed to yourselves: If thy brother trespass against thee, rebuke him; and **if he repent, forgive him**. And if he trespass against thee seven times in a day, and seven times in a day turn again to thee, saying, I repent; thou shalt forgive him. (Luke 17:3–4; read also Luke 13:3, 5)
>
> Repent ye therefore, and be converted, that your sins may be blotted out, when the times of refreshing shall come from the presence of the Lord. (Acts 3:19; read also Acts 2:38; 8:22; Rev. 2:5; 3:19)
>
> We are encouraged to come before God to have our sins forgiven:
>
> If we confess our sins, he is faithful and just to forgive us our sins, and to cleanse us from all unrighteousness. (1 John 1:9)
>
> Again, this teaching comes from the Old Testament:
>
> Have mercy upon me, O God, according to thy lovingkindness: **according unto the multitude of thy tender mercies blot out my transgressions. Wash me** throughly from mine iniquity, and **cleanse me** from my sin (Ps. 51:1–2).
>
> I acknowledged my sin unto thee, and mine iniquity have I not hid. I said, **I will confess my transgressions unto**

> **the LORD; and thou forgavest the iniquity of my sin** Selah. (Ps. 32:5)

David's sins were forgiven according to God's mercy after he openly confessed them before his Creator, whose commandments he had transgressed. He had faith in the God of Abraham, because He was the God of mercy, patience, and loving-kindness. One of David's marvelous confessions can be read in Psalms chapter 51. There is no mention of David doing any works of laws for God to forgive his sins: "For **thou desirest not sacrifice**; else would I give it: thou delightest not in burnt offering. **The sacrifices of God are a broken spirit: a broken and a contrite heart**, O God, thou wilt not despise" (Ps. 51:16–17).

The *animal* sacrifices have become obsolete because they've served their purpose (Heb. 9–10; Eph. 2:15), which was to deliver us to the faith of the Messiah's sacrifice (Gal. 3:24) so that sin's penalty could be removed, thus giving us His promised gift of eternal life (Rom. 6:23; 1 John 2:25). It's still the same today: when we violate God's commandments, we sin (Matt. 5:19; James 2:9–10; 1 John 3:4), wherefore God's law still charges us with the death penalty (Gen. 2:17; 3:3; Rom. 6:23; James 1:15), which enslaves us into sin's bondage. This is the curse of the law. And faith in the Messiah's sacrifice—upon repentance—frees us from that curse, which justifies us, thus reconciling us to God: "But God commendeth his love toward us, in that, while we were yet sinners, Christ died for us. Much more then, being now justified by his blood, we shall be saved from wrath through him. For if, when we were enemies, we were reconciled to God by the death of his Son, much more, being reconciled, we shall be saved by his life. And not only so, but we also joy in God through our Lord Jesus Christ, by whom we have now received the atonement" (Rom. 5:8–11). That is what the works **<ergon>**[27] of the law **<nomos>**[22] (animal sacrifice and ritual laws) could not do (Rom. 8:3), wherefore it was nailed to the tree together with our redeeming Messiah; thus we are no longer in bondage to that penalty: "For sin shall not have dominion over you: **for ye are not under the law <nomos>**[22]**, but under grace**" (Rom. 6:14). Rather, we are dead to it: "Wherefore, my brethren, **ye**

also are become dead to the law <nomos>[22] [animal sacrificial and ritualistic law] **by the body of Christ** [the Messiah's atoning blood]" (Rom. 7:4). The Messiah's sacrificial blood has made the *animal* sacrificial law of no effect, meaning that we're no longer under the bondage of sins penalty, thus dead to its sting—if our sins are repented of.

Repenting of breaking God's commandments, through faith in the Messiah's atoning blood, has freed us from the works of the laws, which never could forgive sins: "But in those sacrifices there is a remembrance again made of sins every year. For **it is not possible that the blood of bulls and of goats should take away sins**" (Heb. 10:3–4; read also verse 11). Let's not forget to praise our eternal God for such an awesome plan. Allelujah! "Behold the Lamb of God, which taketh away the sin of the world" (John 1:29).

After repenting and being forgiven for breaking God's commandments, do we then no longer need to obey His commandments? Are we then allowed to worship Baal; profane His Sabbaths; eat unclean meat; commit adultery, murder, and theft; live covetously; dishonor our parents; and so on? Is it then no longer sin to violate the Ten Commandments? Or do only certain of the Ten Commandments remain in effect after God forgives us for violating them? I really appreciate the vital scriptural points upon which Paul based his epistles, which he commands us to follow: "Be ye followers of me, even **as I also am of Christ**. Now I praise you, brethren, that ye remember me in all things, **and keep the ordinances, as I delivered them to you**" (1 Cor. 11:1–2). The Messiah revealed this to him: "But I certify you, brethren, that the gospel which was preached of me is **not after man**. For I neither received it of man, neither was I taught it, but **by the revelation of Jesus Christ**" (Gal. 1:11–12; Phil. 3:17). Paul, trained directly by the Messiah, kept God's commandments, just as the Messiah did, including the Lord's weekly and annual Sabbaths.

Side Note: I have another challenge for today's anti-Law Christendom. As I slightly touched on a bit earlier, in Acts chapter 21 Paul was falsely charged for teaching the people to forsake the teachings of Moses. This account occurred decades after the Messiah's resurrection. Now please get this: before trial, Paul goes into the temple and performs the complete eight-day purification rituals, according to the ritualistic laws, as instructed in Numbers chapter 6 in the Old Testament Torah scriptures. This is the same Paul who, according to traditional church doctrine, condemns anyone who would dare to keep God's laws and commandments! For the preachers of this doctrine, and their followers, I will ask you a personal question: Did the apostle Paul lose his salvation for keeping God's commandments—especially the traditionally labeled Jewish weekly and annual Sabbaths? The Messiah also kept all of God's commandments perfectly (John 15:10). Did the keeping of commandments put them into legalistic bondage, as is advocated by traditional preachers? I encourage you to study these accounts for yourself to see how Paul once again proved the Torah test in Acts chapter 21 by observing the commandments of Numbers chapter 6, without being condemned for keeping God's commandments. Nevertheless, I will briefly summarize it here.

Luke recorded that Paul's accusations were nothing; they were likely fabricated, trumped-up lies used to frame him. Whatever Luke meant by it, he wrote that it was nothing:

> And they are informed of thee, **that thou teachest all the Jews which are among the Gentiles to forsake Moses**, saying that they ought not to circumcise their children, neither to walk after the customs. What is it therefore? the multitude must needs come together: for they will hear that thou art come. Do therefore this that we say to thee: We have four men which have a vow on them; Them take, and purify thyself with them, and be at charges with them, that they may shave their heads: and all may know that those things, **whereof they were informed concerning thee, <u>are nothing</u>** [likely trumped-up lies]; **but that thou thyself also walkest orderly, and keepest the law.** (Acts 21:21–24)

Accordingly, Paul was not condemning the teachings of Moses, but he kept the law, just as he also himself confirmed in other scriptures: "But this I confess unto thee, that after the way which they call heresy, so worship I the God of my fathers, **believing all things which are written in the law and in the prophets**" (Acts 24:14; read also Acts 26:22). If he did condemn the laws of Moses, it would set up a serious contradiction in him getting purified by a means that he himself—according to traditional Christendom—condemned! These accusers were of the same sect as the one for which he used to be a champion and advocate. Now they condemned *him* for not keeping God's laws in accordance with the Talmud, just as they did the Messiah, for which both of them were killed.

Let's go back to the account in Acts chapters 6–7, where Paul was still a Pharisaic mob ringleader named Saul before he was converted. He, as a commander of that sect of Pharisees, gave consent to his gangsters, who also had specifically been set up to fabricate lies in order to frame Stephen about the exact same issue as the one he was later himself accused of in Acts chapter 21. Acts 6:13–14 specifically states that they set up false witnesses against Stephen to accuse him of speaking against the laws of Moses. Notice on what grounds these false accusers framed Stephen. They applied the Torah test, which requires that if anyone preaches anything other than what the God of Abraham commanded throughout the Torah, such a one must be stoned to death. Now recall how the Pharisees used that commandment to accuse the Messiah, namely by judging Him in accordance with the commandments of their Talmud. Stephen's accusers already knew that such an accusation came with a very certain and absolute assurance from those same religious rulers that it would get Stephen executed as well. And it did, with Saul's consent (Acts 8:1; 22:20). Now, this is the same "God-inspired" Paul who, according to traditional church doctrine, preached that not only Moses's laws but also the Ten Commandments were nailed to the tree already decades before that account in Acts chapter 21.

With that kind of philosophy, the early traditional church fathers invented anti-Torah doctrines in order to justify their lustful, lawless desires, and they passed them on as divine doctrines from God. Aside from the betrayal of the Messiah, for those preachers who profess to be teaching God's Word to use Paul's epistles as a tool or weapon in an effort to erroneously steer the followers of the Messiah away from keeping the Ten Commandments must be one of the greatest betrayals ever foisted upon mankind since the so-called Christian era began.

Please don't get mad at me. I didn't write those words into the scriptures. The God of Abraham, Isaac, and Jacob; the God of Israel; the God who started the fire on the sun and commanded the moon to rotate around the earth; the God who created you and me and gave us breath to live—that non-evolutionary God—inspired Moses to record the purification ordinances in the book of Numbers according to His will. Paul was inspired by that same God to purify himself before Him, according to the ordinances of His laws. That same God also inspired Luke to record those accounts of Paul and Stephen for our admonition and examples (2 Peter 1:21; 2 Tim. 3:16; 1 Cor. 10:11). God inspired these Words of His to be written down for us to see once again that His laws and commandments, His infallible Word, stand uncontradictorily forever, from which not a jot or tittle will be destroyed as long as we can put our feet on this earth (Matt. 5:18), and yet for some time after that (Matt. 24:35). We must choose to believe either the non-evolutionary eternal God of creation or man's evolutionary pagan gods (Deut. 11:26–28; 30:15–20; 1 Kings 18:21). The creator God made us free moral agents and provided us with all the necessary tools to enable us to make our own choices. God knows what's best for us, and offers it to us; but as free moral agents, we must choose; He will not choose for us!

Paul never preached against keeping God's laws and commandments or the law of Moses, including the sacrificial and ritualistic laws and circumcision. But he aggressively preached that a man never was and never will be justified from sin by them, because that leaves out the need for a Savior: "I do not frustrate the grace of God: for if righteousness come by the **law <nomos>**[22] [animal sacrificial laws], then Christ is dead in vain" (Gal. 2:21). If the penalty of sin could be taken away by the animal sacrificial laws, the Messiah wouldn't have needed to be sacrificed for them. We could then sacrifice animals to take away our sins. That never was God's plan. (Read Heb. 10:3–12; Gal. 2:16; 3:10; Hab. 2:4.) And that's the issue that Paul and the Messiah had with Judaism and heathenism, because they were doing all those works to be justified by from sin. And Judaism did not come from God or Moses, but from philosophies of pagan gods with whom the people frequently flirted (as they still are), thereby committing idolatry, which to God is adultery and thus violates the first four commandments and the seventh. That's why God calls the global traditional church system the Babylonian whore. That church has a long history of adulterating every law of the God of Creation; this has been happening literally since the beginning of mankind. These commandments carry the death penalty for their violation.

The traditional anti-Law church doctrines come from the same pagan philosopher who constantly enticed the Israelites to forsake the God of Abraham. That ever-so-clever philosopher is none other than Satan, the devil, who cunningly devised a plan by which he created tremendous enmity between the two sects in order to make them believe that they were opposites. To achieve that enmity, he indoctrinated the early traditional church fathers with an extreme anti-Jew philosophy: **we can't have anything in common with the Jews.** From this philosophy inevitably developed the anti-Torah doctrines, because the deceiver convinced those fathers that the Messiah had condemned the Jews for keeping God's commandments that are written in the Torah. Therefore, because the so-labeled wicked and evil Jews have conveniently laid claim to God's commandments, the traditionalists must condemn them—both the Jews and God's commandments—and stick to their traditional doctrines just as they were passed down from the early anti-Jew church fathers, and preach them as coming directly from God's divine Word. There is also, besides the extreme anti-Jew matter, no shortage of doctrines to reason around the requirement to keep the Ten Commandments—particularly the Sabbath commandment, which they've been able to conveniently label as Jewish and thus extremely burdensome. That has resulted in a lawless lot of Christians who have thereby inevitably rejected the God of the Old Testament. And Satan will not run out of such enticing tricks until he gets thrown into the lake of fire for all eternity. Until then he will only become more aggressive by making the anticommandment/anti-God messiah more tolerant to man's most motivating desires of lust, jealousy, envy, and greed.

Food for Thought: Assuming that the Old and New Testaments are the Word of God and the traditional anti-Law doctrines are also the Word of God, one of two things must be true: either that teaching is contrary to the Holy Scriptures, or the Holy Scriptures exhibit contradictions among the Old and New Testaments. I challenge traditionalists to decipher which is in agreement with the Word of God as a whole, bearing in mind that the Author of the scriptures said the following:

> The scripture cannot be broken (John 10:35).
>
> For God is not the author of confusion... (1 Cor. 14:33).
>
> For verily I say unto you, Till heaven and earth pass, one jot or one tittle shall in no wise pass from the law, till all be fulfilled. (Matt. 5:18)
>
> For I am the LORD, I change not. (Mal. 3:6)
>
> Jesus Christ the same yesterday, and to day, and for ever. (Heb. 13:8)
>
> Every good gift and every perfect gift is from above, and cometh down from the Father of lights, **with whom is no variableness, neither shadow of turning.** (James 2:17)
>
> It was impossible for God to lie. (Heb. 6:18; read also Titus 1:2)

So if there is any contradiction, and if we choose to believe the Messiah's words, the contradiction would have to be elsewhere than in the scriptures, correct?

I'm not suggesting that I'm more righteous than other people. But since traditionalists are judging my family merely because we're observing the Ten Commandments, they're inevitably putting the same judgment onto Paul and the Messiah, because they also observed God's commandments, including the weekly and annual Sabbaths.

The law-done-away doctrines are a deliberate attempt to justify lawlessness. As Jude wrote in verse 4, God's grace is being used as a license to live by lawless doctrines and traditions of this lust-inspired Babylonian world. These principles coincide with the golden calf ordeal and the doctrines of Jeroboam and Balaam in that they all preach man's commandments in the name of the Lord!

Breaking God's commandments exacts the death penalty (Gen. 2:17; 3:3; Matt. 15:4; Rom. 6:23; James 1:15). As we saw earlier, the Messiah took that penalty of ours to the tree, thus doing it away for repentant believers and setting us free from the bondage of that death sentence hanging over our head. Traditional preachers teach the Messiah's doing away of God's commandments to be the very liberty wherewith He set us free; they say that now we don't need to be concerned about keeping or thus breaking them. As usual, it's the opposite of what scriptures say—an apostasy the Messiah warned us would come from the religious leaders of the day: "And he charged them, saying, Take heed, beware of the leaven [sinful, wicked doctrines] of the Pharisees [religious rulers of the day], and of the leaven of Herod [political rulers of the day]" (Mark 8:15). He warned that they would be very serious, cunning, and vicious: "Beware of false prophets, which come to you in sheep's clothing, but **inwardly they are ravening wolves**" (Matt. 7:15).

Paul also gave us the same warnings: "For I know this, that **after my departing shall grievous wolves enter in among you**, not sparing the flock. Also of your own selves shall men arise, speaking perverse things, **to draw away disciples after them"** (Acts 20:29–30; read also Jude 16–19). The Messiah said that false satanic ministers will preach and do wonders **in** His name: "Many will say to me in that day, **Lord, Lord**, have we not **prophesied in thy name**? and **in thy name have cast out devils**? and **in thy name done many wonderful works** [elements of the Torah test]? And then will I profess unto them, **I never knew you: depart from me, ye that work iniquity <anomia>**[12][lawlessness; denial of commandments]" (Matt. 7:22–23). The anti-Law ministers deceive people by cunningly preaching that He (the crucified Lord) is the true Messiah of the Holy Scriptures, while actually advocating a messiah who hates God's commandments and condemns anyone who practices them: "For many shall come **in my name**, saying, **I am Christ** [saying that He—the Lord—is the Messiah]; and shall deceive many" (Matt. 24:5). How can preaching in the name of the Messiah be coming from an anti-God preacher? I will show you that it's going on today, right under our noses, coming from the pope's strategic network of pulpit parrots, Catholic and Protestants alike—namely, the whole traditional church system.

According to these scriptures, false ministers are today performing miracles in His name to deceive us. The Matthew scriptures above are a sure testimony of the Torah test prophecy, because as the Messiah said, they are doing wonders and miracles in His name while promoting anticommandment doctrines. This is a very powerful testimony that the Torah test prophecy is currently coming to pass in the traditional church system. Today's traditional religion is measured by using the Lord's name to do healings, wonders, and whatever suits the flavor of the day, wherewith today's vulnerable traditional-religiously indoctrinated people are easily snared by being cunningly led to believe that healings and wonders can come only through a true prophet of God, without a need to obey His commandments. Therefore, it is not hard for preachers of the anti-Law doctrines to seduce their faithful followers away from the teaching of God's Torah scriptures. As long as the preachers profess to be doing wonders in the name of the Lord, the indoctrinated people will believe that it comes directly from the eternal God of Creation! The Messiah, in whose name they profess to be performing those wonders, said He never knew them because of their anticommandment works. In plain words, God is allowing Satan to do miracles through his ministers to test us to see if we really love Him with all our heart. Please read Deut. 12:28–13:5 again, and you'll see that test prophecy coming alive today in the mainstream traditional church system. Anti-Law/anti-God preachers are using the Lord's name to snare people, thus directly violating the third commandment, and moreover the first tablet, which specifically identifies the non-evolutionary God of Abraham: "Thou shalt not take the name of the LORD thy God in vain" (Ex. 20:7). That is, of course, if you believe in God's commandments!

The message God gives us in Deuteronomy 12:28–13:5, of which Matthew 5:17–18, 7:22–23, and Revelation 22:18–19 are a New Testament confirmation and testimony, is very obvious and clear: if anyone comes and teaches anything—one jot or tittle—other than His teaching in the Torah; if one of the Ten Commandments is not kept and advocated, that teaching cannot have come from the God of Abraham, Isaac, and Jacob!

Furthermore, traditional anti-Law preachers teach that the Messiah's purpose was to specifically move us away from the Torah. Satan has convinced theologians that there are no consequences for breaking the Ten Commandments—the same trick he used to deceive Eve when he convinced her that she had an immortal soul that could not die (Gen. 3:4). They preach that trying to keep God's commandments is sin because, they say, it disconnects you from His grace. If that be so, if the Messiah, the Son of God, came to change as much as a jot or tittle of God's laws, then in accordance with His own commandment in Deuteronomy 12:28–13:5, the Pharisees would have followed God's instructions when they crucified Him for that very purpose. Think about it. The Messiah came to validate this very prophecy, to prove and confirm that He was the promised Messiah of the Torah prophecies by *specifically* testifying that He had not come to make any changes to God's laws: "Think **not** that I am come to destroy the law, or the prophets: I am not come to destroy, but to fulfil. For verily I say unto you, **Till heaven and earth pass, one jot or one tittle shall in no wise pass from the law**, till all be fulfilled. Whosoever therefore shall **break one of these least commandments**, and shall **teach** men so, he shall be called the least in the kingdom of heaven: but whosoever shall **do and**

teach them, the same shall be called great in the kingdom of heaven" (Matt. 5:17–19). But as we saw earlier, the Messiah's testimony did not align with their Judaized talmudic version of the Torah, just as it doesn't align with the traditionalized Christian version of the New Testament congregation! If keeping God's commandments disconnects a person from God's grace, then the Messiah would have also been disconnected from His Father's grace, together with His disciples, because they kept God's commandments according to the Torah. And it was because of their obedience to God's commandments that His mercy and grace followed them.

The very fact that traditional Christendom is advocating an anti-Law messiah is a powerful proof that they have not yet come to know the true Messiah. And they preach the reason for not keeping the Ten Commandments to be that they choose God's grace instead of His commandments. But the Messiah and the apostles make no hint of such a doctrine anywhere in the scriptures; rather, they state the opposite—teaching us to *not* sin, which, according to scriptural interpretation means that we are not to break God's commandments (1 John 3:4; Matt. 5:19; James 2:8–12). Paul specifically clarifies that doctrine: "What then? **shall we sin, because we are not under the law** [animal sacrificial laws]**, but under grace** [the Messiah's sacrifice]**? God forbid**" (Rom. 6:15).

Because we are forgiven for a sin we've repented of does not mean that the commandment that was violated is thereafter abolished and that there is hence no more penalty for breaking it. If that were the case, then each and every scripture in the New Testament that teaches against sinning would be totally in vain. In all of his epistles, Paul emphasizes that the Redeemer of Israel is now manifested, wherewith we have forgiveness of sin, wherefore we are no longer under the animal sacrificial laws, which were never designed to remove the penalties of sin (Heb. 10:3–4). They were designed to remind people of their sins in order to build up their faith in the promised Redeemer, who was yet to be revealed; thus they were a schoolmaster (Gal. 3:19–24).

Thus, the anti-Law advocates have labeled the Old Testament as a book of legalistic law-bearing instructions given by a tyrannical god only for the Jews, and the New Testament as the only instructions for the New Testament church, commanded by an anti-Law messiah who came to set us free from the so-labeled "burdensome, unbearable, and dumb" Jewish commandments of the Old Testament God so that we may live as we will without ever becoming guilty of sin. And their fruits do show that they believe those doctrines. Yes, they have faith in *their* god, but that's *not* the God of Abraham.

Such a profession cannot be made without inventing violent contradictions, of which Paul and Peter warned us (2 Cor. 11:3–15; Gal. 1:6–7; 2 Peter 3:15–17). And such an apostasy makes the eternal God out to be an outdated, ever-changing, and confused evolutionary god, thereby erecting a wall of partition between God and His holy Son. But according to scriptures, that won't happen: "And if a kingdom be divided against itself, that kingdom **cannot** stand" (Mark 3:24; read also Matt. 12:25). Paul was well aware of such anti-Law preachers: "For if he that cometh **preacheth another Jesus** ..." (2 Cor. 11:4). These wall-builders are preaching an anti-Law/anti-Torah and hence anti-God messiah, and not the redeeming Messiah, who did only what His Father commanded Him: "Jesus answered them, and said, **My doctrine is not mine, but his that sent me**" (John 7:16; read also verses 17–18; 8:28). He kept His Father's commandments: "I have kept my Father's commandments" (John 15:10). He commands us to follow in His steps: "He that saith he abideth in him ought himself also so to walk, even as he walked" (1 John 2:6; read also Luke 6:46). He does so if we love Him ("If ye love me, keep my commandments" [John 14:15]) and desire eternal life ("if thou wilt enter into life, keep the commandments" [Matt. 19:17]). The Messiah boldly asks religious hypocrites, "And **why call ye me, Lord, Lord, and do not the things which I say?**" (Luke 6:46).

In John 7:16 the Messiah clearly states that the people who do the will of His Father will know whether a doctrine is of God or of man. What was His Father's will when He spoke this? He said this over a decade before a word of the New Testament was written, and He commanded us to live by every word that proceeds out of the mouth of God: "It is written, Man shall not live by bread alone, but by **every word that proceedeth out of the mouth**

of God" (Matt. 4:4; read also Luke 4:4), which He cited directly from the Torah in Deuteronomy 8:3, thus proving by another Torah test that He was of the God of Abraham. Which of the Ten Commandments or laws did not proceed from the mouth of God? When the writers of the Gospels penned His sayings, they made absolutely no mention of the Messiah having changed a jot or tittle of it. God does not change (Mal. 3:6; James 1:17), and He *will* not change (Heb. 13:8). He cannot lie (Titus 1:2; Num. 23:19; Heb. 6:18), and He does not set up confusion (1 Cor. 14:33). Thus, the Messiah did not come to make any changes to God's commandments and laws (Matt. 5:17–18; Luke 16:17). Paul and all the other apostles believed His statement. Traditional Christians don't, because they have been brainwashed by indoctrination that if they don't believe whatever comes from the pulpit, they will get eternal life in the fires of hell—a fear tactic that by itself has deceived multitudes of people.

So, if a jot or tittle has been removed from God's commandments and laws after the Messiah made these statements—other than what was prophesied to occur—it has been done by Satan's ministers, and none other! That's what Paul related to in his argument with the rulers of his day who falsely accused him of changing the laws: "Having therefore obtained help of God, I continue unto this day, witnessing both to small and great, **saying none other things than those which the prophets and Moses did say should come**" (Acts 26:22). And he specifically stated which changes had thus far occurred through the Messiah's crucifixion and resurrection, of which the prophets of old did write: "That Christ should **suffer**, and that he should be **the first that should rise from the dead**, and should **shew light unto the people** [Israelites]**, and to the Gentiles**" (Acts 26:23). Those are the prophecies of the Old Testament that the Messiah has fulfilled thus far, and there is no mention of abolishing the Ten Commandments. That's why Paul loved the laws and commandments of God: "Wherefore **the law is holy, and the commandment holy, and just, and good"** (Rom. 7:12). As Paul explains in this chapter, they give us direction and conviction in order for us to become more righteous and just before God. And that the creator's commandments and laws are eternal and non-evolutionary is the sole reason that we can always rely on their integrity, validity, and verity; there is nothing in the whole universe that is more reliable.

Paul agreed with the Psalmist, who always praised God for the goodness and righteousness of His laws and commandments:

> With my whole heart have I sought thee: O let me not wander from thy commandments. Thy word have I hid in mine heart, that I might not sin against thee. (Ps. 119:10–11)

> My tongue shall speak of thy word: for all thy commandments are righteousness. Let thine hand help me; for I have chosen thy precepts. I have longed for thy salvation, O LORD; and thy law is my delight. Let my soul live, and it shall praise thee; and let thy judgments help me. I have gone astray like a lost sheep; seek thy servant; for I do not forget thy commandments. (Ps. 119:172–176)

Psalm 119 is the longest chapter in the scriptures, and it praises God's laws and commandments in practically every verse. It really is worth the while to read and study it to get a deeper sense of what God's laws are designed to do to the hearts and minds of His people, His temple, where He wants to dwell.

The thought of God dwelling in my heart overwhelms me, thus helping me to understand why He needs it to become more and more undefiled. God is holy, and for Him to dwell in our heart, our heart must also be holy: "But **as he which hath called you is holy, so be ye holy** in all manner of conversation; Because it is written, **Be ye holy; for I am holy**" (1 Peter 1:15–16; Lev. 11:44).

7a. Does Keeping God's Commandments Forfeit Salvation?

There is a common traditional teaching that is advocated with an evangelistic zeal to the effect that the Ten Commandments play no role in God's plan of salvation. Some go as far as to say that if you keep them, wherewith you supposedly reject the salvation of the Messiah and His grace, you can't be saved, thus you'll burn alive forever in the fires of hell for trying. I've had that phrase thrown in my face a number of times. First of all I will ask those that are drunk on that philosophy, how long is forever? The same people who advocate that philosophy have been indoctrinated with a belief that the Hebrew word **<`owlam>**[1]—which, according to *Strong's Concordance,* means "**forever** - without beginning or end - time out of mind - perpetual - eternity - everlasting," and so on, which the God of the Old Testament repeatedly said was how long His commandments would stand—apparently ended at the stake together with the Messiah's mortal life. This is not the place to argue about when forever expires, because the terms I listed above are a few of the definitions I found in *Strong's Concordance,* which I believe describes the word **<`owlam>**[1] fairly accurately according to how it is used throughout the scriptures. But the scriptures speak for themselves, if we let them. And according to the scriptures, forever is not up yet. So I'll assume that the correct rendering of the word **<`owlam>**[1] is "forever; without end."

But for argument's sake, let's assume that the rendering of **<`owlam>**[1] is as the traditional preachers say it is—that it ended already once at the cross. My next question is to the same drunken traditionalist: if I'm going to burn alive forever in hellfire for keeping the Ten Commandments, when will forever come to its next expiration date? After the Rapture? After the Great Tribulation, when the Messiah returns? After the millennial reign? After the Eighth Day—the great white throne judgment? If forever comes with a certain time limit, as the traditional preachers teach in their fire-and-brimstone sermons, when is it due to expire again? I ask this because, according to the traditional indoctrinated beliefs, it already has expired once, so it should expire again at some point, right? It goes the same for eternal life—to live forever— in God's kingdom; does it also have an expiry date? No offense, but give at least yourself an honest answer for that question.

According to scripture, it's our belief and obedience (faith) to the Torah that allow us to see and understand the prophecies wherewith the Messiah would come and set us free from the bondage of sin, and at liberty with God and man: "Then said Jesus to those Jews which believed on him, If ye continue in my word, then are ye my disciples indeed; And **ye shall know the truth, and the truth shall make you free**. They answered him, We be Abraham's seed, and were never in bondage to any man: how sayest thou, Ye shall be made free?" (John 8:31–33). The Pharisees did not believe that they had any sin, because they were Abraham's descendants. If they had repented for keeping and advocating their traditional talmudic commandments and gone back to keeping God's commandments, the Messiah would have forgiven them.

God's desire is to keep us well forever, for thousands of generations, through always keeping His commandments:

> O that there were such an heart in them, that they would fear me, and **keep all my commandments always**, that it might be well with them, and with their children **for ever <`owlam>**[1]! (Deut. 5:29)

> And **shewing mercy unto thousands** of them [generations] that love me, and **keep my commandments.** (Ex. 20:6)

If the word "thousands" here means even just 1,000, it would translate to 40,000 years. From the time that God spoke this commandment to the Israelites till the crucifixion was close to

1,400 years. That's about 34 generations, leaving at least another 966 generations to fulfill that time span. From the crucifixion until today is another fifty generations. God doesn't say that His commandments will end there, but if they do, it still leaves a balance of over 36,000 years. "Heaven and earth shall pass away, but **my words shall not pass away**" (Matt. 24:35). So it looks like the Ten Commandments have not ended yet, and they never will.

Observing God's commandments fends off disease and assures health: "And said, If thou wilt diligently hearken to the voice of the LORD thy God, and wilt do that which is right in his sight, **and wilt give ear to his commandments, and keep all his statutes, I will put none of these diseases upon thee**, which I have brought upon the Egyptians: **for I am the LORD that healeth thee**" (Ex. 15:26). The pride of the Pharisees through which they enforced their Talmud did not allow God's instructions to enter their mind. "Jesus answered them, Verily, verily, I say unto you, Whosoever committeth sin is the servant of sin. And the servant abideth not in the house for ever: **but the Son abideth ever. If the Son therefore shall make you free** [by redeeming our death penalty]**, ye shall be free indeed"** (John 8:34–36). I'll say it again that He came to set us free from sin's bondage, not from keeping God's commandments.

If the Messiah came to set us free from keeping God's commandments, then we can no longer sin, thus He went through the crucifixion in vain, because there is then no commandment to break, thus no sin in need of repentance, hence no penalty in need of redeeming. Everyone that is born after the crucifixion and resurrection would then not be able to sin. And that is, of course, what a carnal mind desires. But the scriptures state that anyone who professes that there is no sin is a lying deceiver: "**If we say that we have no sin, we deceive ourselves, and the truth is not in us. If we confess our sins** [for breaking commandments]**, he is faithful and just to forgive us our sins** [for breaking commandments], and to cleanse us from all unrighteousness. **If we say that we have not sinned, we make him** [God] **a liar, and his word** [the Messiah—John 1:1] **is not in us**" (1 John 1:8–10). He continues to confirm that God's commandments are to be kept: "He that saith, I know him, and keepeth not his commandments, is a liar, and the truth is not in him" (1 John 2:4). These Scriptures were written decades after the crucifixion.

The Messiah offers eternal life, which Abraham and Moses couldn't. As He explained to the Pharisees earlier (John 5:45–47), if they had believed Moses, who spoke and wrote of Him, they would know and believe Him. But since they had not believed Moses or the prophets, wherefore they had perverted all of God's commandments and laws that God had Moses and the prophets advocate for Him, God had them blinded so that they could not understand that the purpose of the Messiah's First Coming was to free them from the *penalty* of their sins. And since they did not believe that He was the one who could justify them and free them from man's bondage to sin, knowing Him gave them no hope: "If ye believe not that I am he, ye shall die in your sins" (John 8:24).

To truly and fully understand God's plan of salvation, one must understand the role the Messiah plays in each of God's holy day festivals, which He commanded us to keep forever. The Pharisees kept them, but as with the Ten Commandments, they had also been perverted centuries earlier by their idolatrous forefathers: "I hate, I despise **your** feast days, and I will not smell in **your** solemn assemblies. Though ye offer me burnt offerings and your meat offerings, I will not accept them: neither will I regard the peace offerings of your fat beasts. Take thou away from me the noise of **thy** songs; for I will not hear the melody of thy viols" (Amos 5:21–23; read also Isa. 1:14; Lam. 2:6; Mal. 2:3). God called those feast days theirs in the above scripture because they kept them according to their own traditional talmudic standards and customs, wherefore He said He would not even listen to their prayers and songs—He hates them. But God said there would come a time when His Sabbaths (His weekly, annual, and land Sabbaths) will be recovered from the peoples' profaning of them: "Then shall the land enjoy **her** sabbaths, as long as it lieth desolate, and ye be in your enemies' land; even then shall the land rest, and enjoy **her** sabbaths. As long as it lieth desolate it shall rest; **because it did not rest in your sabbaths**, when ye dwelt upon it" (Lev. 26:34–35).

I believe that God inspired the New Testament writers to record the profaning of His Sabbaths also in the New Testament, because the Pharisees were still observing them according to their perverted, Judaized version: "And the **Jews'** passover was at hand, and Jesus went up to Jerusalem" (John 2:13; read also 5:1; 6:4; 7:2; 11:55). And the Messiah confirmed that their disobedience was from not keeping the law: "Did not Moses give you the law, and yet **none of you keepeth the law?**" (John 7:19). Observing God's holy days throughout the year according to his plan reminds God's people of the miraculous role that the Messiah plays in His awesome plan of salvation. That's why He desires and commands us to keep them holy forever. After all, the Messiah will keep them with His faithful followers when He returns (Matt. 26:29; Mark 14:25; Luke 22:18). But He's abhorred by man's feasts; that's why He called them your feasts (Isa. 1:14; Amos 8:10; Mal. 2:3). In modern day terms He would call them something like: **your** New Year, **your** Lent, **your** Easter, **your** Christmas, **your** Halloween, **your** birthday. God calls pagan holidays and ceremonies yours because they do not come from Him. To the displeasure of mainstream traditional Christianity, you can rest assured that Sunday and the pagan holidays will not be observed by the Messiah when He returns to restore this planet to God's standards. His Sabbaths and His feast days will be kept.

By design, God's laws teach of His mercy and grace for mankind. Faithfully and willingly obeying them from the heart is the very essence of our welfare now on this earth, and in God's kingdom later (Deut. 5:33; 30:15–20; Matt. 19:17; Rev. 14:12; 22:14). It allows mercy to flow from one to another, whereby we receive God's mercy and grace. Obedience to them reopens the gate to the tree of life (Rev. 22:14). Without obedience to God's laws, we are without mercy, wherefore we have no forgiveness, without which we are not justified and thus not reconciled to God! So is obedience to God's moral and spiritual laws required for salvation? You be the judge. Without laws, there is no freedom! Not keeping God's commandments and laws has been proven for millennia, without fail, to invite bondage and slavery to mankind by traditional religion, which is an abomination to the God of

Abraham because it enslaves His children! Faith without works is dead, just as much as works without faith is dead (James 2). "For **as the body without the spirit is dead, so faith without works is dead** also" (James 2:26). One thing is certain: we will obey one god or another. It can never be none; neither can it be both. One or the other it will be!

The Messiah leaves no doubt in this matter; there is no confusion: "**No servant can serve two masters**: for either he will hate the one, and love the other; or else he will hold to the one, and despise the other. Ye **cannot serve God and mammon <mammonas>**[20]" (Luke 16:13; read also Matt. 6:24). In plain words, we will keep God's commandments **<entole>**[9], which inherently teach the law of giving, or we will keep man's commandments **<entalma>**[9a], which inherently teach the law of receiving: "I have shewed you all things, how that so labouring ye ought to support the weak, and to remember the words of the Lord Jesus, how he said, **It is more blessed to give than to receive**" (Acts 20:35). Paul says we cannot yield to a worldly god while serving the eternal God: "Know ye not, that **to whom ye yield yourselves servants to obey, his servants ye are** to whom ye obey; whether of **sin unto death** [death for transgressing God's commandments], or of **obedience unto righteousness** [obedience unto God's commandments]?" (Rom. 6:16). What is righteousness? "All thy commandments are righteousness" (Ps. 119:172). Therefore: "Be ye not unequally yoked together with unbelievers: for **what fellowship hath righteousness** [the keeping of commandments] **with unrighteousness <anomia>**[12][commandment-breaking]?" (2 Cor. 6:14).

God gave us free moral agency to choose for ourselves: "I have set before you **life and death, blessing and cursing**: therefore **choose** life" (Deut. 30:19). The decision is ours: "If the LORD be God, follow him: but if Baal, then follow him" (1 Kings 18:21). Read again 1 Samuel chapter 8, where the Israelites choose to be ruled by a human king. God gave them very strong warnings about how they would inevitably end up back in bondage to slavery by choosing a human king. Nevertheless, they voted for their own demise. There are plenty of scriptures that testify to the consequential results of that choice (Neh. 5:1–5; Lam. 5:1–9; Hag. 1:1–6).

We are experiencing those exact same consequences again today on the North American continent. But that's how the Babylonian/democratic-communist system has always operated since its existence. God commands us as free moral agents to choose one god or another and then follow that deity (1 Kings 18:21; Jg. 10:14). Thus we in North America (Canada and the United States) are still voting, which mainstream traditional Christendom has declared a Christian duty. They've been indoctrinated to believe that as followers of the Messiah, we are commanded to vote. For the people who forsook God by trading Him off for an earthly king, this system of democratic voting began shortly after we left Egypt, and no good has ever come from it, nor ever will. That's because it's man-devised and man-desired, which is all about receiving instead of giving. That's why it's ruled by majority vote and not by right or wrong. And the majority votes will typically be lobbied for by the select few controllers who will receive/gain the most by it, even if it means buying (bribing) votes. North America is a true democratic-socialistic death-by-debt communist testimony to that, because we have traded off the Ten Commandments for the ten planks of the *Communist Manifesto.* A majority-rule system stands to gain by the use of the communists' ten planks, and not by the Ten Commandments. (The Ten Commandments and the ten planks of the *Communist Manifesto* are posted on pages 378 to 381).

Numbers chapter 16 holds a very interesting account about God and democracy. Korah rebels against Moses and Aaron because he feels that Moses has become somewhat of a dictator and decides to do something about it. So he starts persuading others to help him to vote for a new leader to replace Moses' cabinet. He persuades two hundred and fifty princes along with over fourteen thousand lay supporters to vote against Moses. Moses and Aaron–together with their King (God)–prepare for the competition, and the election is on. God tells Moses and Aaron to move out of harms way so that He can deal with the renegades without harming them. Moses and Aaron move aside, the earth opens up and swallows almost fifteen thousand rebels.

The earth closes back up, and the ballots are in–Moses and Aaron residing by acclamation, by their King–God. I urge you to read and study that account in Numbers chapter 16 before you go to the polls when election time rolls around.

Then compare the Ten Commandments with the ten planks of the *Communist Manifesto* and judge for yourself which is the better government for mankind. You can find the ten planks to the *Communist Manifesto* in the book Karl Marx and Friedrich Engels published in February of 1848. The planks are also posted on Wikipedia, the free online encyclopedia. If you are honest with yourself, you will see how that move into our North American nation took place very gradually and extremely cunningly through three main institutions of North America: the public education system, the financial system, and the traditional church system. To infiltrate a society with Communist beliefs requires brainwashing which requires all three of those institutions. As a society, we have been indoctrinated through it into believing that it's not only the best way to bring up our children in this country, but that it's the *only* way. That's why it's mandatory in this nation to send our children to public school. And the cunning controlling advocators of the communist system continually demand that the children start attending school at a younger age, because it's *easier* to brainwash a person at a young age. I want to encourage you to read a couple of articles which explain explicitly how the Communist system was–past tense–cunningly infiltrated into the North American continent by indoctrinating its occupants into believing that this Christian-oriented democratic system is Scriptural. These articles can be read online at the following websites:

> ***The Hidden Tyranny***: http://www.biblebelievers.org.au/tyranny1.htm. In this article, Charles A. Weisman interviews one of the Zionist-Jews responsible for infiltrating North America with the Communist program.
>
> ***Protocols of the Learned Elders of Zion***: http://www.biblebelievers.org.au/przion1.htm# is a book about the learned elders of Zion, the very people who implement

the Communist system in countries which they take control of.

The tenth plank of the *Communist Manifesto* calls for free education for all children in public schools. That's where national brainwashing begins. The public schools *and* the private schools are all authorized and thus operating under the same curricular umbrella, but a review of our history in the education sector of the last century or so shows that the private school and home school systems operate at a mere fraction of the cost of the public school system, while the average students come out of the private and home school system with *much* better marks in regard to basic knowledge. I encourage you to read the book about these studies called *Poison Drops in the Federal Senate: The School Question from a Parental and Non-Sectarian Standpoint,* written by Zach Montgomery. The author includes a lot of very interesting studies in his book, and it's full of crime-related stats that boggle one's mind. His studies irrevocably prove that the more money we spend in the public education system, the dumber we become and the more crime we produce. Read it for yourself and draw your own conclusions from that. The book was published in 1886 by Gibson Bros. Printers and Bookbinders. I don't think it's being published today. I downloaded it from a website in pdf format: ***Poison Drops in the Federal Senate***: http://scans.library.utoronto.ca/pdf/3/2/poisondropsinfed00montuoft/poisondropsinfed00montuoft.pdf. It has 150 pages of very sobering information. There are also websites like Amazon.com, where it is sometimes available in used condition. If all else fails, you might find one at bravenewbookstore.com.

Most North Americans–the United States *and* Canada–consider that their nation consists mostly of Bible-believing people. This was true to some degree many decades ago, but now it has become lawless as never before. We have become a greedy, covetous, prideful, and murderous—and thus a man-fearing, self-serving, commandment-hating, and God-denying—nation of people. The Ten Commandments have been removed from parliament, courthouses, schools, and most public places. We hear a lot of uproar from traditional Christians about how upset they are over it. Little do they realize that the Ten Commandments were removed centuries earlier from the traditional anti-Law church system, where they go every Sunday and on the pagan holidays to worship the messiah who removed them. Only in the last few decades have the nation's rulers followed suit by removing them also from the civil and public sectors. I find it so ironic and hypocritical that mainstream traditional Christendom preaches against keeping them in their church, while prayerfully demanding the civil system to obey them and enforce them on the people under the civil rule. God has very extraordinarily special advice for prayers coming from such like hypocrites: "Yet ye have forsaken me, and served other gods: wherefore I will deliver you no more. Go and cry unto the gods which ye have chosen; let them deliver you in the time of your tribulation" (Judges 10:13–14). He is speaking directly to traditional evangelizing commandment-denying hypocrites. He is plainly saying, "You have forsaken me and wholesaled me for Baal, so when you get into trouble, go pray to your pagan sun-god, moon-god, evolutionary god, and whatever gods of this world you took in trade for me, because I will not hear you in your time of trouble!

As God told us in 1 Samuel 8, Ezekiel 8, and Judges 10, if we don't obey His commandments, He will *not* hear our prayers. According to these scriptures, for how long has God not heard the cries of this North American continent? Only when things don't go our way do we scream for His help. But as He said, if we don't keep His commandments, He will not hear our cries! That's a promise from the almighty God Himself! I do not like the sound of it, wherefore (as per His instructions in Revelation 18:4 and 2 Corinthians 6:14–18, which echo the prophecies in Jeremiah chapters 50 and 51), I'm coming out of that Babylonian system as fast as I can, with the help of God.

That's the exact advice from the Torah-abiding, commandment-keeping, Sabbath-keeping, and feast-observing apostle Paul, whom the eternal God inspired to write,

> Be ye not unequally yoked together with unbelievers: for what fellowship hath righteousness [law abiding] with unrighteousness [lawlessness]? and what communion

> hath light [the God of Abraham] with darkness [the god of this world]? And what concord hath Christ with Belial? or what part hath he that believeth with an infidel? And what agreement hath the temple of God with idols? for ye are the temple of the living God; as God hath said, I will dwell in them, and walk in them; and I will be their God, and they shall be my people. Wherefore **come out from among them, and be ye separate**, saith the Lord, and touch not the unclean thing; and I will receive you, And will be a Father unto you, and ye shall be my sons and daughters, saith the Lord Almighty. (2 Cor. 6:14–18; read also Rev. 18:4)

In plain words, God says that a follower of Him cannot have anything in common with the Babylonian customs and traditions of this world! God is not mocked: "Be not deceived; God is not mocked" (Gal. 6:7). Come out of Babylon, my children! (Isa. 48; Jer. chapter 50 and 51; 2 Cor. 6:14–18; Rev. 18:4.)

+ +

Warning! You may be seriously offended if you continue reading!

8. THE CORE OF CORRUPTION IN THE TRADITIONAL RELIGIOUS CIRCLE

I realize that I'm revealing some disturbing and very sobering truths regarding the foundation of the traditional church doctrines and the impact that they have on potentially billions of its faithful followers. I'll give you a fair warning concerning where I stand. If you are strongly opposed and dead set against what you have read so far, you may want to stop reading here, because I will aim straight for the heart and core of the matter in the remainder of this book and arrive at a sobering conclusion. My prayer is that it would provoke the guilty to study, give some direction to the unsure, and encourage the rest. But if you're already offended, you may want to stop reading here.

I have no reason, need, or desire to speak ill or well of the Jews or Gentiles, or of the Catholic/Protestant people, or the Muslims. I must—and do—remain neutral to be able to discern between truth and tradition. My family is not a member of any denominational church, which makes it easier to remain neutral, since we have no man's church doctrines to defend; rather, we have only the Messiah's. And just as He and His early followers did, I admit that I do abhorrently rebuke the traditions of men, wherewith multitudes of sincerely well-meaning people have been misled and deceived, and thereby brought into very serious death-warranting Babylonian bondage.

Please Note: What I am disclosing in this book is in no way to be taken as prejudice. Rather, my prayer is that this information might help traditional churchgoers understand that the doctrines and commandments they hear from the pulpits in the traditional church system are *not* the scriptural truth. I'm not suggesting that these people necessarily know that the doctrines they are being taught and are faithfully following are corrupt. Many of these people have a sincere heart with a true desire to serve the Lord. But they have put their trust into mankind—be it a certain church or a certain pastor—and have been led to believe that they are being nourished with the scriptural truth. There is ample warning in God's Word regarding the dangers of elevating man's traditions to a level where they are being used to indoctrinate people: "Then Peter and the other apostles answered and said, We ought to obey God rather than men" (Acts 5:29; read also 4:19; Prov. 3; Ps. 118:8; Rom. 3:4). The Messiah strictly condemns men's traditions in Matthew chapters 15 and 23, Mark chapter 7, and John chapters 5 through 10. And just like the Pharisees did, these traditional doctrines and commandments are also being preached in the name of the Lord in today's traditional anti-Jew/anti-Law/anti-Torah church system, from which is born an Anti-God philosophy!

A Sad Fact: As a whole, the traditional church system is without any doubt extremely anti-commandment <**entole**>[9], whereby the messiah it advocates is inevitably Satan-inspired because it is extremely opposed to the laws and commandments of the God of Abraham, of Isaac, and of Jacob—the God of Israel / the Israel of God (Gal. 6:16), and of the true Messiah. If that isn't blasphemy toward the creator God, it must be rubbing shoulders with it. The god of this world—Satan, the devil—must be enthralled at the overwhelming success he has achieved by advocating his traditional commandments <**entalma**>[9a] as God's divine commandments <**entole**>[9] wherewith he has deceived and thus ensnared perhaps multiple billions of people via the pharisaic talmudic system for a few millennia, and also through traditional Christendom for a couple of millennia.

Paul confessed in his epistles that his zeal for God—through the god of the Talmud, which is based on the Pharisees' perverted version of God's commandments—caused him to advocate an extremely harsh anti-Messiah program that he had triumphantly preached through his pharisaic membership (Rom. 9:31–10:4;

Gal. 1:10–14; Phil. 3:5–6). This was an extremely powerful control-mongering and authoritative philosophy through which he literally slaughtered many true followers of the true Messiah. Similarly, we have multiple millions—or perhaps billions—of modern-day evangelistic zealots following a similar pattern, by which anti-Law/anti-commandment **<entole>**[9] doctrines are advocated by preaching traditional commandments **<entalma>**[9a] as if they're divinely coming from God. Through this pattern, an anti-God messiah is inevitably born, and these zealots evangelize around the globe under the banner of Christianity, by which they profess to be following the Son of God—the one who professed to be fully keeping God's commandments **<entole>**[9] and who commands His followers to do the same—as an anti-Commandment messiah.

There is one clear doctrinal distinction between the pharisaic Talmudists and traditional Christendom, which is by whose authority their traditions are being taught. Because of the traditional church system's extreme anti-Jew philosophy, which they've inherited from the foundational roots of their mother church—the universal Roman Catholic system, from which they claim to have severed but never really have because they're still divinely attached to her nursery of delicate pagan doctrines—traditional Christendom openly professes that they avoid the use of the Ten Commandments because they were apparently nailed to the tree by their saving messiah to set them at liberty (the freedom from needing to live by them) in order to reconcile them with their god. On the other hand, the Pharisees profess the Talmud to be the very commandments **<entole>**[9] of God. Nevertheless, both of these groups preach their own man-made traditions as divine instructions coming from the eternal God of heaven and earth. And just the same, according to scriptures, both of these doctrinal systems inevitably forsake the creator God by denying His commandments **<entole>**[9] by the use of man-made traditions, which the true Messiah flat out condemned in the New Testament (Matt. 15 and 23; Mark 7; John chapters 5–10).

There are ample warnings in scripture that God will square off with each individual on a one-on-one basis. When He returns,

He will destroy every god on this whole earth, just as He did in Egypt when He passed judgment throughout its kingdom on that Passover night over three thousand years ago: "For I will pass through the land of Egypt this night, **and will smite all the firstborn** in the land of Egypt, both man and beast; **and against <u>all the gods</u> of Egypt I will execute judgment**: **I** am the LORD" (Ex. 12:12; read also Num. 33:4; Ps. 82:1; Zeph. 2:11). Ignorance is no excuse (Hosea 4:6; Isa. 5:13; Rom. 1:20). We must "prove all things" (1 Thess. 5:21). Ezekiel chapters 18 and 33 have a very plain and revealing testimony that every man will answer for himself and that no man needs to be punished for another's sins, unless those sinful doctrines are followed and not severed from and thus repented of. It will be absolutely of no use to tell God that one was taught wrong by a father, mother, husband, wife, preacher, teacher, friend, governor, or king:

> As for his father, because he cruelly oppressed, spoiled his brother by violence, and did that which is not good among his people, lo, even **<u>he</u> shall die in his iniquity**. Yet say ye, Why? doth not the son bear the iniquity of the father? When the son hath done that which is lawful and right, and hath kept all my statutes, and hath done them, **he shall surely live. <u>The soul that sinneth, it shall die</u>** [no immortal soul]**. The son shall not bear the iniquity of the father, neither shall the father bear the iniquity of the son**: the righteousness of the righteous shall be upon him, and the wickedness of the wicked shall be upon him [no inherited sin]. **But if the wicked will turn from all his sins that he hath committed, and keep all my statutes, and do that which is lawful and right, he shall surely live, he shall not die.** All his transgressions that he hath committed, they shall not be mentioned unto him: in his righteousness that he hath done he shall live. (Ezek. 18:18–22; read also chapter 33)

Everyone will have to answer for himself or herself, just as Paul admonished the people: "Work out **your own** salvation with fear and trembling" (Phil. 2:12).

Prophecies clearly indicate that the plagues God has prepared for the rebellious false preachers together with their followers of this age will be much greater than what the judgments of Egypt were. This prophecy applies to people of all nations:

> And this shall be the plague wherewith the LORD will smite all the people that have fought against Jerusalem; **Their flesh shall consume away** while they stand upon their feet, and **their eyes shall consume away** in their holes, and **their tongue shall consume away** in their mouth ... And if the family of Egypt go not up, and come not, that have no rain; **there shall be the plague, wherewith the LORD will smite <u>the heathen that come not up to keep the feast of tabernacles</u>**. This shall be the punishment of Egypt, and the punishment of **<u>all nations</u> that come not up to keep the feast of tabernacles**. (Zech. 14:12, 18–19)

God warned us about these plagues already a few millennia ago: "Then the LORD will make thy plagues wonderful, and the plagues of thy seed, even **great plagues**, and of long continuance, and sore sicknesses, and of long continuance. Moreover **he will bring upon thee all the diseases of Egypt**, which thou wast afraid of; and they shall cleave unto thee [no cure]. Also **every sickness, and every plague, <u>which is not written in the book of this law</u>, them will the LORD bring upon thee, <u>until thou be destroyed</u>**" (Deut. 28:59–61; read Deut. 28:15–68; Lev. 26:14–46). And these plagues, as a Torah test proof, are confirmed in the last chapter of the New Testament scriptures: "For I testify unto every man that heareth the words of the prophecy of this book, **If any man shall add unto these things, God shall add unto him the plagues that are written in this book: And if any man shall take away from the words of the book of this prophecy, God shall take away his part out of the book of life**, and out of the holy city, and from the things which are written in this book" (Rev. 22:18–19). This doesn't leave much wiggle room for the traditional New Testament Christians, who claim that God's word from the Old Testament is burdensome, only for the Jews, outdated, void, and done away, does it?

Tragically, every traditional church denomination professes to be using only the scriptures as their doctrines—except the mother church (Roman Catholic), which triumphantly admits with a degree of pride that they have permission (through the Messiah, they say) to make up their own doctrines as they go. I don't agree with them on that, but I must give them credit for at least being honest about it. They openly laugh at their rebellious daughter churches, the Protestants, calling them liars and hypocrites for professing to be using only the Holy Scriptures, while actually preaching most of *their* (the Catholic Church's) doctrines in their churches. I'll cite a few examples of their boasting, and there are many:

Roman Catholic:

> Regarding the change from the observance of the Jewish Sabbath to the Christian Sunday, I wish to draw your attention to the facts:
>
> 1). That Protestants, who accept the Bible as their only rule of faith and religion, should by all means go back to the observance of the Sabbath. The fact that they do not, but on the contrary observe the Sunday, stultifies them in the eyes of every thinking man.
>
> 2). We Catholics do not accept the Bible as the only rule of faith. Besides the Bible we have the living Church, the authority of the Church, as a rule to guide us. We say, this Church, instituted by Christ to teach and guide man through life, has the right to change the ceremonial laws of the Old Testament and hence, we accept her change of Sabbath to Sunday. We frankly say, yes, the Church made this change, made this law, as she made many other laws, for instance, the Friday abstinence, the unmarried priesthood, the laws concerning mixed marriages, the religion of Catholic marriages and a thousand more laws.

It is always laughable, to see the Protestant churches, in pulpit and legislation, demand the observance of Sunday, of which there is nothing in the Bible. (Peter R. Kraemer: *Catholic Church Extension Society* [Chicago, Illinois, 1975]).

Question: What challenge do Catholics give to Protestants concerning Sunday?
Answer: "The Church changed the observance of the Sabbath to Sunday by rite of the divine, infallible authority given to her by her founder, Jesus Christ. The Protestant, claiming the Bible to be the only guide of faith, has no warrant for observing Sunday". (*The Catholic Universe Bulletin*, August 14, 1942).

"Protestantism, in discarding the authority of the [Roman Catholic] Church, has no good reason for its Sunday theory, and ought logically to keep Saturday as the Sabbath (John Gilmary Shea, in the *American Catholic Quarterly Review*, January 1883).

"It is well to remind the Presbyterians, Baptists, Methodists, and all other Christians that the Bible does not support them anywhere in their observance of Sunday. Sunday is an institution of the Roman Catholic Church, and those who observe the day observe a commandment of the Catholic Church". (Priest Brady, in an address, reported in the *Elizabeth, NJ. News* of March 18, 1903).

There are Protestant authorities who admit to what the Catholic authorities have alluded to:

Anglican/Episcopal:

We have made the change from the seventh day to the first day, from Saturday to Sunday, on the authority of the one holy Catholic Church. (Bishop Seymour, *Why We Keep Sunday, Article 12*)

The Sabbath was binding in Eden, and it has been in force ever since. This fourth commandment begins with the word 'remember,' showing that the Sabbath already existed when God Wrote the law on the tables of stone at Sinai. How can men claim that this one commandment has been done away with when they will admit that the other nine are still binding? (D. L. Moody, *Weighed and Wanting* [New York: Fleming H. Revell Co., 1898] page 47–48).

Methodist:

But, the moral law contained in the ten commandments, and enforced by the prophets, he [Christ] did not take away. It was not the design of his coming to revoke any part of this. This is a law which never can be broken ... Every part of this law must remain in force upon all mankind, and in all ages; as not depending either on time or place, or any other circumstances liable to change, but on the nature of God and the nature of man, and their unchangeable relation to each other. (John Wesley, *The Works of the Rev. John Wesley, A. M.,* vol. 1, ed. John Emory [New York: Eaton & Mains; J. Collord, Printer, 1831], p. 221-222).

Lutheran:

They [Roman Catholics] refer to the Sabbath Day, as having been changed into the Lord's Day, contrary to the Decalogue, as it seems. Neither is there any example whereof they make more than concerning the changing of the Sabbath Day. Great, say they, is the power of the Church, since it has dispensed with one of the Ten Commandments! (Melanchthon, *Augsburg Confession of Faith*, art. 28, approved by Martin Luther, 1530; as published in Henry Jacobs, ed., *The Book of Concord of the Evangelical Lutheran Church* [1911], 63).

++++++++++++++++++++++++++++++++++

My goal is not to condemn or condone the universal Roman Catholic (Babylonian) system, but I must give them credit for being honest by at least admitting that they don't go by the scriptures to establish their doctrines. The traditional church rulers are blatantly lying through their teeth when they claim that they use only God's Word as their doctrines, while actually fearfully cowering behind and advocating their mother church's admittedly man-made customs and traditions as God's divine word!

All traditional Christian churches are Protestant denominations that have supposedly broken away from the Roman mother Catholic Church. They use many of the mother church's doctrines and have traded off some of the former pagan doctrines for other pagan doctrines. Revelation chapters 17 and 18, Isaiah chapter 47, and Jeremiah chapters 50 and 51 describe this whole system quite well. The Roman Catholic system precisely matches the criteria of the great Babylonian whore as described in these scriptures, and the Protestants (protesting Catholics - the traditional Church system) just as adequately suit the criteria for her harlot daughters, because they are still nursing on most of their mother's doctrines. Of course, the Protestant preachers will not admit to this and will take issue with my statement while they lie through their teeth to reason around it. They've made it a habit to badmouth their mother church while hypocritically and cunningly nurturing off her doctrines, most of which come from the deceiver of this world. That deceiver has seminaries full of instrumentally designed traditional/talmudic-style, ready-made, ear-tickling excusing doctrines and commentaries to justify man-made doctrines as divine instructions; preaching them in **the Name of the LORD**, just like the account in Exodus chapter 32 where our fore-fathers proclaimed their sacrificing to the golden calf as **"a feast to the LORD."**

It's true that the reformers severed from a few onerous Babylonian doctrines, but in the same breath they are still nursing on many of the Roman Catholic doctrines, such as the immortal soul doctrine, the trinity doctrine, the pagan holidays (such as New Year's, Epiphany, Lent, Easter, Halloween, Advent, Christmas, birthdays, and the main and most important one, the Roman Catholic / Babylonian identity, their icon, Sunday). Thus they feast on Babylonian doctrines in the name of the Lord.

This is very similar to the account of Jeroboam using a portion of God's truth mixed with pagan doctrines and his own doctrines to successfully turn the Israelites away from the God of Abraham. That's the philosophy with which he devised doctrines for the Israelites to worship the God of Abraham on days and feasts he devised from his own heart, which abhorred God, and thus this caused Him to scatter them:

> So he offered upon the altar which he had made in Bethel the fifteenth day of the **eighth month** [instead of the seventh month, as ordained by God], even in the month which **he had devised of his own heart**; and ordained a feast unto the children of Israel: and he offered upon the altar, and burnt incense. (1 Kings 12:33)

> They **feared the LORD, and served their own gods, after the manner of the nations** [commandments **<entalma>**[9a] of men]. (2 Kings 17:33)

> Also Judah kept not the commandments of the LORD their God, but walked in the **statutes of Israel which they made** [commandments **<entalma>**[9a] of men]. **And the LORD rejected all the seed of Israel, and afflicted them, and delivered them into the hand of spoilers, until he had cast them out of his sight.** (2 Kings 17:19–20)

Remember, the God of Israel has nothing in common with paganism, and He has not changed:

Jesus Christ **the same yesterday, and to day, and for ever.** (Heb. 13:8; read also Mal. 3:6; James 1:17)

The God of Abraham set His children straight to teach them the importance of keeping His Sabbaths holy on His appointed days, by giving them enough manna on the sixth day of the week so that they would have enough to feed them on His seventh-day Sabbath (Ex. chapter 16). But rulers like Jeroboam set their own times and days for worship. And we can clearly see that God does *not* accept that.

Humans surely are stiff-necked, selfish, and control-mongering beasts; else they should have learned from the earlier account of the golden calf, in which God made it specifically clear that He does not accept His name to be mixed with paganism: "And when Aaron saw it [the golden calf, verse 4], he built an altar before it; and Aaron made proclamation, and said, **To morrow is a feast to the LORD**" (Ex. 32:5). They feared the Lord and worshipped paganism in His name, but the God of Abraham blatantly condemned it: "Now therefore let me alone, that my wrath may wax hot against them, and that I may consume them" (Ex. 32:10). Today's society—especially mainstream traditional Christianity, who ought to know better—has not changed for the better. Mankind's desire still remains to serve the Babylonian gods rather than the eternal God. And just like our forefathers of old, mankind still does this in the name of the Eternal, professing to be worshipping the Lord, thus deceiving millions—or perhaps billions—of well-meaning people by it, hence taking the name of the Lord in vain (Ex. 20:7).

Forgive me if this sounds harsh or judgmental, because that is not at all my intention. My heart is crying out to reveal the truth to all who want to hear it. I was a very dedicated follower of that very system for nearly five decades, and what I am writing here is based on my own personal experience in and with that system. As instructed in Isaiah 58:1 and Hosea 5:8, I'm blowing the trumpet and crying aloud to try to wake up the people who are still drunk on that intoxicating system, and warn against the great wrath God has in store for those who know better but, because of the fear of man, choose to keep wallowing in it in whatever ways.

If you are a dedicated follower of that system while you are reading this, I have a good knowledge of how you are feeling at this moment; I've been there. Satan cannot afford to let the people hear the truth about such apostasies, and he'll stop at nothing to prevent this sort of information from gaining any ground—especially in the traditional church system itself, which is inspired by his anti-God messiah, through whom it is preached—for his sole purpose of darkness and destruction in the end. The Messiah cautioned us about Satan's darkness being manifested through man: "And this is the condemnation, that light is come into the world, and **men loved darkness rather than light, because their deeds were evil** (John 3:19). Therefore, I am truly grateful that the eternal God of heaven and earth called me and my family out of that Christianized pagan Babylonian system: "Come out of her, my people, that ye be not partakers of her sins, and that ye receive not of her plagues" (Rev. 18:4). Paul also emphasized it: "Wherefore **come out** from among them, and **be ye separate**, saith the Lord, and touch not the **unclean <akathartos>**[35a] thing; and I will receive you" (2 Cor. 6:17; read also Isa. 48:20; Jer. 50:8, 28; 51:6, 45). Paul is warning God's people to sever from the Babylonian system, which he knew was indulging in unclean **<akathartos>**[35a] things, such as eating unclean foods while sacrificing to pagan gods and worshipping the same.

I realize that this small testimony may not be important to you. But what is important to me is that you might know that as long as you're a part of that system, or supporting it, you will remain blinded (veiled) to God's truth. Only after being called out of that pagan Babylonian anticommandment and hence anti-*God* system can our hearts be unveiled to perceive the scriptural truth. That is our true experience, and it's supported by God's Word. As we saw in section 1, the philosophical traditional indoctrination of this world's gods—the religious Babylonian anti-Torah system—kept us veiled from seeing the truth as long as we played a part in it. (2 Cor. 3:14 to 4:4; John 5:46–47).

If you finish reading this book, I hope and pray that God will open your eyes and ears:

> I counsel thee to buy of me gold tried in the fire, that thou mayest be rich; and white raiment, that thou mayest be clothed, and that the shame of thy nakedness do not appear; and **anoint thine eyes** with eyesalve, **that thou mayest see.** (Rev. 3:18)

> Then the eyes of the blind shall be opened, and the ears of the deaf shall be unstopped. (Isa. 35:5)

And only the God of Israel can open our eyes and ears and thus reveal His prophecies to us. All I can do is share my experience and hope that it might by some tiny measure at the very least provoke you to seek the truth from the Holy Scriptures, so that if and when God calls you out, you will understand and obey His calling. And that is how God speaks and prophesies to us today—through His word in the Holy Scriptures, not through Satan's lawless, commandment-hating, hence anti-God ministers! When we fearfully and faithfully pray to God for wisdom (Ps. 111:10; John 15:16; James 1:5–6), unbiased and unharnessed from the world's traditional Babylonian anti-God system, He unveils our heart, whereby we can then start to understand His prophecies. That is the Messiah's emphasis in John 5:46–47; 9:39 (the whole argument from chapters 5–10); and Paul's emphasis in 2 Cor. 3:14 to 4:4. And God can open our eyes only if we are willing to obey Him (Acts 5:32; Heb. 5:9) and seek Him with an honest, reverent, and unbiased heart and mind (Lev. 26:40–42; 2 Chron. 7:14; James 1:5–6; John 14:13–17; 16:23–27; 1 John 3:22) through His righteous, glorified Son, the Messiah, who does not contradict His Word (John 10:35; Matt. 5:17; Heb. 13:8). May the eternal God grant you that wisdom and understanding in full abundance and in all richness, for His honor and glory; so be it.

==

In the first few sections we briefly reviewed the downfall of the children of Israel, and we reviewed in short how and why the Pharisees invented multiple hundreds of commandments of their own. We saw in Matthew chapter 15 and Mark chapter 7 how God's commandments **<entole>**[9] were automatically forsaken by and through the use of man's traditional commandments **<entalma>**[9a].

Because of their zeal for God, the Pharisees did profess to be keeping His commandments, although in a profaned way. Since the Messiah condemned the use of their Judaized version of God's commandments, the theologians have labeled God's commandments **<entole>**[9] as Judaism! Our Lord and Savior did not condemn their keeping of God's commandments **<entole>**[9], but He violently condemned their Judaizing of them—the adding and taking away of words that God abhorrently forbids: "**Ye shall not add unto the word which I command you, neither shall ye diminish ought from it**, [Why?] **that ye may keep the commandments of the LORD your God** which I command you" (Deut. 4:2; read also 12:32; Prov. 30:6; Rev. 22:18–19). And the Book of Scriptures ends by confirming that same warning (Rev. 22:18–19). That Book of Scriptures begins with Genesis 1:1 and ends with Revelation 22:21.

Why would the Messiah excoriate the Pharisees for forsaking God's commandments if He specifically came to abolish them? Should He not then rather have complimented them for forsaking them? I say no! Read the Messiah's words again; focus specifically on the words *not* and *no* and what they mean: "Think **not** that I am come to destroy the law, or the prophets: I am **not** come to destroy, but to fulfil. For verily I say unto you, Till heaven and earth pass, one jot or one tittle shall in **no** wise pass from the law, till all be fulfilled" (Matt. 5:17–18; read also Luke 16:17). We have reviewed many scriptures so far that plainly explain what is and what is not yet fulfilled, and the purpose behind what is and what is not fulfilled. We learned that what had been fulfilled was not destroyed, or abolished, but brought to its fullness, purpose, and intended goal so that we, through and by His spirit, can likewise keep God's commandments and laws properly to fulfill them as He did; because the faithful keeping of them produces God's sacrificial-type charitable <**agape**>[8] love and mercy within us.

The Messiah gives us strong warnings about people becoming lawless (breaking commandments) in the end time. The pride and covetousness of the Pharisees of His time is a perfect testimony and example of how the love for God and for one another freezes over (waxes cold) when we underestimate the importance of observing God's laws and commandments rather than man's. I believe that we now know that the Scriptural definition of "love" is keeping God's commandments: "By this we know that we love the children of God, when we love God, and **keep <tereo>[21] his commandments <entole>[9]. For this is the love <agape>[8] of God, that we keep his commandments: and his commandments are not grievous** [but rather <**agape**>[8] love]" (1 John 5:2–3). He warned that the commandments of God would not be kept by many people in the end time, wherefore <**agape**>[8] love would logically grow cold: "And because **iniquity** <**anomia**>[12] [lawlessness; the breaking of commandments] shall abound, the **love** <**agape**>[8] of many shall wax cold" (Matt. 24:12). The Messiah makes it very plain that love grows cold when God's laws are not observed. This occurs because mankind is typically more afraid of the visible religious leaders—the gods of this world—than of the invisible creator God of Abraham.

The apostles did not show hatred toward the rulers of that day, but the religious rulers bore extreme hatred toward them. Why? Because the apostles—who were trained by the Messiah—set the importance of God's commandments and laws above the commandments of men. As we learned earlier, that's why they were continually at loggerheads with the religious leaders (Acts 5:25–33; Acts 4:19; Ps. 40:4; 62:8–9; 118:8; Jer. 17:5, 7). The Messiah warned them beforehand that if they would follow Him, the religious leaders would kill them, believing that they were pleasing God:

> Then shall they deliver you up to be afflicted, and **shall kill you**: and **ye shall be hated of all nations for my name's sake.** (Matt. 24:9)

> They shall put you out of the synagogues: yea, the time cometh, that **whosoever killeth you will think that he doeth God service.** (John 16:2)

It holds true that by such works traditionalists are actually pleasing *their* god—Satan—the god of traditional religion.

So we can begin to see that it's the anti-Jew philosophy that has influenced the theologians, hence early church fathers, to invent the anti-Law doctrines, through which today's traditional churches are plagued with an anti-God messiah without knowing it! Why don't they know it? According to God's Word, they can't, for the same reason as the Pharisees; they forsake God's laws and commandments, wherefore the God of Abraham allowed the god of this Babylonian world to also blind/veil their hearts (2 Cor. 3:14–4:4; 11:13–15) from the true light, wherefore God must turn His back on them (Isa. 59:2; Matt. 27:46)! God had to turn His back even on His sinless Son because He purchased the penalty for *our* lawlessness (breaking of commandments). How shall God, as the Creator of the universe, look at a church system that advocates lawlessness as salvation to millions or perhaps multiple billions of people, professing it divinely in His name! Can you see the irony in that?

After explaining the parable of the tares, the Messiah very plainly tells us what the reward will be for commandment breakers at the end of this age: "As therefore the tares are gathered and burned in the fire; so shall it be **in the end of this world**. The Son of man shall send forth his angels, and they shall gather out of his kingdom **all things that offend, and <u>them which do iniquity</u> <anomia>**[12] [breaking of commandments]; **And shall cast them into a furnace of fire** [the second and final (eternal) death]**:** there shall be wailing and gnashing of teeth" (Matt. 13:41–42). He's referring to the end time, which, if you're reading this, testifies that the end has not yet occurred; thus it's yet before us. And should you be guilty of following in the steps of such a Babylonian anti-Law system, you can still come out of her, repent of it, and come to terms with the God of Israel and be saved from His promised wrath (2 Cor. 6:14–18; Rev. 18:4). Read Matthew 13:41–42 again. **The Messiah stated in unmistakable**

terms that commandment breakers will be cast into the lake of fire. It's each one's own choice whose commandments one wishes to follow.

The early church fathers wholesaled God's commandments off for Roman and other pagan customs and traditions, which have been passed down throughout the generations and have thus also been elevated above commandment status through the traditional church system. And once again, since the Jews proudly professed to be keeping God's commandments, traditional Christendom must forsake them ("can't have anything in common with the Jews; the murderers of our LORD" [Constantine's canonized decree]). As we can read throughout the scriptures, whenever God's commandments are not being kept, they always, without fail, get replaced with Egyptian/Babylonian pagan customs and traditions—a system that is symbolically described in Isaiah chapters 47 and 48, Jeremiah chapters 50 and 51, 2 Corinthians chapters 6 and 11, and Revelation chapters 14, 17, and 18 as a very influential Babylonian whore together with her harlot daughters, the mystery religion of lawlessness: "For the **mystery of iniquity <anomia>**[12] [breaking of commandments] **doth already work"** (2 Thess. 2:7).

Apostasies such as I'm trying to expose are likely what the Messiah had in mind while speaking to an end-time church of Pergamos: "But I have a few things against thee, because thou hast there them that hold the **doctrine of Balaam**, who taught Balak **to cast a stumblingblock before the children of Israel, to eat things sacrificed unto idols, and to commit fornication"** (Rev. 2:14). God's true congregation is still called the Israel of God (Gal. 6:16). But because of the anticommandment and hence anti-God philosophy, which is born through the extreme anti-Jew indoctrination of the masses, today's traditional church system is violently pulling people away from God's original instructions in the Torah, thereby also—just like Balaam—creating a stumbling block for the followers of the God of Israel, who is the only true redeeming Messiah and Savior.

If you'll study the accounts of false prophets in the Old Testament, you will see how God allows Satan to subtly indoctrinate people with his concepts and beliefs in such a cunning way that his followers will even sacrifice their lives for him (Satan), believing that they are doing it for the God of Creation. Satan, through his theologically trained ministers, does this in a very gradual and friendly fashion, and in a way that will entice the people in such a seemingly innocent way that they will actually sincerely believe that they are doing it for the Lord God of Creation! I will briefly summarize some of the events that show how the God of Israel allowed the wicked prophet Balak to use an honest prophet, Balaam, to test His children—to very gradually ensnare the Israelites by enticing them with things that appease the carnal mind, thus causing them to commit to things that are an abomination to the God of Israel. This is similar to what Paul alludes to in 2 Thessalonians chapter 2, where he warns against believing lies from lawless indoctrinators.

9. THE DOCTRINE OF BALAAM

We will briefly review what befell the children of Israel after Balak hired Balaam to sabotage their belief in the God of Abraham by putting curses upon them. We will see how the God of Abraham allowed Satan's faithful minister Balak—a god of this world—to work through the prophet Balaam to truly test the Israelites by using the principles of the test prophecy of the Torah to see whether or not they truly loved Him (Deut. 12:28–13:5). Then we will see how the principles of the Balak/Balaam doctrines have become a foundational building block for the doctrines of today's traditional church system, which ought to be a test for its adherents *if* they compare the doctrines with the Word of God. But tragically, traditional Christendom will typically measure the doctrines that come from *their* denomination against the doctrines from other denominations, instead of from God's Word.

Balak was a king of the Moabites who served Baal *(Satan)*. Balaam was an honest prophet, which Balak knew was required to gain access to the God of Israel. Balak was afraid of being overtaken by the children of Israel upon their entry into his territory. He already knew the history of the Israelites and what their God had recently done to other heathen nations around him, because he had witnessed the Amorites get destroyed by that God (Num. 22:2–3), which gave him a very valid reason to be afraid. Balak was too arrogant with too much pride to give in to that God, so he hired someone who had access to the powers of that great God, in hopes to use that power to curse the Israeli army, in an effort to save him from their God's wrath. So Balak figured that Balaam qualified for that position and tried to hire him with high hopes of conquering the Israelites by getting Balaam to put curses upon them for him. So out of the fear of the wrath of the God of Israel—which Balak obviously thought came from the Israelites—he hired Balaam to put curses upon the Israelites in order to save him from such wrath as he had witnessed.

Incidentally, the God of Israel requires that a man fear Him in order to have Him on his side, but Balak had the wrong kind of fear; he feared the Israelite *people*. Balak's god—a god of this world—comes as a friendly giant who uses his ministry to indoctrinate the people with a fear of men, as obviously was the case with Balak. King Saul confessed after he realized that the god of this world had put the wrong fear into him: "And Saul said unto Samuel, I have sinned: for I have transgressed the commandment of the Lord, and thy words: **because I feared the people, and obeyed their voice**" (1 Sam. 15:24).

In Numbers chapters 22 through 24, Balak tried with all his power and might to bribe Balaam into cursing the Israelites for him. He offered Balaam whatever it might take, if only he would curse them for him. Obviously Balak's gods could not do it for him. There is a very good analogy in the scriptures that explains the uselessness of Balak's gods: "Go and cry unto the gods **which ye have chosen**; let them deliver you in the time of your tribulation" (Judg. 10:14). Balak chose to worship and sacrifice to gods who were obviously powerless. And as free moral agents, we are commanded by the God of Israel to choose one or the other: "And Elijah came unto all the people, and said, How long halt ye between two opinions? **if the Lord be God, follow him: but if Baal, then follow him**" (1 Kings 18:21). Satan's servants—the traditional anti-Torah ministers—through traditional commandments, train his followers to fear man, wherefore mankind will typically choose Baal.

Balaam kept telling Balak's messengers that he could not go beyond the commandments of the Lord and therefore could do to the Israelites only what their God told him (Num. 22:18). And it so happened that every time a curse was to be put forth upon the Israelites, they received a blessing instead. And this went on for some time.

Finally, when we get to chapter 25, Satan's mission is accomplished by Balak, through Balaam. As the Israelites started to conquer the last nations of their promised possession, they became attracted to the strangers of that land. Satan devised a plan by encouraging the sons and daughters of the heathen nations to entice the children of Israel to marry them. Through this relationship they started serving and worshipping the gods of the people, which God had forbidden them to do; they were to make no covenants with the strangers, and He gave them plenty of very serious warnings before they crossed the Jordan River:

> Take heed to thyself, **lest thou make a covenant with the inhabitants of the land whither thou goest, lest it be for a snare** in the midst of thee: But ye shall destroy their altars, break their images, and cut down their groves: For **thou shalt worship no other god**: for the LORD, whose name is Jealous, is a jealous God: **Lest thou make a covenant with the inhabitants of the land, and they go a whoring after their gods, and do sacrifice unto their gods** [New Year's, Easter, Christmas, Sunday, birthdays (Jeroboam's doctrines)], **and one call thee, and thou eat of his sacrifice** [unclean meats and/or profaned clean meats]; **And thou take of their daughters unto thy sons, and their daughters go a whoring after their gods, and make thy sons go a whoring after their gods** (Ex. 34:12–16; read also Ex. 23:32–33; Deut. 7:2–6; 12:28–13:7; 2 Cor. 6:14–18; Rev. 2:14).

God's message is crystal clear throughout the scriptures: to be kept (protected) by Him and liberated as His prized possession and children requires one to cling to only His commandments, statutes, and laws.

If the Israelites had applied the Torah test–as God commanded them to in Deuteronomy 12:28–13:7 just before they crossed the Jordan River–they would have been able to tell that Balak and his people were not Torah-abiding people, and thus they could have avoided one of their great downfalls.

I will list a few of the scriptures form the Old and New Testament that pertain to the Balaam doctrines, so you can read and study them to your satisfaction: Numbers chapters 22–25 and 31; Judges chapter 2; 1 Kings chapter 18, 2 Kings chapter 17; 2 Peter 2:15; Jude 1:11; Revelation 2:14.

Remember how Jeroboam caused the Israelites to transgress God's laws in a way in which the Israelites thought that they were worshipping the God of their fathers? Jeroboam may not necessarily have done it to intentionally work against God, but he used doctrines devised by his own thoughts—the commandments of men. He changed the timing of God's worship days and His holy days, and just as in the account of the golden calf (Ex. 32:5–6), the Israelites thought they were doing it in honor of the God of Israel. Even though they had good intentions, God flat-out condemned the works of Jeroboam—the very works (specifically the breaking of Sabbaths) that caused Him to first have the Israelites taken into captivity and then to have them scattered all over the world, through which they lost their identity (Ezekiel chapter 20). Thus He eventually divorced them (Jeremiah 3:8). You will find these accounts in 1 Kings starting in chapter 11, and his doctrinal legacy runs clear through the scriptures and continues to this day! A powerful example is Sunday, which traditional Christendom has labeled the Lord's Day in an effort to justify Satan's abrogation of the true Lord's Sabbath commandment. There is a lot documented in the scriptures about rulers like Jeroboam and Balaam because God wanted us to learn lessons from those accounts. Remember, it will not be of any help to tell God that we were misled by a parent, a preacher, a doctor, or anyone else, because each will answer to Him on his own behalf (Ezek. 18 and 33; Matt. 16:27; Rom. 2:6; Rev. 2:23; 20:12-15; 22:12).

We need to always remember that the God of Israel allows the god of this world to surreptitiously foist pagan atrocities upon us as a test, but He does not accept any worship, nor hear any prayers, that come from a person whose beliefs are tainted with pagan philosophies:

> He said also unto me, Turn thee yet again, and thou shalt see greater abominations that they do. Then he brought me to the door of the gate of the LORD's house which was toward the north; and, behold, there sat women **weeping for Tammuz** [Nimrod's son]. Then said he unto me, Hast thou seen this, O son of man? turn thee yet again, and thou

> shalt see greater abominations than these. And he brought me into the inner court of the LORD's house, and, behold, at the door of the temple of the LORD [symbolically our heart today], between the porch and the altar, were about five and twenty men, with their backs toward the temple of the LORD, and their faces toward the east; and **they worshipped the sun toward the east** [Easter and Easter sunrise service, Sunday worship]. Then he said unto me, Hast thou seen this, O son of man? Is it a light thing to the house of Judah that they commit the abominations which they commit here? for they have filled the land with violence, and have returned to provoke me to anger: and, lo, **they put the branch to their nose**. Therefore will **I also deal in fury: mine eye shall not spare, neither will I have pity: and <u>though they cry in mine ears with a loud voice, yet will I not hear them.</u>** (Ezek. 8:13–18; read also Jg. 10:14; 1 Sam. 8:18)

In the phrase "they put the branch to their nose," the Hebrew text does not indicate whose nose is being referred to. I kind of take that to refer to—as in a modern-day vernacular—sticking the big finger under His [God's] nose. Whether that's the intent or not, the context certainly indicates that the people whom He is referring to here are doing whatever they are doing in order to humiliate Him.

The God of Israel makes it very plain that He will not hear their prayers, not even in a time of need when they are crying aloud for His help. We can't say that He didn't warn us about the consequences of choosing a different god. He delivers His people when they obey Him, but not when they follow other gods: "The Zidonians also, and the Amalekites, and the Maonites, **did oppress you; and ye cried to me, <u>and I delivered you out of their hand</u>. Yet ye have forsaken me, and served other gods: wherefore I will deliver you no more. <u>Go and cry unto the gods which ye have chosen; let them deliver you in the time of your tribulation</u>**" (Deut. 32:37; Judg. 10:14; 1 Kings 18:27; 2 Kings 3:13; Jer. 2:28). I hear from the traditional pulpits that the commandments of the God of Israel are burdensome. Think about this and decide for yourself whose commandments deliver curses and whose commandments deliver blessings! Then, as God commands, choose your gods and pray to them whenever you need deliverance.

In 1 Samuel chapter 8, the Israelites voted for democracy for the second time since God redeemed them from Egyptian bondage and slavery. Study it and you'll see how that enslaved them again into the bondage and slavery of this world's religious-governmental system; by voting for their own king, they inevitably forsook the God of Israel. They were free moral agents, and God allowed them to choose for themselves. So they chose—or, in modern terms, voted—for an earthly king to rule over them, of which the accounts in Nehemiah 5:1–5, Lamentations 5:1–9, and Haggai 1:1–6 are a very powerful and sobering testimony about the extreme bondage with which they were again enslaved a few generations later because of that choice. And the accounts in Mark chapter 7 and Matthew chapters 15 and 23 give very valid testimonies to that control-mongering and hypocritically religious apostasy; these testimonies are still applicable in the modern day. Today's mainstream traditional Christendom is still voting, with the same results. God's voice still tells us today that we can scream into His ears as loud as we will, but while we're ensnared in this world's paganism, He will not hear our prayers!

Studying these accounts reminds me so much of today's traditional Christians. When discussing obedience to God's commandments vs. church traditions, observing God's holy days instead of pagan holidays, keeping God's Sabbath instead of the pagan Sunday, keeping God's dietary and health laws, and the like, the traditionalists will always justify their philosophy by triumphantly pronouncing that it does not matter which days we celebrate and worship or how we do so; that it does not matter what we eat and how we keep ourselves, or how we conduct our lives. The important thing, they say, is that we do the things we do in the Lord's name. In the same breath, they judge commandment-keepers like me for not keeping their pagan holidays and Sundays, and for not eating abominable and unclean things. Study the following scriptures to see how God abhors people that follow after traditions of men: "*Thus saith the*

*LORD; **Cursed be the man that trusteth in man**"* (Jer. 17:5; read also Prov. 3:5–8; Pss. 40:4; 62:5–9; 118:8; Matt. 15:1–20; chapter 23; Mark 7:1–13; Acts 4:19; 5:29).

While reviewing the Bible commentaries, I see that many of them use that exact same lawless philosophy. I find in many areas that they will reference and link Judaism together with God's commandments to surreptitiously connect them to certain accounts that involve grievous and burdensome deeds, in order to portray the Ten Commandments as being responsible for all the burdensome and grievous deeds the Pharisees foisted upon the people under their rule. But in every such case, they take the text out of its context. As a result, they have made God's commandments out to be a burdensome and hard to bear-yoke of bondage, which they label as weak and beggarly rudiments and elements of this world; they interpret the pagan holidays as God's holy days, they label God's dietary and health laws as Jewish and burdensome, and the list goes on and on. Thereby, God's laws and commandments, which He created for our good (Deut. chapter 8; 30:19–20), have been labeled with all the wicked and evil aspects the scriptures have condemned as traditionalism and Judaism. As I've been trying to show, God's commandments are to be kept because they reveal God's sacrificial charitable <**agape**>[8] love to us.

God redeemed His children from bondage and slavery because of His <**agape**>[8] love for them:

> Wherefore say unto the children of Israel, I am the LORD, and **I will bring you out from under the burdens of the Egyptians**, and **I will rid you out of their bondage**, and **I will redeem you** with a stretched out arm, and with great judgments. (Ex. 6:6)

> Ye have seen what I did unto the Egyptians, and how **I bare you on eagles' wings**, and **brought you unto myself.** (Ex. 19:4)

> As described in Deuteronomy 30:15-30, keeping God's commandments promises life - not keeping them guarantees death.

God's love does not cause grief; rather, it allows one to bear it for another: "**Bear ye one another's burdens**, and so **fulfil** <**anapleroo**>[10c] the law of Christ" (Gal. 6:2). I'll say it again; the Messiah kept God's commandments perfect, whereby He attained God's sacrificial-type charitable <**agape**>[8] love, which caused Him to willingly bear our burdens. He *is* God's Word, which inherently includes the Ten Commandments, which is part of every word of God: "And the **Word** [the Messiah] was made flesh, and **dwelt** <**skenoo**>[36] among us." (John 1:14; read also Matt. 4:4; Luke 4:4). God's Word (the Torah) became the Messiah, who dwells (tabernacles) in the heart (temple) of His people.

To say that God's laws can't be kept because they are grievous is to imply that He took the children of Israel out of the Egyptian bondage and slavery only to enslave them with His legal bondage and slavery. That is about as close to blasphemy as it can get, for God's apostles—who continually point out the goodness, holiness, and justness of His commandments—to call the laws by such terms as the theologians and traditional ministers claim they did.

10. TRADITIONAL CHRISTENDOM VS. JEWISM: WALL-BUILDING

By now we know that we cannot yet possess immortality (1 Cor. 15:42–56). The Messiah is the only one from earth who has immortality (1 Tim. 6:16). No one but the resurrected Messiah has entered God's kingdom: "And no man hath ascended up to heaven, but he that came down even the Son of man which is in heaven" (John 3:13; read also Ps. 30:4; Acts 2:29, 34; Heb. 11). Hebrews chapter 11 explains in simple terms that the saints of old have not yet received the promises (verses 13 and 39). It goes on to say that they will not receive them before the very same resurrection upon which today's saints are also waiting (verse 39–40).

A logical reason to explain why the mainstream traditional-Catholic/Protestant-Christian doctrines are taught the way they are, is that the early traditional church fathers—because of their extreme hatred for an all-authoritative God—inevitably caused them to hate His commandments and laws; that's a given (Rom. 8:7). Since many of the Jews professed to be keeping God's commandments in the days of the early traditional church fathers, the hatred of the church fathers built up rapidly and furiously toward the Jews. That's why Constantine the Great made that decree: "can't have anything in common with the Jews; the murderers of our LORD." Since the Pharisaic Jews rejected the events of the Messiah's First Coming, it is safe for the traditional Christians to latch onto it, and they somewhat have. And because those Jews are still waiting for the events of the Second Coming—which they understand as the only coming—the traditional church system cannot and will not have any part of it. So they must again take the opposite approach, and they have invented plenty enough theocracy to have accomplished that mission by indoctrinating their followers with a belief that all is already fulfilled. Thus the fathers have cunningly shifted the events of the Messiah's Second Coming into the realm of His First Coming, because their doctrines indicate—as the fathers triumphantly profess—that the Messiah already fulfilled everything on the tree.

Since the Jews professed their beliefs to be based upon the God of the Old Testament, traditional Christendom must forsake that God—and they have—by advocating an anti-Law/anti-God messiah/god of the New Testament, who is viciously opposed to the commandments and laws of the Old Testament God. Thus, mission accomplished! T*raditional* Christianity now virtually has **nothing** in common with the Jews! And since this doctrine undeniably requires full attainment of the events of both comings, all has been fulfilled in that philosophy, thus not requiring a Second Coming of the Messiah, because they don't need a resurrection! But, Paul condemned exactly such doctrines:

> Study to shew thyself approved unto God [prove doctrine with the Torah test], a workman that needeth not to be ashamed [truth sets us free - John 8:32], rightly dividing the word of truth [separating truth from lies—traditions of men]. But **shun profane and vain babblings** [false doctrines]**: for they will increase unto more ungodliness.** And their word will eat as doth a canker: of whom is Hymenaeus and Philetus; **Who concerning the truth have erred, saying that the resurrection <anastasis>**[67] **is past already** [indicating that all is fulfilled]; and overthrow the faith of some. Nevertheless the foundation of God standeth sure [a foundation goes back to its beginning], having this seal, The Lord knoweth them that are his [by the sign]. And, **Let every one** [Jew and Gentile] **that nameth the name of Christ depart from iniquity.** (2 Tim. 2:15–19)

In Paul's day there were people already preaching that the resurrection was fulfilled. Although traditional Christendom does not blatantly preach that philosophy exactly in that way, based on their doctrines they don't require a resurrection.

What Paul wrote to Timothy harmonizes perfectly with the end-time prophesies written of in Isaiah chapters 56 and 58, in that those who name God as Lord are to depart from lawless and unrighteous living. God commands the people of all races who name Him as their Lord are to keep His Sabbaths. Chapter 56 finishes with God excoriating the shepherds who cannot understand because they use their own ways—traditions of men—to their gain:

> Thus saith the LORD, Keep ye judgment, and do justice: for my salvation is near to come, and my righteousness to be revealed. Blessed is the man that doeth this, and **the son of man that layeth hold on it; that keepeth the sabbath from polluting it**, and keepeth his hand from doing any evil. **Neither let the son of the stranger, that hath <u>joined himself to the LORD</u>, speak, saying, The LORD hath utterly separated me from his people** [the believing Gentiles are not counted separate from His people, the Israelites, which includes the Jews]: neither let the eunuch say, Behold, I am a dry tree. For thus saith the LORD unto the eunuchs that keep my sabbaths, and choose the things that please me, and take hold of my covenant; Even unto them will I give in mine house and within my walls a place and a name better than of sons and of daughters: I will give them an everlasting name, that shall not be cut off. **Also the sons of the stranger, that <u>join themselves to the LORD</u>, to serve him, and to love the name of the LORD, to be his servants, <u>every one that keepeth the sabbath from polluting it</u>, and taketh hold of my covenant; Even them will I bring to my holy mountain, and make them joyful in my house of prayer**: their burnt offerings and their sacrifices shall be accepted upon mine altar; for mine house shall be called an house of prayer for all people. The Lord GOD which gathereth the outcasts of Israel saith, Yet will I gather others to him, beside those that are gathered unto

> him. All ye beasts of the field, come to devour, yea, all ye beasts in the forest. His watchmen are blind: they are all ignorant, they are all dumb dogs, they cannot bark; sleeping, lying down, loving to slumber. Yea, **they are greedy dogs which can never have enough, and they are shepherds that cannot understand: they all look to their own way** [traditions of men]**, every one for his gain**, from his quarter. Come ye, say they, I will fetch wine, and we will fill ourselves with strong drink; and to morrow shall be as this day, and much more abundant. (Isaiah chapter 56)

These are very powerful testimonies from both the Old and New Testaments stating that the Gentiles (strangers) of today who have joined themselves to the Lord (Isa. 56:6), or every one that names the name of Christ (2 Tim. 2:19) as Paul called it, are to keep the Lord's Sabbaths and refrain from breaking commandments, together with the Israelites, which includes the Jews. I know—this statement is absolutely unacceptable to the traditional anti-Jew church society.

Since the Jews are awaiting the First Coming of their Messiah, which we recognize as the Second Coming, the mainstream traditional Christians need to get out of this world before the resurrection. That's why Satan invented the Rapture theory—to bypass the Second Coming, as that's for the Jews. And according to the traditional Babylonian doctrines, upon death they immediately go to heaven, hell, or whatever their destiny might be, thus bypassing the Second Coming and the future resurrections via an immortal soul that they profess to have, hence they do not require a resurrection. But since all must die, the resurrection is man's only hope (1 Cor. 15:12–19).

I will list a few doctrines that I believe had to be invented in order to reason around the need to be tried by the events of the tribulation and whatsoever identifies the apocalyptic events that must come to pass prior to the Messiah's Second Coming, when the first resurrection will occur for His true followers. These are as follows:

1. The new covenant must be fully established in order to already fully obtain salvation. For this, a person must already be immortal in order to enter into God's kingdom immediately upon death without needing to wait for the resurrection. This would take care of the ones that have died.
2. For the so-called Christians yet living at that time, Satan has cunningly invented a theory that would rapture them out of here before the trials get tough. (As explained briefly in the side note in section 5b, this theory is just that—theory! It is Satan's bypass theory). For the believers of this theory, I must ask again, where does faith fit into all this? As we saw in section 5b, by simply using the same scriptures that they've misappropriated and perverted to establish the pretrib Rapture theory shatters it, thus rendering it a bogus doctrine. That is a setup for extreme disappointment and betrayal to believers of it when they find out—perhaps too late—that they believed an ear-tickling, pew-warming, anti-Jew lie. Remember, no lies will enter God's kingdom (Rev. 21:8; 22:15). And God specifically said that He would cause those who don't love the truth (the Torah) to believe strong lies for their own demise (2 Thess. 2:1–13).

Thus, the deceiver's purpose for these doctrines is accomplished: the Messiah's Second Coming—which is the only hope that the Pharisaic Jews have, and which Paul stated in 1 Corinthians chapter 15 is the true hope for all mankind—is not required according to the traditional church doctrines! As the earlier church fathers stated, "we can have nothing in common with the Jews!" Mission accomplished! The traditional church doctrines have nothing in common with the Jews. And they cannot make that claim if they keep God's commandments, God's holy days, and God's dietary and health laws, or if they wait until the first resurrection for the Messiah's Second Coming, which will be after the tribulation. By the way, the true Messiah, and most of His disciples, were also Jewish born, and traditional churchgoers have potentially nothing, or very little at most, in common with them. Thus, Satan's mission to denigrate the validity and verity of the Ten Commandments has been accomplished through the traditional church system. Therefore, that system just might turn to ashes during the Great Tribulation.

These doctrines come from one same sect of theologians, most of which go back to the Gnostic Greeks. Some date back as far as ancient Egypt, the tower of Babel (the birthplace of Babylon), and the garden of Eden. Since the creation of the first man, the controlling sect of humanity has indoctrinated the masses with concepts and theories as to how to get to the highest heaven (the place where God resides) with Satan's roadmap. As we learned earlier, Satan has enticed mankind to forever search for a shortcut to God's throne via his roadmap, as it was with the tower of Babel. And that has been Satan's plan since before man was created, when he convinced many angels to rebel together with him against God. He has attempted to gain access to God's throne ever since he was dethroned: "How art thou fallen from heaven, O Lucifer, son of the morning! how art thou cut down to the ground, which didst weaken the nations! For **thou hast said in thine heart, I will ascend into heaven, I will exalt my throne above the stars of God: I will sit also upon the mount of the congregation** [he will for a season in the end of time - Revelation chapter 13]**, in the sides of the north: I will ascend above the heights of the clouds; I will be like the most High. Yet thou shalt be brought down to hell, to the sides of the pit**" (Isa. 14:12–15; read also Ezek. chapter 28; Luke 10:18). This is Satan's seed, from which philosophies like the pretrib Rapture-bypass theory have sprung, which requires an immortal soul in order to bypass the Great Tribulation and the resurrection. All of this had to be doctored up in order to have **nothing in common with the Jews**—in the name of man's hatred toward the sovereign creator God who created the Ten Commandments.

The Messiah gave us His thoughts on that bypass philosophy:

> Verily, verily, I say unto you, **He that entereth not by the door into the sheepfold, but climbeth up some other**

way [bypass theory]**, the same is a thief and a robber.** (John 10:1)

And He defines the traits of such a thief: **The thief cometh not, but for to steal, and to kill, and to destroy** [wake-up call for the Rapture enthusiasts]**:** I am come that they might have life, and that they might have it more abundantly. (John 10:10)

Paul put a very serious emphasis on that Isaiah prophecy, how through the works of lawlessness Satan will first control his people through the religious masses by exalting himself as God, and then come to absolute naught:

Now we beseech you, brethren, by the coming of our Lord Jesus Christ [after the tribulation—Matt. 24:29; at the last trumpet—1 Cor. 15:52; Rev. 11:15], and by our gathering together unto him [after the resurrection], That ye be not soon shaken in mind, or be troubled, neither by spirit, nor by word, nor by letter as from us, as that the day of Christ [the Lord's Day—Rev. 1:10] is at hand. Let no man deceive you by any means: for that day shall not come, except there come a falling away first, and that man of sin be revealed, the son of perdition; **Who opposeth and exalteth himself above all that is called God, or that is worshipped; so that he as God sitteth in the temple of God, shewing himself that he is God.** Remember ye not, that, when I was yet with you, I told you these things? And now ye know what withholdeth that he might be revealed in his time. For **the mystery of iniquity <anomia>**[12] [lawlessness, opposition to God's commandments] **doth already work:** only he who now letteth will let, until he be taken out of the way. And **then shall that Wicked be revealed, whom the Lord shall consume with the spirit of his mouth, and shall destroy with the brightness of his coming** [the Messiah's Second Coming]**: Even him** [the Messiah], **whose coming is <u>after</u> the working of Satan** [after the tribulation] **with all power and signs and lying wonders** [the ultimate Torah test of all time]. (2 Thess. 2:1–9; read also Dan. 7:25; 11:36; 1 Cor. 8:5; 1 John 2:18; 4:1–3; Rev. chapter 13)

What will the religious anti-Jew people measure the man of sin—Satan—against when he starts to manifest those prophesied miracles? The only truth to truly measure against is the Torah. Since mainstream traditional Christendom blatantly rejects the Old Testament, which contains the Torah, they are left with nothing of truth to measure any doctrines against, except the pulpit parrots' man-made church traditions, which come from the same deceiver who's going to be sitting in the temple doing the prophesied miracles. So, in essence, this is the result:

A Sobering End-Time Event: Everything that Satan will do—the great miracles and wonders like bringing fire down from heaven to impress and deceive all people—will be in perfect harmony with the traditional church doctrines! Why, you ask? Because Satan is the very one who orchestrated those pulpit doctrines in the first place, for the Pharisees and for traditional Christendom—all traditionalists alike throughout the world. God will specifically allow this to come upon mankind in order to test those who profess to be his children (Deut. 12:28–13:5). Satan—for the very purpose of the ultimate test—knows exactly what he needs to do in order to impress those who've already been indoctrinated to follow his doctrines, so that he can use them to persuade even more with his convincing, ear-tickling theories.

People will marvel at his miracles:

And he doeth **great wonders, so that he maketh fire come down from heaven** on the earth in the sight of men, **And deceiveth them that dwell on the earth by the means of those miracles** which he had power to do in the sight of the beast; saying to them that dwell on the earth, that they should make an image to the beast, which

> had the wound by a sword, and did live. And he had power to give life unto the image of the beast, that the image of the beast should both speak, and cause that as many as would not worship the image of the beast should be killed. (Rev. 13:13–15)

All who do not truthfully and diligently follow the Lord God of heaven and earth will be deceived: "And **all** that dwell upon the earth shall worship him, **whose names are not written in the book of life** of the Lamb slain from the foundation of the world" (Rev. 13:8).

We all need to give this a lot of serious thought: who or what will I measure Satan's great works against? How can I be absolutely sure from whom or where those great miracles are coming? It will not be quite so hard for the people who keep God's commandments, because if whoever is sitting in that seat does not keep and advocate all of the Ten Commandments, then it obviously cannot be from God. If you don't keep the Ten Commandments, you have absolutely nothing to measure him against; it will agree with traditional doctrine so much that it will simply impress its members.

I'm not suggesting that he won't be able to deceive those who observe the Ten Commandments, because he will in order to also test them. What I'm saying is that those who do keep God's commandments have much more truth to measure the deceiver's doctrines against than those who don't, thus giving such ones at least a slight leg up—a bit more measuring stick to measure that deceiver against. For example, if that deceiver is not keeping and advocating the Ten Commandments—including the weekly and annual Sabbaths—it's obvious that he's not from the God of the scriptures. What will traditional Christendom measure him against when he will be keeping and advocating Sunday, Christmas, Easter, and many other such doctrines that he himself invented millennia ago to prepare for this great event which God allowed him to orchestrate in order to test the people of this age this one final time? We can all rest assured that Satan will make the most of that event.

Paul specifically warned us about the mysterious, lawless works Satan has propagated through his anti-commandment ministry: "For such are false apostles, deceitful workers, transforming themselves into the apostles of Christ. And no marvel; for **Satan himself is transformed into an angel of light**. Therefore it is no great thing if **his ministers** [anti-Law preachers] **also be transformed as the ministers of righteousness**; whose end shall be according to their works" (2 Cor. 11:13–15). Only when we look at the cause and the effect of false doctrines from such a standpoint as we just have, and then compare it with God's true plan of salvation as revealed in His scriptures by applying the Torah test, can we start to discern between the scriptural truths and the traditional ear-tickling lies. According to traditional "All was fulfilled at the cross" philosophy, we must have already during the last two thousand years experienced the plagues that are to occur just prior to the Messiah's Second Coming, and likewise also the great promises that are to be fulfilled after His Second Coming. Such doctrines harbor an assurance, although false (insurance?), that salvation is already fully established, wherewith comes attached beliefs such as the immortal-soul and trinity doctrines, the going-to-heaven philosophy, the pretrib Rapture theory, and many more anti-Torah beliefs that are required to reason around the need to patiently wait through the tribulation period for the Messiah's return to resurrect His saints.

Let's put this into perspective. If you and I have an immortal soul that immediately upon death goes to heaven (or hell), why would a resurrection be required? We would already be in our destination the very moment we died. When I go to a funeral, I hear phrases like, "Here we are once again, looking at one of our faithful brethren whom God has called home to be with Him in heaven, from now into eternity. His immortal soul is watching us put his body into the ground." It makes me want to jump up and holler out the truth; that's why I rarely go to funerals in the traditional Christian circle.

These are simply ear-itching lies (2 Tim. 4:3–4) coming directly from the deceiver of the world (Rev. 12:9) to fill the seats in the traditional churches. Paul gave strong warnings about man-commanded fables that will be rampant as this era winds down: "Not giving heed to Jewish fables, and **commandments of men, that turn from the truth**" (Titus 1:14). He called the end-time philosophies "doctrines of devils": "Now the Spirit speaketh expressly, that **in the latter times** some shall depart from the faith, giving heed to seducing spirits, and **doctrines of devils; Speaking lies in hypocrisy**; having their conscience seared with a hot iron" (1 Tim. 4:1–2). The belief that we are already immortal is a doctrine of devils that goes all the way back to the deceiver's lie in the garden of Eden: "You shall **not** surely die" (Gen. 3:4), and that doctrine is still believed and preached today by the deceiver's meticulously trained traditional ministers (2 Cor. 11:13–15). But, as we learned in section 6b, we will not be immortal until after the resurrection, which happens at the return of the Messiah at the last trumpet, which will blow toward the end of the tribulation to announce the Messiah's return to put an end to the Great Tribulation (Matt. 24:29; 1 Cor. 15:52; 1 Thess. 4:16; Rev. 11:15). That will be a grievous time for Satan, the devil, because he will at that time—just before he wins over the last few people of this earth—be locked away for one thousand years.

Since the traditional church system has adopted and accepted only the aspects and events of the New Testament (covenant), they triumphantly denounce all the previous covenants. This would have to include the covenants that God made with Abraham, on which hinges the inheritance of the promised Messiah, and thus what He already has done and yet will do for His faithful followers.

So at the present they are without a covenant, as far as God's covenants are concerned. Since their system takes great pride in violently denouncing everything from the Old Testament (including God's laws, commandments, and covenants because they've been labeled as Jewish), they've made covenants with the anti-God, Jew-less messiah of this world's Babylonian religion—but professing it in the name of the Lord. God's laws are which He measures all people (Jews and Gentiles) against to see whether we'll choose Him and His covenants, or Baal's:

> Now therefore, **if ye will obey my voice indeed, and keep my covenant, then ye shall be a peculiar <c@ gullah>[43] treasure unto me above all people**: for all the earth is mine: And ye shall be unto me a kingdom of priests, and an holy nation. (Ex. 19:5–6)

> See, I have set before thee this day **life and good**, and **death and evil**; In that I command thee this day to love the LORD thy God, to **walk in his ways, and to keep his commandments and his statutes and his judgments, that thou mayest live** and multiply: and the LORD thy God shall bless thee in the land whither thou goest to possess it. (Deut. 30:15–16)

Now here comes a pivotal point. It's time to make a decision. It's going to be one god or the other:

> **But if thine heart turn away, so that thou wilt not hear, but shalt be drawn away, and worship other gods, and serve them; I denounce unto you this day, that ye shall surely perish**, and that ye shall not prolong your days upon the land, whither thou passest over Jordan to go to possess it. I call heaven and earth to record this day against you, that I have set before you **life and death, blessing and cursing**: **therefore choose life, that both thou and thy seed may live: That thou mayest love the LORD thy God, and that thou mayest obey his voice, and that thou mayest cleave unto him: for he is thy life, and the length of thy days** that thou mayest dwell in the land which the LORD sware unto thy fathers, to **Abraham**, to **Isaac**, and to **Jacob**, to give them (Deut. 30:17–20).

Everybody that believes in life after death wants what was promised to Abraham, Isaac, and Jacob/Israel, but how can one obtain it without following the instructions that come with it? Traditional Christendom has laid claim to it, but how will they obtain it without joining the same tree into which the Jews are also being grafted? Since traditional Christendom can have nothing in common with the Jews, who are Israelites, I ask: how can Abraham's covenants be separated from Isaac and Jacob/Israel—the Israel of God (Gal. 6:16)? God does not have one plan for the Jews and another plan for the traditional Christians—or Gentiles, as they prefer to be called. We are all one in the Messiah: "There is neither Jew nor Greek, there is neither bond nor free, there is neither male nor female: for **ye are all one in Christ Jesus. And if ye be Christ's** [Isa. 56:6; 2 Tim. 2:19]**, then are ye Abraham's seed, and heirs according to the promise**" (Gal. 3:28–29; read also Rom. 10:12; 1 Cor. 12:13; Gal. 5:6; Eph. 2:14–16; Col. 3:11).

So will we choose to obey God and keep His—not the Jews'—commandments and claim the promises He made through Abraham as we just read in Deuteronomy 30:15–20 and put the anti-Jew enmity philosophy behind us, or will we rather stick with Baal? We must choose:

> How long halt ye between two opinions? if the LORD be God, follow him: but if Baal, then follow him. (1 Kings 18:21)

> Yet ye have forsaken me, and served other gods: wherefore I will deliver you no more. Go and cry unto the gods which ye have chosen; let them deliver you in the time of your tribulation. (Judg. 10:13–14)

That's straightforward. If we want God's blessings, He commands us to keep His commandments and to not make any covenants with anyone but Him. God knows that we will adopt the customs and traditions of whatever god or gods we choose: "Take heed to thyself, **lest thou make a covenant with the inhabitants of the land** whither thou goest, **lest it be for a snare in the midst of thee**" (Ex. 34:12).

God already revealed to the children of Israel over three thousand years ago, while making the old covenant with them, that He would make them to be His priests in His kingdom (Ex. 19:6), and His plans have not changed in the New Testament (1 Peter 2:9; Rev. 1:6; 5:10; 20:6). Traditional Christendom solemnly swears that the old covenant and the Old Testament were for the Jews only. They teach that they—Gentile Christians—will be raptured away before the onset of the tribulation for to be trained as priests, while they watch the non-Christians, *especially* the Jews, and all commandment-keepers and non-churchgoers being tortured and destroyed on earth. I won't argue how many Jews, Israelites, Gentiles, churchgoers, non-churchgoers, or commandment-keepers will perish at that time, because it sounds as though there will be plenty from every sect. But, who stands the better chance to make it; which begs an answer to another question: according to Exodus 19:6 and 1 Peter 2:9, whom did God choose to become His Priests? Answer: His faithful children, Jacob's descendants *and* Gentiles who join themselves to the Lord, the mixed multitude (Ex. 12:38), "the inheritance of the congregation of Jacob" (Deut. 33:4), "the **Israel of God**" (Gal. 6:16)—all who faithfully choose to follow and obey the laws and commandments of the God of Abraham, Isaac, and Jacob/Israel, and thereby lay claim to the promises of the covenants that He made with them, through whom He promised to bless all nations. All (Jews, Israelites, Gentiles) who lay claim to His promises, keep His commandments, and name Him Lord will be conformed into scriptural-spiritual Israelites (Rom. 8:29): "I will place salvation in Zion for Israel My Glory ... **the Israel of God**" (Isa. 46:13; Gal. 6:16).

God says repeatedly that His laws and commandments have blessings and life; and without them is curses and death! He commands us to choose, make up our mind whom we will serve, and then follow that god (1 Kings 18:21–24). Then, when tribulations come, we are to pray to that god or those gods whom we've chosen. He will not choose for us. God wants us to choose Him for what He is and what He has in store; we are not to choose merely because we don't like the alternative, which is hell and death. Fear of the enemy is a wrong fear. We are to fear the God of Abraham:

> And **fear not them** [Satan's ministers, the gods of this world] which kill the body, but are not able to kill the soul: but rather **fear him** [the God of Abraham] which is able

to destroy both soul and body in hell. (Matt. 10:28; read also Luke 12:5)

The **fear of the LORD** is the beginning of wisdom: a good understanding have all they that do his commandments: his praise endureth for ever. (Ps. 111:10)

Let us hear the conclusion of the whole matter: **Fear God, and keep his commandments: for this is the whole duty of man.** (Eccl. 12:13)

Throughout the scriptures God likens mankind's relationship with Him to a marriage relationship. God was married to the Israelites; they were His wife (Jer. 3:14; 31:32; Hosea 2:19-20; Rom. 11:5). And because of their continual committing of adultery with other gods, He divorced her (Jer. 3:8). Once a wife has been divorced and defiled, the former husband cannot take her back (Deut. 24:4); thus their hope was gone (Ezek. 37:11). Since their husband—God in the Messiah—died, they are freed from that divorce and may marry whom they will (Rom. 7:2; 1 Cor. 7:39). And the Messiah did forgive them before He died: "Then said Jesus, **Father, forgive them**; for they know not what they do" (Luke 23:34). So now if they so **choose**, they can get grafted back into the original tree: "And they also, **if they abide not still in unbelief, shall be graffed in: for God is able to graff them in again**" (Rom. 11:23; read also 1 Cor. chapter 7). That's the only tree into which any person can be grafted—Jew or Gentile. Once grafted in, a person can also be cut off again (Rom. 11:22); this is not good for the "once saved" advocates. God desires all to become His wife, but He will marry only virgins—the ones that are not flirting with Baal (committing idolatry/adultery) and his influences and trappings (Rev. 14:4).

As revealed in Leviticus chapter 26 and Deuteronomy chapters 28 through 32, Moses was clearly prophesying about a time that is still before us—the latter days (Deut. 4:30; 31:29)—when God will gather His scattered children from all nations in a greater exodus. That's when God will truly circumcise our hearts and minds, making it possible to keep His commandments properly, thus enabling us to inherently love God and others from our heart, because His sacrificial-type charitable <**agape**>[8] love will be inherently inscribed into it for eternity. All prophecies after these are expanded upon what Moses already prophesied before they crossed the Jordan River; and they vividly depict the Messiah's return to deliver salvation to all believing Jews and Gentiles while He ushers in the new covenant, after which all will know God and there'll be no sinning, because Satan together with his influences will be locked away! But as for today, Satan is still ruling this world and thus still influencing us with the man-desired lustful trappings of his religious-political Babylonian system.

10a. A New Wall of Enmity

I believe that we can now conclude the fact that the Protestant doctrines hinge fully on a universal mixture (Constantine's adoption of all willing non-Jewish religions) of an extreme Romanized, Constantinized, Luthernized, Freemasonry anti-Jew philosophy, upon which an anti-Law/anti-Torah, and hence anti-God messiah is cunningly borne (1 John 2:22). As we touched on earlier, the true Messiah removed the wall of partition from between the Jews and Gentiles, which was established upon a fixed hatred between them (Eph. 2:14–15). That wall of hatred was not built by God, but by the religious ruling Rabbis and Pharisees. Because of the anti-Law Christians' extreme hatred for the commandment-requiring God, whereby they inevitably hate His so-labeled Jewish commandments (Rom. 8:7), they literally blame and condemn the commandment-keeping people, particularly the Jews alone, for the crucifixion of the Messiah.

That was Martin Luther's theme in many, or rather most, of his later writings, sermons, and books. I know that the teachers of this law-done-away system will take issue with this statement. But they cannot deny the facts, because the results of their anti-Jew/anti-Law/anti-Torah and hence anti-God commandment-hating teaching—the fruit of their labor—is a very strong testimony to it, as I believe I've exposed. The Messiah explained that religion very dramatically:

> **Beware of false prophets, which come to you in sheep's clothing, but inwardly they are ravening wolves** [Satan's anti-God ministers]**. Ye shall know them by their fruits** [which will not be in alignment with the Torah]**.** Do men gather grapes of thorns, or figs of thistles? Even so every good tree bringeth forth good fruit; but a corrupt tree bringeth forth evil fruit. A good tree cannot

bring forth evil fruit, neither can a corrupt tree bring forth good fruit. Every tree that bringeth not forth good fruit is hewn down, and cast into the fire. Wherefore **by their fruits ye shall know them.** Not every one that saith unto me, Lord, Lord, shall enter into the kingdom of heaven; **but he that doeth <u>the will of my Father</u> which is in heaven** [what was His Father's will when He said this?]. Many will say to me in that day, **Lord, Lord, have we not prophesied in thy name? and in thy name have cast out devils? and in thy name done many wonderful works** [the wonders of the Torah test prophecy]**?** And then will I profess unto them, I **never** knew you: **depart from me, ye that work iniquity <anomia>**[12] [God-hating commandment breakers]. (Matt. 7:15–23)

He couldn't have stated it any clearer that no matter what miracles or how many wonders one does in His name, those who do not practice the Ten Commandments are unknown by Him and as such will have no part in Him. One cannot love God and deny His commandments; neither can one hate God and keep His commandments. Professing to love God and not keeping His commandments is an oxymoron if there ever was one: "And hereby we do know that we know him, if we keep his commandments. **He that saith, I know him, and keepeth not his commandments, is a liar, and the truth is not in him**" (1 John 2:3–4). I know this sounds harsh, but hang on, because we'll prove it yet more.

Anyone who does not profess that the Messiah is of God is anti-Messiah: "Who is a liar but he that denieth that Jesus is the Christ? He is antichrist, that denieth the Father and the Son" (1 John 2:22; read also 1 John 4:3; 2 John 1:7).

Ponder this: How can one profess that the Messiah is God, or of God, while in the same breath indoctrinating hundreds of millions, or perhaps billions, of people with a philosophy that professes a messiah who commands his followers to not keep His Father's commandments, of which He said not one jot or tittle would pass? The

> Messiah made ongoing testimonies to prove that He was the Son of the God of Abraham. He did that by performing miracles and wonders and fulfilling prophecies from the Old Testament **specifically** without changing a jot or tittle of God's laws and commandments. That's how His faithful followers knew with all certainty that He was the promised Messiah of which the prophets had testified and written—they applied the Torah test. If He had made any changes, that test would have disqualified Him as Messiah. God and His Son are not divided, but the traditional anticommandment philosophy has erected a very subtle and distinctive wall between them.

Of such are the doctrines of devils: "Now the Spirit speaketh expressly, that **in the latter times** some shall depart from the faith, giving heed to seducing spirits, and **doctrines of devils; Speaking lies in hypocrisy; having their conscience seared** with a hot iron" (1 Tim. 4:1–2). By professing that the Ten Commandments are abolished, thus making it impossible to sin, the conscience is automatically seared—thus feeling no guilt. My loving mother, whom God has put to rest until the resurrections, used to say, "To do a sinful deed without feeling guilty, one must first bite the head off of one's conscience and spit it out."

Thus these church fathers have craftily and purposely added a new wall of partition between the traditional professing New Testament Christians and the Jews—actually all keepers of the so-labeled Jewish Ten Commandments. That wall is the dividing page between what are commonly called the Old and New Testaments. The apostles called the whole of the scriptures God's Word and taught that this Word was authored, inspired, and interpreted by the one unchanging eternal God of heaven and earth:

> **All scripture is given by inspiration of God**, and is profitable for doctrine, for reproof, for correction, for instruction in righteousness: That the man of God may be perfect, thoroughly furnished unto all good works. (2 Tim. 3:16–17)

> Knowing this first, that **no prophecy of the scripture is of any private interpretation**. For the prophecy came not in old time by the will of man: **but holy men of God spake as they were moved by the Holy Ghost** [Spirit]. (2 Peter 1:20–21)

While the Messiah walked on this earth, there was no New Testament, and there would not be until over a decade later. It's evident in all the scriptures that the apostles worked off of the Old Testament scrolls because that's all they had. And traditional Christianity preaches to not use the Old Testament in today's church because it apparently contradicts the New, wherefore the Messiah supposedly abolished it.

Because of the added dividing page, when you talk to traditional churchgoing Christians about keeping God's commandments, the Lord's Sabbath, God's holy days, and God's dietary and health laws, they immediately snarl phrases at you like "Those burdensome, weak, and beggarly elements were for the Jews! Jesus did away with them on the cross! You're going to burn alive forever in hell with the rest of the commandment keepers and Jews, because by keeping the Ten Commandments you're rejecting the Messiah and God's grace!" This raises a very serious question: did the Messiah and His disciples reject God's grace by keeping God's commandments? They kept even the so-labeled burdensome Jewish weekly and annual Sabbaths. They were literally circumcised. Twenty years after the Messiah apparently did away with God's commandments and laws, Paul went through the eight-day purification rituals of Numbers chapter 6. Will they all end up in the fires of hell for that, to burn alive for all eternity together with commandment keepers like me? God forbid! The Messiah said that He kept His Father's commandments so that His Father's sacrificial-type charitable **<agape>**[8] love could dwell in Him. And He encourages us to do the same, in order that His sacrificial-type charitable **<agape>**[8] love may dwell in us also: "If ye keep my commandments, ye shall abide in my love **<agape>**[8]; even as I have kept my Father's commandments, and abide in his love **<agape>**[8]" (John 15:10).

The traditional Christians see no chance for a Jew—or any commandment keeper—to be saved. Why not? For the simple reason that a part of the Jews' doctrines contain the commandments <**entole**>[9] of the God of heaven and earth instead of the commandments <**entalma**>[9a] of Satan's traditional evolutionary Babylonian gods. Both systems, Judaism and traditional Christendom, have their share of man-made traditions; that's not the real debate here. Which gods are identified by the commandments they keep is the challenge, because if you keep God's commandments, you must keep the Lord's weekly and annual Sabbaths (the identifying sign) and His dietary and health laws, and the world will see you as a peculiar person. To a traditional Christian this makes one look foolishly Jewish and stupid; that's the real problem. And Satan, by advocating his messiah's commandments <**entalma**>[9a] through his ministers, will stop at nothing to pervert scriptures by mixing truth with lies in order to doctor up theocracy with which to tickle ears by reasoning around the need to obey God's commandments—particularly the identifying ones, such as the Sabbaths and the dietary laws.

But then again, God said in the Old *and* New Testaments that His children would be a priesthood of peculiar treasured people unto Him (Ex. 19:5; Deut. 14:2; 26:18; Ps. 135:4; Titus 2:14; 1 Peter 2:9). According to *Strong's Concordance*, both the Hebrew and Greek words they translated into English by using the word "peculiar" relate to "something very special - a jewel - ownership." Satan hates the thought of God treasuring His people in that way, because that causes some to obey the commandments <**entole**>[9] of the God of heaven and earth instead of the commandments <**entalma**>[9a] of his god/messiah of this Babylonian world religion (Acts 4:19; 5:29; Pss. 40:4; 62:8–9; 118:8; Jer. 17:5–7). Mixing truth (God's commandments) with lies (Satan's commandments—traditions of men) is how Satan has made God's commandments of no effect today through the traditional church system. That's exactly how Satan invented the Talmud a few millennia ago, through the rabbis and Pharisees. And he has indoctrinated both of these sects with *sobering* success.

Inset: It's no wonder that the Jews hate the Christians so much. Although many of them do not acknowledge or recognize the aspects of the First Coming of the Messiah, they do know that the messiah advocated by traditional Christendom cannot be the Messiah of which the God of Abraham prophesied through the prophets of old. The Messiah of the scriptures does not fit the description of either the Talmud or traditional Christendom. But the Jews do know with all certainty that the true Messiah will not separate Himself from God His Father by condemning His commandments and laws. I'm in full agreement with them on that point.

When being contested by typical traditional Christians, I often hear them state, "All these thousands of preachers can't be wrong!" But I ask, what if they *are* wrong? There is no safety in numbers. It's almost always the opposite, especially when it comes to matters that revolve around the laws of the scriptures, because, as it clearly states in Romans 8:7, the carnal mind hates God, wherefore it cannot accept His laws. That speaks for the majority of mankind, because Satan has deceived the whole world (Rev. 12:9). We can see right there why God warned us to not just go with the flow; the whole world is deceived, and that's an absolute majority. So maybe the preachers could be wrong. Just like you and me, they are also part of the deceived world, aren't they? God forbids a person to justify lawlessness even if everyone else—the whole world—is doing it: "Thou shalt not follow a multitude to do evil" (Ex. 23:2; read also Ezek. chapters 18 and 33). That's why the Messiah always referred to only a small remnant whenever He spoke of His own of this era.

I know it's easy and comfortable to blend in with a crowd of like-minded people and follow them, to justify the common traditions; after all, that's democracy. It's a common philosophy in the Roman/universal/Catholic (Babylonian socialistic communistic democratic Freemason) society in which we live today: the majority *must* be right; that's why people vote. A president gets voted in by selling the most votes. By far, most of the votes are bought and rigged by the wealthier controlling class of people and by the corporations who need certain laws changed and tax laws added, removed, or amended for their gain. That's why the Pharisees invented the Talmud. It worked as an incredibly powerful tool to use God's laws and their own laws in a mixture formulated for a guaranteed success for their arguments with the people whom they controlled through oppression. That's what the Messiah excoriates them for in Matthew chapter 23. They used portions of God's laws only as an authoritative dictate to put their congregational members on a guilt trip, mixed with their traditional talmudic laws in such ways that they would always gain by it. That's why the Messiah told the people to do as they say but not as they do. They spoke of God's truth, but their works/fruits were the exact opposite, to their gain.

I will ask all lower- and middle-class voters, has the majority vote ever done one single thing by which you truly benefited? I don't know of any, but that's how democratic majority rule works. We keep voting in "better" people to run the nations, only to unveil more and more corruption and miserable failure, thus creating more wars each time. For God's chosen people, that majority-rule democracy began in 1 Samuel chapter 8, which testified its total failure in Nehemiah chapter 5, Lamentations chapter 5, and Haggai chapter 1, and this is still going on today in our traditional religious-democratic society, which has almost 100 percent support of traditional Christendom. The book of Amos is not long, and I suggest that you read it. In it God explains exactly how—by which methods—the rich oppress and suppress the poor, and what the outcome of that will be.

We—as a nation of people—are still in high hopes of voting in a better person or group of people to run the government for us, by which the majority will benefit, and mark my words, which are backed by scriptures: **that won't happen** until the Messiah returns to rule this earth by God's laws and commandments—a rod of iron. And the Messiah is not campaigning to sell votes! He's an autocrat—a monarchist—, and as such he will have total, complete, and **absolute** power and authority, not answering to a single human being, not even to the pope or any of his Freemason ministers who control the ballots. And, disappointing as it may be to the democratically voting Christians, the Messiah will not be voted into, or out of office! His taking office will not depend on one single vote! Thus bribery and campaigning will become totally valueless, and God's laws—by which He will rule—will not change a jot or tittle for any person's advantage.

That's the very reason man hates God and His laws (Rom. 8:7); He does no favors to place one man unfairly above another, and mankind can't stand those kind of laws: "For **there is no respect of persons with God**" (Rom. 2:11; read also Acts 10:34; Gal. 2:6; Eph. 6:9; Col. 3:25; 1 Peter 1:17). He can't even be bought off. He simply does not accept bribes; He abhors them: "For the LORD your God is God of gods, and Lord of lords, a great God, a mighty, and a terrible, **which regardeth not persons, nor taketh reward** [no bribes]" (Deut. 10:17). Man's wealth or clout in society or church will have absolutely no advantage: "How much less to him that accepteth not the persons of princes, **nor regardeth the rich more than the poor**? for they all are the work of his hands" (Job 34:19). Once He takes office, we're stuck with Him forever, without an expiry date. Except for traditional Christendom, forever did not end at the cross. And I see that as a good thing; Lord, come quickly and save us from ourselves: "He which testifieth these things saith, **Surely I come quickly. Amen. Even so, come, Lord Jesus"** (Rev. 22:20).

I have some wonderful, exciting, and peculiar news! In very simple and literal terms, God's plan since before the foundation of the world has been to conform His faithful followers into spiritual Israelites—a plan that He does not reveal to theologians: "I thank thee, O Father, Lord of heaven and earth, because **thou hast hid these things from the wise and prudent**, [theologians; traditional preachers] and hast revealed them unto babes [those who humbly seek God's truth]" (Matt. 11:25; read also Ps. 8:2; Luke 10:21; 1 Cor. 1:19, 27; 2:8). Why so? Because God knows, as the prophets and apostles have warned, and as the Gospel accounts of the scribes and Pharisees testify, and as mainstream traditional Christendom proves today, that such control-mongering glory seekers only pervert God's truths to the destruction of mankind, always to feed man's never-ending hunger for control because of his never-ending thirst for blood and revenge. And these anti-Law preachers do it by tainting the Messiah as an anti-Torah and hence anti-God Savior, which inevitably separates God from His Son. Thus, these wall-builders are a living testimony to this. But God will not be mocked (Gal. 6:7).

We must remember that God conforms His obedient followers into the image of His firstborn Son, the life-giving Messiah, who was born a Jew that kept God's commandments and laws and statutes! So also did His early followers, whom He also trained to observe God's Sabbaths, God's holy days, and God's dietary and health laws. Nowhere are they shown to observe the pagan New Year's day, Lent, Easter, Christmas, Halloween, Sunday, or birthdays. And the Messiah tells us to follow in His footsteps:

> If ye love me, keep my commandments **<entole>**[9]. (John 14:15)
>
> If thou wilt enter into life, keep the commandments **<entole>**[9]. (Matt. 19:17)
>
> And **why call ye me, Lord, Lord, and do not the things which I say?** (Luke 6:46)
>
> John confirmed it again about sixty years after the crucifixion:
>
> He that saith he abideth in him ought himself also so to walk, **even as he walked.** (1 John 2:6)

Did the Messiah or any of His apostles walk in the way of paganism by celebrating things like Christmas (Jer. 10:1–5; Acts 19:24), Easter (1 Kings 11:5, 33; 2 Kings 23:13; Jer. 7:18; 44:17–25; Acts 19:24), Sunday (Ezek. 8:14–18), or birthdays (Gen. 40:20–22; Job 1:4–5; Matt. 14:6–10)? The scriptures are full of examples in which God condemns pagan customs and traditions, because they all come from gods of the commandment-hating God-denying religious societies. He said that the keepers (preservers) of God's commandments that have the faith of the Messiah will be in God's kingdom: "Here is the patience of the saints: **here are**

they that keep the commandments of God, and the faith of Jesus" (Rev. 14:12; read also Rev. 12:17; 22:14).

That dividing page between the Old and New Testament—the new wall of partition—is used by traditional Christendom as a scapegoat in an effort to pound off the Lord's Sabbaths (Gen. 2:2–3; Ex. 20:8–11; 31:14–18; Lev. 23; Deut. 5:12–15; Mark 2:27–28) for the pagan Sunday (Ezek. 8), God's holy days (Lev. 23; Deut. 16) for pagan holidays (Ex. 32:1–6; 1 Kings 12:33; Isa. 1:12–14; Jer. 10:1–5; 44:17–19; Hos. 2:11; Amos 8:10; Gal. 4:10), etc. Anything and everything that requires obedience in a way that openly identifies one as a follower of the God of Israel, the eternal God of heaven and earth—the God whom the Jews profess to be following—instead of the pagan Babylonian god of their traditional church system, is violently denounced and condemned by chucking it over that new wall of partition into what they have labeled as the burdensome and grievous works and curses of the old Jewish commandments and laws of a god that—according to that philosophy—is a confused, tyrannical, legalistic, and evolutionary/ever-changing Old Testament god. That's what gives them the audacity to blatantly condemn anyone who practices the Ten Commandments. Thus they've adopted an evolutionary god/messiah who changes his commandments, as is lustfully desired and required by their church's traditional doctrines, hence church commandments **<entalma>**[9a]—the traditions of men! Thus, Constantine's decree 'can't have anything in common with the Jews' is still sacred text to the Catholic and Protestant alike - thus having much in common.

11. WHAT DOES ALL THIS MEAN?

Since the traditional church doctrines hinge solely on the fact that the prophesied events of the First and Second Comings of the Messiah are already fulfilled, it has ignorantly and systematically removed the need for a resurrection, whether they know it or not. But ignorance is no excuse (Hos. 4:6; Ezek. chapters 18 and 33). This may well be the biggest apostasy to ever have plagued Christian society in the history of the Christian era! The result of this system seems to be a mixture of some doctrines of the Pharisees and some of the Sadducees cunningly syncretized and hidden within the witchcraft-sorcery religion of someone like Simon Magus. I'll explain what I mean.

The Sadducees believe only in the written Torah but do not believe in a resurrection of the dead. The Pharisees place the oral Torah—the Talmud / the traditional commandments **<entalma>**[9a] of men (Matt. 15; Mark 7; Gal. 1:14; Col. 2:8, 22)—above the written Torah, but they do believe in the resurrection. But because of their self-righteousness and pride (Rom. 9:31–10:3), they overlooked the need of the Messiah's First Coming as the ultimate sacrifice to redeem them. Thus they argue that the Messiah was not the Son of God or their Passover Lamb, let alone their Lord and King. These two sects must have had a church split, because they were both of the Jews. And both groups had many followers.

Based on these facts, it's very likely that someone like Simon Magus—the one who tried to buy the Holy Spirit with money (Acts 8:18)—may have adopted a few doctrines from each of those Pharisaic groups, mixed them with his demon-driven witchcraft religion, which was already extremely popular ("All gave heed," Acts 8:10), thus enhancing it even more, thereby appeasing the appetite of almost any kind of traditional belief system. In the religiously confused world in which we live today, such a modern one-size-fits-all, universal, control-mongering, Babylonian, Romanized, Catholic, Magusized, law-done-away, liberty-preaching, once-saved, pretrib Rapture religion becomes very appealing to almost any group of people who are in search of carnal comfort.

This is very logical, because that's exactly what Roman emperor Constantine the Great did in the first third of the fourth century. He amalgamated all the religious groups of his day into one universal (Roman Catholic) religious belief system, whereby he accepted and adopted the pagan doctrines, witchcraft, theology, and whatever customs and traditions they brought along with them—as long as they had nothing in common with the Jews! And tyrannical philosophers after that time, such as Martin Luther and Adolf Hitler, played very key roles in the sustaining of the anti-Law/anti-Jew/anti-Torah doctrines through which an anti-God messiah is surreptitiously preached, thus deceiving multitudes of sincere and faithful people.

Luke recorded a vivid account about the popular philosophy of Simon Magus that supports the above-described philosophy: "But there was a certain man, called Simon, which beforetime in the same city used sorcery, and bewitched the people of Samaria, giving out that himself was some great one: **To whom they all gave heed**, from the least to the greatest, saying, **This man is the great power of God**. And to him they had regard, because that **of long time he had bewitched them with sorceries**" (Acts 8:9–11).

> **Note:** Samaria was the capital of many of the ten so-called lost tribes of Israel. That's where many of them ended up after God had them scattered (2 Kings 17; Acts 8:1). Jerusalem was the capital of many Jews. So Simon the sorcerer had indoctrinated—bewitched—many Israelites and Jews.

Luke recorded that all—great and small—gave heed to Simon because they sized him up as a man of God. Accordingly, his religion would likely have included a universal concoction of customs and traditions similar to what Constantine the Great had after he amalgamated all the beliefs of his day. There were Jews and also many other Israelites in Samaria at that time, so Simon must have also amalgamated the beliefs of the Pharisees and of the Sadducees as part of his universal people-pleasing, ear-tickling religion. After all, Luke said they were all pleased with his witchcraft religion.

Because of the great works with which he impressed the people, the people were convinced that his abilities had to come from the God of Abraham. After all, that's where miracles come from, right? The true apostles knew immediately that he was a fraud—full of wickedness—because they could measure Simon against the commandments of the God of Abraham using the Torah test, wherefore they were not deceived by him. Simon obviously measured up against the Talmud, because there's no record of the Pharisees disputing him; rather, they gave heed to him.

That's exactly how I picture the great deceiver of the end time when he sets up his throne in the temple / church system to pull off the ultimate Torah test of all time—the acid test, as it might be termed today. There will be only a few people who will be able to measure him against the truth of the God of Abraham because there are only very few people in the world today who keep God's commandments. As I mentioned earlier, the same deceiver who's setting up that throne has already—over a few millennia—trained thousands or perhaps millions of his ministers, through which he has indoctrinated multiple billions of people into his ways of thinking. He will have very little, if any, resistance from them, because they are already trained to believe in his doctrines as coming from the God of Abraham; they profess and teach his doctrines on *his* Sunday and pagan holidays - in the name of the Lord!

Of those who do keep God's commandments, there will also be some who are deceived into not keeping them proper, just like the Pharisees who keep God's commandments according to their Talmud. I hope not, but I may also be deceived; Satan has deceived the whole world, and I'm still in this world. But I have great hope and faith in the God of Creation that He will intervene in the time of need—that's what He has promised for those who keep His commandments. Nevertheless, it will be a tremendous test of faith for those who have to go through that time. In the Olivet Discourse, as the Messiah spoke to His disciples regarding the end time—the time of the Great Tribulation—He warned about how the false preachers will deceive people in His name: "And Jesus answered and said unto them, **Take heed that no man deceive you**. For many shall come **in my name**, saying, **I am Christ**; and shall deceive many" (Matt. 24:4–5). The Messiah promised to save those who endure to the end: "And many false prophets shall rise, and shall deceive many. And because iniquity **<anomia>**[12] [lawlessness; anticommandment advocation] shall abound, the love of many shall wax cold. But **he that shall endure unto the end, the same shall be saved**" (Matt. 24:11–13).

There are multiple hundreds of Protestant denominations in this world today. Every one of them uses at least a few of their own traditional doctrines in order to be distinct from all the other denominations. They all claim that theirs is the true Church because they are the only one to be using only the Holy Scriptures as their doctrines. Immediately we can know one thing for certain: there can be only one of two things here; only one of them is true, or none! That's very simple math. If they were all using only the Holy Scriptures; they would all agree as one, right? The Messiah said He would build His congregation, not congregations. He's not divided! According to the traditional denominations' own doctrines, as soon as there's more than one, only one, at the very most, can be true! According to Old Testament scriptures, there is only one: "**Hear, O Israel: The LORD our God is one LORD** And thou shalt love the LORD thy God with all thine heart, and with all thy soul, and with all thy might" (Deut. 6:4–5). According to New Testament scriptures, there is only one:

> And Jesus answered him, The first of all the commandments is, **Hear, O Israel; The Lord our God is one Lord** And thou shalt love the Lord thy God with all thy heart, and with all thy soul, and with all thy mind, and with all thy strength: this is the first commandment. (Mark 12:29–30; also John 17:3; 1 Cor. 8:4)

> One Lord, one faith, one baptism, One God and Father of all. (Eph. 4:4–6; read also 2:14–16; Mark 12:32; Rom. 3:30; 10:12; 1 Cor. 8:6; 1 Tim. 2:5; James 2:19)

There is **one** Lord, **one** Israel, **one** faith, **one** baptism, **one** tree, **one** root-system. The Lord our God is **one**! Not two, not a trinity, but **one** Lord God!

The traditional church system is all about controlling the masses, a teaching that comes directly from the pope, whose indoctrination most certainly comes from someone like Simon the sorcerer—not Simon Peter the apostle, as they profess.

11a. The Universal Mother-Harlot and her Daughters

I will sum up only briefly what appears to be the foundational structure and outcome of the traditional religious system when compared and measured against the scriptures with the Torah test. I encourage you to read the supporting scripture references I use in this section and see for yourself what message God had the prophets of old write down for our admonition, and then draw your own unbiased conclusions based on what you read in the scriptures.

The Babylonian witchcraft religion as described in the scriptures closely matches the criteria of the religious anti-Law doctrines of the traditional church system that I'm trying to reveal in my books—a system that has been plagued with extreme Pharisee-like glory-seeking and powerful control-mongering elements. The immortal-soul doctrine helps to overcome the hidden antiresurrection elements by syncretizing the traditional doctrines with some of the doctrines of the Sadducees. Now, if such a religion were legitimate, it would be able to send their followers to heaven, hell, purgatory, or perhaps some happy hunting ground immediately after they died. And the traditional church system is preaching such doctrine. I often hear them claim that their last breath here on earth is their first breath in heaven, made possible only by the immortal soul that they profess to have; hence, a resurrection is not required. This is where serious witchcraft comes into play. There you have it in a nutshell.

I believe that the doctrines of the Roman emperor–State / Pope-Church religious system, universally mixed with Simon Magus's witchcraft/sorcery doctrines, were conceived and borne upon such a Babylonian foundation. It certainly meets the criteria of the Babylonian whore, who is portrayed as a mother of many in Jeremiah chapters 50 and 51; Isaiah chapters 21,

47, and 48, and Revelation chapters 7, 14, and 17–19. And the Protestant system (reformed protesting Catholics, or traditional Christendom), qualifies as an extremely effective and efficient global mega-network of her harlot daughters. It's like a spiderweb that blankets the whole earth, drawing people unawares into the harlotry system (the Vatican). Isaiah prophesied that this Babylonian mother of harlots would feel very confident that she was the only church and that she would never lose her children or become widowed: "I am, and none else beside me; I shall not sit as a widow, neither shall I know the loss of children" (Isa. 47:8; read also Rev. 18:7).

Many protesting daughter groups broke away from the universal Roman Catholic system—the mother—and started new church denominations believing that they had broken free from the corruption of that Babylonian whore. It's true that they severed because of a few onerous Babylonian doctrines, but to this very day all of these groups still preach many, or most, of that mother's doctrines, particularly the doctrines that identify her, such as the following:

- the Sunday Sabbath and the pagan holidays—the Babylonian icon
- the immortal soul
- the Catholics' admittedly confusing and irreconcilable trinity doctrines
- the separation of the Old and New Testaments in an effort to make the Ten Commandments go away, mainly to abrogate the requirement to keep the Lord's weekly and annual Sabbaths.
- an anti-Law/anti-Torah philosophy resulting in an anti-God messiah

And there are many more doctrines through which they have created an intermediary messiah, of which Mary the mother of the Messiah and the queen of heaven is one, who overruled God together with His eternal commandments and laws, thus turning God into an outdated, confused, and miserable God of the so-labeled Old Jewish Testament, and then claiming himself to be the new evolutionary god of the New Testament church who changes according to the requirements of their Christianized Babylonian pagan customs and traditions—the traditions of men.

All of these doctrines are prescribed to accomplish one main goal: to present God's Word to people in a way that will steer them away from the Ten Commandments of the eternal God of heaven and earth, mainly to justify not having to keep the commandments that identify which god or gods one serves—namely the first tablet (Ex. 20:2–11). The first tablet identifies the true eternal God as the only Redeemer, and as the creator God of heaven and earth. The fourth commandment—the Lord's Sabbath commandment—is by far the most offensive to traditional Christendom, because in today's religiously confused Babylonian sun god–worshipping society, it sticks out like a sore thumb, thus causing a great potential for persecution, wherefore they will have no part of it.

Thus, that mother did not really lose any children. Instead, the Protestant system has become an extremely effective and efficient network for her, by which her family has victoriously expanded globally, in unfathomable leaps and bounds. Millions—or perhaps billions—of these people are likely Israelites, because they have been scattered all over the world and lost their identity, and they have a long history of living in paganism and thus enjoying anti-God doctrines. But as God says in the scriptures referenced above, she will become naked, widowed, and desolate (exposed and utterly destroyed) when the Messiah returns to take over the rule of this Satan-inspired religious world (Isa. chapter 47; Rev. chapters 17, 18, and 20). Of course, the rulers of that system have indoctrinated their followers—with much flavor—into believing that they will be raptured away by Satan's bypass theory (the revised tower of Babel) before the pangs of the tribulations begin.

This paints a vivid picture of the modern, globally commercialized Babylonian system, which has solely for gain gotten religiously drunk on the wine of the wrath of that harlot's fornication (Rev. 14:8; 17:2; 18:3; Jer. 51:7). Through lustful trappings (ear-itching doctrines—1 Tim. 4:1–2; 2 Tim. 4:3–4), controlling groups such as kings, popes, traditional church leaders, governments, commercial giants, corporate societies, etc. are intoxicated with the bloodstained doctrines of her delicately relished and religiously flavored paganized money-gobbling system (New Year's, Epiphany, Easter, Christmas, Sunday, Lent, Halloween, and birthdays, to name a few). Observing pagan holidays and times is termed in the scriptures as idolatry (Lev. 19:26; Deut. 18:14; Gal. 4:10), which to God is adultery (flirting with other gods - harlotry), which was the very cause for Him to scatter and eventually divorce Israel some 2,600 years ago (Jer. 3:8; 2 Kings chapter 17; Ezekiel chapters 20 and 23;). And He has given no indication that He has any more tolerance today to trade or mix His commandments and laws with paganism than before. Rather, with the Holy Spirit available to us today to help us keep His commandments proper in their spiritual intent, violating His commandments is even more serious now than in the days before the Holy Spirit was available to the laymen.

When the Great Tribulation begins, God will start housekeeping in the churches (Ezek. 9:6; 1 Peter 4:17), because that is where His name is most viciously defiled by using it in vain to man's gain through traditional doctrines of men to snare multitudes of people, as forewarned in Deuteronomy chapters 12, 13, and 18. And only those with God's identifying sign or mark will be spared—first from Satan's wrath, and then ultimately from God's wrath. (Read Ex. 13:9; 31:13–18; Deut. 6:1–8 ; 11:13, 18; Ezek. 9:4–6, 10; 20:12, 20; Rev. 7:3; 9:4; 12:17; 14:1; 20:4; 22:4.) By the time God finishes housekeeping, there will be a very small remnant of people left—namely a tithe (Isa. 1:9; 6:12–13).

I encourage you to study that Babylonian system by starting where it got its name in Genesis chapters 10–11: "Therefore is the name of it called **Babel <Babel>**[48]; because the LORD did there confound the language of all the earth" (Gen. 11:9). In most of the 260 times that the word "Babylon" is mentioned in scripture, it is portrayed as a very influential and powerful entity in which the wickedness and evils of this Satan-inspired world thrive and dwell in enticing ways to snare and spoil those who testify to believe in the God of Abraham. I will list a few of the references—particularly the ones that reference the book of Revelation: Isa.

13:19; 21:9; chapters 47–48; Jer. chapters 50–51; Rev. chapters 14–18. A study of these texts shows that the Babylonian church system is symbolically portrayed as the mother of harlots, who has multitudes of followers, including the whole Protestant system (because they never really severed from most of her Babylonian customs and traditions—her delicacies).

Now, if you will compare the Ten Commandments with the ten planks of the *Communist Manifesto*, you will see that the Babylonian system has used (past tense) the "free" public education system together with the traditional church system to cunningly indoctrinate (brainwash) the people of the North American nations (and other Israelitish nations as well) into believing in a lawless society being a liberated and God-fearing nation of people. This commandment-defying nation of people will feel God's undiluted wrath (Rev. 14:8–11) coming down on them if they do not repent in time (2 Cor. 6:17; Rev. 18:4).

For the Protestant people—preachers and their followers alike—who profess to not be following the universal Roman Catholic system; I encourage you to watch the video link below. See for yourself in the 'Amazing Facts' documentary how the 'mother of harlots' is bringing her 'harlot daughters' back into her fold: http://www.youtube.com/watch?v=7kgxEvIDoGs

If the link is no longer available, I have downloaded it and will send you a DVD copy of it if you will request it. Send me your request by email or by postal service together with your mailing address.

12. REVERSING THE CURSES

I realize that this book has probably been a hard read for some of you, especially for dedicated supporters of the traditional church system. It was not easy to write, and I want to try to end it on a positive note, because there is light for God's people! Stephen was stoned to death for openly exposing the murderous rulers of an atrocity similar to that which I've termed today's traditional Christendom: "**Ye stiffnecked and uncircumcised in heart and ears, ye do always resist the Holy Ghost** [Spirit]**: as your fathers did, so do ye**" (Acts 7:51; read also Matt. 15; Mark 7). And he will be rewarded by and in the first resurrection for holding on to the truth—enduring to his end (Acts 7:54–60).

The only way to correct this situation is to reverse the curses of Leviticus 26:14–39 and Deuteronomy 28:15–68. And the only way it can be accomplished is for the people of the nation to obey God's instructions and petition Him to apply His promised blessings:

> If they shall confess their iniquity [their/our own], and the iniquity of their fathers [their/our root system], with their trespass which they trespassed against me, and that also they have walked contrary unto me; And that I also have walked contrary unto them, and have brought them into the land of their enemies; if then their uncircumcised hearts be humbled, and they then accept of the punishment of their iniquity [repentance from the breaking of commandments]: Then will I remember my covenant with Jacob, and also my covenant with Isaac, and also my covenant with Abraham will I remember; and I will remember the land" (Lev. 26:40–42).

In plain words, God says that if we will sever from and repent of following the lawless doctrines of our fathers, and repent from our own lawlessness—the breaking of commandments—and repent for causing God to turn His back on us, He will forgive those transgressions and heal the land. That sounds awesome. After all, He is the God who prevents diseases and heals people who obey Him and keep His commandments: "And said, If thou wilt diligently hearken to the voice of the LORD thy God, and wilt do that which is right in his sight, and wilt **give ear to his commandments, and keep all his statutes, I will put none of these diseases upon thee**, which I have brought upon the Egyptians: for **I am the LORD that healeth thee**" (Ex. 15:26).

God keeps His promises and reverses His curses through our faith in Him, by His grace: "If I shut up heaven that there be no rain, or if I command the locusts to devour the land, or if I send pestilence among my people [curses]; **If my people, which are <u>called by my name</u>** [those having total faith in Him]**, shall humble themselves, and pray, and seek my face, and turn from their wicked ways** [repentance]; **then will I hear from heaven, and will <u>forgive their sin</u>, and will <u>heal their land</u>**" (2 Chron. 7:13–14). John graciously reminds us that that deal is still on for us today: "If we confess our sins, he is faithful and just to forgive us our sins, and to cleanse us from all unrighteousness" (1 John 1:9). God's blessings are immeasurable. He promises to give us a hundred times what we lose for His name's sake now, and afterward eternal life, if we obey Him and keep His commandments: "And Jesus answered and said, Verily I say unto you, There is no man that hath left house, or brethren, or sisters, or father, or mother, or wife, or children, or lands, for my sake, and the gospel's, But **he shall receive an hundredfold now** in this time, houses, and brethren, and sisters, and mothers, and children, and lands, with persecutions; **and in the world to come eternal life**" (Mark 10:29–30; compare with Lev. 26:1–13 and Deut. 28:1–14). God has awesome blessings for people who obey Him.

With that understanding and mind-set, fearfully, reverently, and humbly come before the merciful God and Father of heaven and earth with a repentant, contrite spirit and broken heart (Ps. 34:18; 51:17; Isa. 57:15) and petition Him to apply His blessings to this sinful nation, which He promises in Leviticus 26:1–13 and Deuteronomy 28:1–14 for keeping His commandments. If this is done in fear of the creator God, He will answer, because this is His wish and will for us. God always keeps His promises, and let's not forget to continually praise Him for that.

So there is hope! With today's tremendously incomprehensible global economic downturn, the prophecies of Leviticus chapter 26 and Deuteronomy chapter 28, which foretold of the lawless time in which we're living today, become very powerful, more meaningful, and more real and clearer by the day. Scriptures prove that God keeps His word and promises, which are still valid testimonies for us (1 Cor. 10) that are being fulfilled today—the latter days, which are upon us. In Deuteronomy 4:30–40 blessings are promised for obedience to God when tribulations come in the latter days—that's now. In chapters 30 and 31 He warns us about how we will corrupt ourselves in the latter days by using man's ways instead of His ways, for which evil will inevitably befall us if we do not repent in time. (Read also Ps. 118:8; Prov. 3; Acts 5:29; Rom. 3:4; and James 4:4.) Our generation is a living testimony to these prophecies. God is about to come down on the wickedness of this nation with both feet to deliver tremendous undiluted wrath! Thoughts of God's wrath cause me to tremble with fear, repent of the old and wicked ways, turn to Him, and practice His commandments, in order to hopefully avoid His wrath, or at least lessen the stripes.

North America—Canada and the United States—has been blessed tremendously in the previous few generations (about AD 1800 to the early 1900s), beyond any generation on record. In the last few decades, God and His commandments have had to take the backseat, or rather the trunk, so that perhaps He can get out and push when needed. And after the push, He can get back into the trunk and shut up. His commandments **<entole>**[9] got buried—hence forsaken—by commandments **<entalma>**[9a] of men through traditional church doctrine (Matt. 15; Mark 7). Political rulers—of which most are Freemasons—followed suit by also removing God's commandments from public and civil properties, because that is their agenda. Ironically, the traditional Christians are screaming and pawing the ground because of it! I don't understand why, because whether they know it or not, God got kicked out of their traditional church system decades, or perhaps centuries, before the politicians did. We need to wake up and come to grips with the one and only non-evolutionary eternal God of Creation, repent, and keep His commandments. But I can't see national repentance in the near agenda, in which case desolation and destruction are likely inevitable. It's a promise from the only one who has the power to keep promises—the Creator of the universe Himself! We are already enslaved in terrible bondage by debt; thus we are in captivity with no way out in sight. As the Messiah stated in Matthew 7:15–22, on a national scale, we're reaping the fruits of our labors in the name of so-called modern-day liberty!

Although national repentance is extremely unlikely, there still remains hope for you and me! Remember, safety is not in big numbers. The Messiah always referred to only a small remnant, and never a big crowd, when He spoke about His own. He did it before, when out of the whole world full of people He saved eight people who believed in Him—Noah and his family (Gen. 7:7; 1 Peter 3:20)—although the whole world mocked them for the whole 120 years (which is how long Noah spent building the ark). The world mocked him for believing the God of Creation—for having faith in the invisible God. God saved three from Sodom and Gomorrah (Gen. 19:15, 26). He saved two of the Hebrew children (Israelites) that left Egypt (Num. 26:65). Notice how the numbers are trending downward.

The whole chapter 17 in the gospel of John is devoted to the Messiah's prayer, in which He pleaded with God His Father and petitioned Him to protect His own. He specifically petitioned God to not remove His chosen disciples from this earth, but to keep <**tereo**>[21] (guard/protect) them while they were on this earth just as He had kept <**tereo**>[21] them while walking with them (verses 12 and 15). Please note that there is no mention of a secret rapture, but that He will openly keep <**tereo**>[21] (guard/protect) His own on this earth. He has the power to do it, as numerous testimonies show throughout the scriptures. And it requires an unwavering and unmixed faith in Him alone to be able to believe it.

<u>12a. Man Does Not Have Inherited Sin</u>

How can you and I be saved from the certain coming wrath? I know it looks hard or impossible because the common traditional church doctrines teach that we have inherited sin hanging over our heads, over which we have little or no control. Contrariwise, the scriptures are full of references showing that each person will answer for his own. Therefore, even if the whole nation is cursed, you and I need not be partakers of that certain coming wrath. No man's salvation needs to be jeopardized or lost because of another man's wrongs. The following scriptures explain it in very simple, easy-to-understand, and unmistakable terms:

> Yet say ye, Why? **doth not the son bear the iniquity of the father** [don't we have inherited sin]**? When the son hath done that which is lawful and right, and hath kept all my statutes, and hath done them, he shall surely live** [no inherited sin]**. <u>The soul that sinneth, it shall die</u>** [no immortal soul]. The son shall **not** bear the iniquity of the father, **neither** shall the father bear the iniquity of the son: the righteousness of the righteous shall be upon him, and the wickedness of the wicked shall be upon him [each will account for his own]. (Ezek. 18:19–20; read also chapter 33; Job 34:11; Jer. 17:10; Matt. 16:27; Rom. 2:6–9; 14:12; 2 Cor. 5:10; Rev. 2:23; 20:12; 22:12).

And once again, Paul echoes the same principles in the New Testament—yet another Torah test proof: "Wherefore, my beloved, as ye have always obeyed, not as in my presence only, but now much more in my absence, **work out your own salvation** with fear and trembling" (Phil. 2:12).

As we can read in the accounts of Noah's family (Gen. 7), Lot's family in Sodom (Gen. 19), the account of the plagues placed upon the Egyptians for enslaving the Israelites (Ex. chapters 5–14), the Israelites taking possession of the wicked Heathen Nations (Deut. 9), Daniel's three friends in the fiery furnace (Dan. 3), and Daniel in the lion's den (Dan. 6), God does not destroy the righteous with the unrighteous (Ezek. 18; 33). God is still the same today (Heb. 13:8). God does not change; He is not evolutionary (Mal. 3:6; James 1:17). Praise His holy name! If God were an evolutionary god—one who changes—as is preached from the theologically trained traditional pulpits, we could never rely on His word, because it might have changed the day before, or this morning.

How can we prove that God is not evolutionary without going back to God's word in the Torah to see whether it agrees with it or not?: "... searched the scriptures daily, whether those things were so [a true Torah test]" (Acts 17:11). The Bereans had only the Old Testament scriptures—the Torah—to confirm whether or not the apostles were preaching God's truth to them. What a splendid testimony of a true Torah test proof! If the apostles had preached of any changes from the Old Testament commandments and laws, the Bereans would have had to disagree with them. But there's no indication of such a dispute, wherefore we know that the apostles advocated no changes. Praise, honor, and glory be to the God of Abraham, because we can absolutely depend on His unchanging and non-evolutionary eternal Word yesterday, today, and forever, from eternity to eternity. True believers—commandment keepers—will always be able to prove all doctrines with God's non-evolutionary word—Allelujah!

If we consider the wicked and evil traditions of our fathers, repent and turn away from them, and turn to God's ways, He will save us:

> **Now, lo, if he beget a son, that seeth all his father's sins which he hath done, <u>and considereth, and doeth not such like,</u> That hath not eaten upon the mountains** [social welfare pension system; communism], **neither hath lifted up his eyes to the idols of the house of Israel** [pagan customs and traditions], **hath not defiled his neighbour's wife** [no adultery], **Neither hath**

oppressed any [not been covetous or greedy], **hath not withholden the pledge** [kept his promise; paid his debt], **neither hath spoiled by violence** [not taken another's possessions by force], **but hath given his bread to the hungry** [a genuine giver—loved his neighbor], **and hath covered the naked with a garment** [cared about the neighbor's needs], **That hath taken off his hand from the poor** [has not oppressed or taken advantage of the poor], **that hath not received usury nor increase** [has not charged interest or gains], **hath executed my judgments** [judged according to God's laws], **hath walked in my statutes** [lived according to His laws]; **<u>he shall not die for the iniquity of his father</u>** [no inherited sin], **he shall surely live.** As for his father, because he cruelly oppressed, spoiled his brother by violence, and did that which is not good among his people, lo, even he shall die in his iniquity. Yet say ye, Why? doth not the son bear the iniquity of the father? When the son hath done that which is lawful and right, and hath kept all my statutes, and hath done them, he shall surely live. **The soul that sinneth, it shall die. The son shall not bear the iniquity of the father, neither shall the father bear the iniquity of the son: the righteousness of the righteous shall be upon him, and the wickedness of the wicked shall be upon him** [each will give account to God for his own]. (Ezek. 18:14–20)

As always, it's confirmed in the New Testament:

And I saw the dead, small and great, stand before God; and the books were opened [the scriptures]: and another book was opened, which is the book of life [the book in which God has recorded our deeds (our works)]: and **the dead were judged out of those things which were written in the books, according to their works** [a personal/individual record]. And the sea gave up the dead which were in it; and death and hell delivered up the dead which were in them: and **they were judged**

> **every man according to their works** [each his own—no inherited sin]. (Rev. 20:12–13; read also Matt. 16:27; 2 Cor. 11:15; Phil. 2:12; Rev. 2:23; 18:6)

The scriptures will be opened together with the book of our personal records, and they will be compared; this will be every person's ultimate and final Torah test.

Most of us have been traditionally indoctrinated with the belief that if we don't continue in the traditional ways of our fathers, we'll go straight to hell and burn alive for all eternity—eternal life in hellfire! Again, as we just read, that runs exactly contrary to the scriptures: "But if the wicked will turn from all his sins that he hath committed, and keep all my statutes, and do that which is lawful and right, he shall surely live, he shall not die. All his transgressions that he hath committed, they shall not be mentioned unto him: in his righteousness that he hath done he shall live" (Ezek. 18:21–22). As Paul confirmed in the New Testament, everyone will be judged according to his or her own works (Phil. 2:12).

The Eternal God desires for all people to repent of their wickedness and live:

> Have I any pleasure at all that the wicked should die? saith the Lord GOD: and not that **he should return from his ways, and live**? But when the righteous turneth away from his righteousness, and committeth iniquity, and doeth according to all the abominations that the wicked man doeth, shall he live? All his righteousness that he hath done shall not be mentioned: in his trespass that he hath trespassed, and in **his** sin that **he** hath sinned, **in them shall he die**. Yet ye say, The way of the Lord is not equal. Hear now, O house of Israel; Is not my way equal? are not your ways unequal? When a righteous man turneth away from his righteousness, and committeth iniquity, and dieth in them; **for his iniquity that he hath done shall he die** [the wicked alone will die for his sins]. Again, when the wicked man turneth away from his wickedness that he hath committed, and doeth that

> which is lawful and right, he shall save his soul alive. **Because he considereth, and turneth away from all his transgressions that he hath committed, he shall surely live, he shall not die** [each man can save himself by turning away from sin: "... work out your own salvation" (Phil. 2:12)]. Yet saith the house of Israel, The way of the Lord is not equal. O house of Israel, are not my ways equal? are not your ways unequal? Therefore I will judge you, O house of Israel, **every one according to his ways**, saith the Lord God. **Repent, and turn yourselves from all your transgressions; so iniquity shall not be your ruin.** Cast away from you all your transgressions, whereby ye have transgressed; and make you a new heart and a new spirit: for why will ye die, O house of Israel? For **I have no pleasure in the death of him that dieth**, saith the Lord God: wherefore **turn yourselves** [repent]**, and live ye.** (Ezek. 18:23–32; read also 33:11; Eph. 4:22–23; 1 Tim. 2:4; 2 Peter 3:9)

That scripture speaks plainly for itself, and it's easy to understand. It explains in very simple and unmistakable terms how you and I can be saved, no matter what the rest of the world does, including the traditional church system and our ancestors.

As explained in the end-time prophecies in Isaiah 56:1–6 and 58:13–14, and Jeremiah 17:21–27; God specifically promises blessings for those who delightfully keep His Sabbaths holy. Throughout the Gospels, the Messiah liberates and heals people who come to Him because of the faith they have in Him, and they do so on His Sabbaths. The Lord's Sabbath foreshadows a time of liberation. God's kingdom will consist of people who keep His commandments through faith in the Messiah (Matt. 5:19; 19:17; Rev. 12:17; 14:12; 22:14). His commandments are not burdensome (Matt. 11:28–30; 1 John 5:2–3), but liberating (James 1:25; 2:12; Rom. 7:12, 22). In the Gospel accounts, the Pharisees constantly accuse the Messiah and His disciples of breaking the Sabbath commandment—which they truly did, but only according to the Talmud. The issue was never whether to keep it or not, but always how to keep it. The Messiah performed many miracles on His Sabbath days to teach us that the Sabbath was made for man to be liberated. The Pharisees created hundreds of regulations—dos and don'ts—as to how and how not to keep the Sabbath, thus making it impossible to do anything without breaking at least one or more of the regulatory rules from the Talmud. This turned the Lord's Sabbath into bondage.

Side Note: The Messiah made many wonderful examples about the liberating aspects of the LORD's Sabbath by healing people:

> And he was teaching in one of the synagogues **on the sabbath**. And, behold, there was a woman which had a spirit of infirmity **eighteen years**, and was bowed together, and could in no wise lift up herself. And when Jesus saw her, he called her to him, and said unto her, Woman, thou art loosed from thine infirmity. And he laid his hands on her: and **immediately she was made straight, and glorified God**. And **the ruler of the synagogue answered with indignation, because that Jesus had healed on the sabbath day**, and said unto the people, There are six days in which men ought to work: in them therefore come and be healed, and not on the sabbath day. The Lord then answered him, and said, **Thou hypocrite, doth not each one of you on the sabbath loose his ox or his ass from the stall**, and lead him away to watering? And **ought not this woman, being a daughter of Abraham, whom Satan hath bound, lo, these eighteen years, be loosed from this bond on the sabbath day?** And when he had said these things, all his adversaries were ashamed: and all **the people rejoiced for all the glorious things that were done by him.** (Luke 13:10–17)

The believers rejoiced, and God was glorified by it.

In some other accounts it states that the people being healed were actually touching the fringe on the Messiah's garment: "And a woman having an issue of blood twelve years, which had

spent all her living upon physicians, neither could be healed of any, Came behind him, and touched the **border <kraspedon>**[75] [tassel; fringe of Num. 15:38–39] of his garment: and immediately her issue of blood stanched. (Matt. 9:20-22; 14:36; Mark 6:56; Luke 8:43-44). Those tassels represent the commandments of God (Num. 15:37–41). The woman in Luke 8 had spent all she had on doctors, totally in vain. One must wonder if the Pharisees owned a pharmaceutical outlet, because they were ticked off that the Messiah healed her for free. She touched the tassel on the Messiah's garment, and she was instantly healed; that's liberating.

Thus we faithfully and patiently take comfort and great hope in the awesome promises of God, especially in times of strife as we see today, wherefore we ought to take it very serious and humbly petition God to protect us in such times. He promises very powerful protection in Leviticus chapter 26, Deuteronomy chapter 28, and John chapter 17, but it's conditional: to be protected by the eternal God of heaven and earth means keeping the commandments of that same God—all ten of them. Don't be fooled into believing Satan's lies, which he has foisted upon us through the traditional church system, which declares those scriptures to be outdated, Jewish, burdensome, unbearable (anything but good), and obsolete. In the same book from which Satan has cooked up those perverted and corrupt doctrines, God warns us that when tribulations come in **the latter days**, we are to take heed to keep His commandments (Deut. 4:30; 31:29). And we can be quite certain that the tribulations will get much worse in the near future. My prayer today is that you will take an honest inventory of your own spirituality and petition the Eternal God of heaven and earth accordingly. Do it for yourself, and to your Creator's honor and glory.

We can learn a lot from King Solomon on this matter. Being the wisest man to ever have lived, he wrote quite a book about his experiences in life. He became extremely wealthy and had virtually everything he could imagine having. God inspired him to dedicate pretty much the whole book of Ecclesiastes to explaining how he came to realize at the end of his life that everything he had achieved and gained for himself turned out to be totally in vain. Solomon winds down toward the end of the book by declaring that all is vanity: "**Vanity of vanities**, saith the preacher; **all is vanity**" (Eccl. 12:8). And he concludes his story by warning us about what really is important in the end: "Let us hear the conclusion of the whole matter: **Fear God, and keep his commandments:** for this is the whole duty of man. For God shall bring every work into judgment, with every secret thing, whether it be good, or whether it be evil" (Eccl. 12:13–14; read also Rev. 20:12–13). So, he says, since everything else is simply in vain, keep God's commandments, because that's what's going to matter in the end! It takes the faith in and of the Messiah to be able to understand and keep God's commandments properly. And God gives His spirit to every person who obeys Him, through which one can keep His commandments in their proper spiritual intent.

I stand to be corrected and by all means am open for debate and discussion on these matters, from a scriptural perspective. Please don't hurl stones at me yet for sharing these truths. But if you must, so be it!

Please do not take information such as this from me or any man; for your own safety, check it out in the scriptures. I don't mean to say that you shouldn't believe another man, but that your salvation has too high a price tag to place it into the hands of *any* man. That is very dangerous, and it is the very reason for books such as this. I am not telling you to believe me, but please allow information such as this to at least provoke you to "prove all things" from the Holy Scriptures (1 Thess. 5:21), including the scriptures themselves! And the scriptures can be proven, as I've explained in section 4 of my first book, *The Commandments of God*. There I explain that I will always take an unambiguous scripture that will speak for itself in plain and unmistakable terms. So if I then happen to come across an ambiguous scripture that seems to contradict an unambiguous scripture, I have the Messiah's absolute assurance (John 10:35) that it cannot and will not contradict the unambiguous scripture. Then I can undoubtedly know and admit that I do not fully understand the ambiguous scripture, with the wonderful assurance from our savior. That's how the scriptures interpret themselves: "Knowing this first, that **no prophecy of the scripture is of any private interpretation**" (2 Peter 1:20). Then, most importantly, apply the Torah test to confirm its validity and verity for today.

When it comes to scriptural laws, Paul's epistles are the easiest to pervert to suit a lawless mind-set. And Peter gives us a very good warning about ALL of Paul's hard-to-understand scriptures (2 Peter 3:15–17). I thank God for inspiring Peter to warn us about such an important element. So, when you study them with the mind-set that you believe what God says, and that His Son cannot and will not contradict His Word (John 10:35); you can then know, without a "shadow of turning" (James 1:17), that God's Word is infallible. It heals, it is life, and it holds true, binding from eternity to eternity: For ever, O LORD, thy word is settled in heaven (Ps. 119:89).

Think about it and draw your own conclusions. I pray that you use the Holy Scriptures to make your decisions. That is our obligation, and my prayer for all; so be it!

May God open our eyes and bless us with His understanding, as He promises in Psalms 111:10–112:1! Any good coming out of this book comes from God. Any errors would come from me!

==

Cornie Banman, Box 292, La Crete, Alberta, Canada, T0H 2H0.
Phone: 780–928–3679
Website: http://corniebanman.com
E-mail: cornieb@sis.net

==

13. HEBREW/GREEK/ENGLISH CONCORDANCE

[1] Hebrew word for "forever" #5769 **`owlam**, o-lawm'; or lolam; from 5956; properly, concealed, i.e. the vanishing point; generally, **time out of mind (past or future)**, i.e. (practically) **eternity**; frequentatively, adverbial (especially with prepositional prefix) **always**:--alway(-s), ancient (time), any more, **continuance**, **eternal**, (for, (n-))ever(-lasting, -more, of old), lasting, long (time), (of) old (time), **perpetual**, at any time, **(beginning of the) world (+ without end)**. Pages 1, 14, 52, 94, 115, 143, 188, 201, 276, 277.

[2] Hebrew word for "charge" #4931. **mishmereth**, mish-meh'-reth; fem. of **4929**; watch, i.e. the act (custody), or (concr.) the sentry, the post; obj. preservation, or (concr.) safe; fig. observance, i.e. (abstr.) duty or (obj.) a usage or party:--charge, keep, or to be kept, office, ordinace, safeguard, ward, watch. Pages 2, 65, 83.

= #**4929**. rmvm mishmar, mish-mawr'; from **8104**; a guard (the man, the post or the prison); a deposit (fig.); also (as observed) a usage (abstr.), or an example (concr.):--diligence, guard, office, prison, ward, watch.

= #**08104**. shamar, shaw-mar'; a primitive root; properly, to hedge about (as with thorns), i.e. guard; generally, to protect, attend to, etc.:--beward, be circumspect, take heed (to self), keep(-er, self), mark, look narrowly, observe, preserve, regard, reserve, save (self), sure, (that lay) wait (for), watch(-man).

[3] Hebrew word for "commandment" #4687. **mitsvah**, mits-vaw'; from **6680**; a command, whether human or divine (collectively, the Law):--(which was) commanded(-ment), law, ordinance, precept. Pages 2, 65, 83, 164.

= #**6680**. hwu tsavah, tsaw-vaw'; a primitive root; (intensively) to constitute, enjoin:--appoint, (for-)bid, (give a) charge, (give a, give in, send with) command(-er, -ment), send a messenger, put, (set) in order.

[4] Hebrew word for "statutes" #2708. **chuqqah**, khook-kaw'; feminine of **2706**, and meaning substantially the same:--appointed, custom, manner, ordinance, site, statute. Pages 2, 65, 83, 93, 143, 164, 201.

= #**2706**. choq, khoke; from **2710**; an enactment; hence, an appointment (of time, space, quantity, labor or usage):--appointed, bound, commandment, convenient, custom, decree(-d), due, law, measure, X necessary, ordinance(- nary), portion, set time, statute, task.

= #**2710**. chaqaq, khaw-kak'; a primitive root; properly, to hack, i.e. engrave (Judges 5:14, to be a scribe simply); by implication, to enact (laws being cut in stone or metal tablets in primitive times) or (gen.) prescribe:--appoint, decree, governor, grave, lawgiver, note, pourtray, print, set.

[5] Hebrew word for "law" #8451, **towrah**, to-raw'; or **torah** {toraw'}; from **3384**; a precept or statute, especially the **Decalogue** or **Pentateuch** :--**law**. Pages 2, 63, 64, 65, 83, 88, 89, 164, 171, 174.

* The Pentateuch is the first five books of the Scriptures, which contain the Decalogue. The Decalogue is the Ten Commandments.

* Word #**3384**. yarah, yaw-raw'; or (2 Chr. 26:15) yara; {yaw-raw'}; a primitive root; properly, to flow as water (i.e. to rain); transitively, to lay or throw (especially an arrow, i.e. to shoot); figuratively, to point out (as if by aiming the finger), **to teach**:--(+) archer, cast, **direct**, **inform**, **instruct**, lay, shew, shoot, **teach(-er,-ing)**, through.

[6] Hebrew word for "Israel" #3478. **Yisra'el**, yis-raw-ale'; from **8280** and **410**; he will rule as God; Jisrael, a symbolical name of Jacob; also (typically) of his posterity: --Israel. Page 2.

= #**8280**. sarah, saw-raw'; a primitive root; to prevail:--have power (as a prince).

= #**410**. 'el, ale; shortened from **352**; strength; as adjective, mighty; especially the Almighty (but used also of any deity):--God (god), X goodly, X great, idol, might(-y one), power, strong. Compare names in "-el."

= #**352**. 'ayil, ah'-yil; from the same as **193**; properly, strength; hence, anything strong; specifically a chief (politically); also a ram (from his strength); a pilaster (as a strong support); an oak or other strong tree:--mighty (man), lintel, oak, post, ram, tree.

= #**193**. 'uwl, ool; from an unused root meaning to twist, i.e. (by implication) be strong; the body (as being rolled together); also powerful:--mighty, strength.

[7] Hebrew word for "season" #4150. **mow`ed**, mo-ade'; or moled {moade'}; or (feminine) moweadah (2 Chronicles 8:13) {mo-awdaw'}; from **3259**; properly, an appointment, i.e. a fixed time or season;

specifically, a festival; conventionally a year; by implication, an assembly (as convened for a definite purpose); technically the congregation; by extension, the place of meeting; also a signal (as appointed beforehand):--appointed (sign, time), (place of, solemn) assembly, congregation, (set, solemn) feast, (appointed, due) season, solemn(-ity), synogogue, (set) time (appointed). Pages 2, 114, 115, 118, 143.

= #**3259**. ya`ad, yaw-ad'; a primitive root; to fix upon (by agreement or appointment); by implication, to meet (at a stated time), to summon (to trial), to direct (in a certain quarter or position), to engage (for marriage): -agree,(maxke an) appoint(-ment,a time), assemble (selves), betroth, gather (selves, together), meet (together), set (a time).

[8] Greek word for "love" #26. **agape**, ag-ah'-pay; from 25; love, i.e. affection or benevolence; specially (plural) a love-feast:--(feast of) charity(-ably), dear, love. Pages 25, 26, 28, 43, 45, 56, 64, 67, 78, 79, 80, 81, 82, 83, 86, 87, 91, 103, 108, 109, 123, 146, 147, 156, 157, 163, 164, 168, 173, 180, 181, 182, 186, 219, 229, 243, 248, 249, 300, 301, 311, 312, 328, 332.

[8a] Greek word for "love" #25. **agapao**, ag-ap-ah'-o; perhaps from agan (much) (or compare 5689); to love (in a social or moral sense):--(be-) love(-ed). Pages 26, 156.

[9] Greek word for "commandments" #1785. **entole**, en-tol-ay'; from 1781; injunction, i.e. an authoritative prescription:--commandment, precept. Pages 25, 26, 28, 30, 37, 38, 39, 40, 41, 45, 46, 49, 61, 102, 123, 146, 155, 157, 173, 186, 219, 220, 238, 247, 254, 255, 256, 281, 288, 289, 299, 300, 301, 333, 337, 351.

[9a] Greek word for "commandments" #1778. **entalma**, en'-tal-mah; from 1781; an injunction, i.e. religious precept:-- commandment. Pages 30, 38, 39, 40, 46, 49, 60, 61, 101, 102, 155, 157, 186, 217, 219, 220, 238, 247, 254, 259, 281, 288, 289, 296, 300, 333, 338, 339, 351.

[10] Greek word for "fulfill" #**4137**. **pleroo**, play-ro'-o; from **4134**; to **make replete**, i.e. (literally) to cram (a net), level up (a hollow), or (figuratively) to furnish (or imbue, diffuse, influence), satisfy, execute (an office), finish (a period or task), verify (or coincide with a prediction), etc.:--accomplish, X after, (be) complete, end, expire, **fill (up)**, fulfil, (be, **make) full** (come), **fully preach**, perfect, supply. Pages 25, 42, 63, 66, 88, 110, 163, 168, 169, 170, 171, 183.

[10a] Greek word for "full" #**4134**. **pleres**, play'-race; from **4130**; **replete**, or covered over; by analogy, **complete**:--**full**. Page 131, 169, 171.

= **#4130**. pletho, play'-tho; to "fill" (literally or figuratively (imbue, influence, supply)); specially, to fulfil (time):--**accomplish**, **full (... come)**, furnish.

= **#3378**. **anapleroo**, an-ap-lay-ro'-o; from 303 and **4137**; **to complete**; by implication, to occupy, supply; figuratively, to **accomplish (by coincidence or obedience)**:--**fill up**, **fulfill**, occupy, supply. Page 33.

[10b] Greek word for "fulfilling" #4138. **pleroma**, play'-ro-mah; from **4137**; repletion or completion, i.e. (subjectively) what fills (as contents, supplement, copiousness, multitude), or (objectively) what is filled (as container, performance, period):--which is put in to fill up, piece that filled up, fulfilling, full, fulness. Pages 64, 87, 109, 170, 171.

[10c] Greek word for "fulfill" #378. **anapleroo**, an-ap-lay-ro'-o; from 303 and **4137**; to complete; by implication, to occupy, supply; figuratively, to accomplish (by coincidence ot obedience):--fill up, fulfill, occupy, supply. Page 312.

[11] Greek word for "spirit" #4151. **pneuma**, pnyoo'-mah; from 4154; a current of air, i.e. breath (blast) or a breeze; by analogy or figuratively, a spirit, i.e. (human) the rational soul, (by implication) vital principle, mental disposition, etc., or (superhuman) an angel, demon, or (divine) God, Christ's spirit, the Holy Spirit:--ghost, life, spirit(-ual, -ually), mind. Compare 5590. Pages 26, 68, 119, 211, 239.

[12] Greek word for "lawlessness" and "iniquity" #458. **anomia**, an-om-ee'-ah; from 459; illegality, i.e. **violation of law** or (genitive case) **wickedness**:-- **iniquity**, X **transgress**(**-ion of**) **the law**, **unrighteousness**. Pages 34, 65, 270, 281, 301, 302, 303, 319, 330, 342.

[13] Greek word for "righteous" #1342. **dikaios**, dik'-ah-yos; from 1349; equitable (in character or act); by implication, innocent, holy (absolutely or relatively):--just, meet, right(-eous). Page 37.

[13a] Greek word for "ordinances" #1345. **dikaioma**, dik-ah'-yo-mah; from **1344**; an equitable deed; by implication, a statute or decision:--judgment, justification, ordinance, righteousness. Page 37.

= **#1344**. dikaioo, dik-ah-yo'-o; from 1342; to render (i.e. show or regard as) just or innocent:--free, justify(-ier), be righteous.

[14] Greek word for "fulfilled" #1096. **ginomai**, ghin'-om-ahee; a prolongation and middle voice form of a primary verb; to cause to be ("gen"-erate), i.e. (reflexively) to become (come into being), used with great latitude (literal, figurative, intensive, etc.):--arise, be assembled,

be(-come, -fall, -have self), **be brought (to pass)**, (be) come (to pass), continue, be divided, draw, be ended, fall, **be finished**, follow, be found, **be fulfilled**, + God forbid, grow, happen, have, **be kept**, be made, be married, be ordained to be, partake, pass, be performed, be published, require, seem, be showed, X soon as it was, sound, be taken, be turned, use, wax, will, would, be wrought. Pages 42, 66, 110, 122, 163, 169, 170, 171, 173, 183.

[15] Hebrew word for "sanctified" #6942. **qadash**, kaw-dash'; a primitive root; to be (causatively, make, pronounce or observe as) clean (ceremonially or morally):--**appoint**, bid, **consecrate**, **dedicate**, defile, **hallow**, (be, **keep) holy**(-er, place), **keep**, prepare, proclaim, purify, **sanctify**(-ied one, self), X wholly. Pages 53, 73, 187, 202, 214.

[15a] Hebrew word for "consecrate" #5144. **nazar**, naw-zar'; ... specifically, **to set apart (to sacred purposes)**, i.e. **devote**:--**consecrate**, separate(-ing, self). Page 187.

= **#1510.** eimi, i-mee'; the first person singular present indicative; a prolonged form of a primary and defective verb; I exist (used only when emphatic):--am, have been, X it is I, was. See also 1488, 1498, 1511, 1527, 2258, **2071,** 2070, 2075, 2076, 2771, 2468, 5600.

= **#2071.** esomai, es'-om-ahee; future of **1510;** will be:--shall (should) be (have), (shall) come (to pass), X may have, X fall, what would follow, X live long, X sojourn.

[16] Greek word for "are" #1526. **eisi**, i-see'; 3d person plural present indicative of 1510; they are:--agree, **are**, be, dure, X is, were. Page 55, 56.

[17] Hebrew word for "Shiloh" #7886. **Shiyloh**, shee-lo'; from 7951; tranquil; Shiloh, an epithet of the Messiah:--Shiloh. Page 57.

[18] Hebrew word for "mixed" #6154. **`ereb**, ay'-reb; or mereb (1 Kings 10:15), (with the article prefix), {eh'-reb}; from 6148; the web (or transverse threads of cloth); also a mixture, (or mongrel race):--Arabia, mingled people, mixed (multitude), **woof**. Page 59.

[19] Hebrew word for "reward" #7810. **shachad**, shakh'-ad; from **7809**; a donation (venal or redemptive):--**bribe**(-ry), gift, present, reward. Page 59.

= 07809. shachad, shaw-khad'; a primitive root; to donate, i.e. bribe:--hire, give a reward.

[20] Greek word for "church" #1577. **ekklesia**, ek-klay-see'-ah; from a compound of 1537 and a derivative of 2564; a calling out, i.e.

(concretely) a popular meeting, especially a religious congregation (Jewish synagogue, or Christian community of members on earth or saints in heaven or both):-- assembly, church. Page 67.

[20a] Hebrew word for "congregation" #06952. **q@hillah**, keh-hillaw'; from **6950**; an assemblage:--assembly, congregation. Page 67.

= **06950**. qahal, 'kaw-hal'; a primitive root; to convoke:--assemble (selves) (together), gather (selves) (together).

[21] Greek word for "keep" #5083. **tereo**, tay-reh'-o; from teros (a watch; perhaps akin to 2334); to guard (from loss or injury, properly, by keeping the eye upon; and thus differing from 5442, which is properly to prevent escaping; and from 2892, which implies a fortress or full military lines of apparatus), i.e. to note (a prophecy; figuratively, to fulfil a command); by implication, to detain (in custody; figuratively, to maintain); by extension, to withhold (for personal ends; figuratively, to keep unmarried); by extension, to withhold (for personal ends; figuratively, to keep unmarried):--**hold fast**, keep(- er), **(pre-, re-) serve**, **watch**. Pages 67, 99, 123, 163, 301, 352.

[22] Greek word for "law" #3551. **nomos**, nom'-os; law (through the idea of prescriptive usage), genitive case (regulation), **specially**, **(of Moses** (including the volume); **also of the Gospel**), or figuratively (a principle):--**law**. Pages 81, 84, 104, 182, 250, 252, 253, 254, 255, 256, 259, 260, 262, 263, 266.

[23] Greek word for "transgressions" #3847. **parabasis**, par-ab'-as-is; from **3845**; violation:--breaking, transgression. Page 81.

= #**3845**. parabaino, par-ab-ah'-ee-no; from 3844 and the base of 939; to go contrary to, i.e. violate a command:--(by) transgress(-ion).

[24] Greek word for "finished" #5055. **teleo**, tel-eh'-o; from **5056**; to end, i.e. **complete**, execute, conclude, discharge (a debt):--**accomplish**, make an end, expire, fill up, **finish**, go over, pay, perform. Page 82, 108.

[24a] Greek word for "end" **#5056. telos**, tel'-os; from a primary tello (to **set out for a definite point or goal**); properly, the point aimed at as a limit, i.e. (by implication) the conclusion of an act or state (termination (literally, figuratively or indefinitely), result (immediate, ultimate or prophetic), purpose); specially, an impost or levy (as paid):- -+ continual, custom, end(-ing), finally, uttermost. Pages 82, 87, 88, 157, 188.

[24b] Greek word for "perfected" #5048. **teleioo**, tel-i-o'-o; from **5046**; to complete, i.e. (literally) accomplish, or (figuratively) consummate (in character):--consecrate, finish, fulfil, make) perfect. Page 83.

= **#5046**. teleios, tel'-i-os; from 5056; complete (in various applications of labor, growth, mental and moral character, etc.); neuter (as noun, with 3588) completeness:--of full age, man, perfect.

[24c] Greek word for "perfect" #5046. **teleios**, tel'-i-os; from **5056**; complete (in various applications of labor, growth, mental and moral character, etc.); neuter (as noun, with 3588) completeness:--of full age, man, perfect. Page 83.

[25] Greek word for "repent" #3340. **metanoeo**, met-an-o-eh'-o; from 3326 and 3539; to think differently or afterward, i.e. reconsider (morally, feel **compunction**):--repent. Page 87.

[26] Greek word for "baptized" #907. **baptizo**, bap-tid'-zo; from a derivative of 911; to **immerse**, submerge; to make whelmed (i.e. **fully wet**); used only (in the New Testament) of ceremonial ablution, especially (technically) of the ordinance of Christian baptism:--Baptist, baptize, wash. Page 87.

[27] Greek word for "work" #2041. **ergon**, er'-gon; from a primary (but obsolete) ergo (to work); **toil** (as an effort or occupation); by implication, an act:--deed, doing, **labour**, work. Pages 104, 106, 107, 134, 250, 260, 262.

[28] Greek word for "are" #2076. **esti**, es-tee'; third person singular present indicative of 1510; he (she or it) is; also (with neuter plural) they are:--**are**, be(-long), call, X can(-not), come, consisteth, X dure for a while, + follow, X have, (that) is (to say), make, meaneth, X **must needs**, + profit, + **remaineth**, + wrestle. Page 116, 144, 157.

[29] Hebrew word for "quarters" #1366. **g@buwl**, gheb-ool'; or (shortened) gbul {gheb-ool'}; from 1379; properly, a cord (as twisted), i.e. (by implication) a boundary; by extens. the territory inclosed:--border, bound, coast, X great, landmark, limit, quarter, space. Page 118.

[30] Hebrew word for "trumpet" #4536. **salpigx**, sal'-pinx; perhaps from 4535 (through the idea of quavering or **reverberation**); a **trumpet**:--trump(-et). Page 120, 121, 123, 124, 129.

[31] Hebrew word for "sounded" #4537. **salpizo**, sal-pid'-zo; to **trumpet**, i.e. **sound a blast** (literally or figuratively):--(**which are yet to**) **sound** (a trumpet). Page 121, 124.

[32] Hebrew word for "trumpet" #8643. **t@ruw`ah**, ter-oo-aw'; from **7321**; clamor, i.e. acclamation of joy or a battle-cry; especially clangor of trumpets, as an alarum:--alarm, blow(- ing) (of, the) (trumpets), joy, jubile, loud noise, rejoicing, shout(-ing), (high, joyful) sound(-ing). Page 122.

[32a] Hebrew word for "alarm" #**7321. ruwa`**, roo-ah'; primitive root; to mar (especially by breaking); figuratively, to **split the ears (with sound)**, i.e. shout (for alarm or joy):--blow an alarm, cry (alarm, aloud, out), destroy, make a joyful noise, smart, shout (for joy), **sound an alarm**, triumph. Page 125.

[33] Greek word for "last" #2078. **eschatos**, es'-khat-os; a superlative probably from 2192 (in the sense of contiguity); **farthest**, **final** (of place or time):--ends of, last, **latter end**, lowest, **uttermost**. Pages 124, 180, 239.

[34] Hebrew word "trumpet" #7782. **showphar**, sho-far'; or shophar {sho-far'}; a cornet (as **giving a clear sound**) or curved horn:--cornet, **trumpet**. Page 125.

[35] Greek word for "uncleanness" #167. **akatharsia**, ak-atharsee'-ah; from **169**; impurity (the quality), physically or morally:-- uncleanness. Page 198, 203.

[35a] Greek word for "unclean" #**169. akathartos**, ak-ath'-ar-tos; from 1 (as a negative particle) and a presumed derivative of 2508 (meaning cleansed); impure (ceremonially, morally (lewd) or specially, (demonic)):--foul, unclean. Page 131, 203, 204, 205, 206, 207, 209, 210, 212, 215, 298.

[35b] Greek word for "common" #**2839. koinos**, koy-nos'; probably from 4862; **common**, i.e. (literally) **shared by all** or several, or (ceremonially) profane:--common, defiled, **unclean**, unholy. Page 204, 205, 206, 209, 210, 211, 212.

[35c] Greek word for "defileth" #**2840. koinoo**, koy-no'-o; from **2839**; **to make (or consider) profane** (ceremonially):--call common, defile, **pollute**, unclean. Page 206, 210.

[36] Greek word for "dwelt" #4637. **skenoo**, skay-no'-o; from **4636**; to tent or encamp, i.e. (figuratively) to occupy (as a mansion) or (specially), to reside (as God did in the Tabernacle of old, a symbol of protection and communion):-- dwell. Page 131, 132, 312.

[36a] Greek word for "tabernacle" #**4633. skene**, skay-nay'; apparently akin to **4632** and **4639**; a tent or cloth hut (literally or figuratively):--habitation, tabernacle. Page 132.

= **4632**. skeuos, skyoo'-os; of uncertain affinity; a vessel, implement, equipment or apparatus (literally or figuratively (specially, a wife as contributing to the usefulness of the husband)):--goods, sail, stuff, vessel.

= **4639**. skia, skee'-ah; apparently a primary word; "shade" or a shadow (literally or figuratively (darkness of error or an adumbration)):-- shadow.

[36b] Greek word for "tabernacle" **#4636. skenos**, skay'-nos; from **4633**; a hut or temporary residence, i.e. (figuratively) the human body (as the abode of the spirit):--tabernacle. Page 132.

[36c] Greek word for "tabernacle" #4638. **skenoma**, skay'-no-mah; from 4637; an encampment, i.e. (figuratively) the Temple (as God's residence), the body (as a tenement for the soul):-- tabernacle. Page 132.

[37] Hebrew word for "soul" #5315. **nephesh**, neh'-fesh; from **5314**; properly, **a breathing creature**, i.e. animal of (abstractly) vitality; used very widely in a literal, accommodated or figurative sense (bodily or mental):--any, appetite, beast, body, breath, creature, X dead(-ly), desire, X (dis-)contented, X fish, ghost, + greedy, he, heart(-y), (hath, X jeopardy of) life (X in jeopardy), lust, man, me, mind, mortally, one, own, person, pleasure, (her-, him-, my-, thy-)self, them (your)-selves, + slay, soul, + tablet, they, thing, (X she) will, X would have it. Page 137, 201, 222, 223, 224, 233.

[37a] Hebrew word for "breathe" **#5314. naphash**, naw-fash'; a primitive root; **to breathe**; passively, to **be breathed upon**, i.e. (figuratively) refreshed (as if by a **current of air**):--(be) **refresh** selves (-ed). Page 136.

[37b] Hebrew word for "breathed" #5397. **n@shamah**, nesh-awmaw'; from 5395; a puff, i.e. wind, angry or vital breath, divine inspiration, intellect. or (concretely) an animal:--blast, (that) breath(-eth), inspiration, soul, spirit. Page 137.

[37c] Hebrew word for "spirit"/"breath" #7307. **ruwach**, roo'-akh; from **7306**; wind; by resemblance breath, i.e. a sensible (or even violent) exhalation; figuratively, life, anger, unsubstantiality; by extension, a region of the sky; by resemblance spirit, but only of a rational being (including its expression and functions):--air, anger, blast, breath, X cool, courage, mind, X quarter, X side, spirit((-ual)), tempest, X vain, ((whirl-))wind(-y). Page 135, 136, 223.

= **07306**. ruwach, roo'-akh; a primitive root; properly, to blow, i.e. breathe; only (literally) to smell or (by implication, perceive (figuratively, to anticipate, enjoy):--accept, smell, X touch, make of quick understanding.

[38] Hebrew word for "keep" #8104. **shamar**, shaw-mar'; a primitive root; properly, to hedge about (as with thorns), i.e. guard; generally, to protect, attend to, etc.:--beward, be circumspect, take heed (to self), keep(-er, self), mark, look narrowly, observe, preserve, regard, reserve, save (self), sure, (that lay) wait (for), watch(-man). Page 143, 163, 237.

[39] Greek word for "meat" #1035. **brosis**, bro'-sis; from the base of **977**; (abstractly) **eating** (literally or figuratively); by extension (concretely) **food** (literally or figuratively):--eating, food, meat. Page 143.

= #**977**. bibrosko, bib-ro'-sko; a reduplicated and prolonged form of an obsolete primary verb (perhaps causative of **1006**); to **eat**:--eat.

= #**1006**. bosko, bos'-ko; a prolonged form of a primary verb (compare **977**, **1016**); to pasture; by extension to, fodder; reflexively, to graze:--**feed**, keep.

= #**1016**. bous, booce; probably from the base of 1006; an ox (as grazing), i.e. an animal of that species ("**beef**"):--ox.

[39a] Greek word for "drink" # 4213. **posis**, pos'-is; from the alternate of **4095**; a drinking (the act), i.e. (concretely) a draught:--drink. Page 143.

= #**4095**. pino, pee'-no; occurs only as an alternate in certain tenses; to imbibe (literally or figuratively):--drink.

[40] Greek word for "to come" #3195. **mello**, mel'-lo; a strengthened form of **3199** (through the idea of expectation); to intend, i.e. be about to be, do, or suffer something (of persons or things, especially events; in the sense of purpose, duty, necessity, probability, possibility, or hesitation):--about, after that, be (almost), (that which is, things, + which was for) to come, intend, was to (be), mean, mind, be at the point, (be) ready, + return, shall (begin), (which, that) should (after, afterward, hereafter) tarry, which was for, will, would, be yet. Page 144, 145.

= #**3199**. melo, mel'-o; a primary verb; to be of interest to, i.e. to concern (only third person singular present indicative used impersonally, it matters):--(take) care.

[40a] Greek word for "now" #3568. **nun**, noon; a primary particle of present time; "now" (as adverb of date, a transition or emphasis); also as noun or adjective present or immediate:--henceforth, + hereafter, of late, soon, present, this (time). See also **3569**, **3570**. Page 144.

= **#3569**. tanun, tan-oon'; from neuter plural of 3588 and 3568; the things now, i.e. (adverbially) at present:--(but) now.

= **#3570**. nuni, noo-nee'; a prolonged form of 3568 for emphasis; just now:--now. See Greek **3568 (nun)**

[41] Greek word for "subtlety" #3834. **panourgia**, pan-oorg-ee'-ah; from 3835; adroitness, i.e. (in a bad sense) trickery or sophistry:--(cunning) craftiness, subtilty. Page 147.

[42] Greek word for "simplicity" #572. **haplotes**, hap-lot'-ace; from 573; singleness, i.e. (subjectively) sincerity (without dissimulation or self-seeking), or (objectively) generosity (copious bestowal):--bountifulness, liberal(-ity), simplicity, singleness. Page 147.

[43] Hebrew word for "peculiar treasure" #5459. **c@gullah**, segoollaw'; feminine passive participle of an unused root meaning to shut up; wealth (as closely shut up):--jewel, peculiar (treasure), proper good, special. Page 54, 201, 324.

[44] Greek word for "peculiar" #4047. **peripoiesis**, per-ee-poy'-ay-sis; from 4046; acquisition (the act or the thing); by extension, preservation:--obtain(-ing), peculiar, purchased, possession, saving. Page 154.

[45] Greek word for "rest" #4520. **sabbatismos**, sab-bat-is-mos'; from a derivative of **4521**; a "sabbatism", i.e. (figuratively) the repose of Christianity (as a type of heaven):--rest. Page 155.

[45a] Greek word for "Sabbath" **#4521**. **sabbaton**, sab'-bat-on; of Hebrew origin (**7676**); the Sabbath (i.e. Shabbath), or day of weekly repose from secular avocations (also the observance or institution itself); by extension, a se'nnight, i.e. the interval between two Sabbaths; likewise the plural in all the above applications:--sabbath (day), week. Page 141, 142.

= **#7676**. shabbath, shab-bawth'; intensive from **7673**; intermission, i.e (specifically) the Sabbath:--(+ every) sabbath.

= **#7673**. shabath, shaw-bath'; a primitive root; to repose, i.e. desist from exertion; used in many implied relations (causative, figurative or specific):--(cause to, let, make to) cease, celebrate, cause (make) to fail, keep (sabbath), suffer to be lacking, leave, put away (down), (make to) rest, rid, still, take away.

[45b] Greek word for "day" #2250. **hemera**, hay-mer'-ah; feminine (with 5610 implied) of a derivative of hemai (to sit; akin to the base of 1476) meaning tame, i.e. gentle; day, i.e. (literally) the time space

between dawn and dark, or the whole 24 hours (but **several days** were **usually** reckoned by the Jews as inclusive of the parts of both extremes); figuratively, a period (always defined more or less clearly by the context):--age, + alway, (mid-)day (by day, (-ly)), + for ever, judgment, (day) time, while, years. Page 141, 142.

[46] Greek word for "kept" #5442. **phulasso**, foo-las'-so; probably from 5443 through the idea of isolation; to watch, i.e. be on guard (literally of figuratively); by implication, to preserve, obey, avoid:-- beward, keep (self), observe, save. Page 163.

[47] Hebrew word for "because" #6118. **`eqeb**, ay'-keb; from 6117 in the sense of 6119; a heel, i.e. (figuratively) the last of anything (used adverbially, for ever); also result, i.e. **compensation**; and so (adverb with preposition or relatively) **on account of**:--X **because**, by, end, for, if, **reward**. Page 163.

[48] Hebrew word for "Babel" # 0894. **Babel**, baw-bel'; from 1101; **confusion**; **Babel** (i.e. Babylon), including Babylonia and the **Babylonian empire**:--**Babel**, **Babylon**. Pages 166, 190, 347.

[49] Greek word for "ready" #1451. **eggus**, eng-goos'; from a primary verb agcho (to squeeze or throttle; akin to the base of 43); near (literally or figuratively, of place or time):--from, at hand, **near**, nigh (at hand, unto), ready. Page 168, 177, 178.

[50] Greek word for "destroy" #2647. **kataluo**, kat-al-oo'-o; from 2596 and 3089; to loosen down (disintegrate), i.e. (by implication) to demolish (literally or figuratively); specially (compare 2646) to halt for the night:--destroy, dissolve, be guest, lodge, come to nought, overthrow, throw down. Page 168.

[51] Greek word for "mourn" #2875. **kopto**, kop'-to; a primary verb; to "chop"; specially, to beat the breast in grief:--cut down, lament, mourn, (be-)wail. Compare the base of **5114**. Page 179.

= **#5114**. tomoteros, tom-o'-ter-os; comparative of a derivative of the primary temno (to cut; more comprehensive or decisive than 2875, as if by a single stroke; whereas that implies repeated blows, like hacking); more keen:--sharper.

[52] Greek word for "power" #1411 **dunamis**, doo'-nam-is; from **1410**; force (literally or figuratively); specially, miraculous power (usually by implication, a miracle itself):--ability, abundance, meaning, might(- ily, -y, -y deed), (worker of) miracle(-s), power, strength, violence, mighty (wonderful) work. Page 179.

= **#1410**. dunamai, doo'-nam-ahee; of uncertain affinity; to be able or possible:--be able, can (do, + -not), could, may, might, be possible, be of power.

[53] Greek word for "kept" #5432. **phroureo**, froo-reh'-o; from a compound of 4253 and 3708; to be a **watcher in advance**, i.e. to mount guard as a sentinel (post spies at gates); figuratively, to **hem in**, **protect**:--**keep** (with a garrison). Page 180, 182.

[54] Hebrew for "unclean" #2931. **tame'**, taw-may'; from **2930**; foul in a relig. sense:--defiled, + infamous, polluted(-tion), unclean. Page 201, 205, 206, 214.

= **#2930. tame'**, taw-may'; a primitive root; to be foul, especially in a ceremial or moral sense (contaminated):--defile (self), pollute (self), be (make, make self, pronounce) unclean, X utterly.

[54a] Hebrew word for "tamah" #2933. **tamah**, taw-maw'; a collateral form of 2930; to be impure in a religious sense:--be defiled, be reputed vile. Page 214

[55] Hebrew word for "purify" #2891. **taher**, taw-hare'; a primitive root; properly, to be bright; i.e. (by implication) to be pure (physical sound, clear, unadulterated; Levitically, uncontaminated; morally, innocent or holy):--be (make, make self, pronounce) clean, cleanse (self), purge, purify(-ier, self). Page 202.

[56] Hebrew word for "garden" #1593. **gannah**, gan-naw'; feminine of **1588**; a garden:--garden. Page 202.

= **#1588**. gan, gan; from **1598**; a garden (as fenced):--garden.

= **#1598**. ganan, gaw-nan'; a primitive root; to hedge about, i.e. (generally) protect:--defend.

[57] Greek word for "kill" #615. **apokteino**, ap-okay-ti'-no; from 575 and kteino (to slay); to kill outright; figuratively, to destroy:- -put to death, kill, slay. Page 221.

[58] Greek word for "body" #4983. **soma**, so'-mah; from 4982; the body (as a sound whole), used in a very wide application, literally or figuratively:--bodily, body, slave. Page221.

[59] Greek word for "soul" #5590. **psuche**, psoo-khay'; from **5594**; breath, i.e. (by implication) spirit, abstractly or concretely (the animal sentient principle only; thus distinguished on the one hand from **4151**, which is the rational and immortal soul; and on the other from **2222**, which is mere vitality, even of plants: these terms thus exactly

correspond respectively to the Hebrew 5315, 7307 and 2416):--heart (+ -ily), life, mind, soul, + us, + you. Page 221, 223, 224, 229, 239.

= #**5594**. psucho, psoo'-kho; a primary verb; to breathe (voluntarily but gently, thus differing on the one hand from 4154, which denotes properly a forcible respiration; and on the other from the base of 109, which refers properly to an inanimate breeze), i.e. (by implication, of reduction of temperature by evaporation) to chill (figuratively):--wax cold.

[11] Greek word for "spirit" #**4151**. **pneuma**, pnyoo'-mah; from 4154; a current of air, i.e. breath (blast) or a breeze; by analogy or figuratively, a spirit, i.e. (human) the rational soul, (by implication) vital principle, mental disposition, etc., or (superhuman) an angel, demon, or (divine) God, Christ's spirit, the Holy Spirit:--ghost, life, spirit(-ual, -ually), mind. Compare 5590. Page 26, 68, 119, 239.

= #**2222**. zoe, dzo-ay'; from 2198; life (literally or figuratively):--life(-time). Compare 5590.

[60] Greek word for "destroy" #622. **apollumi**, ap-ol'-loo-mee; from **575** and the base of **3639**; to destroy fully (reflexively, to perish, or lose), literally or figuratively:--destroy, die, lose, mar, perish. Page 221.

= #**575**. apo, apo'; a primary particle; "off," i.e. away (from something near), in various senses (of place, time, or relation; literal or figurative):--(X here-)after, ago, at, because of, before, by (the space of), for(-th), from, in, (out) of, off, (up-)on(-ce), since, with. In composition (as a prefix) it usually denotes separation, departure, cessation, completion, reversal, etc.

= #**3639**. olethros, ol'-eth-ros; from a primary ollumi (to destroy; a prolonged form); ruin, i.e. **death**, punishment:--destruction.

[61] Greek word for "hell" #1067. **geenna**, gheh'-en-nah; of Hebrew origin (1516 and 2011); valley of (the son of) Hinnom; ge-henna (or Ge-Hinnom), a valley of Jerusalem, used (figuratively) as a name for the place (or state) of everlasting punishment:--hell. Page 221, 222, 223, 225, 226.

= #**2348**. thnesko, thnay'-sko; a strengthened form of a simpler primary thano than'-o (which is used for it only in certain tenses); to die (literally or figuratively):--be dead, die.

[62] Greek word for "book of life" #2222. **zoe**, dzo-ay'; from **2198**; life (literally or figuratively):--**life**(-time). Compare **5590**. Page 222, 223.

= **#2198**. **zao**, dzah'-o; a primary verb; to live (literally or figuratively):--life(-time), (a-)live(-ly), quick.

[37] Hebrew word for "soul" #5315. **nephesh**, neh'-fesh; from 5314; properly, a breathing creature, i.e. animal of (abstractly) vitality; used very widely in a literal, accommodated or figurative sense (bodily or mental):--any, appetite, beast, body, breath, creature, X dead(-ly), desire, X (dis-) contented, X fish, ghost, + greedy, he, heart(-y), (hath, X jeopardy of) life (X in jeopardy), lust, man, me, mind, mortally, one, own, person, pleasure, (her-, him-, my-, thy-)self, them (your)-selves, + slay, soul, + tablet, they, thing, (X she) will, X would have it. Page 137, 201, 223, 224, 233.

[63] Greek word for "death" #2288. **thanatos**, than'-at-os; from **2348**; (properly, an adjective used as a noun) death (literally or figuratively):--X deadly, (be ...) death. Page 222, 224, 225, 226.

[64] Greek word for "hell" #86. **hades**, hah'-dace; from 1 (as negative particle) and 1492; properly, unseen, i.e. "**Hades**" or the place (state) of departed souls:--**grave**, hell. Page 222, 224, 225, 226.

[65] Hebrew word for "die" #4191. **muwth**, mooth; a primitive root: to die (literally or figuratively); causatively, to kill:--X at all, X crying, (be) dead (body, man, one), (put to, worthy of) death, destroy(-er), (cause to, be like to, must) die, kill, necro(-mancer), X must needs, slay, X surely, X very suddenly, X in (no) wise. Page 223.

[66] Hebrew word for "hell" #7585. **sh@'owl**, sheh-ole'; or shol {shehole'}; from 7592; **Hades** or the world of the dead (as if a subterranean retreat), including its accessories and inmates:--grave, hell, pit. Page 224.

[67] Greek word for "resurrection" #386. **anastasis**, an-as'-tas-is; from **450**; a standing up **again**, i.e. (literally) a resurrection from death (individual, genitive case or by implication, (its author)), or (figuratively) a (moral) recovery (of spiritual truth):--**raised to life again**, resurrection, rise from the dead, that should rise, **rising again**. Page 224, 314.

= **#450**. anistemi, an-is'-tay-mee; from 303 and 2476; to stand up (literal or figurative, transitive or intransitive):--arise, lift up, raise up (again), rise (again), stand up(-right).

[68] Greek word for "dead" #3498. **nekros**, nek-ros'; from an apparently primary nekus (a corpse); dead (literally or figuratively; also as noun):--dead. Page 224.

[69] Hebrew word for "Hinom" #2011. **Hinnom**, hin-nome'; probably of foreign origin; Hinnom, apparently a Jebusite:--Hinnom. Page 225, 226.

[70] Greek word for "hell" #5020. **tartaroo**, tar-tar-o'-o; from Tartaros (the deepest abyss of **Hades**); to incarcerate in eternal torment:--cast down to hell. Page 226.

[71] Greek word for "quickening" #2227. **zoopoieo**, dzo-op-oyeh'-o; from the same as 2226 and 4160; to (re-)vitalize (literally or figuratively):--make alive, give life, quicken. Page 238.

[72] Greek word for "establish" # 2476. **histemi**, his'-tay-mee; a prolonged form of a primary stao stah'-o (of the same meaning, and used for it in certain tenses); to stand (transitively or intransitively), used in various applications (literally or figuratively):--abide, appoint, bring, **continue**, covenant, **establish**, **hold up**, lay, **present**, **set (up)**, stanch, stand (by, forth, still, up). Page 123, 246.

[73] Hebrew word for "believe" #539. **'aman**, aw-man'; a primitive root; properly, to build up or support; to foster as a parent or nurse; figuratively to render (or be) firm or faithful, to trust or believe, to be permanent or quiet; **morally to be true or certain**; once (Isa. 30:21; interchangeable with 541) to go to the right hand:--hence, assurance, **believe**, bring up, **establish**, + fail, **be faithful** (of long continuance, stedfast, sure, surely, **trusty**, verified), nurse, (-ing father), (put), trust, turn to the right. Page 250.

[74] Greek word for "Passover" #3957. **pascha**, pas'-khah; of Chaldee origin (compare 6453); the **Passover** (the meal, the day, the festival or the special sacrifices connected with it):--Easter, Passover. Page 250.

[75] Greek word for "border" #2899. **kraspedon**, kras'-ped-on; of uncertain derivation; a margin, i.e. (specially), a fringe or tassel:--border, hem. Page 359.

- -

NOTE: All emphasis like words **bolded** is by me. The phrases 'Greek (or Hebrew) word for "___", are added by me. The page numbers following the definitions are added by me, only to show where that definition is used in the book.

==

THE TEN COMMANDMENTS OF THE LORD

Table 1: Love Toward God
First Commandment: "I am the LORD thy God, which have brought thee out of the land of Egypt, out of the house of bondage. Thou shalt have no other gods before me."
Second Commandment: "Thou shalt not make unto thee any graven image, or any likeness of any thing that is in heaven above, or that is in the earth beneath, or that is in the water under the earth: Thou shalt not bow down thyself to them, nor serve them: for I the LORD thy God am a jealous God, visiting the iniquity of the fathers upon the children unto the third and fourth generation of them that hate me; And shewing mercy unto thousands of them that love me, and keep my commandments."
Third Commandment: "Thou shalt not take the name of the LORD thy God in vain; for the LORD will not hold him guiltless that taketh his name in vain."
Fourth Commandment: "Remember the sabbath day, to keep it holy. Six days shalt thou labour, and do all thy work: But the seventh day is the sabbath of the LORD thy God: in it thou shalt not do any work, thou, nor thy son, nor thy daughter, thy manservant, nor thy maidservant, nor thy cattle, nor thy stranger that is within thy gates: For in six days the LORD made heaven and earth, the sea, and all that in them is, and rested the seventh day: wherefore the LORD blessed the Sabbath day, and hallowed it."

Table 2: Love Toward Others.
Fifth Commandment: "Honour thy father and thy mother: that thy days may be long upon the land which the LORD thy GOD giveth thee."
Sixth Commandment: "Thou shalt not kill."
Seventh Commandment: "Thou shalt not commit adultery."
Eight Commandment: "Thou shalt not steal."

<u>Ninth Commandment:</u> "Thou shalt not bear false witness against thy neighbour."
<u>Tenth Commandment:</u> "Thou shalt not covet thy neighbour's house, thou shalt not covet thy neighbour's wife, nor his manservant, nor his maidservant, nor his ox, nor his ass, nor any thing that is thy neighbour's."

- -

The first commandment starts with Exodus 20 verse 2, not verse 3, as we commonly see it displayed. Verse 2 clearly identifies which God is the Lord that can save—the one who delivered His children out of the Egyptian bondage and slavery! The first and fourth Commandments identify which is the true God, whom we are to serve if we desire His blessings. The fourth one (the Sabbath commandment), has been abolished by the traditional church fathers for many centuries already. So if you leave out verse 2, the eternal God's identity is gone, and you have another god; this is what is happening in today's traditional Christianity, thus creating the allowance needed to flavor God's commandments with Baal's customs whilst still calling them holy!

<u>Matthew 22:36–40:</u> Master, which is the great commandment in the law? Jesus said unto him, Thou shalt love the Lord thy God with all thy heart, and with all thy soul, and with all thy mind. This is the first and great commandment. And the second is like unto it, Thou shalt love thy neighbour as thyself. On these two commandments hang all the law and the prophets.

<u>Deuteronomy 4:2; 12:32:</u> Ye shall **not add** unto the word which I command you, **neither shall ye diminish ought from it**, that ye may keep the commandments of the LORD your God which I command you ... What thing soever I command you, observe to do it: thou shalt **not add** thereto, **nor diminish** from it.

<u>Revelation 22:18–19:</u> For I testify unto every man that heareth the words of the prophecy of this book, **If any man shall add**

unto these things, God shall add unto him the plagues that are written in this book: And **if any man shall take away from the words** of the book of this prophecy, God shall take away his part out of the book of life, and out of the holy city, and from the things which are written in this book.

==

THE TEN PLANKS OF THE COMMUNIST MANIFESTO

First Plank. Abolition of property in land and application of all rents of land to public purposes.

Second Plank. A heavy progressive or graduated income tax.

Third Plank. Abolition of all right of inheritance.

Fourth Plank. Confiscation of the property of all emigrants and rebels.

Fifth Plank. Centralisation of credit in the hands of the State, by means of a national bank with State capital and an exclusive monopoly.

Sixth Plank. Centralisation of the means of communication and transport in the hands of the State.

Seventh Plank. Extension of factories and instruments of production owned by the State; the bringing into cultivation of waste-lands, and the improvement of the soil generally in accordance with a common plan.

Eighth Plank. Equal liability of all to labour. Establishment of industrial armies, especially for agriculture.

Ninth Plank. Combination of agriculture with manufacturing industries; gradual abolition of the distinction between town and country, by a more equitable distribution of the population over the country.

Tenth Plank. Free education for all children in public schools. Abolition of children's factory labour in its present form and combination of education with industrial production.

(Taken from Wikipedia, the free online encyclopedia) <http://en.wikipedia.org/wiki/The_Communist_Manifesto>

A quite informative copy can also be downloaded from the following Website:
<http://www.marxists.org/archive/marx/works/download/pdf/Manifesto.pdf >

==

Many of us are familiar with going to Church on Sunday to hear the singing of hymns and evangelical songs. We hear speakers talking about their walk with the Lord and how we ought to follow after their pattern. Preachers give sermons on topics that they claim to be from the Holy Scriptures, wherefore they will tell us to take heed and follow their instructions. It may become very moving.

But do we ever stop to think where these church doctrines really come from? How often and how sincerely do we check these doctrines with the scriptures, as God instructs us to do? We are encouraged in scripture to compare the church doctrines with the Word of God. I know from my own experience that this is a hard challenge that dedicated churchgoers—which I was for almost fifty years—find very hard to do without becoming biased, for the fear of not wanting to be betrayed by a trusted preacher.

I challenge you to the task! Do not pass judgment on any minister, but check the doctrines for the spiritual welfare and safety of you and your family, and to God's honor and glory.

With Love, God Bless!
Cornie Banman

ABOUT THE AUTHOR

Cornie Banman has worked in the sawmill industry for three decades. He and his wife, Sara, have one daughter and live in Alberta, Canada. Banman's first book, The Commandments of God, was published in 2011. Visit him online at http://corniebanman.com.

Printed in the United States
By Bookmasters